Simulated Annealing: Issues and Concerns

Edited by **Brian Maxwell**

CLANRYE
INTERNATIONAL

New Jersey

Published by Clanrye International,
55 Van Reypen Street,
Jersey City, NJ 07306, USA
www.clanryeinternational.com

Simulated Annealing: Issues and Concerns
Edited by Brian Maxwell

International Standard Book Number: 978-1-63240-466-4 (Hardback)

Printed in the United States of America.

Contents

Preface

A comprehensive account based on the issues and concerns related to the field of Simulated Annealing has been illustrated in this book. Simulated annealing is a probabilistic meta-heuristic which is utilized for solving both continuous and discrete optimization problems. It is widely used in resolving complex optimization problems due to its advantages over other solution methods. This book gives a detailed account on different aspects of simulated annealing. It covers single and multiple objective applications to provide the readers with extensive knowledge of SA and its various applications. It serves the objective of assisting students and researchers in their related activities by providing practical insights into the subject. The book has been compiled with the contributions of renowned experts and practitioners in this field.

All of the data presented henceforth, was collaborated in the wake of recent advancements in the field. The aim of this book is to present the diversified developments from across the globe in a comprehensible manner. The opinions expressed in each chapter belong solely to the contributing authors. Their interpretations of the topics are the integral part of this book, which I have carefully compiled for a better understanding of the readers.

At the end, I would like to thank all those who dedicated their time and efforts for the successful completion of this book. I also wish to convey my gratitude towards my friends and family who supported me at every step.

Editor

Single Objective

Mean Field Annealing Based Techniques for Resolving VLSI Automatic Design Problems

Gholam Reza Karimi and Ahmad Azizi Verki

Additional information is available at the end of the chapter

1. Introduction

The neuro-computing approaches based on Hopfield model were successfully applied to various combinatorial optimization problems such as the traveling salesman problem [1-3], scheduling problem [4], mapping problem [5], knapsack problem [6,7], communication routing problem [8], graph partitioning problem [2,9,10], graph layout problem [11], circuit partitioning problem [12,13].

MFA, as a neuro-computing technique, is applied for solving combinatorial optimization problems [1,2,4-8,10,13] , cell placement problem [14].

MFA combines the *annealing* notion of SA approach with the collective computation property of *Hopfield neural networks* to obtain optimal solution for np-hard problems.

We begin our study with the review of basic concepts of MFA techniques and describe the applied use of this technique to solve the problems in high speed Integrated Circuits (IC) design and in addition we applied a modified MFA algorithm to solve VLSI relocation problem [15].

1.1. Annealing

Annealing is a mechanical process in which material is slowly cooled allowing the molecules to arrange themselves in such a way that the material is less strained thereby making it more stable.

If materials such as glass or metal are cooled too quickly its constituent molecules will be under high stress lending it to failure (breaking) if further thermal or physical shocks are encountered. Slowing the cooling of the material allows each molecule to move into a place it feels most comfortable, i.e., less stress.

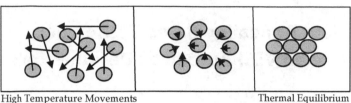

High Temperature Movements   Thermal Equilibrium

Figure 1. Molecules movement at the cooling process

As the material is kept at a high temperature the molecules are able to move around quite freely thus reducing stress on a large scale, indeed if the material is made too hot it will move into the liquid state allowing free movement of the molecules. As the material is cooled the molecules are not able to move around as freely but still move limited distances reducing stress in regional areas. The result is a material with significantly less internal stress and resistant to failure due to external shock.

The statistic mechanic is a domain in physics that describes the process of slow cooling of *Hamiltonian Ising* for particles or spins with high degree of freedom until they accede on their equilibrium states. The particles that are cooling, on solid state, provide a framework to characteristics improvisation of intricate and large systems. Now this idea is stated inside optimization algorithms to resolve various cases of problems.

1.2. Hopfield Neural Network (HNN)

The Hopfield Network is a fully connected network of simple processing units, V_i , with numerically weighted symmetric connections, T_{ij}, between units V_i and V_j. processing units have states (either discrete in {0, 1}, or continuous in [0, 1] depending on whether the discrete or the continuous version of the network is being considered). Each processing unit performs simple and identical computations which generally involve summing weighted inputs to unit, applying an internal transfer function, and changing state if necessary. The power of the Hopfield model lies in the connections between units and the weights of these connections [16]. An Energy function was defined by Hopfield on the states of the network (values of all units). The energy function, E, in its simplest form is:

$$E = -\frac{1}{2}\sum_{i=1}^{N}\sum_{j=1}^{N} T_{ij}V_jV_i + \sum_{i=1}^{N} V_iI_i \tag{1}$$

Where V_i denotes the current state (value) of the *ith* neuron and I_i denotes its bias. Hopfield utilized the fact that the $E(\vec{V_i})$ is a *Liapunov* function (bounded from below) to show that, from any starting state, the network would always converge to some energy function minimum upon applying a sequence of asynchronous local state updates (that locally reduce energy).

To solve any particular problem, first a decision must be made on how to set the network parameters T and I, so that minimization of the problem objective function and enforces satisfaction of the problem constraints; this process is termed 'mapping' the problem onto the network. Hopfield gives the motion equation of the *ith* neuron:

$$\frac{dU_i}{dt} = \frac{U_i}{\tau} - \frac{\partial E(\vec{v_i})}{\partial v_i}, U_i = \frac{\partial E_H(\vec{v_i})}{\partial v_i} \tag{2}$$

Where E is energy function in term of V_i and E_H is *Hopfield term* of energy function. Totally Eq. 2.is motion (updating) equation of state of neurons and its output is U_i. Usually a simple nondecreasing monatomic output function in term of U_i like $g(U_i)$ is applied torelate U_i to the states. Typically this function is a step function or a hyperbolic tangent function. τ is a constant number as the weighting factor of U_i. Thereforea Hopfield Neural Network minimizes a cost function that is encoded with its weights by implementation of *gradient descent*. For more details see [16]

2. MFA technique

As it mentioned before, MFA merges collective computation and annealing properties of Hopfield neural Networks and SA, respectively, to obtain a general algorithm for solving combinatorial optimization problems. MFA can be used for solving a combinatorial optimization problem by choosing a representation scheme in which the final states of the discrete variables (spins or neurons) can be decoded as a solution to the problem. In fact the space of problem is mapped to the space of MFA variables (spins) and there will be a one-to-one relation between two spaces. This is called *encoding*. Then, an energy function is formulated in term of spins with a structure that is based on essence of problem whose global minimum value corresponds to an optimum solution of the problem. MFA is expected to compute the optimum solution to the target problem, starting from a randomly chosen initial state, by minimizing this energy function. Steps of applying MFA technique to a problem can be summarized as follows:

1. Choose a representation plan which encodes the configuration space of the target optimization problem using spins. In order to get a good performance, number of possible configurations in the problem domain and the spin domain must be equal. That means there must be a one-to-one mapping between the configurations of spins and the problem.
2. Formulate the cost function of the problem in terms of spins to derive the energy function of the system. Global minimum of the energy function should correspond to the global minimum of the cost function.
3. Derive the mean field theory equations using formulated energy function. Derive equations are used for updating averages (expected values) of spins.
4. cooling schedule
5. Set suitable parameters of the energy function and the cooling schedule to obtain efficient algorithm.

These main steps are same for various types of optimization problems and are explained at the following sections.

2.1. Encoding

The MFA algorithm is derived by analogy to *Ising* and *Potts* models which are used to estimate the state of a system of particles, called spins, in thermal equilibrium. In *Ising* model, spins can be in one of the two states represented by0 and 1, whereas in Potts model they can be in one of the K states and the configuration of the problem determines which one has to be used.

For *K*-state *Potts* model with n_s spins, the states of spins are represented using n_s K-dimensional vectors.

$$S_i = [S_{i1}, \dots, S_{ik}, \dots, S_{iK}] \text{ for } 1 \leq i \leq n_s \qquad (3)$$

Just one of the components of S_i is 1 and the others are 0. That means *ith* spin must be at one of the K- states.

$$\sum_{k=1}^{K} S_{ik} = 1 \text{ for } 1 \leq i \leq n_S \qquad (4)$$

For encoding of VLSI circuit design problem, for example, each spin vector corresponds to a cell in the circuit or a module in the placement. Hence, number of spin vectors is equal to the number of cells or modules; n_c. Dimension K of the spin vectors is equal to the number of empty part of overall circuit space or empty spaces of the placement. That means we can divide the circuit space (chip area or die surface)to K parts and fill every part just by one and only one of the circuit elements [12, 13]. Therefore when a spin is assigned in *kth* state that means its corresponding cell or module (circuit element) is placed on *kth* space or part of circuit or placement.

2.2. Energy function formulation

In the MFA algorithm, the aim is to find the spin values minimizing the energy function of the system. In order to achieve this goal, the average (expected) value $V_i = \langle S_i \rangle$ of each spin vector S_i is computed and iteratively updated until the system stabilizes at some fixed point.

$V_i = \langle S_i \rangle$ *for* $1 \leq i \leq n_c$ and $V_i = [v_{i1}, \dots, v_{ik}, \dots v_{iK}]$ So:

$$[v_{i1}, \dots, v_{ik}, \dots v_{iK}] = [\langle S_{i1} \rangle, \dots \langle S_{ik} \rangle, \dots, \langle S_{iK} \rangle] \text{ for } 1 \leq i \leq n_c \qquad (5)$$

v_{ik} is probability of finding spin i at state k and can take any real value between 0 and 1. When the system is stabilized, v_{ik} values are expected to converge to 0 or 1.As the system is a Potts glass we have the following constraint:

$$\sum_{k=1}^{K} v_{ik} = 1 \text{ for } 1 \leq i \leq n_c \qquad (6)$$

This constraint guarantees that each Potts spin S_i is in one of the K states at a time, and each cell is assigned to only one position for encoded configuration of the problem. In order to construct an energy function it is helpful to associate the following meaning to the values v_{ik}, for example:

$$v_{ik} = P\{\text{spin } i \text{ is in position } k\} \text{ for } 1 \le i \le n_c, 1 \le k \le K(P\{\} \text{ is probability function}) \qquad (7)$$

v_{ik} is the probability of finding spin i at state k. If $v_{ik} = 1$, then spin i is in state k and the corresponding configuration is $V_i = S_i$.

Locating spin i at stat k relevant to type of target problem has some costs and actually energy function calculates these costs. Example given, for circuit partitioning problem, utilizing the interconnection cost and the wire-length cost for VLSI placement problem are common cost functions and are used to formulating energy function of these target problems [12-14].

The interconnection cost is represented by E_c that for the circuit is total length of internal connections between circuit components or the cost of the connections among the circuit partitions. It is clear that if all of the circuit elements are located in one place and overlaps together, the interconnection cost (total wire length) becomes 0 and it is not acceptable. This is what we mean *illogical minimization* of interconnection cost energy function. So another term of the energy function must be applied for penalizing illogical minimization of first cost function. This term is represented by E_p. For example, this term is imbalanced partitioning for circuit partitioning problem and overlap between modules for VLSI placement problem [13, 14].The total energy function, E_t, is sum of both terms:

$$E_t = E_c + \alpha \times E_p \qquad (8)$$

Where α parameter is introduced to maintain a balance between the two opposite terms of total energy function.

2.3. Derivation of the mean field theory equations

Mean field theory equations, needed to minimize the total energy function E_t, can be derived as follow:

$$\phi_{ik} = -\frac{\partial E(V)}{\partial v_{ik}} \qquad (9)$$

The quantity ϕ_{ik} represents the *k*th element of the *mean field vector* effecting on spin i. Using the mean field values, average spin values, v_{ik}, can be updated.

$$v_{ik} = \frac{e^{\phi_{ik}/T}}{\sum_{n=1}^{K} e^{\phi_{in}/T}} \text{for} 1 \le i \le nc, 1 \le k \le K \qquad (10)$$

Where T is the temperature parameter which is used the relax the system iteratively and is managed with a cooling schedule program.

2.4. Energy difference and cooling schedule

A teach iteration of algorithm, the mean field vector effecting on a randomly selected spin is computed. Then, spin average vector is updated. This process is repeated for a random sequence of spins until the system is stabilized for the current temperature. The system is observed after each spin vector update in order to detect the convergence to an equilibrium state for a given temperature.

If the total energy does not decrease in most of the successive spin vector updates, this means that the system is stabilized for that temperature. Then, T is decreased according to the cooling schedule by a decreasing factor and the iterative process restarted again with new temperature. To reduce the complexity of energy difference computation an efficient scheme could be used.

$$\Delta E_{ik} = \phi_{ik}\,\Delta v_{ik} \; so \; \Delta E = \sum_{k=1}^{K} \phi_{ik}\,\Delta v_{ik} \, where \; \Delta v_{ik} = v_{ik}(new) - v_{ik}\,(old) \qquad (11)$$

Depending to complexity of problem, the cooling program could be in one stage or more stages in order to reach faster and better result. In some problems like circuit partitioning problem the applied cooling schedule is simply in one stage (t_f is decreasing factor):

$$T_{new} = T_{old} \times t_f \; for \; 0 < t_f < 1 \qquad (12)$$

Actually cooling schedule controls amount of acceptable cost increasing moves and the efficiency of the algorithm. Clearly for very large temperatures almost any change will be accepted while as the temperature is reduced the chance that a positive cost change will also be accepted is reduced.

2.5. Total MFA algorithm

The total format of MFA for various kind of problem is represented as:

1. Get the initial temperature T_0, and set $T = T_0$
2. Initialize the spin averages $V = [v_{11}, ..., v_{ik}, ..., v_{n_c K}]$
3. While temperature T is in the cooling range DO:
3.1. While E is decreasing DO:
3.1.1. Select the ith spin randomly.
3.1.2. Compute mean field vector corresponding to the ith spin: $\phi_{ik} = -\dfrac{\partial E(V)}{\partial v_{ik}}$
3.1.3. Compute the summation: $\sum_{n=1}^{K} e^{\phi_{in}/T}$
3.1.4. Compute new spin average vector: $v_{ik}(new) = e^{\phi_{ik}/T} / \sum_{l=1}^{K} e^{\phi_{il}/T}$
3.1.5. Compute new spin average vector: $\Delta E = \sum_{k=1}^{K} \phi_{ik}\,(v_{ik}(new) - v_{ik})$
3.1.6. Update the spin average vector: $v_{ik}(new) = v_{ik}$
3.2. Decrease the temperature: $T = T \times t_f$

Inside the algorithm some notes must be considered. Selection of initial temperatures is crucial for obtaining good quality solutions. Typically spin averages initialize with an equal values plus a small disturbing part that is randomly valued but this is not an eternal rule. Adding this disturbing part causes the spins exit their stable states and their movement starts. Selecting balance factors in energy function has important role for efficiency of the algorithm.

3. VLSI Relocation problem using MFA technique

In modern VLSI physical design, Engineering Change Order (ECO) optimization methods are used to mitigate model placement problems such as hot spots and thermal dissipation that are identified at a given layout at post-routing analysis that is an evaluation stage after placement stage. The relocation problem is defined as adding an additional module to a model placement in order to solve problems at a manner that similarity of the resultant placement to the model placement is kept.

Our presented MFA-based technique is modified form which was applied for cell placement problem in [14] by adding some considerations relating to particular characteristics of the local relocation problem.

3.1. Cell placement problem

Placement is the process of determining the locations of circuit devices on a die surface. ItisanimportantstageintheVLSIdesignflowbecauseitaffectsroutability, performance, heat distribution, and to a less extent, power consumption of a design.

Traditionally, it is applied after the logic synthesis stage and before the routing stage. Since the advent of deep submicron process technology around mid-1990, interconnect delay, which is largely determined by placement, has become the dominating component of circuit delay. As a result, placement information is essential even in early design stages to achieve better circuit performance.

The circuit is presented with a hyper-graph $\Omega(C, N)$, that consists of a set C representing the cells circuit, a cell weight function of the circuit, a hyper-edge set N representing the nets of the $\omega_{cell}: C \to \mathcal{N}$ and a net weight function $\omega_{net}: N \to \mathcal{N}$ where $\mathcal{N}$ represents the set of natural numbers. Space of circuit is a rectangular grid of clusters with P rows and Qcolumns where the cells will be placed.

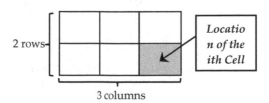

Figure 2. Cell location on spin space configuration

As presented before in the K-state Potts model of S spins, the states of spins re represented using S K-dimensional vectors. To apply MFA technique for cell placement problem the circuit layout space is mapped to a grid space with P rows and Q columns. If the number of cells be C_L, the number of spins that encode the configuration of problem is C_L $(P \times Q)$-dimensional Potts spins so there would be a total of $|C_L| \times P \times Q$ two-state variables. To decreasing the number of spins that encode the configuration of problem, they are separated to two types: row and column spins. Therefore there would be P row spins and Q column spins and totally $|C_L| \times (P+Q)$ spins[14].For example for a circuit space with 2 rows and 3 columns if the row spin vector of *ith* cell is $v_{ip}^r = [0,1]$ and its column spin vector is $v_{iq}^c = [0,0,1]$ that means this cell is located at second row and third column of configuration space as Fig. 2.

3.1.1. Energy function formulation

Energy function in the MFA algorithm corresponds to formulation of the cost function of the cell placement problem in terms of spins. Since the MFA algorithm iterates on the expected values of the spins, the expected value of the energy function is formulated. The gradient of the expected value of the energy function is used in the MFA algorithm to compute the new values to update spin vectors in order to minimize the energy function. The applied cost energy for this problem is routing cost energy that is calculated approximately. It is not feasible to calculate the exact routing length for two reasons. Firstly, a feasible placement is not available during the execution of some algorithms; secondly, the computation of the exact routing cost necessitates the execution of the global and the detailed routing phases which are as hard as the placement phase. Commonly used approximations are the *semi-perimeter* method or *Half Perimeter Wire Length* (HPWL) method.

Using the expected values of spins, the probability of existence of one or more cells of *nth* net in *pth* row and *qth* column is calculated and applying HPWL method routing length cost is obtained. Different weights for row and column routing length costs could be considered.

If the routing cost is used as the only factor in the cost function, the optimum solution is mapping all cells of the circuit to one location in the layout. This placement will reduce the routing cost to zero but obviously it is not feasible. Hence, a term in the energy function is needed which will penalize the placements that put more than one cell to the same location. This term is called the overlap cost. This term is calculated by multiplying the probabilities of being *ith* and *jth* cells in same location. The total energy functionE_t, is:

$$E_t = E_{vrc} + E_{hrc} + \beta \times E_o \tag{13}$$

where E_{vrc}, E_{hrc} and E_o are vertical routing cost, horizontal routing cost and overlap cost respectively.The parameter β is balance factor between routing and overlap cost functions.

3.1.2. Half Perimeter Wire Length (HPWL) method

A very simple and widely used cost function parameter is the interconnect wire length of a placement solution; this can be easily approximated using the bounding box method. This wire length estimation method draws a bounding box around all ports in a given net, half the perimeter of this box is taken as the net's interconnect length approximation. The *half perimeter wire length* (HPWL) estimation for minimally routed two and three port nets gives an exact value.

3.2. Local relocation using MFA technique

Our method executes local relocation on a model placement where an additional module is added to it for modification with minimum number of displacement. The model placement is a given placement of the circuit that needs modification. MFA based method resolves the problem in less time and hardware in compare to SA-based method. In addition, the runtime of solution is mostly independent of size and complexity of input model placement. Our proposed MFA algorithm is optimized by adding the ability of rotation of modules inside an energy function called *permissible distances preservation energy* that will be defined at section 3.2.6. This in turn allows more options in moving the engaged modules. Finally, a three-phase cooling process governs convergence of problem variables called neurons or spins.

The relocation problem is formulated as follows:

Input: A model placement including a set of modules and a net list or hypergraph representation of circuit, the additional module with its coordinates and the incident nets.

Output: Local relocated placement

Objective: Fast relocation with minimum number of displacements and more similarity

Constraint: No overlap between modules and preservation of permissible distances

There are four classified approaches to the problem of inserting an extra module into a model placement.

i.   The additional elements are inserted into unoccupied "whitespace" areas as much as possible.
ii.   Before additional logic elements are inserted, an effort is made to predict the amount of whitespace area required; this whitespace is distributed over the chip. If the prediction is accurate (or conservative), the added elements can be placed within the available space.
iii. The third approach is to simply insert or resize the required logic elements, and begin the optimization process from scratch.
iv.   The fourth approach is to insert additional logic elements without considering overlaps.

Our approach matched the fourth approach above. The MFA relocation algorithm removes overlaps by moving or rotating modules. Note that all of the movements and rotations must observe some permissible distances that will be explained in the following sections. Feasibility of problem depends on topology of placement and similarity. It is clear that selecting a big part of model placement as the relocation range may cause a feasible solution but causes more unsimilarity.

3.2.1. Local relocation algorithm

The proposed relocation algorithm consists of two stages:

i.   Construction of MFA vectors and calculation of permissible distances from a proper relocation range around additional module.
ii. Local Relocation with MFA

At first stage, given the model placement and an additional module with its coordinates, the small area around the additional module is scanned to find proper range that has enough free space as the *local relocation range,* then necessary information that will be used at the second stage are extracted. At second stage, MFA algorithm starts to move or rotate some modules (movable modules) considering critical distances criteria using information of first stage. All of the seconcepts like movable modules, permissible distances and critical distances are defined at the following sections.

3.2.2. Calculation of permissible distances and construction of MFA vectors

The first stage of local relocation algorithm has to extract information of hypergraph representation of selected part of model placement as inputs of second stage, such as P, Q and sets C and N and MFA input vectors. The selected part of model placement is called the local *relocation range* and must has enough free space or dead space for inserting an extra module.

Selecting size and position of relocation rang depends on size of additional module and desirable similarity between model placement and relocated placement. It is clear that selecting bigger part of a model placement as a relocation range may cause more unsimilarity. So, this algorithm seeks around additional module in different directions considering relocation range limitation to find desirable range.

After relocation range determination, its underlying modules are classified into two groups:

First group includes modules that are completely inside the relocation range and are *movable modules.* Second group consists of modules that just overlap with relocation range and must have fixed position during relocation because they form a frame around movable modules and are *fixed modules.*

Actually if we assume the model placement as a puzzle, this frame is just a piece of it. It's clear that after local relocation, this piece must fit on its location again so any movement or rotation from inside modules must preserve vertical and horizontal distances between outer ones. Fig. 3.a shows the relocation range and its underlying modules on the model placement. Fig. 3.b shows local relocated placement of Fig. 3.a.

Dashed square is the relocation range and black module is the additional module. Modules marked as "o" are outer modules and those marked as "i" are inner modules. In our method we have used MFA with discrete variable for relocation, so the problem's configuration must encode to discrete space. As a result, the width and height of relocation range are divided into equal spans that form some columns and rows respectively. The rows and columns that are occupied with modules are marked. The outer modules are then separated into four sets: up boundary modules, down boundary modules, left boundary modules and right boundary modules.

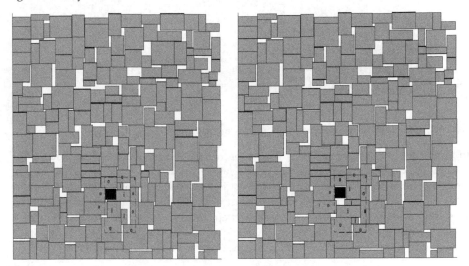

Figure 3. a) Relocation range and it sunder lying modules. b) Local relocated placement using MFA

3.2.3. Calculating permissible distances

For each row or column, two modules are determined as its boundary module. *Permissible distance* of every row or column is obtained with calculating distance between left boundary module and right boundary module of that row or distance between up boundary module and down boundary module of that column respectively. Fig. 4.a shows coordinates of a module. Left-down corner and right-top corners of a module are considerable here. Right-top corner coordinate of module "i" is obtained.

$$xw_i = x_i + w_i \ , yh_i = y_i + h_i \qquad (14)$$

For each row or column, two modules are determined as its boundary modules. Fig. 4.b represents boundary modules of the relocation range shown in Fig. 3.

In Fig. 4.b row and column permissible distances are computed using Eq. 15 considering coordinates of the boundary modules of that row or column. Subscribe "o" Refers to outer modules, Rpd_i and Cpd_i represent *ith* row's *jth* column's permissible distances.

$$Rpd_i = x_{oi} - xw_{oi}, \; Cpd_i = y_{oj} - yh_{oj} \tag{15}$$

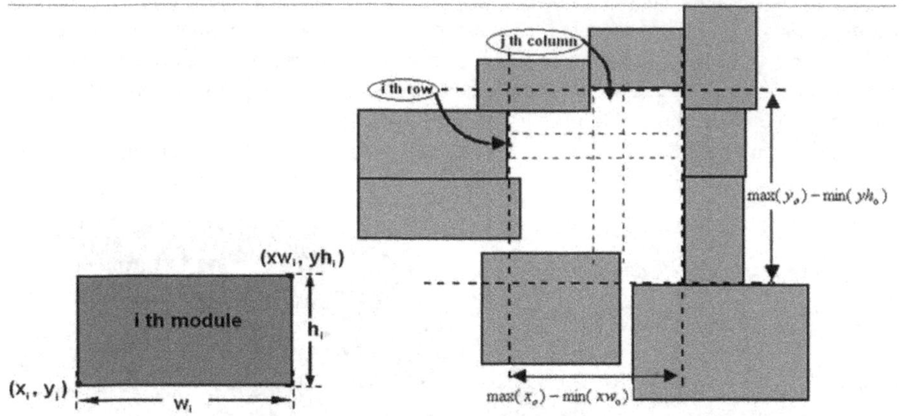

Figure 4. a) Coordinates of a module   b) Boundary modules

In main algorithm sum of widths or heights of modules that are located in the same row or column are calculated and results are not permitted to exceed permissible distance of that row or column. For decreasing number of variables and calculations, outer modules that must have fixed position are laid aside and just inner modules that are movable enter MFA algorithm. In addition extra module as an overlap maker module enters the algorithm but it stays on its location during algorithm. Some of outer modules that advance inside the inner modules area could enter MFA algorithm to prevent some undesirable locating.

3.2.4. Construction of MFA initial average spin vectors based on the position of movable modules (mapping)

In addition extra module as an overlap maker module enters the algorithm too but it stays on its location during algorithm. Some of outer modules that advance inside the inner modules area could enter MFA algorithm to prevent some undesirable locating. We divided inner modules area to P rows and Q columns. Minimum value between all of the heights and widths of the modules is obtained. Then the width and height of relocation range are divided to this obtained value and rounded to integer values that are number of columns and rows; Q and P. We define position of a module with two vectors at MFA space, one for representing its vertical position and another one for its horizontal position. These vectors have P and Q elements respectively and for module "m" these vectors are shown with v_m^r and v_m^c that finally form overall matrices as v^r and v^c. Every element of above mentioned vectors called spin (neuron) and sum of values of these elements is equal to 1. Left-down corner coordinate of a module determines its position, that means if this point locates in range of ith row and jth column, ith element of v_m^r and jth element of v_m^c is set to 1 and others to 0 as:

$$v_m^r = [0 \quad \cdots \quad 1 \quad \cdots \quad 0] \quad , \quad v_m^c = [0 \quad \cdots \quad 1 \quad \cdots \quad 0] \tag{16}$$

$$\underbrace{\qquad}_{1:\,i\text{-}1} \underbrace{\ }_{i} \underbrace{\qquad}_{i+1:\,P} \qquad \underbrace{\qquad}_{1:\,j\text{-}1} \underbrace{\ }_{j} \underbrace{\qquad}_{j+1:\,Q}$$

To construct precision vertical and horizontal vectors we used a pseudo-trigonometric method. Module position is determined using its left-down corner distance with left-down corner of relocation range with coordinate as (x_{rr}, y_{rr}). Fig. 5 shows the relocation range of Fig. 3 and its incident inner modules that are darker one. We used a special value to normalize these distances. This value is Euclidean distance between left-down corner of relocation range and a point with coordinate of inner modules maximum "x" and maximum "y" as:

$$Sd = \sqrt{(\max(x_{in}) - x_{rr})^2 + (\max(y_{in}) - y_{rr})^2} \tag{17}$$

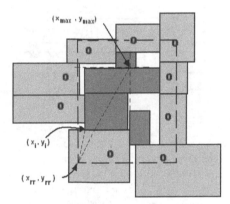

Figure 5. Relocation range and its inner modules for construction of MFA initial average spin vectors

Then for calculating row vector of a module, its vertical distance with left-down corner of relocation range is obtained and then normalized as Eq. 18. Same calculation is done for column vector.

$$vd_i = \frac{y_i - y_{rr}}{Sd} \, , \, hd_j = \frac{x_j - x_{rr}}{Sd} \tag{18}$$

Eq. 19 represents normalized total horizontal and vertical ranges. Horizontal range is divided into P parts and vertical range into Q parts. The algorithm then determines position of modules based on their vd_i and hd_j values in comparison to P and Q obtained spans.

$$\text{Horizontal range} = \left(\frac{\min(x_{in}) - x_{rr}}{Sd} \, , \, \frac{\max(x_{in}) - x_{rr}}{Sd} \right), \tag{19}$$

$$\text{Vertical range} = \left(\frac{\min(y_{in}) - y_{rr}}{Sd} \, , \, \frac{\max(y_{in}) - y_{rr}}{Sd} \right)$$

For module "m", being in the *ith* vertical span causes the *ith* element of v_m^r to become 1 and being in the *jth* horizontal span causes the *jth* element of v_m^c to be equal to 1. In MFA space that means probability of finding module "m" at row "i" and column "j" is 1. v^r and v^c are initial average spin vectors as two inputs of MFA algorithm. Fig. 6 shows the flowchart of first stage of MFA local relocation algorithm.

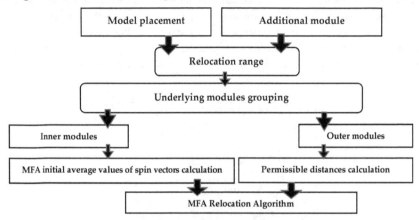

Figure 6. The flowchart of first stage of Local relocation

3.2.5. MFA relocation algorithm

At every epoch of MFA Algorithm one of the movable modules is selected randomly for mean field vector calculation from a random select list that includes movable modules with unconverged average spin vectors, and then selected module's average spin vector are updated using this vector. At the end of every epoch spin of every average vector that is greater than "0.9" is set to 1 and others are set to 0 and this vector is deleted from random select list because it has converged.

3.2.6. Energy functions

MFA Algorithm moves modules to minimize a total energy function. Our MFA relocation algorithm's total energy function is summation of three energy functions. First of all is routing cost function or wire length energy that is sum of vertical and horizontal routing costs and the algorithm minimizes it. Second one is the overlap cost and avoids algorithm to locate more than one module in same location. In MFA probability of being a module in row "i" and column "j" in the same location is computed for all of the modules. The energy term is formulated corresponding to the overlap cost as Eq. 7 in cell-placement problem [14]. In Eq. 20, ω_i and ω_j are constant values as the weights of modules "i" and "j" and are given from a module weight function that is used to encode the areas of modules. These values are some of input values of the algorithm and ω_i for module "i" is related to its area. v_{ip}^r is the probability of finding module "i" in one of the Q locations at row "p", and v_{jq}^c is the probability of finding module "i" in one of the P locations at column "q", respectively.

Last energy function that supervises preserving permissible distances is *permissible distances preservation energy* or E_{pd}. When a selected module moves to a location, the summation of widths and heights of the modules that are in the same column or row are calculated and are compared to permissible distance of that row and column. If these values exceed the permissible distances first the selected module is rotated and the summation and comparison is done again. If the problem still exists the value of E_{pd} and total energy increases respectively. In Eq. 21, E_t, E_w and E_o are total energy function, routing cost or wire length energy function and overlap energy function, respectively. α and β are balance factors between E_w, E_o and E_{pd} .α and β are constant during simulation and are used to increase or decrease importance of every energy functions in total energy function related to others.

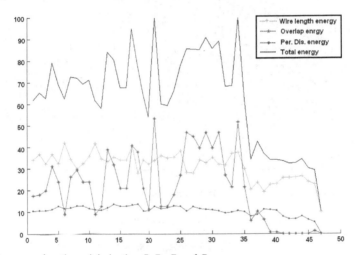

Figure 7. The energy function minimization: E_t, E_w, E_o and E_{pd}

$$E_o = \frac{1}{2} \sum_i \sum_{j \neq i} \omega_i \omega_j \times P\{\text{Modules i and j are in the same location}\} =$$

$$\frac{1}{2} \sum_i \sum_{j \neq i} \omega_i \omega_j \sum_{p=1}^P \sum_{q=1}^Q P\{\text{Module i is in location pq}\} \times P\{\text{Module j is in location pq}\} \quad (20)$$

$$= \frac{1}{2} \sum_i \sum_{j \neq i} \omega_i \omega_j \sum_{p=1}^P \sum_{q=1}^Q v_{ip}^r v_{iq}^c v_{jp}^r v_{jq}^c$$

$$E_t = E_w + \alpha \times E_o + \beta \times E_{pd} \quad (21)$$

Fig. 7 shows energy function and its parameters, wire length cost, overlap energy and permissible distances preservation energy. At the final epoch, where all of the spins converge, overlap and permissible distances preservation energies become 0 and wire length cost is minimized, therefore total energy is minimized too.

3.2.7. Cooling Schedule

For local relocation problem the cooling process is realized in three phases, slow cooling followed by fast cooling and then very fast cooling(or *quenching*).Eq. 22 shows the cooling schedule algorithm. T_{r0}, T_{c0}, T_r and T_c are horizontal and vertical initial temperatures and horizontal and vertical current temperatures of system, respectively.

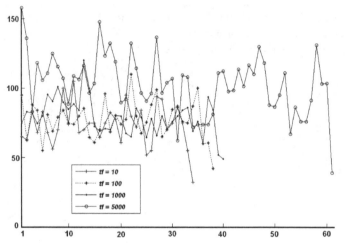

Figure 8. The total energy function minimization for three values of t_f: 10, 100, 1000 and 5000

$$if\ (0.8 \times T_{r0} \leq T_r \& 0.8 \times T_{c0} \leq T_c):T_r = 0.95 \times T_r\ ;\ T_c = 0.95 \times T_c$$

$$elseif\ (0.35 \times T_{r0} \leq T_r \leq 0.8 \times T_{r0} \& 0.35 \times T_{c0} \leq T_c \leq 0.8 \times T_{c0}):$$

$$T_r = 0.8 \times T_r\ ;\ T_c = 0.8 \times T_c$$

$$elseif\ (0.35 \times T_{r0} \geq T_r \& 0.35 \times T_{c0} \geq T_c) :T_r = 0.65 \times T_r\ ;\ T_c = 0.65 \times T_c \qquad (22)$$

end

Due to having vertical and horizontal spins two initial temperatures are calculated at the first of algorithm according to vertical and horizontal sizes of problem and a constant factor is called initial temperature factor or t_f like Eq. 23.

$$T_{r0} \propto t_f \times P\ ,T_{c0} \propto t_f \times Q \qquad (23)$$

Fig. 8 represents total energy minimization during algorithm iterations for three different values of t_f as 10, 100 and 1000. It is clear that changing this factor causes changing number of iterations and also minimum value of total energy function.

On the other hand, setting this factor to insufficient values (specially too high values) may cause unconvergence or unacceptable results, so the range of this factor is limited and according to our experiments is less than 5000.

The cooling process continues until either 90% of the spins are converged or temperature reduces below 1% of initial temperature. So when current temperature is below the 35% of initial temperature, a very fast phase of cooling process moderates the unconverged spins very fast.

At the end of this process, the variable with maximum value in each unconverged spin is set to 1 and all other variables are set to 0.

Fig. 9 shows the flowchart of second stage of MFA local relocation algorithm.

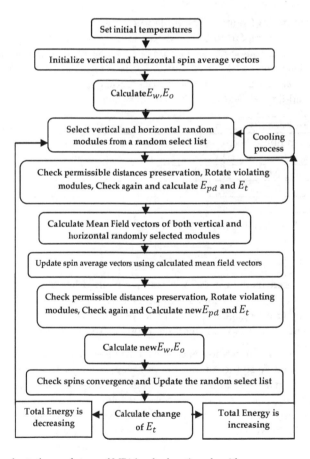

Figure 9. The flowchart of second stage of MFA local relocation algorithm

3.2.8. Experimental results

We implemented the proposed algorithm on a 2.4GHz Intel Pentium IV with 512MB memory using MATLAB 7.2.0.232 (R2006a) in WINDOWS operating system. We applied the proposed algorithm to the relocation of n300a, n200a, and n100a, which are distributed in GSRC benchmarks in [17].

For every benchmark five different problems were resolved using our proposed algorithm and maximum and average runtime of 10 runs of them are presented in Table 1. Results show that our MFA based algorithm is faster than SA-based proposed method in SA-based relocation method in [18] because the number of displacements is limited to the number of movable modules of problem and the problem is local relocation. Actually relocation range reflects on number of displacements and also similarity of resultant placement with model placement.

Results show runtimes of our proposed algorithm almost do not depend on the size of benchmark circuit in compare to the method represented in SA-based proposed method, actually size of local relocation range and numbers of movable modules of each problem are the main parameters here. Also feasibility of local relocation solution, to guarantee the similarity of resultant placement with model placement depends on the existence of enough dead space near additional module so that the relocation rage becomes limited and small.

Benchmark	MFA Local Relocation			SA
	Min. runtime (Sec.)	Average runtime (Sec.)	Max. runtime(Sec.)	Min. runtime (Sec.)
n100	2.0	2.37	2.52	1.0
n200	3.2	3.62	3.72	9.0
n300	3.7	3.92	3.96	60.8

Table 1. MFA Local Relocation results for GSRC benchmarks

4. Conclusion

Briefly, Our proposed method as a local solution method has less displacement and by taking advantages of MFA algorithm in comparison to SA algorithm and localizing problem (that reduces number of engaged modules) and therefore by having less variables, is faster. Also having less number of movable modules causes more similarity *if the solution is feasible*.

Selection of modules for relocation is based on the range that includes enough free space around the extra module so the runtimes of our proposed algorithm almost do not depend on the size of benchmark circuit in compare to the SA-based method, actually size of local relocation range and numbers of movable modules of each problem are the main parameters. Applying ability of rotation of modules inside a fixed distance controller energy function as permissible distances preservation energy and three phases cooling process are main properties of our employed MFA algorithm. Results show our method is almost independent of size and complexity of model placement.

Although the use of SA provides for escaping from the local minima, it results in an excessive computation time requirement that has hindered experimentation with the Boltzmann machine. In order to overcome this major limitation of the Boltzmann machine, a mean field approximation may be used. In mean field network, the binary state stochastic neurons of the Boltzmann machine are replaced by deterministic analogue neurons. A simple formulation of the Traveling Salesman Problems energy function is described which, in combination with a normalized Hopfield-Tank neural network, eliminates the difficulty in finding valid tours[1]. This technique, as the one of the bases of MFA algorithm, is applicable to many other optimization problems involving n-way decisions (such as VLSI layout and resource allocation) and is easily implemented in a VLSI neural network. The solution quality is shown to be dependent on the formation of elements of the problem configuration which are influenced by the constraint penalties and the temperature as what is borrowed from SA technique. The applied algorithm for local relocation problem is modified form of which is applied for cell placement problem. The cooling schedule has three stages that the final stage is very fast cooling with decreasing factor 0.65 that may be what you mean *quenching*. Otherwise other two stages with decreasing factors 0.95 and 0.8 are not so fast and have *annealing* essence. For more information about this topic, one can refer to [1].

Author details

Gholam Reza Karimi and Ahmad Azizi Verki
Electrical Engineering Department, Engineering Faculty- Razi University, Kermanshah, Iran

5. References

[1] VandenBout, D. E. & Miller, T. K. (1989). Improving the performance of the Hopfield-Tank neural network through normalization and annealing, *Biological Cybernetics*, Volume 62, Number 2, Pages 129-139.

[2] Peterson, C.& Soderberg, B. (1989). A new method for mapping optimization problems on to neural networks, *International Journal of Neural Systems*, vol.1 (3), pp. 3–22.

[3] Takahashi, Y. (1997). Mathematical improvement of the Hopfield model for TSP, feasible solutions by synapse dynamical systems. *Neurocomputing*, vol. 15 pp. 15–43.

[4] Gislen, L.; Peterson, C. & Soderberg, B. (1992).Complex scheduling with Potts neural networks," *Neural Computation*, vol. 4, pp. 805–831.

[5] Bultan, T. & Aykanat, C. (1992). A new mapping heuristic based on mean field annealing, *Journal of Parallel and Distributed Computing*, vol. 16, pp. 292–305.

[6] Ohlsson, M.; Peterson, C. & Soderberg, B. (1993). Neural networks for optimization problems with inequality constraints - the knapsack problem, *Neural Computation*, vol.5 (2), pp. 331–339.

[7] Ohlsson, M. & Pi, H. (1997).A study of the mean field approach to knapsack problems, *Neural Networks*, vol. 10(2), pp. 263–271.

[8]   Hokkinen, J.; Lagerholm, M.; Peterson, C. & Soderberg, B. (1998).A Potts neuron approach to communication routing, *Neural Computation*, vol. 10, pp. 1587–1599.

[9]   Herault, L. & Niez, J. (1989). Neural networks and graph k-partitioning, *Complex Systems*, vol. 3, pp. 531–575, 1989.

[10] VandenBout, D.E. & Miller, T.K. (1990). Graph partitioning using annealing neural networks, *IEEE Transaction on Neural Networks*, vol.1(2), pp. 192–203.

[11] Cimikowski, R. &Shope, P. (1996).A neural-network algorithm for a graph layout problem, *IEEE Transactions on Neural Networks*, vol. 7 (2), pp. 341–345.

[12] Yih, J.S. & Mazumder, P. (1990). A neural network design for circuit partitioning, *IEEE Transactions on Computer-Aided Design*, vol.9, pp. 1265–1271.

[13] Bultan, T. & Aykanat, C. (1995). Circuit partitioning using mean field annealing, *Neurocomputing*, vol. 8, pp. 171–194.

[14] Aykanat, C.; Bultan, T. & Haritaoglu, I. (1998). A fast neural-network algorithm for VLSI cell Placement, *Neural Networks*, vol. 11 pp. 1671–1684.

[15] Karimi, G.R.; AziziVerki, A. & Mirzakuchaki, S. (2010). Optimized Local Relocation for VLSI Circuit Modification Using Mean Field Annealing, *ETRI Journal*, Volume 32, Number 6.

[16] Hopfield, J.J. & Tank, D.W. (1985). "Neural" Computation of Decisions in Optimization Problems, *Biological Cybernetics*, vol. 52, pp. 141-152.

[17] http://vlsicad.eecs.umich.edu/BK/CompaSS

[18] Yanagibashi, K.; Takashima, Y. & Nakamura, Y. (December 2007). A Relocation Method for Circuit Modifications, *IEICE TRANS, FUNDAMENTALS*, vol.E90–A, NO.12.

Chapter 2

Simulated Quenching Algorithm for Frequency Planning in Cellular Systems

Luis M. San-José-Revuelta

Additional information is available at the end of the chapter

1. Introduction

This chapter focuses on a specific application of two Natural Computation (NC)-based techniques: Simulated Quenching (SQ) and Genetic Algorithms (GA): the problem of channels' assignment to radio base stations in a spectrum efficient way. This task is known to be an NP-complete optimization problem and has been extensively studied in the last two decades. We have decided to include both SQ and GA in the chapter so as o give an academic orientation to this work for readers interested in practical comparisons of NC methods.

According to this point of view, our main interest is in describing and comparing the performances of these algorithms for solving the channel allocation problem (CAP). Therefore, the aim of our work is not the full theoretical description of SQ and GA. Surely, some other chapters in this book will cover this issue.

There exists an important research activity in the field of mobile communications in order to develop sophisticated systems with increased network capacity and performance. A particular problem in this context is the assignment of available channels (or frequencies) to based stations in a way that quality of service is guaranteed. Like most of the problems that appear in complex modern systems, this one is characterized by a search space whose complexity increases exponentially with the size of the input, being, therefore, intractable for solutions using analytical or simple deterministic approaches (Krishnamachari, 1998; Lee, 2005). An important group of these problems –including the one we are interested in– belong to the class of NP-complete problems (Garey, 1979).

Simulated Quenching (SQ) belongs to the family of Simulated Annealing (SA)-like algorithms. Simulated Annealing is a general method for solving these kind of combinatorial optimization problems. It was originally proposed by (Kirkpatrick, 1983) and (Černy, 1985). Since then, it has been applied in many engineering areas. The basic SA algorithm can be considered a generalization of the local search scheme, where in each step of the iterative process a neighbour s' of each current solution s is proposed at random. Then s is only replaced by s' if cost does not rise. The main problems of SA are: (i) the possibility to get trapped in local minima, and (ii) the large computational load that leads to slow algorithms.

Both of the algorithms described in this chapter try to solve these drawbacks. The first one, SQ, speeds up the algorithm by quickly reducing the temperature in the system, though, in the process, the advantage of SA, i.e. convergence to the global optimum, is defeated (Ingber, 1993). Due to this, SQ is termed as a greedier algorithm in terms of computational load compromising for the global optimum. Besides, the proposed method, occasionally allows moves to solutions of higher cost according to the so-called Metropolis criterion (Metropolis, 1953) (see section 4.1). However, Duque et al. (Duque, 1993) point out that the main drawback they found was to get trapped to a local minimum (by a misplaced transition) with a low chance to get out of it.

The problem of convergence to suboptimal solutions can be efficiently addressed with another NC-based technique, the GAs. These algorithms are based on he principle of natural selection and survival of the fittest, thus constituting an alternative method for finding solutions to highly-nonlinear problems with multimodal solutions' spaces. GAs efficiently combine explorative and exploitative search to avoid convergence to suboptimal solutions. Unlike many other approaches, GAs are much less susceptible to local optima, since they provide the ability to selectively accept successive potential solutions even if they have a higher cost than the current solution (Mitchell, 1996).

This chapter focuses on the application of these methods to solve the channel allocation problem found in cellular radio systems. In this kind of systems, the frequency reuse by which the same channels are reused in different cells becomes crucial (Gibson, 1996). Every cell is allocated a set of channels according to its expected traffic demand. The entire available spectrum is allocated to a cluster of cells arranged in shapes that allow for uniform reuse patterns. Channels must be located satisfying certain frequency separation constraints to avoid channel interference using as small a bandwidth as possible. Considering this framework, the CAP fits into the category of multimodal and NP-complete problems (Krishnamachari, 1998; Garey, 1979; Hale, 1980; Katzela, 1996).

The *fixed* CAP –see section 3.2– has been extensively studied during the past decades. A comprehensive summary of the work done before 1980 can be found in (Hale, 1980). When only the co-channel constraint is considered, the CAP is equivalent to an NP-complete graph coloring problem (Sivarajan, 1989). In this simpler case, various graph-theoretic approaches have been proposed (Hale, 1980; Sivarajan, 1989; Box 1978; Kim, 1994).

From the point of view of NC, some procedures based on NNs (Funabiki, 1992; Hopfield, 1985; Kunz, 1991; Lochite, 1993) and SA or SQ (Duque, 1993; Kirkpatrick, 1983; Mathar, 1993) have already been considered. SA-SQ techniques generally improve the problem of convergence to local optima found with NNs, though their rate of convergence is rather slow (specially in SA), and a carefully designed cooling schedule is required. On the other hand, several GA-based approaches have been applied to solve the CAP: For instance, (Cuppini, 1994) defines and uses specific genetic operators: an asexual crossover and a special mutation. A disadvantage of such crossover is that it can easily destroy the structure of the current solution and, thus, make the algorithm harder to converge. In (Lai, 1996), Lai and Coghill represented the channel assignment solution as a string of channel numbers grouped in such a way that the traffic requirement is satisfied. The evolution is then proceeded via a *partially matched crossover operator* (PMX) –this type of crossover has also been used in (Ghosh, 2003)– and basic mutation. Two years later, Ngo and Li (Ngo, 1998) suggested a GA that used the so-called *minimum separation encoding scheme*, where the number of 1's in each row of the binary assignment matrix corresponds to the number of channels allocated to the corresponding cell. Authors stated that this algorithm outperforms the NN-based approach described in (Funabiki, 1992).

The particularities of the GA shown in section 5 are, mainly, a low computational load and the capability of achieving good quality solutions (optimal, minimum-span, solutions) while maintaining satisfactory convergence properties. The probabilities of mutation and crossover of the GA are on-line adjusted by making use of an individuals' fitness dispersion measure based on the Shannon entropy (San José, 2007). This way, the diversity of the population is monitored and the thus obtained method offers the flexibility and robustness peculiar to GAs.

Another closely related problem that we are not going to deal with is the determination of a lower bound for the *span* (difference between the largest channel used and the smallest channel used) in channel assignment problems. For instance, (Mandal, 2004) and (Smith, 2000) address this problem when proposing solutions to the CAP.

The chapter is organized in the following sections:

- The first section (section 2) presents a brief introduction to the frequency (or channel) allocation problem. As mentioned above, there exist many good articles covering this problem, and our main purpose is to introduce the basic references of SQ and GAs applied to the CAP, to pose the problem as well as to describe a first motivation to research into this field.
- Next, section 3 explains mathematically the interference and traffic constraints that define the CAP.
- Sections 4 and 5 are devoted to the detailed description of both the proposed SQ and the GA-based algorithms for frequency allocation, respectively. The first one is mainly based on the method proposed in (Duque, 1993), though incorporating some improvements concerning the weakest aspects outlined in the conclusions of the work of Duque et al. Important concepts such as the specific *cooling procedure* and the *neighbourhood production* are here described. On the other hand, the genetic algorithm included in section 5 is based on our previous work in the field of NC-based strategies for approaching not only the frequency allocation problem (San José, 2007), but also digital communications (San José, 2008) or image processing problems (San José, 2009), most of them using GAs.
- Finally, the last section of the chapter is devoted to the description of the numerical results, with special emphasis on the comparison between Neural Networks (NNs), SQ

and GAs: advantages and drawbacks of each of them are here explained. For the sake of comparison, a set of well-known problem instances was selected since they have been used in most of the papers related to this problem, thus allowing a direct comparison.

2. The Channel Assignment Problem (CAP)

2.1. Interference constraints

As mentioned in the Introduction, frequency reuse is a key issue in current mobile communication systems. It is well known that the co-channel interference caused by frequency reuse is the most restraining factor on the overall system capacity in wireless networks. Therefore, the main purpose is the simultaneous use of a given radio spectrum while maintaining a tolerable level of interferences. Specifically, each system cell is assigned a set of channels according to the expected traffic demand. This assignment of channels must satisfy the following constraints:

- **Co-site constraint (CSC)**: channels assigned to the same cell must be separated by some minimum spectral distance.
- **Co-channel constraint (CCC)**: the same channel cannot be simultaneously assigned to certain pairs of cells. The *co-channel reuse distance* is the minimum distance at which the same channel can be reused with acceptable interference (Katzela 1996).
- **Adjacent channel constraint (ACC)**: any pair of channels in different cells must have a specified minimum distance (Funabiki, 2000).

The channel assignment algorithm must also take into account the specified traffic profile (number of channels) required in each cell. These non-uniform cell demand requirements imply that those cells with a higher traffic demand will need the assignment of more channels.

2.2. Problem definition

Let us consider the problem where a set of c channels must be assigned to n arbitrary cells (in this work we consider only the *fixed* CAP, where the channels are permanently assigned to each cell; the reader interested in *dynamic* and *hybrid* schemes can see (Gibson, 1996; Hale, 1980; Katzela 1996).

In our problem formulation we assume that the total number of available channels is given –it can be determined by either the available radio spectrum or the lower bound estimated by a graph-theoretic method (Mandal, 2004; Smith, 2000). Without loss of generality, channels can be assumed to be evenly spaced in the radio frequency spectrum. Thus, using an appropriate mapping, channels can be represented by consecutive positive integers. Therefore, the interference constraints are modelled by an $n \times n$ *compatibility matrix* **C**, whose diagonal elements c_{ii} represent the co-site constraint, i.e., the number of frequency bands by which channels assigned to cell i must be separated. The non-diagonal elements c_{ij} represent the number of frequency bands by which channels assigned to cells i and j must differ. When this compatibility matrix is binary, the constraints can be expressed more simply: if the same channel cannot be reused by cells i and j, then $c_{ij}=1$, and, otherwise, $c_{ij}=0$.

The traffic demand is modelled by means of an n-length demand vector $\mathbf{d}=[d_1,d_2,...,d_n]^T$, whose elements represent the number of channels required in each of the cells. For instance, Fig. 1 shows the four demand vectors that will be used in the simulations' section.

$$d_1^T = [1\ 1\ 1\ 3]$$
$$d_2^T = [5\ 5\ 5\ 8\ 12\ 25\ 30\ 25\ 30\ 40\ 40\ 45\ 20\ 30\ 25\ 15\ 15\ 30\ 20\ 20\ 25]$$
$$d_3^T = [8\ 25\ 8\ 8\ 8\ 15\ 18\ 52\ 77\ 28\ 13\ 15\ 31\ 15\ 16\ 57\ 28\ 8\ 10\ 13\ 6]$$
$$d_4^T = [10\ 11\ 9\ 5\ 9\ 4\ 5\ 7\ 4\ 8\ 8\ 9\ 10\ 7\ 7\ 6\ 4\ 5\ 5\ 7\ 6\ 4\ 5\ 7\ 5]$$

Figure 1. Traffic demand vectors for the benchmark problems considered.

The assignment to be generated is denoted by an $n{\times}c$ binary matrix $\mathbf{A}$, whose element a_{ij} is 1 if channel j is assigned to cell i, and 0 otherwise. This implies that the total number of 1's in row i of matrix $\mathbf{A}$ must be d_i (see Fig. 2).

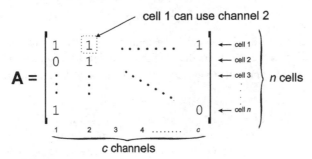

Figure 2. Structure of the allocation matrix A.

The cost due to the violation of interference constraints can be written as

$$J_1 = J_{CSC} + J_{ACC} \tag{1}$$

where J_{CSC} and J_{ACC} represent, respectively, the costs due to the violations of the co-site and the adjacent channel constraints. The first one can be written as

$$J_{CSC} = \lambda_{CSC} \sum_x^n \sum_{i,i\neq j}^{n_x} \sum_j^{n_y} \Phi(f_i^x, f_j^x) \tag{2}$$

where parameter λ_{CSC} weighs the relative importance of CSC and $\Phi(f_i^x, f_j^x)$ is a measure of the co-site constraint satisfaction. This parameter equals 0 only if the difference between channels i and j of cell x is $|f_i^x - f_j^x| \geq c_{xx}$, and 1 otherwise. f_α^β represents the assigned frequency for the αth channel of cell β, and n_α is the number of channels in the αth cell.

On the other hand, the cost due to the adjacent channel constraint violation is obtained as

$$J_{ACC} = \lambda_{ACC} \sum_{x\neq y}^n \sum_y^n \sum_i^{n_x} \sum_j^{n_y} \Psi(f_i^x, f_j^y) \tag{3}$$

where

$$\Psi(f_i^x, f_j^y) = \begin{cases} 0 & \text{if} \quad |f_i^x - f_j^y| \ge c_{xy} \\ 1 & \text{otherwise} \end{cases} \tag{4}$$

Parameter λ_{ACC} in Eq. (3) is set to weigh the relative importance of the adjacent channel constraint. Finally, the cost due to the violation of the traffic demand requirements is modelled as

$$J_{TRAFF} = \lambda_{TRAFF} \sum_i^n \left(d_i - \sum_j a_{ij} \right)^2 \tag{5}$$

Gathering all the costs, the final cost function to be minimized is

$$J = J_{CSC} + J_{ACC} + J_{TRAFF} \tag{6}$$

If the traffic demand requirements are incorporated implicitly by only considering those assignments that satisfy them, then the cost function can be expressed by $J=J_1=J_{CSC}+J_{ACC}$, subject to $\sum_j a_{ij} = d_i, \forall i$. For that reason, the fitness function to be used in the algorithms is given by $\rho=1/J$.

Finally, the estimation of parameters λ_{CSC} and λ_{ACC} has been achieved using the same inhomogeneous 25-cell network used by Kunz and Lai in (Kunz, 1991) and (Lai, 1996), respectively. After analyzing the number of iterations required for a proper convergence for different values of λ_{CSC} and λ_{ACC}, the optimal values for the weights λ_{CSC} and λ_{ACC} were found to be close to 1 and 1.3, respectively.

It is important to note that the most important difference between different pairs of λ_{CSC} and λ_{ACC} is the required computational load for each of them, since the number of generations required to converge proportionally acts on the execution time. This way, a precise computation of both λ_{CSC} and λ_{ACC} is indispensable to get an efficient allocation algorithm.

3. Simulated quenching algorithm for CAP

3.1. Basic concepts

As mentioned in the Introduction, SQ is methodology proposed to speed up the standard SA algorithms when applied to solve difficult (NP-complete) optimization problems. The original SA method can be viewed as a simulation of the physical annealing process found in nature, e.g., the settling of a solid to its state of minimum energy (ground state). SQ is stronger based on physical intuition though it loses some mathematical rigor.

Generally speaking, an optimization problem consists of a set of S configurations (or solutions) and a cost function J that determines, for each configuration s, its cost $J(s)$. Local search is then performed by determining the neighbours s' of each solution s. Thus, a neighbour structure $N(s)$ that defines a set of possible transitions that can be proposed by s has to be defined.

When performing local search, in each iteration of the algorithm, a neighbour s' of s is proposed randomly, and s will only be replaced by s' if cost does not increase, i.e., $J(s')\leq J(s)$. Obviously, this procedure terminates in a local minimum that may have a higher cost than the global optimal solution. To avoid this trapping in a suboptimal solution, our proposed SQ method occasionally allows "uphill moves" to solutions of higher cost using the so-called Metropolis criterion (Metropolis, 1953). This criterion states that, if s and $s' \in N(s)$ are the two configurations to choose from, then the algorithm continues with configuration s' with a probability given by $\min\{1,\exp(-(J(s')-J(s))/t)\}$, with t being a positive parameter that gradually decreases to zero during the algorithm. Note that the acceptance probability decreases for increasing values of $J(s')-J(s)$ and for decreasing values of t, and that cost-decreasing transitions are always accepted (see Fig. 3).

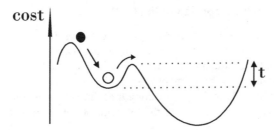

Figure 3. SQ allows uphill moves up to a cost proportional to the instantaneous temperature t.

Mathematically, SA-SQ can be modelled as an inhomogeneous Markov process, consisting of a sequence of homogenous chains at each temperature level t (Duque, 1993). Under this framework, it has been shown (Aarts, 1989; Geman, 1984) that there exist two alternatives for the convergence of the algorithm to the globally minimal configurations. On the one hand (homogenous case), asymptotic convergence to a global minimum is guaranteed if t is lowered to 0, and if the homogenous chains are extended to infinite length to establish the stationary distribution on each level. On the other hand (inhomogeneous case), convergence is guaranteed, irrespective of the length of the homogenous chains, if t approaches 0 logarithmically slow.

The problem arising here is that just the enumeration of the configuration space has an exponential time complexity and, in practice, some approximation is required. The formal procedure is to choose a *cooling schedule* to decide for:

- the start condition (initial temperature, t_0).
- the rule for decreasing the temperature.
- the equilibrium condition.
- the stop condition (final temperature, t_F).

The initial temperature should be chosen high enough in order to allow that most of the proposed transitions pass the Metropolis criterion. Hence, at the start of the algorithm, an explorative search into the configuration space is intended. Later on, the number of accepted transitions decreases as $t\to 0$. Finally, when $t \approx 0$, no more transitions are accepted and the algorithm may stop. As a consequence, the algorithm converges to a final configuration representing the solution of the optimization problem.

As (Duque, 1993) shows, when doing this most cooling schedules lean on the homogenous variant and try to establish and maintain equilibrium on each temperature level by adjusting the length of the Markov chains and the cooling speed.

According to this, the main steps required for solving an optimization problem applying SQ involves that, first, the problem must be expressed as a cost function optimization problem by defining the configuration space S, the cost function J, the neighbourhood structure N. Next, a cooling schedule must be chosen, and, finally, the annealing process is performed.

3.2. Simulated quenching applied to the CAP

In order to apply SQ to solve the CAP, we have to formulate the CAP as a discrete optimization problem, with S, J and N defined. In section 3.2 we have already presented the problem together with its mathematical characterization: a mobile radio network of n radio cells, each of them capable to carry any of the n available channels. The channel assignment is given by binary matrix $\mathbf{A}$, with $a_{ij}=1$ meaning that channel j is assigned to cell i. Since the traffic demand is modelled by vector $\mathbf{d}$, the total number of 1's in row i of matrix $\mathbf{A}$ must equal d_i.

The cost function J is then given by Eq. (6) that quantifies the violation of the interference constraints defined in section 3.1. Thus $J(s)$ reaches its minimum of zero if all constraints are satisfied.

In this work we will use the same simple strategies for generating the neighbourhood than those used in (Duque, 1993) but with probabilities specifically tuned for our application: (i) *single flip*: just switching on or off channel i in cell j, –this procedure mimics the mutation operation that will be described later in the GAs context, and (ii) *flip-flop*: replacing at cell j one used channel with one unused.

Considering the particularities of the channel allocation problem with hexagonal cells, the same channel should be reused as closed as possible. To approach this goal, the *basic flip-flop* is modified as follows: (ii-1) a cell j is chosen at random, (ii-2) from all the channels not used in cell j, the channel that is most used within the nearest cells to j that may share that channel with cell j is switched on, (ii-3) one of the channels previously used at cell j is randomly selected and switched off. This *modified flip-flop* is used in conjunction with the basic one.

For the cooling schedule we have implemented of a mixture of different cooling schemes –(Aarts, 1989; Huang, 1986; Romeo, 1989)– with a polynomial-time approximation behaviour. The initial value of the temperature is set to assure a user specified transitions' acceptance ratio. For that, first, t is set to 0, and then it is iteratively changed until the desired acceptance ratio is reached. Our simulations worked fine with acceptance ratios between 0.55 and 0.6.

Temperature decrement follows a restriction proposed by Huang et al. (Huang, 1986): the decrease ΔJ in the average cost between two subsequent temperatures t and t' should be less than the standard deviation of the cost (on level t). After some calculus (Huang, 1986; Romeo, 1989) this rule is expressed as

$$t' = t \exp\left(-\frac{\lambda t}{\sigma}\right) \tag{7}$$

Since testing for the establishment of equilibrium at a specific t would involve an unacceptable monitoring load, Huang et al. (Huang, 1986) approximate this check in two respects: (i) a Gaussian form for the equilibrium distribution is assumed, whose average and standard deviation are estimated from the Markov chain itself, and (ii) the process is considered stationary if the ratio of the number of accepted transitions, their costs being in a 2δ-legth interval, to the total number of accepted transitions, reaches a stable value $erf(2\delta/\sigma)$. In those cases where the criterion for stationarity can not be reached the length of the chain is bounded proportionally to the number of configurations which can be reached in one transition.

The final temperature is reached if a substantial improvement in cost can no more be expected. In (Huang, 1986; Duque 1993) this is monitored by comparing the difference between the maximum and minimum costs encountered on a temperature level with the maximum single change in cost on that level. If they are the same, the process is assumed to be trapped in a local minimum and the algorithm is stopped.

Numerical experiments show that once being trapped into a suboptimal solution (suboptimal minimum) it is almost impossible to get out of it. Technical literature has described simple approaches to partially improve this situation such as tuning the neighbourhoods to prefer flip-flops which resolve existing interference, or preset violations and to disadvantage those that introduce new ones.

Another solution is based on occasionally allowing arbitrary long jumps while preserving a fast cooling schedule. These long jumps open up the possibility to detrap from any minimum in a single transition, without being questioned by a maybe long chain of acceptance decisions. A simple method for producing these long jumps is to extend the basic transitions –flip-flops– to a chain of consecutive ones. By properly adjusting the chain length, this allows to tunnel through a hill of the cost function landscape in one single jump, instead of painfully working to its top just to fall down into the next valley.

4. Genetic algorithm for CAP

This section describes a low complexity GA (known as μGA) that is applied to solve the channel assignment problem. Next sections present the proposed method, particularizing the concepts to the CAP for a better understanding.

4.1. Basic concepts

The golden rule of GAs is that a set of potential solutions (*population*) can be represented with a predetermined encoding rule. At every iteration k, each potential solution (*chromosome*) is associated to a *fitness* value, $\rho_i(k)$, in accordance to its proximity to the optimal solution. Considering the problem of frequencies assignment, the goal is to avoid violating any of the constraints described in section 3.1, while satisfying the traffic demand in each cell and minimizing the required overall bandwidth.

The initial set of potential solutions, $\mathcal{P}[0]$ (population at k=0), is randomly generated when no *a priori* knowledge of the solution is available (in our specific CAP, some a priori information is available and will help to generate the initial population –see (Lai, 1996). Let us denote $P[k] = \{u_i\}_{i=1}^{n_p}$ to the population at iteration k, with n_p being the number of individuals u_i per generation. In our problem, u_i consists of a string structure containing all the channels required for each base station (see Fig. 4). This way, each string represents a particular assignment for all the base stations. By assigning, the number of elements in each string to satisfy the required number of channels for each cell, such computations can be effectively ignored in the objective function.

Figure 4. Schematic representation of the chromosome structure for the CAP. Channels for each base station are coded consecutively into the chromosome.

The number of individuals that constitute the population, n_p, is an important issue to be addressed. In (Lai, 1996), Lai and Coghill suggest that a reasonable choice should be in the range 30-110 in order to have a large variability within the population. Since we propose a μGA, the population size would be much smaller, in the range 10-20.

4.2. Genetic operators

Once individuals are generated and given a fitness value, the next step consists in applying the *genetic operators*, mainly *mutation* and *crossover*, to those individuals selected using a fitness-based selection algorithm (Fig. 5 shows the pseudocode that outlines the main steps of the proposed GA). This selection procedure is based on a biased random selection, where the fittest individuals have a higher probability of being selected than their weaker counterparts. This way, the probability of any individual to be selected is $P_i(k) = \rho_i(k) / \sum_{j=1}^{n_p} \rho_j(k)$, with $\rho_i(k)$ being the fitness of the ith individual in the population during the kth iteration of the algorithm. The simplest way to implement this concept is based on a *roulette wheel*, where the size of each slot in the wheel is proportional to the individual's fitness (Mitchell, 1996).

```
0. GENERATE POPULATION P[0]
1. DO{
        1.1 EVALUATE FITNESS OF INDIVIDUALS IN P[k]
        1.2 DO{
                SELECTION (ROULETTE WHEEL)
                APPLY GENETIC OPERATORS:
                        PMX CROSSOVER (PROBABILITY p_c)
                        MUTATION (PROBABILITY p_m)
                }
                WHILE NEW GENERATION NOT COMPLETED
        1.3 EXECUTE CREATE-ELITE
        }
        WHILE {TERMINATION CRITERIA = NO}
2. PRINT BEST ASSIGNMENT SOLUTION u_i

FUNCTION CREATE-ELITE:
{
        SELECTION OF BEST INDIVIDUALS
        MUTATION (PROBABILITY p_m)
        ELITE = MUTATED ELITE + NOT-MUTATED ELITE
        INSERT ELITE INTO POPULATION:
                P[k+1]=INSERT(ELITE,P[k])

}
```

Figure 5. Pseudocode of the proposed GA.

The main genetic operators are:

- **Mutation**: the mutation operator modifies specific individuals with probability p_m, changing the value of some concrete positions in the encoding of individual u_i. The number of positions within the encoding of the channels of each cell that are candidates for possible mutation is half the number of channels present at that base station. Both the specific positions and the new values are randomly generated, and mutation is performed with probability p_m. Notice that this genetic operator promotes the exploration of different areas of the solutions space. A low level of mutation serves to prevent any element in the chromosome from remaining fixed to a single value in the entire population, while a high level of mutation will essentially result in a random search. Hence, probability p_m must be chosen carefully in order to avoid excessive mutation. To maintain a good balance between such extremes a good initial value for p_m is 0.02-0.05 (Lai, 1996; Grefenstette, 1986). In our application, $p_m(0)=0.04$.
- **Crossover**: the crossover operator requires two operands (*parents*) to produce two new individuals (*offspring*), which are created merging parents by crossing them at specific internal points. This operation is performed with probability p_c. Since parents are selected from those individuals having a higher fitness, the small variations introduced within these individuals are intended to also generate high fit individuals.

Simulation results show that with the *simple crossover* operator, a significant number of the generated configurations have the same frequency assigned to a group of base stations that interfere with each other. To alleviate this problem we have implemented the *partially matched crossover* operator (Lai, 1996). This operator partitions each string into three randomly chosen portions. When this operator encounters that the same frequency has been assigned more than once, it solves this conflict by rearranging the conflicting elements in each string –see (Lai, 1996) for a detailed description. Our range for p_c is [0.35, 0.85].

4.3. Elitism, termination criteria and convergence

The proposed algorithm also implements an elitism strategy, where the elite for $\mathcal{P}[k+1]$ is formed by selecting those individuals from both the elite of $\mathcal{P}[k]$ and the mutated elite of $\mathcal{P}[k]$ having the highest fitness value in the population. The mutation of the elite is performed with a probability $p_{m,e}=0.25p_m$. No crossover is performed on the elite.

This elitist model of the GA presents some convergence advantages over the standard GA. Using Markov chain modelling, it has been proved that GAs are guaranteed to asymptotically converge to the global optimum –with any choice of the initial population– if an elitist strategy is used, where at least the best chromosome at each generation is always maintained in the population (Bhandari, 1996).

The whole procedure is iterated until a termination criterion is satisfied. In our simulations, the search is terminated when there are no significant changes between the maximum and minimum values of the objective function in any two successive generations. Notice that, it can not be guaranteed that a valid solution is found in a finite number of iterations. Besides, the time required to compute an optimal solution increases exponentially with the size of the problem (Beckmann, 1999; Kunz, 1991; Funabiki, 1992). Thus, it is necessary to develop approximate methods capable of finding at least a near-optimum solution within a reasonable amount of time.

However, Bhandari et al. provided the proof that no finite stopping time can guarantee the optimal solution, though, in practice, the GA process must terminate after a finite number of iterations with a high probability that the process has achieved the global optimal solution. Note that, in our problem, the optimal string is not necessarily unique and there may be many strings that provide the optimal value (Bhandari, 1996).

In our proposed GA, the coding scheme guarantees that the traffic demand is always satisfied. However, in hard assignment instances it can be impossible to minimize the cost function to zero, i.e., some of the interference constraints may be violated by the generated assignment. In those cases where the optimal solution is not achieved in a finite time, invalid assignments should be resolved by manually assigning more frequencies to the affected cells (thus yielding a span that is larger that the lower limit). Nevertheless, none of the proposed test problem instances led to this situation.

At the end, the string u_i corresponding to the highest fit chromosome is finally chosen as the channel allocation problem solution.

4.4. Diversity and related genetic operators

Convergence properties become notably improved with the introduction of procedures to adjust the parameters in order to achieve and maintain a good population diversity. This diversity is a crucial issue in the performance of any evolutionary algorithm, including GAs: standard GAs have a tendency to converge prematurely to local optima, mainly due to selection pressure and too high gene flow between population members (Ursem, 2002). A high selection pressure will fill the population with clones of the fittest individuals and it may result in convergence to local minima. On the other hand, high gene flow is often determined by the population structure. In simple GAs, genes spread fast throughout the population, and diversity quickly declines.

On the other hand, one of the main drawbacks of standard GAs is their excessive computational load: the application of the genetic operators is often costly and the fitness function evaluation is also a very time-consuming step. Besides, population sizes n_p normally are 100, 200 or even much higher −for instance, (Ursem, 2002) uses n_p=400 individuals. The method used in this paper works with much smaller population sizes, in the order of 10 to 20 individuals. An elite of 3 individuals is selected and the crossover and mutation probabilities depend on the Shannon entropy of the population (excluding the elite) fitness, which is calculated as

$$\mathcal{H}(\mathcal{P}[k]) = -\sum_{i=1}^{n_p} \rho_i^*(k)\log\rho_i^*(k) \tag{8}$$

with $\rho_i^*(k)$ being the normalized fitness of individual u_i, i.e.,

$$\rho_i^*(k) = \frac{\rho_i(k)}{\sum_{i=1}^{n_p}\rho_i(k)} \tag{9}$$

When all the fitness values are very similar, with small dispersion, $\mathcal{H}(\mathcal{P}[k])$ becomes high and p_c is decreased −it is not worthwhile wasting time merging very similar individuals. This way, the exploration character of the GA is boosted, while, conversely, exploitation decreases. On the other hand, when this entropy is small, there exists a high diversity within the population, a fact that can be exploited in order to increase the horizontal sense of search. Following a similar reasoning, the probability of mutation is increased when the entropy is high, so as to augment the diversity of the population and escape from local suboptimal solutions (exploitation decreases, exploration becomes higher). Therefore, we have that probabilities p_m and p_c are directly/inversely proportional to the population fitness entropy, respectively.

Finally, some exponentially dependence on time k is included in the model −making use of exponential functions− in order to relax, along time, the degree of dependence of the genetic operators' probabilities on the dispersion measure.

The complexity of the thus obtained GA is notably decreased since crossover is applied with a very low probability (and only on individuals not belonging to the elite), and the diversity control scheme allows the algorithm to work properly with a much smaller population size.

5. Numerical results

This section evaluates the performance of the proposed algorithms in terms of convergence and solution accuracy under different conditions. Radio base stations are considered to be located at cell centers and the traffic is assumed to be inhomogeneous, with each cell having a different and *a priori* known traffic demand. Following the ideas shown in (Lai, 1996), the initial population is constructed using the available *a priori* information, i.e., the algorithm assigns a valid string of frequencies to all the cells following a simple approach: first, the algorithm attempts to assign a set of valid frequencies to as many base stations as possible. In the event that valid frequencies cannot be located to some of the cells, they are then randomly assigned.

5.1. Benchmark problems

In order to evaluate the performances of the proposed methods and compare them to other approaches, performance is analyzed using the set of thirteen benchmark problems defined in (Sivarajan, 1989) (also used in (Funabiki, 2000) as well as problems 1, 2 and 4 from (Ngo, 1998) (we will refer to these problems with numbers 14, 15 and 16). The characteristics of the first 13 benchmark instances can be found in (Sivarajan, 1989). The definition of problems 14, 15 and 16 are summarized in Table 1, where all the channel demand vectors were shown in Figure 1, and the compatibility matrices are: C_1 (matrix in Example 1, page 846, in (Sivarajan, 1989)), C_2 (matrix in Fig. 3 (c) (Funabiki, 1992), p. 435) and C_3 (matrix in Fig. 3 (a) (Funabiki, 1992), p. 435). The total number of frequencies varies from 11 to 221. Benchmark problem 15 belongs to a particular set of useful benchmark tests for cellular assignment problems called *Philadelphia problems*. Notice that (Sivarajan, 1989) presents some variations from the original Philadelphia problems, which were first presented by Anderson (Anderson, 1973) in the early 70's. These problems constitute, by far, the most common set of benchmark problems for channel assignment algorithms, making it possible to compare the obtained solutions with previously published results. Notice that problems 1–4 and 9–14 consider the three constraints defined in the beginning of section 3.1, while problems 5–8, 15 and 16 consider only the co-channel and co-site constraints.

Problem No.	No. of Cells	Lower Bound	Compatibility Matrix	Demand Vector
14	4	11	C_1	d_1
15	21	221	C_2	d_2
16	25	73	C_3	d_4

Table 1. Specifications of benchmark problems No. 14, 15 and 16.

As an example, Fig. 6 shows the cellular geometry of the Philadelphia problem with $n=21$ cells (the cluster size for CCC is $N_c=7$).

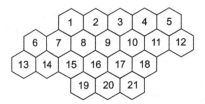

Figure 6. Cellular geometry for the Philadelphia benchmark problem with $n=21$ cells.

5.2. Adjustment of parameters and convergence performance

In this section, the convergence properties of the proposed methods are studied. Results shown in Table 2 are average values over 25 trials for each problem. The parameters to be set in the GA are: the number of iterations n_g, the initial mutation and crossover probabilities, the population size n_p, and the parameters of functions $p_c(k)$ and $p_m(k)$. After several trials that helped to fine tune the parameters ensuring that the computation is manageable, the optimal values were found to be:

- Number of fitness evaluations: 100 (for problem 14), 25,000 (problems 5–8 and 11), 50,000 (problems 12, 15 and 16), 75,000 (problem 13), 100,000 (problems 1–4), 150,000 (problem 10) and 300,000 (problem 9). If the values corresponding to problems 10, 12, 14 and 16 are compared to those shown in (Ngo, 1998) it can be seen that these values mean a reduction of 75% (in problems 15, 12 and 16) and 62.5% (in problem 10) with respect to the number of iterations needed in (Ngo, 1998); in problem 14 both approaches require 100 iterations. Notice that, since not every offspring needs to be evaluated in each generation, the number of fitness evaluations is a more representative parameter of the performance than the number of generations.
- Initial crossover probability, $p_c(0)$: this parameter is set to 0.35 in problems 5–8 and 11–16, while instances 1–4, 9 and 10 showed better results with 0.25.
- Initial mutation probability, $p_m(0)$: 0.04 for all the problems.
- Population size, n_p: 10 individuals, except in problems 1–4, 9 and 10, which required 20.
- Simulations show that $\lambda_{CSC}=1$ and $\lambda_{ACC}=1.3$ lead to faster convergence as compared to $\lambda_{ACC}=1$. This result is in accordance to (Lai, 1996), where $\lambda_{ACC\text{-}optimal}=1.1/2$ was obtained.

On the other hand, the SQ algorithm has been implemented with a mixture of standard and modified *flip-flops* (described in section 4.2). Problems 5–8, 11–12, 14–16 are solved with a configuration of 50-70% of modified flip-flops, while problem instances 1–4, 9, 10 and 13 used 20-40% of modified flip-flops. The remaining cases, in all problem instances, were implemented with standard flip-flops. To explain this experimental adjustment, just notice that the more complex is the problem instance, the more explorative must be the global search for solutions in order to avoid convergence to suboptimal local minima.

Comparative results are shown in Table 2. The performance is measured using the percentage of convergence to the solutions, defined as the ratio of the total number of successful convergence to the total number of runs. Table 2 shows the results for problems 10, 12, 14, 15 and 16, whose convergence properties have been previously studied by Ngo and Li using a GA-based scheme (Ngo, 1998) and by Funabiki and Takefuji, who applied a NN-based algorithm to solve these instances (Funabiki, 1992).

Problem No.	Percentages of convergence (%)			
	Funabiki & Takefuji's NN (Funabiki, 1992)	Ngo & Li's MGA (Ngo, 1998)	Proposed μGA	Proposed SQ
10	-	21	24	15
12	23	80	86	78
14	100	100	100	100
15	77	92	90	95
16	9	99	99	98

Table 2. Comparison between convergence results.

Results show that both GA or SQ based procedures outperform the convergence results of the neural network for solving the fixed CAP. The four approaches converge properly in 100% of cases in problem 14. In problems 12, 15 and 16, both genetic methods converge more frequently than the neural network-based approach, and SQ is slightly better than GA in problem 15, while marginally worse in problems 12 and 16. In problem 15 the GA shows a little bit worse convergence results than (Ngo, 1998) (only in about 2%) while SQ moderately improves the MGA. In spite of that, the proposed method involves fewer computational load than that required by (Ngo, 1998) (see Table 3) and the complexity of the SQ method is intermediate between that of the standard GA (MGA) and that of the proposed μGA. In contrast, the μGA presents notably better convergence in problems 10 and 12, where MGA and SQ offer very similar results. In essence, in problems 12, 15 and 16 algorithms exhibit very similar results, with the μGA being less complex.

5.3. Computational complexity

Table 3 shows the execution times required to solve these problems. Bold figures show the CPU time normalized to the time required to solve problem 15 using the μGA.

It can be seen how the computational burden of the proposed method is about 20% lower than that of the standard GA by Ngo and Li (Ngo, 1998) (18% in problem 15, 23% in problem 12, and 20% in problems 10 and 16).

On the other hand, the SQ method shows larger execution times in order to obtain similar convergence figures (as noticed in previous sections). Only in problem No. 15 SQ requires less computational load than the MGA algorithm, although, even in this problem, the μGA obtained the results faster. Notice that this reduction in the computational load observed in

GA-based approaches is achieved maintaining a very similar –or even better– percentage of convergence (Table 2) and with the three approaches getting optimal conflict-free solutions.

	MGA (Ngo, 1998)		µGA		SQ	
10	4.129	**26.12**	3.285	**20.78**	6.101	**38.61**
12	0.959	**6.07**	0.738	**4.67**	1.022	**6.468**
14	0	**0**	0	**0**	0.01	**0.06**
15	0.192	**1.22**	0.158	**1**	0.189	**1.196**
16	0.284	**1.80**	0.226	**1.43**	0.386	**2.443**

Table 3. Execution times (in seconds) for benchmark problems 10, 12, 14, 15 and 16. CPU: AMD Athlon XP 2100+ 1.8 GHz. Bold figures show the CPU time normalized to the time required to solve problem 15 using the µGA

Comparing the values given in Table 3 for (Ngo, 1998) with the specific values reported in the original author's paper, a small difference can be observed. The reason is that the algorithm has been programmed and run in a different computer and language. In order to get the comparative figures shown in Table 3, both methods were similarly programmed and run in the same computer environment.

5.4. Optimal solutions

Now, different search techniques are compared when they run without any time constraint and an optimal solution is guaranteed. Figure 7 shows the execution times for three different algorithms: (i) the IDA (Iterative Deepening A) algorithm (Nilsson, 1998), which offers a quite simple algorithm that can solve large problems with a small computer memory, (ii) the so-called BDFS (Block Depth-Fist Search) real-time heuristic search method proposed in (Mandal, 2004), (iii) the proposed GA, and (iv) the proposed SQ method. For the sake of comparison, we have chosen the same number of cells and number of channels than in (Mandal, 2004).

It can be seen first that the BDFS algorithm produces an increasing average speedup over the IDA method. On the other hand, the proposed µGA outperforms BDFS (and, hence, IDA) whenever the complexity of the problem becomes considerable. In these cases, the running time of the µGA is about 20% smaller than the BDFS. Only in the three simplest cases (a: $n=5$, $c=3$), (b: $n=5$, $c=4$) and (c: $n=7$, $c=3$), the minimum computational load required to implement the µGA is larger than the BDFS, though still much better than the IDA.

When SQ is used, results show that for simple configurations, computational load is approximately that of the GA-based method. However, as complexity (in terms of the number of channels) is increased, the computational load of the SQ procedure tends towards that of the IDA algorithm. These results are in accordance with those outlined in the other numerical simulations.

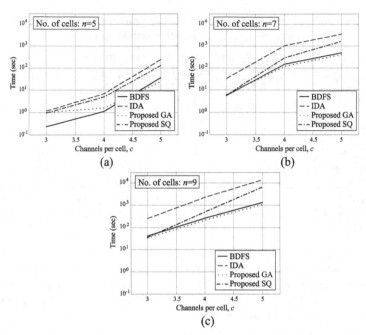

Figure 7. Execution time performance comparison between three different methods for CAP.

5.5. Performance with harder instances

To conclude this analysis of the performance of the proposed methods, two more cases that are more difficult have been studied. Their main characteristics are shown in Table 4.

	No. of Cells, n	d	ACC	CCC	CSC
A	21	$2d_3$	Yes	Yes	Yes (c_{ii}=5)
B	21	$4d_3$	Yes	Yes	Yes (c_{ii}=5)

Table 4. Definition of benchmark instances A and B.

Our methods are going to be compared with the GA-based approach by Funabiki et al. (Funabiki, 2000). Using the μGA the best assignments we were able to find required 855 and 1713 channels, for problems A and B, respectively, while the method in (Funabiki, 2000) required slightly higher values, 858 and 1724 (results are shown in Table 5). On the other hand, the SQ method requires 855 and 1715 channels, respectively. Thus, in case A –which is a bit simpler than case B- both SQ and GA achieve near optimal results, while in case B –a rather more complex network- SQ requires two more channels than the GA, and 9 less than the NN method. In terms of computation times, the μGA took 11.86 and 23.76 seconds, for problems A and B, respectively; the other GA-based algorithm took about 16.73 and 32.8

seconds, respectively, and, finally, the SQ approach took 15.20 and 37.15 seconds, respectively (see Table 6). This means a reduction in time of 38–41% in favour of the proposed μGA method, while the NN and SQ approaches showed very similar execution times.

	μGA	NN (Funabiki, 2000)	SQ
A	855	858	855
B	1713	1724	1715

Table 5. Best assignments for benchmark instances A and B.

	μGA	NN (Funabiki, 2000)	SQ
A	11.86	16.73	15.20
B	23.76	32.80	37.15

Table 6. Computation time for benchmark instances A and B.

6. Conclusions

NC-based algorithms (GA and SQ) have been proven to fit very well for solving complex NP-complete problems such as the fixed channel allocation problem. Both of them show good convergence properties and reduced computational load. We have solved 18 different benchmark instances with successful results, proving, this way, the accuracy, flexibility and robustness of the proposed methods. Making use of several well-known benchmark instances, their performances have been shown to be superior to those of the existing frequency assignment algorithms in terms of computation time, convergence properties and quality of the solution. Even when compared to one of the best previous approaches –based on a NN-based scheme–, GA and SQ methods have been able to find better solutions to the most complex benchmarks tested.

While both the μGA and SQ offer similar computational load, convergence properties and quality of the solution for simple and moderately-simple benchmark instances, the proposed μGA shows the most reduced computational load when applied to complex problems.

Author details

Luis M. San-José-Revuelta
University of Valladolid, Spain

Acknowledgement

This work has been partially supported by Spanish project TEC2010-21303-C04-04.

7. References

Aarts, E. & Korst, J. (1989). *Simulated annealing and Boltzmann machines*, Wiley (New York).

Anderson, L.G. (1973). A simulation study of some dynamic channel assignment algorithms in a high capacity mobile telecommunications system, *IEEE Trans. Commun.* Vol. 21 (1973) 1294–1301.

Beckmann, D. & Killat, U. (1999). A new strategy for the application of genetic algorithms to the channel assignment problem, *IEEE Trans. Vehicular Tech.*, 48 (1999) 1261–1269.

Bhandari, D., Murthy, C.A. & Pal, S.K. (1996). Genetic algorithm with elitist model and its convergence, *International Journal on Pattern Recognition and Artificial Intelligence*, Vol. 10, No. 6 (1996) 731–747.

Box, F. (1978). A heuristic technique for assignment frequencies to mobile radio nets, *IEEE Trans. Vehicular Technol.*, Vol. 27 (1978) 57–64.

Černy, V. (1985). Thermodynamical approach to the travelling salesman problem: an efficient simulation algorithm, *J. Opt. Theory Appl.*, Vol. 45 (1985) 41-51.

Cuppini, M. (1994). A genetic algorithm for channel assignment problems, *Eur. Trans. Telecommunications and Related Technology*, Vol. 5, No. 2 (1994) 285–294.

Duque-Antón, M. Kunz, D. & Rüber, B. (1993), Channel assignment for cellular radio using simulated annealing, *IEEE Trans. on Vehicular Technology*, Vol. 42 (1993) 14–21.

Funabiki, N. & Takefuji, Y. (1992). A neural network parallel algorithm for channel assignment problems in cellular radio networks, *IEEE Trans. Vehicular Technol.*, Vol. 41 (1992) 430–437.

Funabiki, N., Okutani, N. & Nishikawa, S. (2000). A three-stage heuristic combined neural-network algorithm for channel assignment in cellular mobile systems, *IEEE Trans. Vehicular Technol.*, Vol. 49 (2000) 397–403.

Garey, M.R. & Johnson, D.S. (1979). *Computers and Intractability: A Guide to the Theory of NP-Completeness*, W.H. Freeman and Co., New York, 1979.

Geman, S. & Geman, D. (1984). Stochastic relaxation, Gibbs distributions and the Bayesian restoration of images, *Trans. Patt. Anal. Mach. Intell.*, Vol. 6 (1984) 721–741.

Ghosh, S.C., Sinha, B.P. & Das, N. (2003). Channel assignment using genetic algorithm based on geometric symmetry, *IEEE Trans. on Veh. Techl.*, Vol. 52, No. 4 (2003) 860–875.

Gibson, J.D. (Ed.) (1996). *The Mobile Communications Handbook*, CRC Press.

Grefenstette, J.J. (1986). Optimization of control parameters for genetic algorithms, *IEEE Trans. Syst. Man and Cybern.*, Vol. 16 (1986) 122–128.

Hale, W.K. (1980). Frequency assignment: theory and applications, *Proceedings of the IEEE 68* (1980) 1497–1514.

Hopfield, J.J. & Tank, D.W. (1985). Neural computation of decisions in optimization problems, *Biol. Cybern.*, Vol. 52 (1985) 141–152.

Huang, M.D. & Romeo, F., Sangiovanni-Vicentelli (1986). Am efficient general cooling schedule for simulated annealing, Proc. IEEE ICCAD-86, Santa Clara, CA (1986) 381–384.

Ingber, L. (1993). Simulated annealing: practice and theory, *Mathematical and Computational Modeling*, Vol. 18 (1993) 29–57.

Katzela, I. & Naghshineh, M. (1996). Channel assignment schemes for cellular telecommunic-ation systems: a comprehensive survey, *IEEE Personal Commun.*, Vol. 3 (1996) 10–31.

Kim, S. & Kim, S.L. (1994). A two-phase algorithm for frequency assignment in cellular mobile systems, *IEEE Trans. Vehicular Technol.*, Vol. 43 (1994) 542–548.

Kirkpatrick, S., Gelatt, C.D. & Vecchi, M.P. (1983). Optimization by simulated annealing, *Science,* Vol. 220 (1983) 671–680.

Krishnamachari, B. & Wicker, S.B. (1998). Global search techniques for problems in mobile communications, Wireless Multimedia Laboratory, School of Electrical Engineering, Cornell University, 1998.

Kunz, D. (1991), Channel assignment for cellular radio using neural networks, *IEEE Trans. Vehicular Technol.*, Vol 40 (1991) 188–193.

Lai, W.K. & Coghill, G.G. (1996). Channel assignment through evolutionary optimization, *IEEE Trans. Vehicular Technol.*, Vol. 45 (1996) 91–96.

Lee, A.J. & Lee, C.Y. (2005). A hybrid search algorithm with heuristics for resource allocation problem, *Information Sciences,* Vol. 173 (2005) 155–167.

Lochite, G.D. (1993). Frequency channel assignment using artificial neural networks, *Proc. of the 8th IEE Int. Conf. on Antennas and Propagation*, Vol. 2 (1993) 948–951.

Mandal, S., Saha, D. & Mahanti, A. (2004). A real-time heuristic search technique for fixed channel allocation (FCA) in mobile cellular communications, *Microprocessors and Microsystems*, Vol. 28 (2004) 411–416.

Mathar, R. & Mattfeldt, J. (1993). Channel assignment in cellular radio networks, *IEEE Trans. Vehicular Technol.*, Vol. 42 (1993) 647–656.

Metropolis, N., Rosenbluth, A., Rosenbluth, M., Teller, A. & Teller, E. (1953). Equation of state calculations by fast computing machines, *J. Chem. Phys.*, Vol. 21 (1953) 1087-1092.

Mitchell, M. (1996). *An Introduction to Genetic Algorithms*, The MIT Press, Cambridge, MA.

Ngo, C.Y. & Li, V.O.K. (1998). Fixed channel assignment in cellular radio networks using a modified genetic algorithm, *IEEE Trans. Vehicular Technol.*, Vol. 47 (1998) 163–172.

Nilsson, N.J. (1998). *Artificial Intelligence: a New Synthesis*, Morgan Kaufmann Publisher, Los Altos, CA.

Romeo, F.I. (1989). Simulated annealing: Theory and applications to layout problems, *Memo UCB/ERL M89/29, Univ. California, Berkeley*, (Mar. 1989).

San-José-Revuelta, L.M. (2007). A New Adaptive Genetic Algorithm for Fixed Channel Assignment, *Information Sciences*, Vol. 177, No. 13 (2007) 2655–2678.

San-José-Revuelta, L.M. (2008). A hybrid GA-TS technique with dynamic operators and its application to channel equalization and fiber tracking, in *"Local Search Techniques: Focus on Tabu Search"*, I-Tech Education and Publishing, Vienna, Austria. Editor: W. Jaziri (2008) 106–142.

San-José-Revuelta, L.M. (2009). Fuzzy-aided tractography performance estimation applied to Brain magnetic resonance imaging, *Proc. 17th European Signal Processing Conference (EUSIPCO 2009)* (2009) Glasgow, Scotland.

Sivarajan, K.N., McEliece, R.J. & Ketchun, J.W. (1989). Channel assignment in cellular radio, *Proc. of the 39th IEEE Vehicular Technol. Conf.* (1989), 846–850.

Smith, D.H., Hurley, S. & Allen, S.M. (2000). A new lower bound for the channel assignment problem, *IEEE Trans. on Veh. Tech.*, Vol. 49 (2000) 1265–1272.

Ursem, R.K. (2002). Diversity-guided Evolutionary Algorithms, *Proc. Int. Conf. on Parallel Problem Solving from Nature VII (PPSN VII)*, (2002) Granada, Spain, 462–471.

Chapter 3

Optimal Sizing of Harmonic Filters in Electrical Systems: Application of a Double Simulated Annealing Process

Laurence Miègeville and Patrick Guérin

Additional information is available at the end of the chapter

1. Introduction

Many fields including management science, computer science, electrical and industrial engineering bring into play a number of combinatorial optimisation problems that consist in finding the global minimum of a cost function that may possess several local minima over a finite or infinite set of solutions. In practice, excellent results have been obtained by using local search algorithms for a wide variety of issues, leading thus to a growing interest in theoretical results. However, many problems are still open as a challenge. In the current chapter, the authors present their experience in using a double simulated annealing (SA) optimisation process applied to the search for the optimal sizing of harmonic filters placed in a distribution electrical system. The effectiveness of the SA algorithm will be herein argued and illustrated on a distribution system so as to characterise the suitable placement of filtering devices that leads to a minimum required power. One of its main benefits compared with a popular genetic algorithm for example is to supervise the configuration space at every moment and to control the convergence process.

Nowadays, harmonic filters are widely installed in distribution systems for harmonic current filtering to achieve harmonic distortion reduction. The extent of this benefit depends greatly on the filtering system placement. Then, the problem focuses on several formulations about filters locations, their types and sizes. In the past, many efforts were put into the capacitor placement for reactive power compensation [1] even with a distorted substation voltage [2]. Many optimisation methods have found a practical application in this problem and the fuzzy logic [3], the simulated annealing [4], as well as the genetic algorithm [5] have been tested on it. A less attention has been paid for harmonic filters. A formulation has been proposed in [6] with analytical expressions, which have been solved by a graphic method. The placement and sizing of a single filter have been also studied in [7] by a graphic approach. More recently, an equivalent resistance approach [8] has been applied to the location of a single-tuned passive filter.

In the present chapter, the problem is formulated to minimise the filtering power with respect to the bus voltage constraints by limiting the harmonic currents passing through the filtering system. Corresponding to the harmonic currents either drawn by a passive filter or injected by an active filter, the filtering currents are calculated not to cancel the resulting harmonic voltages as proposed in [9], but to bring their magnitude within the limits recommended by the standards [10]. The optimisation of the filter size is then applied separately for each harmonic order by means of a double SA process ruled by two distinctive objective functions and the results are known in terms of filtering power to install with the resultant harmonic voltages expected on the distribution network.

As the number of busbars able to receive harmonic filters is usually limited in industrial plants or on board power systems, all the possible configurations can be individually considered and analysed thanks to a fast harmonic simulation schedule using the analytical models of static converters. Consequently, the search for the suited number of filters, their best location and their respective dimensioning power can be properly conducted.

The present chapter will clearly stress on the promising results provided by the SA theory when dealing with practical optimisation issues, like the placement and the sizing of harmonic filters that it deals with. The real power system of an electric propulsion ship will be then considered for illustration purposes.

2. Simulated annealing overview

The SA process is motivated by an analogy to annealing in solids. The idea comes first from a paper published by Metropolis et al. in 1953 [11]. An algorithm was then proposed to simulate the cooling of a material in a heat bath. This is a process known as annealing. The structural properties of a material that is heated past melting point and cooled afterwards depend on the rate of cooling. In consequence, if the liquid is cooled slowly enough, thermal mobility is lost and large crystals well ordered are formed, which is the state of minimum energy for the system. Conversely, if the liquid is cooled quickly, the crystals contain imperfections and the process becomes a simulated quenching that cannot ensure the achievement of a low energy state.

Metropolis's algorithm simulates the cooling process by gradually lowering the temperature of the system until it converges to a steady frozen state. In 1982, Kirkpatrick et al. [12] took the idea of the Metropolis's algorithm and applied it to optimisation problem. The SA process is then used to search for feasible solutions and converge to an optimal solution.

The popularity of the SA theory comes from its ability to solve complex combinatorial optimisation problems which purpose is to develop an efficient technique for finding minimum or maximum values of a function with many degrees of freedom and many local minima. Based on principles of physics, a combinatorial problem can be viewed as a thermodynamic system where all the equilibrium properties can be resolved by standard statistical mechanical methods [13]. Then, states in thermodynamic usage are identified with solutions in a combinatorial optimisation problem. Energy in thermodynamics is the cost function to be minimised in a SA process. The solution space of the optimisation problem is explored by a probabilistic hill climbing search which step size is controlled by a parameter T that plays the same role of the temperature in the physical system. Therefore, the abstract system can be described as if it was a thermal physical system which aim is to locate the ground state (i.e. optimal solution) while the temperature declines.

In a typical SA process, the initial temperature is set sufficiently high. A new state X_j is generated incrementally from the current state X_i by randomly selecting and proposing a move from a set of predefined ones.

Let the energy of the current state be $f(X_i)$ and the energy of the new one be $f(X_j)$. The probability that a proposed move is accepted or rejected in the SA theory is determined by the Metropolis criterion (1):

$$P(\Delta f_{ij}) = \min\left\{1,\ P_{Boltz} = \exp(-\frac{\Delta f_{ij}}{kT})\right\} \qquad (1)$$

where

$\Delta f_{ij} = f(X_j) - f(X_i)$ is the proposed energy change,
k is a constant known as Boltzmann's constant relating temperature to energy.

It can be then appreciated that if the energy is decreased, the so-called Boltzmann probability P_{Boltz} is greater than the unity. In that condition, the change is arbitrarily assigned to a probability $P(\Delta f_{ij})$ equal to one, which means that the system always moves to this state. Conversely, if the energy is increased, the new state is accepted using the acceptance distribution p_{ij}, as stated in (2):

$$p_{ij} < P_{Boltz} \qquad (2)$$

where

p_{ij} stands for a uniform random number between 0 and 1.

When the proposed move is accepted, the new state becomes the current state; when it is rejected, the current state remains unchanged. Therefore, by controlling the temperature T, the probability of accepting a hill climbing move which results in a positive Δf_{ij} is also controlled and the exploration of the state space too.

The driving mechanism of the SA process is described in Figure 1. The process of selecting and proposing a move is repeated until the system is considered in thermal equilibrium. Then, the temperature is reduced according to a temperature schedule and the system is allowed to reach thermal equilibrium again. Then, as the temperature of the system declines, the probability of accepting a worse move is decreased. This is the same as gradually moving to a frozen state in physical annealing. The process is finally stopped when no significant improvement is expected by further lowering temperature. At this point, the current state of the system is the solution to the optimisation problem.

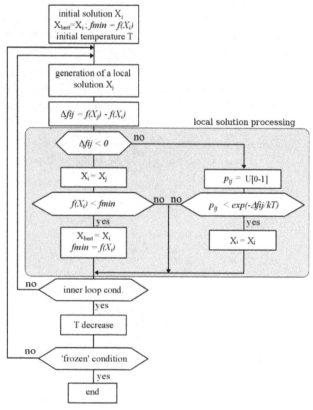

Figure 1. SA algorithm

The major advantage of a SA process over other methods is its ability to avoid becoming trapped in local minima. The algorithm employs a random search which not only accepts changes that decrease the objective function, but also some changes that can increase it. In consequence, a worse move can be accepted temporarily by leading subsequently to an improving solution. Then, the system sometimes goes uphill as well as downhill. However, the lower the temperature, the less likely is any significant uphill excursion.

Most of the practical applications of the SA theory are in complex problem domains, where algorithms either did not exist or performed poorly. Among the considerations which have led to the choice of a SA process for solving the current issue are its ease of implementation and its flexibility in applications to complex optimisation problems, especially ones where a desired global extremum can be hidden among many poorer local extrema. Besides, compared to some other popular methods like genetic algorithms, a SA process offers a far well mastered solution space to explore. Indeed, it can be appreciated that the neighbourhood becomes smaller as the global optimal solution is closer, which makes the search process easier and speeds up the convergence. It is also important to ensure that this condition is met when thinking about one's problem. For all those reasons, a SA process applied to the search for the optimal placement and power sizing of harmonic filters on large-scale electrical systems can be considered as a suitable optimisation method.

3. Problem statement

3.1. Network representation

The present harmonic filtering study is based on the usual assumptions about the symmetry of the electrical network, the balance of the harmonic currents generated by the non-linear loads, and the independence between the harmonic orders. As a result, a single phase network is considered and the analysis is carried out for each individual harmonic order. Then, the relationship between nodal harmonic currents and voltages is defined through the admittance matrix [14], as follows:

$$\mathbf{I}_h = \mathbf{Y}_h \cdot \mathbf{V}_h \tag{3}$$

where

I_h : the vector of the nodal harmonic currents,
Y_h : the harmonic admittance matrix,
V_h : the vector of the nodal harmonic voltages,
h : the harmonic order.

The nodal admittance matrix is obtained from the impedance of every network component and the nodal currents are given from the harmonic currents generated by the non-linear loads.

In industrial distribution systems, loads are supplied through transformers by different voltage levels according to their rated power. Due to the voltage supplies, the filtering current is modified by the transformer ratio when the filter is connected to the primary or to the secondary side of the transformer. In consequence, the comparison between the set of solutions requires considering a per-unit system.

Let V_n be a vector composed of the nominal nodal voltages. The admittance matrix formulation (3) can be then rewritten in an equivalent system where the relationship (5) between nodal harmonic currents and voltages becomes independent from the nominal nodal voltages.

$$\mathbf{V}_n \cdot \mathbf{I}_h = \mathbf{V}_n{}^2 \cdot \mathbf{Y}_h \cdot \frac{\mathbf{V}_h}{\mathbf{V}_n} \qquad\qquad (4)$$

$$\mathbf{i}_h = \mathbf{y}_h \cdot \mathbf{v}_h \qquad\qquad (5)$$

where

$\mathbf{i}_h = \mathbf{v}_n \cdot \mathbf{I}_h$: the vector of the equivalent injected currents in kVA,

$\mathbf{y}_h = \mathbf{V}_{n^2} \cdot \mathbf{Y}_h$: the equivalent admittance matrix in kVA,

$\mathbf{v}_h = \dfrac{\mathbf{V}_h}{\mathbf{V}_n}$: the vector of the equivalent voltages in %.

Besides, an active filter connected to the node k can be considered as a current source which injects a current jh_k on the network. A passive filter can be also modelled by a current source which magnitude would represent the harmonic current that must be drawn by the filter. In this last case, the phase angle depends on the harmonic voltage at the coupling node. All the additional currents produced by the set of filters are intended to reduce the harmonic voltages at each busbar. The location of these filters is defined in a node list called *ListFilter*. Assuming a given number of filters, the harmonic voltages are deduced from (6):

$$\mathbf{v}_h = \mathbf{z}_h \cdot (\mathbf{i}_h + \mathbf{j}_h) \qquad\qquad (6)$$

where

j_h is the vector of the filtering current and $z_h = y_h^{-1}$ the equivalent impedance matrix.

3.2. Optimisation process

The aim of the current optimisation problem is to minimise the total filtering power to connect to the grid while the voltage standards are met for each nodal harmonic voltages. Prior to the search for the optimal current to be injected, it is necessary to answer a first question about the possibility to obtain a current vector j_h able to reduce the voltages within the limiting levels v_{limit} at each node. For this reason, a double SA process is applied, as illustrated by the complete flow chart of figure 2. The purpose of the first one is to minimise the harmonic voltages, while checking if a filtering solution is existing or not.

In cases where no filtering solution can be found, the simulated voltage annealing is fully processed and returns the total filtering current j_{total} able to check a minimum gap between the nodal harmonic voltages and their expected limits. Instead, when the voltage constraints are properly respected, the voltage annealing is partially processed. Once a local solution is achieved, the procedure is switched to a simulated current annealing which purpose is to minimise the total filtering current j_{total} that meets the voltage requirements. The search space is actually the same regardless of the nature of the SA process; what is however different is the objective function, as will be argued further in the subsection 3.2.2.

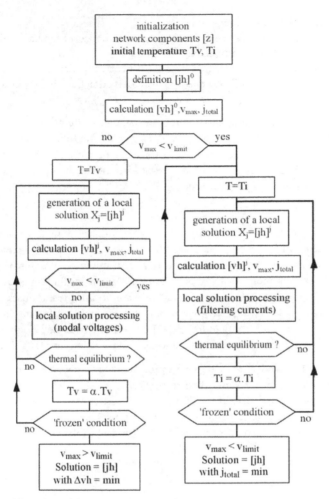

Figure 2. General flow chart of the optimisation procedure

The implementation of the algorithm is detailed further below and the focus is on the major parts of the procedure that can influence the behaviour of the SA approach to optimisation.

3.2.1. Initialisation procedure

When thinking about any optimisation problem, one of the first considerations is to start with a suitable set of initial parameters in order to ensure a good algorithm performance, which means the quality of the solution returned and a reasonable computation time [15]. The initialisation procedure deals first with the definition of the problem's data linked to the specific application. It consists herein of the following input data:

- the electrical system's components,
- the initial vector current $j_h{}^0$, assessed from the cancellation of the harmonic voltages at each node where a filter is connected,
- the resultant voltages $v_h{}^0$, calculated from the network impedances,
- the maximum voltage amplitude v_{max} initially observed in the whole electrical system,
- the total filtering current j_{total}.

The initialisation procedure also starts with the parameters settings for the SA process, i.e. the cooling schedule that consists of the initial temperature and the rules for lowering it as the search for the optimal solution progresses. Each of these specific features will be introduced and explained, regarding the current issue about the optimal placement and sizing of harmonic filters in electrical systems.

- Starting temperature

In a typical SA process, the initial temperature is set sufficiently high to allow a move to almost any neighbourhood state. However, if the temperature starts at a too high value, the search may move to any neighbour and thus transform it into a random search, at least in the early stages. At the moment, there is no known method for finding a suitable starting temperature for a whole range of problems. An idea is to use the information on the cost function difference between one neighbour and another one to calculate a correct initial temperature. Another method suggested in [13] is to rapidly heat the system until a certain proportion of worse solutions are accepted and then slow cooling can start.

In the current application where a double SA process is considered, two initial temperatures for the voltage and the current annealing respectively are set as defined in (7) and (8). The both relationships mean that a 60% tolerance is allowed as regards the acceptance of an unfavourable harmonic voltage equal to twice the required limits and a jump of 30% in the amplitude of the average current is accepted with a same 60% tolerance.

$$T_v = -\frac{2 \times \max(\mathbf{v}_{limit})}{\ln(0.6)} \tag{7}$$

$$T_i = -\frac{0.3 \times \sum\limits_{q \in ListFilter} \left| j_{hq}{}^0 \right|}{\ln(0.6)} \tag{8}$$

- Final temperature

It is usual to let the temperature decrease until it reaches zero. However, this can make the algorithm run for too long, which should be a major drawback. In practice, the stopping criterion is a suitably low temperature, since the chances of accepting a worse move are almost the same when the temperature is null. In other words, the stopping criterion is met when the system is frozen at the current temperature; that is, no better or worse moves are being accepted.

- Cooling schedule

The temperature decreases during the search according to a function known as the cooling (or annealing) schedule. The way in which the temperature declines is critical to the success of the algorithm. Theory states that the number of iterations to execute at each temperature should be large enough to reach the thermal equilibrium.

In the literature, several theoretical and empirical control schemes are suggested [16-19] and can be categorised into classes such as monotonic schedules, geometric schedules, quadratic schedules and adaptive cooling schedules. Actually, many attempts have been made to derive or suggest good annealing schedules. Several comparative studies on the large variety of proposed cooling strategies are discussed in [20-22].

In a conventional SA process, the way to decrement the temperature is a simple linear method. By declining the temperature constantly, it provides the search with a higher transition probability in the beginning of the search and lower probability towards the end of the search. An alternative is a geometric decrease by a constant factor α $(0 < \alpha < 1)$. Then, experience shows that α should lie between [0.8 – 0.99], with better results found in the higher end of the range. However, the higher the value of α, the longer it will take to decrement the temperature to the stopping criterion.

The proposed annealing procedure tested on the minimum power sizing scheduling problem involves the above cooling schedule known as an exponential schedule (9), with a coefficient α equal to 0.95 in order to compromise between computation time and optimisation performance.

$$T(t) = T_0 \cdot \alpha^t \tag{9}$$

where t (for 'time') is the step count and T_0 is the starting temperature.

- Iterations at each temperature

The final decision to make is the number of iterations to consider at each temperature. A constant number seems to be an obvious scheme. An alternative is to dynamically change this number as the algorithm progresses. At lower temperature, it is advisable to set a large value so that the local optimum can be fully explored. At higher temperatures, the number of iterations can be less.

In the current issue, the number of steps N_{steps} was set in connection to the number of possible harmonic filters $N_{filters}$ to connect to the grid, as given in (10):

$$N_{steps} = n \cdot (N_{filters} + 2) \tag{10}$$

where n is a suitably large integer ($n \cong 200$), defined to achieve the thermal equilibrium prior to a next temperature change.

3.2.2. Problem specific decision

Another set of decisions to make is specific to the problem to solve and is presented further below.

- Neighbourhood structure

When thinking about the problem of optimal filtering power sizing, the choice of the way to move from a current solution to another one is questioned. This means that a neighbourhood is to be defined. A relevant study is proposed in [23].

In the present application, the generator of random changes in the configuration is based on a varying neighbourhood as the algorithm progresses. The amplitude of the filtering current is then randomly selected in a solution space according to (11):

$$J_{hk}{}^{j} = \beta(T) \cdot J_{hk}{}^{i} \tag{11}$$

$$\begin{cases} k = 1, .., N_{nodes} \\ i : \text{index of the current state} \\ j : \text{index of the new state} \\ \beta : \text{weight factor depending on the temperature parameter } T = T_v \text{ or } T_i \end{cases}$$

Consequently, as the temperature declines, the weight coefficient β is adjusted as a function of T_v or T_i depending on whether the SA process is applied to the harmonic voltages or to the filtering currents and the neighbourhood is gradually restricted, which ensures the success of the convergence process towards the expected global optimum.

- Cost function

Then, a cost function that models the current problem to solve is needed. As it will be calculated at every step of the algorithm, this objective function must be also easy and fast to calculate.

As the proposed algorithm (Figure 2) involves a double SA, a test procedure is systematically performed in order to assess whether or not the annealing process should be applied to the voltage or to the current according to the gap observed between the maximal nodal voltage newly calculated and the required limits. If the nodal voltage is thus more than the specified requirements, a voltage annealing is applied; conversely, if the standard is met, a current annealing is conducted. Then, the following stages of the algorithm are those of a conventional SA scheme like previously described in section 2.

In consequence, two distinctive objective functions can be referred depending on the nature of the SA process executed. When the problem shows no filtering solution, it means that no injected current goes to providing remedies for a reduction of the harmonic voltages below the standards. The objective is then specifically directed at decreasing as far as possible the nodal harmonic voltages to closely approximate the specified limits. Thus, the appropriate cost function (12) is defined as the standard deviation between the harmonic voltages and their threshold values over all the electrical system's nodes.

$$\min[\Delta v_h] = \min\left[\sqrt{\frac{1}{N} \cdot \sum_{k=1}^{N_{nodes}} (v_{hk} - v_{limit\,k})^2}\right] \tag{12}$$

Instead, when the voltage conditions are satisfied, the existence of a global optimum is clearly confirmed. The voltage annealing process is limited to the success of a local search which already guarantees a solution that works. Then, it automatically switches to a simulated current annealing which optimisation process is naturally applied to the harmonic currents injected by the filters connected to the grid. In that second instance, the objective is to minimise the total filtering current j_{total} that preserves the voltage requirements. The resultant cost function is therefore defined by (13) with respect to the constraint (14) on each nodal harmonic voltage v_{hk}. The returned value of the total filtering power is then minimal while the maximal nodal voltage meets the expected limits.

$$\min[j_{total}] = \min\left[\sum_{q \in ListFilter} |j_{hq}|\right] \tag{13}$$

$$v_{hk} \leq v_{limit\,k} \quad \forall k = 1,.., N_{nodes} \tag{14}$$

It can be appreciated that the minimum filtering power is obtained for the locations defined by the list of nodes *(ListFilter)* initially proposed. The optimal placement on the distribution network is then determined by testing all the possible combinations of the filters connections. In practice, the number of configurations is often small due to the limited number of busbars able to accept harmonic filters. As a result, an optimal process is not required to determine the 'best' configuration corresponding to the minimum value of the filtering power. Besides, the minimum power is not necessarily the best solution retained by an electrical engineer who must take into account many other technical and economical considerations. It seems then better to give the optimal solution for each configuration and to leave the engineer to select the best strategic choice afterwards.

4. Application to a ship power system

Tested on several real power systems, the above optimisation technique is presently implemented into a software package developed in C language. The example of an aboard ship power system is proposed further below so as to point out the benefit of the SA process to a very practical issue regarding harmonics and power quality in electrical systems.

4.1. Description of the power system

The electrical ship network of figure 3 is composed of six busbars with three voltage levels: 690V, 400V and 230V. Four 1.8MVA generators supply the 690V busbar *(TPF1)*. The main powerful loads including the electric propulsion system are then connected directly to it. The propulsion system is made up of two variable speed drives *(MP_BD, MP_TD)* with a twelve-pulse structure. Five low voltage busbars, i.e. one 400V busbar on the port side and another one on the starboard side in addition with three 230V busbars, distribute the energy everywhere aboard ship. According to their rated voltage, they supply the onboard equipment: two winches *(MT_BD, MT_TD)*, the lighting system, several UPS units and battery chargers. Every load is modelled at each node by an equivalent linear impedance or by an equivalent source of current for the converters and the fluorescent lighting. The detailed specifications of the power system are given in the tables 8, 9, 10 of the appendix.

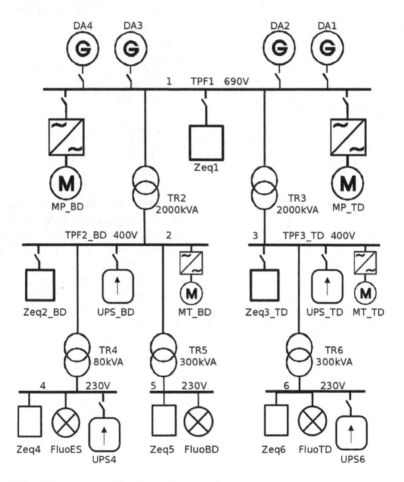

Figure 3. Single line diagram of the aboard ship network

The above-mentioned non linear loads inject harmonic currents in the network, which induces unfavourable resultant voltages. The IEC standard limits harmonic voltages according to the specifications given in the table 1. Nevertheless, the shipyard imposes even lower levels in order to guarantee a better power quality on the low voltage distribution system which might supply sensitive equipment.

harmonic order (h)	5	7	11	13
IEC – V_h (%)	6	5	3.5	3
shipyard - V_h(%) on 690V	3.5	3.5	3	3
shipyard - V_h(%) on 400V & 230V	3.5	3.5	1.2	1.2

Table 1. Harmonic voltage limits

n° busbar	1	2	3	4	5	6
$V_{h=11}$ (%V_n)	4.88	5.40	5.43	5.46	5.40	5.49

Table 2. Harmonic voltage: 11th order in configuration A

n° busbar	1	2	3	4	5	6
$V_{h=5}$ (%V_n)	3.28	3.74	3.88	4.59	4.06	5.41

Table 3. Harmonic voltage: 5th order in configuration B

4.2. Study statement

The two most stringent configurations will be presented and discussed further below. The first one relates to the study of the 11th harmonic order when the ship is travelling at full speed with three diesel engine generators running (configuration A). The second one involves the study of the fifth harmonic order when the ship is on berth with only one diesel engine generator operating (configuration B). Given the harmonic currents introduced by the non-linear loads of the electrical system as mentioned in the table 9 of the appendix, the simulation of the power system for the both configurations above shows the results of the table 2 and the table 3 respectively. It can be appreciated that the resulting voltage levels for the 11th harmonic order extend far beyond the limits set by the requirements. When simulating the harmonic voltages for the 5th order when the ship is in dock, the specified limits are not exceeded on the 690V busbar only. A filtering schedule is however required on the other busbars. The choice of the most suitable placement is then questioned: is it better to plan filtering on the 400V busbar or on the 230V busbar? The proposed optimisation procedure makes it possible to get answers to that critical question.

As displayed in figure 3, the electrical system shows six nodes and thus offers six possible placements for active or passive filters. With six possible locations, the number of filters can vary from one to six. A complete analysis to determine the most suitable placement(s) to select requires sixty-three case studies. With the support of the implemented software, all the combinations are examined in 9.3 seconds of CPU time with a personal computer fitted out with an Intel© CoreDuo T8100, 2.1GHz processor. Among the list of the possible filtering solutions, the most relevant ones will be presented and argued in the following section.

In order to ensure that the optimisation procedure works well, several variables have been saved at each temperature of the SA process as the search for the optimal solution moves forward. The progress of the filtering power and the nodal voltages is then reported at the end of the computation procedure in order to control the performance of the convergence towards the global optimal solution.

4.2.1. Eleventh harmonic order in the configuration A

•   Filters on the 690V busbar

The present study considers a single filter connected to the main 690V busbar *(TPF1)*, at the same location than the propulsion system injecting the greatest harmonic currents. The optimal filtering power provided by the proposed algorithm amounts to 158.9kVA, as mentioned in the table 4.

Filtering power (kVA)							Harmonic voltage (%V_n)					
1	2	3	4	5	6	total	1	2	3	4	5	6
158,9	-	-	-	-	-	158,9	0,39	0,93	0,93	1,20	0,97	1,20
15,0	50,4	44,1	-	-	-	109,5	1,79	0,93	1,10	1,20	0,97	1,20
143,1	-	-	0,8	1,2	2,0	147,1	0,67	1,20	1,20	1,03	0,99	0,90

Table 4. Filtering of the 11th harmonic order on the 690V busbar – Configuration A

It can be then noticed that the resultant harmonic voltage is very low at the filtering node whereas it becomes very close to the specified limits at the other nodes 4 and 6. The voltage requirements are however met at every busbar, even though the limit value of 1.2% is reached on the 230V busbars that are the farthest from the filter's location.

From the sixty-three possible combinations, thirty-two of them assume that one filter at least is to connect at *TPF1*. These solutions however offer different results according to the filtering nodes considered. For example, three filters connected to the 690V and 400V busbars require a lower total power of 109.5kVA as displayed in the table 4, with harmonic voltages at the nodes 4 and 6 still maintained within the specified limits. This solution is actually the best one. When considering another possible combination with harmonic filters on the 690V and 230V busbars respectively, the proposed solution shows a large filter to connect at *TPF1* in addition with smaller ones distributed on the three 230V busbars, in compliance with the harmonic voltages within the specified requirements of the table 1. Even though the total filtering power is slightly lower than that obtained with a single filter placed on the 690V busbar, common sense tell us that the global cost of the filtering system may be higher due to a minimum cost required by the placement of filters with their associated equipment such as cables and breakers. Then, the connection of too small filters might be no economically interesting.

Figure 4 indicates the progress of the main variables during the SA procedure. The graphs show a convergence of the voltage up to the fixed limit while the filtering power decreases towards an optimal value corresponding to the power distribution that minimises the total power. It must be however noticed that the filtering power represents only the magnitude of the current j_h that would be injected by an active filter. The variations of its phase angles which are not reported herein, could explain the greatest fluctuations of the harmonic voltages while power remains constant.

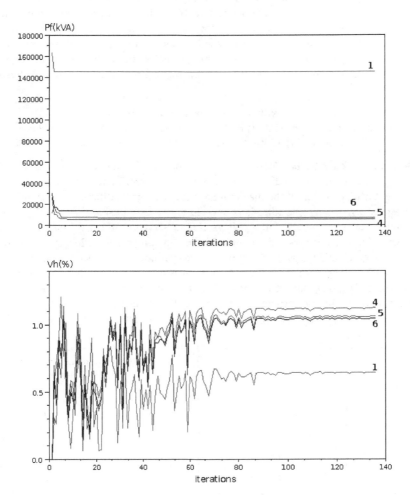

Figure 4. Filtering power and harmonic voltages – Combination {1,4,5,6} for h = 11 – (Conf. A)

• Filters on the 400V busbars

The second group of combinations presented below assumes that filters are placed on the 400V busbars together with some additional ones connected to the 230V busbars. The table 5 and Figure 5 show the resultant harmonic voltages and the filtering power progress during the optimisation procedure. When only one filter is connected to *TPF2* or *TPF3*, the specified limits on harmonic voltages cannot be respected. The optimisation procedure returns then the optimal power sizing associated with the lowest maximal harmonic voltage observed in the electrical system. An alternative is to place two filters on the both 400V busbars: then, the harmonic voltages are within the limit values, whatever the voltage levels throughout the electrical system. Compared with the placement of a single filter on the 690V busbar *(TPF1)*:

-      the convergence is achieved with a lower total power of 104.6kVA,
-      the resultant voltage on the 690V is higher but remains below the requirements,
-      the harmonic voltages on the 230V busbars at nodes 4 and 6, reach the limit of 1.2%.

When filtering the 230V busbar (node 4 or 6) in addition with the both 400V busbars, the results compared with the previous one do not change significantly regarding the total power. Only the distribution of the maximal harmonic voltages is different according to the nodes. Besides, when only one filter is connected to the 400V busbar (TPF2 or TPF3) and several smaller ones to the 230V, the voltage limit observed on the 400V busbar with no filter is exceeded. It can be however noted in Figure 5 the progress in reducing the involved harmonic voltages. Initially, when the annealing temperature is high, some large increases in the harmonic voltages are accepted and some areas far from the optimum are explored. As execution continues and the temperature falls, fewer uphill excursions are tolerated with smaller magnitude. This performance is typical of the SA algorithm. Even if the voltage amplitudes remain greater than the specified limits, the returned values are the best expected ones.

Filtering power (kVA)							Harmonic voltage (%V_n)					
1	*2*	*3*	*4*	*5*	*6*	*total*	*1*	*2*	*3*	*4*	*5*	*6*
-	*114,5*	-	-	-	-	*114,5*	1.66	1.40	2.25	1.03	1.34	2.34
-	-	*119,5*	-	-	-	*119,5*	1.51	2.11	1.49	2.34	2.14	1.35
-	*55,1*	*49,5*	-	-	-	*104,6*	1.94	0.92	1.10	1.20	0.96	1.20
-	*49,7*	*51,9*	*0,3*	-	-	*101,9*	2.02	1.16	1.10	1.20	1.19	1.20
-	*56,6*	*46,0*	-	-	*0,7*	*103,3*	1.98	0.93	1.20	1.20	0.97	1.16
-	*73,6*	-	*3,0*	-	*17,8*	*94,4*	2.37	1.21	2.44	1.20	1.23	1.35

Table 5. Filtering of the 11th harmonic order on the 400V busbar – Configuration A

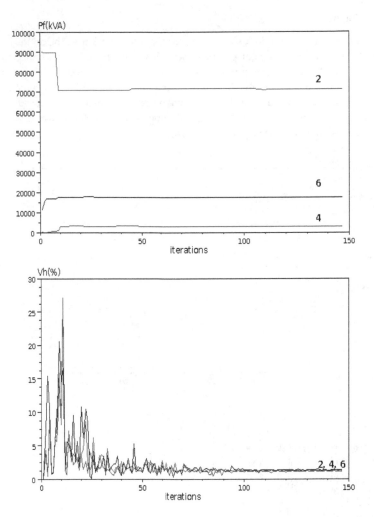

Figure 5. Filtering power and harmonic voltages – Combination {2,4,6} for h = 11 - (Conf. A)

- Filters on the 230V busbars

The analysis of the combinations involving one, two or three harmonic filters on the 230V busbars as displayed in the table 6, leads to the same conclusion: whatever the number of filters connected, none of the proposed solutions are able to fit the harmonic voltage requirements. It can be however noticed that a filtering solution on the 230V busbars could be considered if the harmonic voltage limits were less severe. For example, the table 6 shows that the combination of three filters connected to the nodes 4, 5, 6 respectively could meet the requirements set by the IEC Standard (i.e. 3.5% for h=11).

- Concluding remarks

Among the different solutions discussed above for the configuration A, the optimal filtering solution that offers a minimal total power is achieved with three filters, connected to the nodes 2, 3, 4 respecttively, as shown in Figure 6. However, when thinking about some other considerations like the cost involved by the connection of an additional filter (outputs, protecting devices, etc...), the decision to make can be greatly influenced. Then, a comparison with the gain offered on the total filtering power and the power quality of the electrical system would be worthwhile considering.

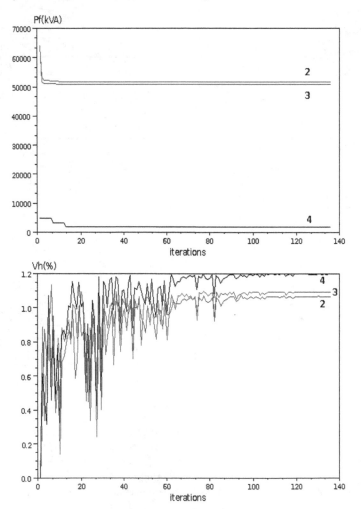

Figure 6. Filtering power and harmonic voltages – Combination {2,3,4} for h = 11 - (Conf. A)

Filtering power (kVA)							Harmonic voltage (%Vn)					
1	2	3	4	5	6	total	1	2	3	4	5	6
-	-	-	9,4	-	-	9,4	4.66	4.93	5.21	2.04	4.93	5.28
-	-	-	-	30,4	-	30,4	4.08	3.73	4.64	3.88	3.02	4.72
-	-	-	-	-	29,9	29,9	4.08	4.62	3.76	4.72	4.63	2.82
-	-	-	6,5	22,7	23,9	53,1	3.50	3.22	3.38	1.36	1.76	1.79

Table 6. Filtering of the 11th harmonic order on the 230V busbar – Configuration A

4.2.2. Fifth harmonic order in the configuration B

- Filters on the 690V / 400V / 230V busbars

Except in the situation where only one filter is located at the node 4 or 5 (230V), every other filters combination allows to meet the harmonic voltage specifications. The table 7 and Figure 7 illustrate the main results for the new configuration. Nevertheless, it can be noted that the filtering power can vary greatly in a ratio from 1 to 4 according to the selected connection point. Then the maximum power level near to 51kVA is achieved with a filter connected to the node 1 or 2 while the minimum value of 14.5kVA is obtained with a filtering applied to the nodes 4 and 6.

The proper working of the optimisation process can be then appreciated: the implemented procedure allows to assess a suitable filtering power in compliance with the specified limits set to 3.5% for the fifth harmonic while minimising the total power involved. This also highlights the interest to search for the optimal number and placement of harmonic filters to connect to the grid. In the proposed example, the placement of two filters at the nodes 4 and 6 allows to solve the matter whereas a single filter connected to the node 4 cannot meet the voltage requirements for a similar filtering power near to 14 kVA.

5. Conclusion

This chapter deals with a new technique to optimise the both placement and sizing of the harmonic filters to connect to a distribution system. Then, the problem is solved by a combinatorial optimisation method using successively two SA processes. The objective is to reduce the harmonic voltages with respect to the standards and to achieve a minimum power size in view of maximum savings in the equipment cost.

The optimisation technique has been implemented into a software package and tested on several real power systems. The tables of results giving information about the optimal filtering power and the resultant harmonic voltages allow fast comparisons between numerous configurations.

Filtering power (kVA)							Harmonic voltage (%Vn)					
1	2	3	4	5	6	total	1	2	3	4	5	6
50,7	-	-	-	-	-	50,7	1.41	1.86	1.98	2.71	2.17	3.50
	51,1					51,1	1.41	1.34	1.98	2.10	1.61	3.50
-	-	37,9	-	-	-	37,9	1.85	2.32	1.98	3.19	2.65	3.50
-	2,2	36,3	-	-	-	38,5	1.83	2.28	1.98	3.14	2.60	3.50
-	-	37,4	0,7	-	-	38,1	1.85	2.31	1.98	2.98	2.63	3.50
-	-	-	13,5	-	-	13,5	2.81	3.13	3.40	3.53	3.45	4.92
-	-	-	-	-	29,6	29,6	2.18	2.64	2.42	3.50	2.96	1.79
-	-	-	1,9	-	12,6	14,5	2.73	3.17	3.17	3.44	3.50	3.50
-	0,7	0,6	1,6	-	12,1	15	2.72	3.16	3.15	3.50	3.49	3.50

Table 7. Filtering of the 5th harmonic order on the 690V/400V/230V busbar – Configuration B

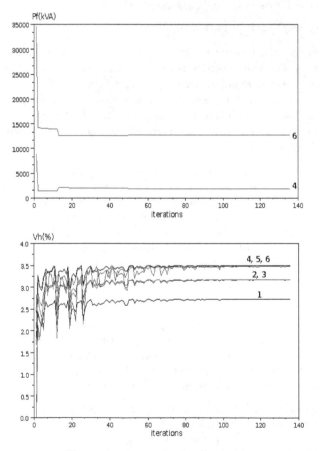

Figure 7. Filtering power and harmonic voltages – Combination {4,6} for h = 5 - (Conf. B)

The analysis of every one can provide several equivalent solutions in terms of total power but shows different voltage distributions. The practical cases discussed in this chapter conclude that for a similar filtering power, some other practical considerations like the minimum cost of the filter installation, the available place aboard ship, the expected power quality at the moment and the further system evolution, must also be taken into account so that the best solution can be suitably identified.

Consequently, the optimisation method associated with the implemented software must be considered as an interesting support for the engineer in charge of the placement of harmonic filters onto the grid. Also given practical purposes, the use of the calculation tool should make easier the harmonic filters sizing and provide a good starting point to make the right decision in terms of filtering solutions. Improvements of power quality together with the optimisation of the power to install in electrical distribution systems are today a critical challenge that deserves our undivided attention.

Appendix

The specifications of the power system described in figure 3 are summarised in the following table 8 and table 10. The impedance of the cables is neglected due to their small length. The harmonic analysis is achieved from the currents injected by the non linear loads given in the table 9.

ref.	U_n (V)	P (kW)	Q (kvar)
Zeq1	690	160	126
Zeq2_BD	400	315	237
Zeq3_TD	400	300	225
Zeq4	230	56	#0
Zeq5	230	40	#0
Zeq6	230	56	#0
DA1-DA3	690	1180	11800 (Scc)
DA4	690	OFF	OFF

Table 8. Linear load parameters

order h Irms(A)	5	7	11	13
MP_BD	0	0	53.7	38.8
MP_TD	0	0	53.7	38.8
MT_BD	46.5	24.7	14.4	9.75
MT_TD	46.5	24.7	14.4	9.75
UPS_BD	30.2	18.6	15.2	9.3
UPS_TD	30.2	18.6	15.2	9.3
Fluo_ES	5.4	0.8	0.4	0.4
UPS4	1.6	1.0	0.8	0.5
Fluo_BD	8.9	1.3	0.6	0.6
Fluo_TB	8.9	1.3	0.6	0.6
UPS6	1.6	1.0	0.8	0.5

Table 9. Harmonic currents (A) injected by the non linear loads of the power system

ref.	U_{1n} (V)	U_{2n} (V)	S_n (kVA)	u_{cc} (%)
TR3	690	400	2000	5.5
TR4	690	400	2000	5.5
TR5	400	230	300	6
TR6	400	230	300	6
TR8	400	230	80	5.5

Table 10. Parameters of the power transformers

Author details

Laurence Miègeville
Department of Electrical Engineering, POLYTECH Nantes, University of Nantes, France
Research Institute on Electrical Energy of Nantes Atlantique, St Nazaire, France

Patrick Guérin
Department of Industrial Engineering and Maintenance,
IUT Saint-Nazaire, University of Nantes, France
Research Institute on Electrical Energy of Nantes Atlantique, St Nazaire, France

6. References

[1] Grainger J.J., Lee S.H (1981) Optimal size and location of shunt capacitors for reduction of losses in distribution feeders. IEEE Trans. on Power Application System, vol. PAS-100, pp. 1105-1118.

[2] Wu Z.Q, Lo K.L (1995) Optimal choice of fixed and switched capacitors in radial distributors with distorted substation voltage. IEE Proc. Generation Transmission Distribution, Vol. 142, n° 1, pp 24-28.

[3]   Saric A.T, Calovic M.S, Djukanovic M.B (1997) Fuzzy optimisation of capacitors in distribution systems. IEE Proc. Generation Transmission Distribution, Vol. 144, n° 5, pp 415-422.

[4]   Chiang H.D, Wang J.C, Darling G (1995) Optimal capacitor placement, replacement and control in large-scale unbalanced distribution systems. IEEE Trans. on Power Systems, Vol.10, n°1, pp 356 - 362.

[5]   Masoum M.A.S, Ladjevardi M, Jafarian A, Fuchs E.F (2004) Optimal placement, replacement and sizing of capacitor banks in distorted distribution networks by genetic algorithms. IEEE Trans. on Power Delivery, vol. 19, n°4, pp. 1794-1801.

[6]   Dai X, Gretsch R (1994) Optimal compensator currents for the reduction of the harmonic distortion in networks, Part 1: analytic solution, Part 2: graphic solution. ETEP, Vol. 4, n°4, pp 301-307, pp 309-313.

[7]   Guérin P, Miègeville L, Bizien A (1999) Optimal placement and size of a single harmonic filter. In: 8th European Conference on Power Electronics and Applications, Lausanne, Switzerland, Session D3.7.

[8]   Chang G.W, Chu S.Y, Wang H.L (2002) A new approach for placement of single-tuned passive harmonic filters in a power system. IEEE Power Engineering Society Transmission and Distribution Conference, vol. 2, issue Summer, pp. 814-817.

[9]   Mikolajuk K (1996) The problem of harmonic compensators location. ETEP, Vol. 6, n°6, pp 397-400.

[10] Guérin P, Miègeville L (2007) Optimal Placement and Sizing of Harmonic Filters Aboard an Electric Propulsion Ship. IET Generation, Transmission and Distribution, Vol. 1, Issue 4. pp. 613-618.

[11] Metropolis N, Rosenbluth A.W, Rosenbluth M.N, Teller A.H, Teller E (1953) Equation of state calculation by fast computing machines. Journal of Chemical Physics, n°21, pp 1087-1091.

[12] [12] Kirkpatrick S, Gelatt C.D, Vecchi M.P (1983) Optimization by simulated annealing. Science, Vol. 220, n°4598, pp 671-680.

[13] Dowsland K.A (1995) Simulated annealing in modern heuristic techniques for combinatorial problems (ed. Reeves, C.R.). McGraw-Hill.

[14] [14] Arrillaga J, Arnold C.P, Harker B.J (1983) Computer modelling of electrical power systems. John Wiley & Sons, ISBN 047110406X.

[15] [15] Shojaee K, Shakouri G, Behnam Taghadosi M (2010) Importance of the initial conditions and the time schedule in the Simulated Annealing. Publisher Sciyo, Simulated Annealing, Theory with Applications 292 p. ISBN 978-953-307-134-3. pp 217-224.

[16] Hajek B (1988) Cooling Schedules for Optimal Annealing. Mathematics of Operations Research, vol. 13, n°2, pp 311-329.

[17] Huang MD, Romeo F, Sangiovanni-Vincentelli A (1986) An efficient general cooling schedule for simulated annealing. Proceedings of the IEEE International Conference on Computer Aided Design, Santa Clara, USA, pp 381-384.

[18] Thompson J, Dowsland KA (1995) General cooling schedules for a simulated annealing based timetabling system. Proceedings of the first International Conference on the practice and Theory of Automated timetabling, Napier University, Edinburgh.

[19] Azizi N, Zolfaghari S (2004) Adaptive temperature control for simulated annealing: a comparative study. Computer & Operations Research, Elsevier, n°31, pp 2439-2451.

[20] Stander J, Silverman B (1994) Temperature schedules for simulated annealing. Statistics and Computing, 4, pp 21-32.

[21] Lin C.K.Y, Haley K.B, Sparks C (1995) A comparative study of both standard and adaptive versions of threshold accepting and simulated annealing algorithms in three scheduling problems. European Journal of Operational Research, 83, pp 330-346.

[22] Nourani Y, Andresen B (1998) A comparison of simulated annealing cooling strategies. Journal Phys. Math. Gen. N°31, pp 8373-8385.

[23] Alizamir S, Rebennack S, Pardalos P.M (2008) Improving the neighbourhood selection strategy in Simulated Annealing using the optimisation stopping problem. Publisher InTech, Simulated Annealing 420 p. ISBN 978-953-7619-07-7, pp 363-382.

Chapter 4

Simulated Annealing in Research and Applications

Ivan Zelinka and Lenka Skanderova

Additional information is available at the end of the chapter

1. Introduction

Simulated annealing (SA) [16], [17], [14]), belongs among those algorithms which allow steps after which the value of the objective function will deteriorate. It can thus be seen again as the local extensions of classical methods of searching. The SA is similar to hill climbing, but differs in the fact that the individual is able to overcome local extremes. However, inspiration for this formulation of statistical mechanics had been found in the description of the physical annealing process of a rigid body. In this analogy, namely during annealing of metals with unstable crystal lattice, there is a stabilization of loose particles in an optimal state, i.e. the formation of a stable crystal lattice. Such a metal has much better properties. The process is carried out by heating the metal at high temperatures to the melting point and then very slowly cooling it. Cooling is done slowly enough to eliminate unstable particles and the metal has acquired the requisite optimal quality. In the early 1980s, Kirkpatrick, Gelatt and Vecchi (Watson Research Center of IBM, USA) and independently Cerny (Department of Theoretical Physics, Comenius University in Bratislava, former Czechoslovakia) proposed solutions to the problem of finding the global minimum of combinatorial optimization analogous to the procedure of the annealing rigid body.

This chapter introduces simulated annealing in special applications focused on deterministic chaos control, synthesis and identification. The first one discusses the use of SA on evolutionary identification of bifurcations, i.e. positions of control parameters of the investigated system related to that event.

The second application discusses the possibility of using SA for the synthesis of chaotic systems. The systems synthesized here were based on the structure of well-known logistic equations. For each algorithm and its version, repeated simulations were conducted and then averaged to guarantee the reliability and robustness of the proposed method. The third and last application is focused on deterministic spatiotemporal chaos realtime control by means of selected evolutionary techniques, with SA. Realtime-like behavior is specially defined and simulated with a spatiotemporal chaos model based on mutually nonlinear joined n equations, so-called Coupled Map Lattices (CML). Investigation consists of different case studies with increasing simulation complexity. For all algorithms each simulation was repeatedly evaluated in order to show and check the robustness of the methods used. All data were processed and used in order to obtain summarized results and graphs. The most significant results are carefully selected, visualized and commented on in this chapter.

1.1. Simulated annealing

Simulated annealing ([16], and by [14]) is a generic probabilistic meta-algorithm for the global optimization problem. SA is a robust general optimization method that is based on the work of [17]. It simulates the annealing of a metal, in which the metal is heated-up to a temperature near its melting point and then slowly cooled to allow the particles to move towards an optimal energy state. This results in a more uniform crystalline structure and so the process allows some control over the microstructure. SA has been demonstrated to be robust and capable of dealing with noisy and incomplete real-world data. This makes SA suitable for engineering applications.

SA is a variation of the hill-climbing algorithm. Both start off from a randomly selected point within the search space. Unlike in hill-climbing, if the fitness of a new candidate solution is less than the fitness of the current solution, the new candidate solution is not automatically rejected. Instead it becomes the current solution with a certain transition probability $p(T)$. This transition probability depends on the change in fitness ΔE and the temperature T. Here temperature is an abstract control parameter for the algorithm rather than a real physical measure. The algorithm starts with a high temperature which is subsequently reduced slowly, usually in steps. On each step, the temperature must be held constant for an appropriate period of time (i.e. number of iterations) in order to allow the algorithm to settle into a thermal equilibrium, i.e. a balanced state. If this time is too short, the algorithm is likely to converge to a local minimum. The combination of temperature steps and cooling times is known as the annealing schedule, which is usually selected empirically. By analogy with metallurgical processes, each step of the SA algorithm replaces the actual solution by a randomly generated solution from the neighborhood, chosen with a probability depending on the difference between the corresponding function values and on a global parameter, so-called temperature - T. Temperature is decreasing during the process. The current solution changes almost randomly when T is large, but increasingly downhill as T goes to zero. The allowance for uphill moves saves the method from becoming stuck at the local minimum. Simulated annealing is a stochastic algorithm depending on parameters as follow:

$$SA = (M, x_0, N, f, T_0, T_f, \alpha, n_T), \tag{1}$$

meaning of parameters is:

- **M**: space of possible solutions
- x_0: initial solution, randomly selected
- $N(x, \sigma)$: Normal distribution
- f: The cost function
- T_0: initial temperature.
- T_f: stopping temperature (temperature of crystallization)
- n_T: number of iterations of Metropolis algorithm
- α: temperature reduction $\alpha : T \to T', T' < T$, usually $T' = \alpha \times T$. Parameter α is usualy in the range 0.8 - 0.99.

In the real world any object consists of particles. Physical state can be described by vector $\mathbf{x} = (x_1, x_2, ..., x_n,)$ describing particle position for example. This state is related to energy $y = f(\mathbf{x})$. If such system is on the same temperature T long enough, then the probability of existence of such states is given by Boltzmann distribution. The probability that the system is in state $\mathbf{x}$ is then given by

$$\frac{e^{-f(\mathbf{x})/T}}{Q(T)} \tag{2}$$

with

$$Q(T) = \sum_x e^{-f(\mathbf{x})/T} \tag{3}$$

where summarization is going over all states x. For a sufficiently small T the probability that the system will be in state x_{min} with minimal energy $f(\mathbf{x_{min}})$ is almost 1. In the 50's simulation of annealing was suggested by means of Monte Carlo method with a new decision function 4.

$$P(x \to x_0) = \begin{cases} 1, & for f(x) < f(x_0) \\ e^{-(f(x)-f(x_0))/T} & for f(x) \geq f(x_0) \end{cases} \tag{4}$$

The function of this decision is whether new state x (when for example one particle will change its position) is accepted or not. In the case that x is related to lower energy then the old state it is replaced by a new one. On the contrary, x is accepted with probability $0 < P(x \to x_0) < 1$. If r is random number from $[0, 1]$, then new state is accepted only if $r < P(x \to x_0)$. In (4) T has an important influence on probability $P(x \to x_0)$ when $f(x) \geq f(x_0)$; for big T any new state (solution) is basically accepted, for a low T states with higher energy are only rarely accepted. If this algorithm (Metropolis algorithm) is repeated for one state in a sufficient number of repetitions, then the observed distribution of generated states is basically Boltzmann distribution. This makes it possible to execute SA on a PC. The SA, repeating Metropolis algorithm for decreasing temperature then uses the final state T_n like initial state for the next iteration x_m with $T_m = T_n - \varepsilon$. Variable ε is arbitrary small number. Pseudocode for SA is

Randomly selected initial solution x_0 from all possible solutions M ;
$x* := x_0$;
Set initial temperature $T_0 > 0$;
$T := T_0$;
Select decrement function $\alpha(t)$ and final temperature T_f ;
repeat
    for i := 1 to n_T **do**
        begin randomly select x from set of all possible neighbor $N(x_0)$;
          $\Delta f := f(x) - f(x_0)$;
          if $\Delta f < 0$
            then begin $x_0 := x$; move to a better solution is always accepted
              if $f(x) < f(x*)$
                then $x* := x$ update the best solution
              end
            else begin randomly select r from uniform distribution on the interval (0,1);
              if $r < e^{-\Delta f}/T$
                then $x_0 := x$ moving to a worse solution otherwise the current solution
remains unchanged

```
        end
    end
    T := α(T) ;
until T < T_f ;
```
x* is an approximation of the optimal solution

2. Case study 1: Evolutionary identification of bifurcations

This part introduces an overview of possible use of SA on bifurcation, i.e. catastrophic events, detection (for a more detailed description, see [43]). Catastrophic events here means Thom's catastrophes that can be used under certain conditions to model chaotic dynamics and bifurcations, that appear in the nonlinear behavior of various dynamical systems. The main aim of this work is to show that SA are capable of the bifurcations of chaotic system identification without any partial knowledge of internal structure, i.e. based only on measured data. In this part we will discuss mainly SA results. The system selected for numerical experiments here is the well-known system logistic equation derived from predator - prey system. For each algorithm and its version, simulations have been repeated 50 times. Our world, mostly consisting of nonlinear systems, is full of our i.e. human, technology that is less or more reliable. Technological systems are mostly, like their natural counterparts, nonlinear and complex and very often show chaotic as well as catastrophic behavior according to Thom's catastrophe theory, [1], [3] and [4], that describes sudden changes in the dynamical system (well developed and described for so called gradient systems) behavior under slightly changing (usually) external conditions. These changes, depending on one or more parameters, can be modeled like the special N dimensional surfaces in the so-called parameter space, see for example [1]. As an example of such systems (and catastrophic events), we can mention systems such as electrical networks (blackout,...), economic systems (black Friday, NY stock market 1929,...), weather systems (Lorenz model of weather born via series of bifurcations modeled by Thom's catastrophes, see [1]), civil construction failure (bridge collapse, etc), complex systems (self-criticality and spontaneous system reconstruction leading to the better energetic stability) and more. Different mathematical models, of which one possibility is the aforementioned Thom's catastrophe theory, model such events. Our aim in this paper is to show that it is possible to use SA to identify such events on mathematical models of such systems and/or it is possible to use SA to design technological systems in such a way that the possibility to reach regimes exhibiting sudden changes in their behavior (i.e. catastrophe events) is minimized. This study is an extension of our previous research in [9] and [10].

Identification of bifurcations has been done in this research so that Lyapunov exponent is calculated in its absolute value, see Figure 6. Zero values on this cost function landscape (multiple global extremes) then indicate for what parameter A bifurcations occur. In order to locate all these zero values SA is used. They advantage is to overcome multiple local extremes that are present in used cost function. They cannot be wiped out, because of chaotic nature of studied problem.

2.1. Chaos, Thom's catastrophes and bifurcations

Bifurcations just described in the previous section can be modeled by Thom's catastrophe theory. This theory, [1]-[4], describes sudden changes in the system behavior under slightly changing (usually) external conditions. These changes, depending on one or more parameters, can be modeled like the special N dimensional surfaces in the so-called parameter space. Each point in the parameter space represents one of the possible system configurations. Those points which are part of the so-called catastrophic fold (surface, plane, ...) are related to system parameter configuration when a system is changing its behavior (moment when bifurcation occurs). When a system control parameter is changed then the point in the parameter space moves and the moment when it crosses through the catastrophic fold changes, then behavior of the system is changed. This change can mean in reality changes in periodicity as well as switching to chaotic dynamic and/or also more drastic changes in the systemâ's physical structure and behavior. Such changes then can lead, in reality, to real catastrophes like aircrafts crashing, dam failure, collapse of a building or power network, etc. As demonstrated in [1] on the Lorenz system (weather model), born of chaos can be understood as a way through the series of bifurcations Thom's catastrophes. Mutual relation between Thom's catastrophes and bifurcations is thus clear.

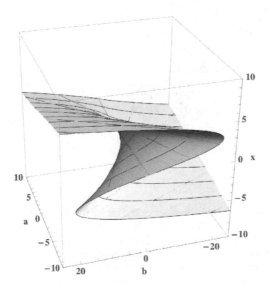

Figure 1. Catastrophe surface - Fold.

2.2. Experiment setup

Experiments have been designed as described in the Table 1. Each experiment was repeated 50 times and the results are reported in the Results section. All simulations have been done on a special grid computer. This grid computer consists of 16 XServers, each 2x2 GHz Intel Xeon, 1 GB RAM, 80 GB HD i.e. 64 CPUs.

2.2.1. Used algorithms

For the experiments described here (SA) [16] had been used. The control parameter settings have been found empirically and are given in Table 1 (SA).

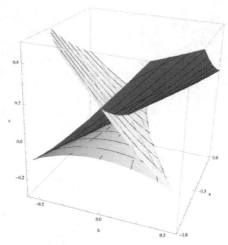

Figure 2. Catastrophe surface - Swallowtail.

No. of particles	100
σ	0.5
Tmin	0.000
Tmax	10000
α	0.98

Table 1. SA setting

2.2.2. Lyapunov exponents

Lyapunov exponents are another member of the family of universal features of deterministic chaos. They are numbers which basically express the divergence (or also convergence) of the state trajectories of a dynamic system. The exponents can be calculated relatively simply, both for discrete-time systems and for continuous-time systems. As will be explained later, Lyapunov exponents are closely related to the structure of the state space, which (in dynamic systems theory) is represented by an array of arrows determining the time development of the system at each point of the space. The development of the system in this space is then represented by a (usually) continuous curve [25]. Illustrative example of different behavior is depicted in Figure 3 and 4. Figure 3 shows the state space of a simple dynamic system along with two different time developments starting from two different initial conditions, which only differ by $x = 0.01$ in the x-axis. The behavior in the two cases is entirely different. Figure 4 shows different behavior. Hence, the behavior of a dynamical system is determined by its physical structure, which in the mathematical description is represented by the state space whose quantifiers can be Lyapunov exponents. If one is to follow colored arrows in Fig. 3, it can be noticed that they are separating with increasing time. On the other hand in Fig. 4 they after certain time occupy the same set of points in the state space, in this case called limit cycle. This observation can be described in a mathematical way by the Lyapunov exponents λ_i, see Equation (5), see [13].

$$\lambda_i = \lim_{t \to \infty} \frac{1}{t} \ln \frac{l_i(t)}{l(0)} \tag{5}$$

The structure of the exponents can help assess whether chaotic behavior is present in the system or not. Lyapunov exponent is a measure of the extension or contraction of the i_{th} semimajor axis of the ellipsoid. For graphic reasons, Lyapunov exponents are arranged by magnitude, i.e. $\lambda_1 \geq \lambda_2 \geq \ldots \geq \lambda_m$, where m is the dimension of the phase space; this is referred to as the Lyapunov exponents spectrum. For a chaotic trajectory, one Lyapunov exponent at least must be positive, although, in addition, the existence of any asymptotic periodicity must be ruled out to confirm the chaotic nature - see, e.g., [44]. In other words, the possibility that the trajectory converges to some periodic orbit with t → ∞ must be eliminated. But it is just this requirement that can pose a problem in practice if the dynamic system is investigated during a finite time interval only. Chaotic systems with more than one Lyapunov exponent are referred to as hyperchaotic, see [2]. Lyapunov exponents are closely related to Kolmogorov-Sinai entropy and kind of fractal dimensions also called Kaplan-Yorke (Lyapunov) dimension.

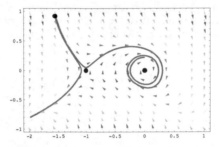

Figure 3. State space trajectory for a dynamic system with 2 singular points s_1 and s_2. On the position s_1 = {0,0} is repellor and at the position s_2 = {−1,0} saddle. Start points of both trajectories diverge despite fact that this coordinates (x_1 = {-1.56, 0.92} and x_2 = {-1.57, 0.92}) are very close.

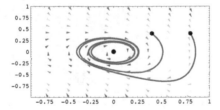

Figure 4. Different behavior can be observed when both trajectories will start in different part of state space. Despite its bigger difference in starting possition (x_1 = {0.4, 0.4} and x_2 = {0.8, 0.4}) trajectories merge together after certain time.

2.2.3. The cost function

The main idea of this part is to identify bifurcation (in the general sense related to Thom's catastrophes, see [1]) by means of EAs. For this purpose a logistic equation has been selected (simplified model of predator-prey system), see (6) and [5]. Logistic equation is very simple model of predator - prey system, that exhibit rich set of complex behavior for different values of control parameter A. For more details see [5].

$$x_{n+1} = Ax_n \left(1 - x_n\right) \tag{6}$$

The bifurcation diagram, [5] (i.e. system dependence on control parameter), of this system is depicted in Figure 7. The Lyapunov exponents of that system, related to parameter A, are depicted in 5 and 6. Simply: when the Lyapunov exponent is negative, the system has deterministic behaviour, when it is positive, the system is chaotic. When the Lyapunov exponent $\lambda = 0$ then bifurcation can be observed in the system behaviour. Then, to find these moments, we need to locate those parameters A for which the Lyapunov exponent $\lambda = 0$. It is enough to use absolute value and then we get Figure 5 and 6. Figure 6 represents the cost function landscape, where values with Lyapunov exponent = 0 are related settings of A for which bifurcation occurs. One can see that this surface is very erratic chaotic, and thus suitable candidates to find cost values with 0 are heuristics such as evolutionary algorithms. Cost function, used for depicting Figure 6, is given by (8) which is an absolute value of (7), see [5], variable d in (7) is the difference between two nearby trajectories. Function $f(x)$ in Equation 7 is in this case logistic equation 6. Graphically is Equation 7 and 8 depicted in Figure 5 and 6. EAs were used to search for $f_{cost} = 0$. Difference between Equation 5 and 7 is mainly in fact that Equation 5 calculate λ from function describing given system, while Equation 7 is based on recorded numerical data.

$$\lambda = \frac{1}{n} \ln \frac{d_n}{d_0}$$
$$d_0 = \left| x_i - x_j \right|$$
$$\dots$$
$$d_n = \left| x_{i+n} - x_{j+n} \right|$$

$$(7)$$

$$f_{cost} = |(\lambda)|$$

$$(8)$$

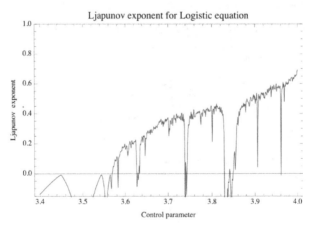

Figure 5. Dependence of Lyapunov exponent on parameter A of Equation (6), see (7)

2.2.4. Experimental results

Results obtained in all experiments are reported in Table 2 (SA) and Table 3 that show minimal, maximal and average cost values given by experimentation. Table 4 shows localized positions of bifurcations.

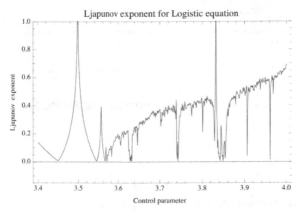

Figure 6. An absolute value of dependence of Lyapunov exponent on parameter A Equation (6), see (8)

Maximum	63358
Average	34728
Minimum	9946

Table 2. SA Cost Function Evaluations

Min	Average	Max
2×10^{-9}	9.2×10^{-6}	2×10^{-2}

Table 3. Cost values

Value of arameter A	3.543	3.568	3.632	3.742	3.847
Hit		23	12	32	19	14

Table 4. The coordinates (value of parameter *A*) of bifurcations (upper row) and number of its successful (approximative) identifications (bottom row).

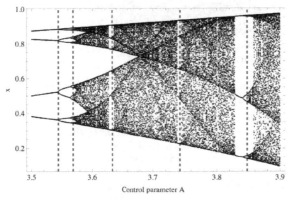

Figure 7. Composed picture show identified bifurcations (red dashed lines) that are in exact correlation with Lyapunov exponent, compare Figure 5 and 6 and Table 4, also [9], [10].

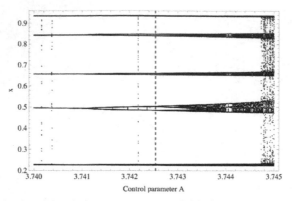

Figure 8. Identified and non-identified bifurcations, see also [9], [10].

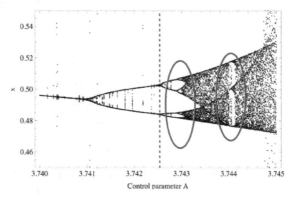

Figure 9. Identified and non-identified bifurcations, zoom from Figure 8, see also [9], [10].

SA in basic versions has been used in a simple system (6), called logistic equation, to localize bifurcations. Simulations were repeated 50 times. Based on results reported in the previous section it can be stated that:

1. **Simulations.** All simulations has been successfully finished by localization of the bifurcation event, see Table 4.

2. **Precision.** Located bifurcations were localized with high precision, however, not exactly, see Figure 7-10. Geometrically it can be interpreted so that the system is at the edge of a catastrophic model or almost before crossing the fold on the surface of Thom's catastrophe manifold. Our opinion is that such non-precise localization can be useful, when applied to a real system and bifurcation can cause real damage, which means that the evolutionary search for bifurcations on a real system can be stopped very near to the bifurcation position. Figures 7-10 clearly show, that there are a lot of other bifurcations that were not localized by the SA that was used, which imply better settings of SA or acceptable value of λ (see Localized bifurcations below), is probably possible. This is open question for further experiments.

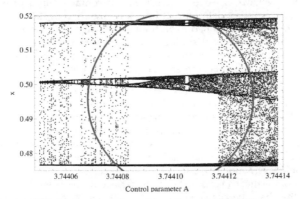

Figure 10. Non-identified bifurcations, zoom from Figure 9, see also [9], [10].

3. **Chaotic systems.** Besides well known logistic equation, other systems such as Ikeda, Burger, Delayed Logistic, etc. can be selected. The logistic equation system (derived from predator prey system) has been chosen because it is well known, and well investigated. Other systems (like those mentioned above) are now in the process of investigation.

4. **Simulation environment and software.** Software used for all calculations, numerical simulations and visualizations was the well known *Mathematica*. Thanks to fact that Mathematica is an integrated environment, the time scale for each simulation was in minutes. It is clear that when C++ or another fast programming language would be used, then time scale of simulation should be much shorter and thus real use of this approach on real systems is possible.

5. **Localized bifurcations.** It is important to note that only main bifurcations have been localized. Bifurcations at exact positions were undiscovered, which implies space for future research, i.e. better algorithm setting, cost function improvement, etc. Figures 7-10 clearly show, that there are a lot of other bifurcations that were not localized by the SA, so the question is: what is the limit for EAs to be used on this kind of task, or what will be better settings for it? The bifurcations were determined by the same SA in repeated simulations. Localized bifurcation implies that $\lambda = 0$, however because SA is numerical algorithm, working with certain preciseness, successful localization has been set for $\lambda < 10^{-1}$.

In the light of our previous experiments described in [11], [12] and [13] it is clear that evolutionary techniques are capable of solving a wider class of problems in the chaos research domain.

3. Case study 2: Chaos synthesis

This part introduces the notion of chaos synthesis by means of evolutionary algorithms and develops a new method for chaotic systems synthesis, [13]. This method is similar to genetic programming and grammatical evolution and is being applied along with evolutionary algorithms: differential evolution, self-organizing migrating, genetic algorithm, simulated annealing and evolutionary strategies. The aim of this investigation is to synthesize new and simple chaotic systems based on some elements contained in a pre-selected existing chaotic system and a properly defined cost function. The investigation consists of two case studies based on the aforementioned evolutionary algorithms in various versions. For all algorithms, 100 simulations of chaos synthesis were repeated and then averaged to guarantee the reliability and robustness of the proposed method. The most significant results were carefully selected, visualized and commented on in this chapter.

Deterministic chaos, discovered by [21] is a fairly active area of research in the last few decades. The Lorenz system produces a well-known chaotic attractor in a simple three-dimensional autonomous system of ordinary differential equations, [21], [22]. For discrete chaos, there is another famous chaotic system, called the logistic equation [23], which was found based on a predator-prey model showing complex dynamical behaviors. These simple models are widely used in the study of chaos today, while other similar models exist (e.g., canonical logistic equation [24] and 1D or 2D coupled map lattices, [25]). To date, a large set of nonlinear systems that can produce chaotic behaviors have been observed and analyzed. Chaotic systems thus have become a vitally important part of science and engineering at the theoretical as well as practical levels of research. The most interesting and applicable notions are, for example, chaos control and chaos synchronization related to secure communications, amongst others.

The aim of the present investigation is to show that EA-based symbolic regression (i.e., handling with symbolic objects to create more complex structures) is capable of synthesizing chaotic behavior in the sense that mathematical descriptions of chaotic systems are synthesized symbolically by means of evolutionary algorithms. The ability of EAs to successfully solve this kind of black-box problems has been proven many times before (see, for example, [26], [27]), and is proven once again here in this paper.

3.1. Cost function

The cost function was in fact a little bit complex decision function. The cost function used for chaos synthesis, comparing with other problems is quite a complex structure which cannot be easily described by a few simple mathematical equations. Instead, it is described by the following algorithm procedure:

1. Take a synthesized function and evaluate it for 500 iterations with and a sampling step of $\Delta A = 0.1$.

2. Check if each value of A for all 500 iterations is unique or if some data are repeated in the series (the first check for chaos, indirectly). If the data are not unique, then go to step 5 else go to step 3.

3. Take the last 200 values, and for each value of A, calculate its Lyapunov exponent.

4. Check the Lyapunov exponent: If the Lyapunov exponent is positive, write all important data (synthesized functions, number of cost function evaluations, etc.) into a file. Then, repeat the simulation for another synthesized system by going to step 1.

5. If the data are not unique, i.e., if the Lyapunov exponent is not positive, return an individual fitness, and sum all values whose occurrences in the dataset from step 1 are more than 1 (simply, it returns the occurrences of periodicity, quasi-periodicity – higher penalization of an individual in the evolution).

More brief and simple description of above algorithmically defined cost function can be also done as in Equation 9.

$$Data[f_{synt, 1}, ..., f_{synt, 500}] := f_{synt, k+1} = f_{synt, k}(x_{start}), \ k \in [1, \ 500]$$
$$\begin{cases} if \ Data[f_{synt, 1}] \neq Data[f_{synt, 2}] \neq .... \neq Data[f_{synt, 500}] \\ then \ \{calculate \ \lambda \ for \ Data[f_{synt, 300}, \cdots, f_{synt, 500}] \ , \ if \ \lambda > 0 \ write \ all \ to \ file \\ else \ penalize \ individual \end{cases} \quad (9)$$

The input to this cost function is a synthesized function and the output is the fitness (quality) of the synthesized function (i.e., the individual in the population). In the cost function, it was tested twice to see if the behavior of the just-synthesized formula is really chaotic. The first test was done in step 2 (unique appearance in the data series) and the second one, in step 4, where the Lyapunov exponent was tested numerically [5].

The reason why in step 5) the sum of the non-unique data appearances was returned is based on the fact that the evolution is searching for minimal values. In this case, the value 2 means that some data element appears in the 500-data series twice, and 1 would means that there is no periodicity and thus synthesized system is possible candidate for chaos.

To make sure that the results so obtained are correct, all written synthesized functions were used for automatic generation of bifurcation diagrams and Lyapunov exponents, as further discussed below.

3.2. Simulations and results

SA algorithms have been applied 100 times in order to find artificially synthesized functions that can produce chaos. All of these experiments were done using the *Mathematica* software. The primary aim of this comparative study is not to show which algorithm is better or worse, but to show that symbolic regression is able to synthesize some new (at least in the sense of mathematical description and behavior) chaotic systems.

Based on the results from experiments, two different sets of figures were created. The first set shows the performances of different algorithms from different points of view (see [13]), the second set (Figure 11 - Figure 14) shows behaviors of the selected synthesized programs, i.e., bifurcation diagrams. The synthesized programs are also appended to each figure in the form of the mathematical formula. Figure 15 shows an example of the so-called program length histogram, generated from 100 simulations. Program length (in *Mathematica* command: LeafCount, denoted as LC) means a number of elements that create a mathematical formula. As a summary, the following statements are presented:

As a summary, the following statements are presented:

- **Result verification.** To be sure that the results as presented in the paper are correct, all written synthesized functions were used for automatic generation of bifurcation diagrams and Lyapunov exponents.

- **Simulation results.** Based on the results (see selected Figures 11 - 14) and the selected bifurcation diagrams, it can be stated that all simulations give satisfactory results and that evolutionary synthesis of chaos is capable of solving this class of problems.

- **Range of chaos and interval of observation.** During evolutions, chaos was searched by focusing on interval [0, 4], based on the a priori known behavior of the logistic equation

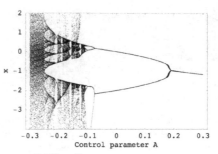

Figure 11. Bifurcation diagram of $\dfrac{2A(2x-1)}{A+x^2}\ldots$

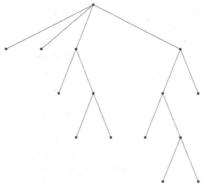

Figure 12. ... and its tree representation.

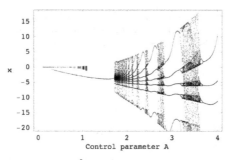

Figure 13. Bifurcation diagram of $\dfrac{2Ax(-A^2-2x)}{A+x^2}\ldots$

whose elements were used in the evolution. Despite the a priori known information, a few chaotic systems were located also outside of this interval. That was due to the fact that a part of the chaotic behavior was inside the interval [0, 4] and thus EA was able to identify it. From these facts, it is clear that EA are able to locate chaos in a wider range than those expected from some textbook exemplary systems.

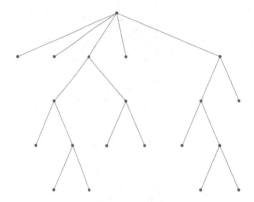

Figure 14. ... and its tree representation.

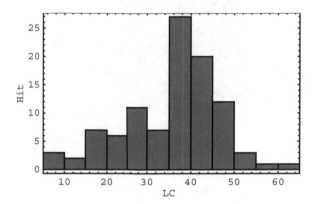

Figure 15. Histogram of LC for DERand1Bin

- **Exemplary system synthesis.** Based on the fact that the logistic equation (its elements and range) is used for chaos synthesis, it is logical to expect that during evolution (if repeated many times) the original system should also be synthesized. That event was also observed a few times, exactly in the mathematical form Equation (6). Some selected bifurcation diagrams of synthesized systems are depicted in Figures 16 - 19.

- **Mutual comparison.** When comparing all algorithms, it is obvious that these algorithms produced good results. Parameter setting for the algorithms was based on a heuristic approach and thus there is a possibility that better settings can be found there. Based on these results, it is clear that for symbolic synthesis via analytic programming any evolutionary algorithm can be used.

- **Engineering design.** It is quite clear that evolutionary synthesis of chaos can be applied to engineering design of devices based on chaos (signal transmission via chaos, chaos-based encryption, and so on). Based on principles and results reported in this paper, it should be possible to synthesize systems with some precisely defined chaotic features and attributes.

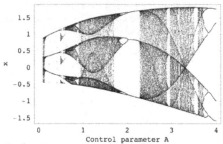

Figure 16. Another synthesized system.

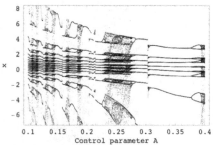

Figure 17. Another synthesized system.

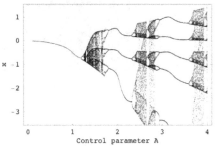

Figure 18. Another synthesized system.

4. Case study 3: Evolutionary control of CML systems

This contribution introduces a continuation of an investigation on deterministic spatiotemporal chaos realtime control by means of selected evolutionary techniques. Realtime-like behavior is specially defined and simulated with a spatiotemporal chaos model based on mutually nonlinear joined *n* equations, so called Coupled Map Lattices (CML), see [25]. SA algorithms have been used for chaos control here. For modeling of spatiotemporal chaos behavior, so-called coupled map lattices were used based on a logistic equation to generate chaos. The main aim of this investigation was to show that evolutionary algorithms, under certain conditions, are capable of control of CML deterministic chaos, when the cost function is properly defined as well as parameters of a selected evolutionary algorithm. Investigation consists of four different case studies with increasing simulation complexity.

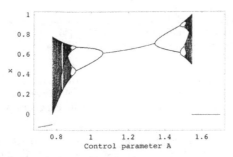

Figure 19. Another synthesized system.

For all algorithms each simulation was repeated 100 times to show and check the robustness of the methods used. All data were processed and used in order to obtain summarizing results and graphs. Many methods were adapted for the so-called spatiotemporal chaos represented by coupled map lattices (CML). Control laws derived for CML are usually based on existing system structures, Schuster H. G. (1999), or using an external observer, Chen G. (2000). Evolutionary approach for control was also successfully developed in, for example, Richter H. and Reinschke K. J. (2000), Richter H. and Reinschke Kurt J. (2000a), Richter H. (2002), Zelinka I. (2006). Many published methods of deterministic chaos control (DCC) were (originally developed for classic DCC) adapted for so-called spatiotemporal chaos represented by CML, given by (10). Models of this kind are based on a set of spatiotemporal (for 1D, Figure 20) or spatial cells which represents the appropriate state of system elements. A typical example is CML based on the so-called logistic equation, [23], [5], [29], which is used to simulate the behavior of system which consists of n mutually joined cells via onlinear coupling, usually noted as #. A mathematical description of the CML system is given by Equation (10). The function which is represented by $f(x_n(i))$ is arbitrary I discrete system in this case study logistic equations have been selected to substitute $f(x_n(i))$.

$$x_{n+1}(i) = (1-\varepsilon)f(x_n(i)) + \frac{\varepsilon}{2}(f(x_n(i-1)) + f(x_n(i+1))) \qquad (10)$$

The main aim of this part is to show that evolutionary algorithms (EA) are capable of controlling (as was also shown for temporal DCC in [31], [32] CML as well as deterministic methods without internal system knowledge operating with CML as with a black box. The

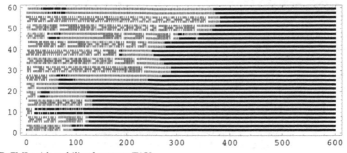

Figure 20. 1D CML with stabilized pattern T1S2

ability of EAs to successfully work with a problematic kind of black box have been proven; see for example realtime control of plasma reactor, [34], [35], [36] or CML non realtime control by evolutionary algorithms [37], [38], [39]. This part is organized as follows. The first part outlines the motivation of this investigation.

This is followed by a brief survey of evolutionary algorithms which follow, along with a brief description of the idea of CML chaos control and the evolutionary algorithms that were used. Evolutionary chaos control is then studied, and finally experimental results are reported, followed by the conclusion.

The main question in the case of this participation was whether EAs are able to control and stabilize chaotic systems like CML, and if they are able to control CML like a black box system, i.e. when the structure of controlled system is unknown. All experiments here were designed to check this idea and confirm or refute this idea. Comparison has been done with a control based on analysis of a CML system, [40], [28] and analytic derivation of control law for CML. Behavior of a controlled CML is as demonstrated in Figure 21 - Figure 23. A snapshot of front-wave stabilization of a CML is depicted here. Figure 21 is the initial phase of front-wave. It is clearly visible that it is fully random. Figure 21 shows the CML after 60 iterations a pattern-like structure is visible there. The last snapshot was made after 344 iterations the CML has been successfully stabilized. Thus, the main aim was to stabilize CML with the quality as standard controlling techniques.

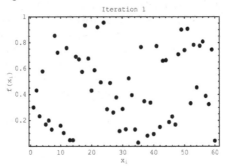

Figure 21. Succesfull stabilization of CML in T1S3 pattern - start.

4.1. CML control

4.1.1. Parameter setting

The control parameter settings have been found empirically and are given in Table 5. The main criterion for this setting was to keep the same setting of parameters as much as possible and, of course, the same number of cost function evaluations as well as population size. Individual length represents the number of optimized parameters (number of pinning sites, values...). Compared to previous [38], the length of experiments has been an individual set of 1 or 2, according to the case study. In [38] and [41], individual length was equal to the number of pinning sites, which has increased complexity of calculations. To simplify simulations here, a simple presumption has been taken into consideration instead of an exact number of pinning sites as in [38], their periodicity has been estimated in the evolution, i.e. if parameter for

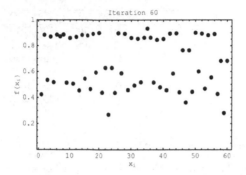

Figure 22. Succesfull stabilization of CML in T1S3 pattern - iteration 60.

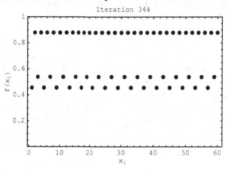

Figure 23. Succesfull stabilization of CML in T1S3 pattern - pattern is stabilised.

the pinning site was, for example, 4th, then each 4th site has been used for pinning value application, etc... In total 4 case studies has been selected and used in this experiment:

- **Case Study A**: - Pinning Value Estimation.
- **Case Study B**: - Pinning Sites Position Estimation.
- **Case Study C**: - Minimal Pinning Sites Position Estimation.
- **Case Study D**: - Minimal Pinning Values and Sites Position Estimation.

see [13].

4.2. Used hardware

CML control in this case study has been done on a special grid computer, as opposed to a simple PC as in [41]. This grid computer, called Emanuel, consists of two special Apple servers, the bigger one is based on 16 XServers, each 2x2 GHz Intel Xeon, 1 GB RAM, 80 GB HD i.e. 64 CPUs. The second one is created from 7 Apple Minimacs CoreDuo i.e. number of accessible CPUs is 14. In total there were 78 CPUs available. Emanuel was used for calculations in two ways. The first one was focused on use of each CPU like a single processor and thus a rich set of statistically repeated experiments were not a time problem. In the second

Case Study	A	B	C	D
No. of particles	10	10	10	10
σ	0.5	0.5	0.5	0.5
k_{max}	66	66	66	66
T_{min}	0.0001	0.0001	0.0001	0.0001
T_{max}	1000	1000	1000	1000
α	0.95	0.95	0.95	0.95
Individual Length	1	1	1	2

Table 5. SA setting for case studies A, B, C and D

way Emanuel was used like grid machine to increase speed of selected simulations reported in this book. This does not mean that this class of problems can be solved only on special computers. All solved problems and reported case studies in this book can also be done on a single PC. Of course in different time scale.

4.2.1. Cost function

The fitness (cost function) has been calculated by using the distance between the desired CML state and actual CML output, Equation (11). The minimal value of this cost function, which guarantees the best solution, is 0. The aim of all simulations was to find the best solution, i.e. a solution that returns the cost value 0. This cost function was used for the first two case studies (pinning values setting, pinning sites setting). In the next (last) two case studies, cost function (12) was used. It is synthesized from cost function (11) so that two penalty terms are added. The first one, p_1, represents the number of pinning sites used in the CML. The second one, p_2, is added here to attract the attention of the evolutionary process on the main part of cost function. If this were not done, then mainly p_1 would be optimized and the results would not be acceptable (proved by simulations). Indexes i and j are coordinates of the lattice element, $CML_{i,j}$ is i_{th} site (equation) in j_{th} iteration. For all simulations of T_1S_1 the stabilized state was set to $S_1 = 0.75$, and for T_1S_2 to period $S_2 = (0.880129, 0.536537)$, i.e. CML behavior was controlled to this state.

Knowledge (at least approximate) about complexity and variability of the cost function used is very important. Such knowledge can be important when the class of optimizing algorithms is selected. Thus a few ideas and examples have been selected here to show complexity and its dependence on chaotic system parameter setting. How complex such a cost function can be is clearly visible from Figure 24 and Figure 25. It is clearly visible, that cost function is partly chaotic and for a certain pinning value, global minimum representing stabilization is accessible. The chaoticness of such a graphical representation is caused by the fact that calculations are based on a chaotic system. If the average value (over many of such runs) were to be calculated, then we would get graphs with a smooth curve. However, because our simulations were running on a single run, not over a lot of them, Figure 24 and Figure 25 are real representations of the landscape of our cost function. Our simulations were run over such, or a similar, landscape. It is also important to note that for each simulation of CML, the exact shape and its chaoticness can be slightly different from the previous one, due to the sensitivity of initial conditions. It is clear that the complexity of the cost function that was used is big, despite the simple mathematical description. Also, suitable stabilizing combination of control parameters depends on the number of CML iterations (after a certain number of iterations the combination is permanent) and configuration (T₁S₁,₂) of stabilized state.

$$f_{cost} = \sum_{i=1}^{30} \sum_{j=a}^{b} \left| TS_{i,j} - CML_{i,j} \right|^2$$

$TS_{i,j}$ – target state of CML   (11)

$CML_{i,j}$ – actual state of controlled CML

$\{a,b\} = \{80,100\}$ for T_1S_1 and $\{a,b\} = \{580,600\}$ for T_1S_1

$$f_{cost} = p1 + \left(p2 + \sum_{i=1}^{30} \sum_{j=a}^{b} \left| TS_{i,j} - CML_{i,j} \right| \right)^2$$

$TS_{i,j}$ – target state of CML

$CML_{i,j}$ – actual state of controlled CML   (12)

p1 – number of actually selected pinning sites

p2 – 100, heuristically set weight constant

$\{a,b\} = \{80,100\}$ for T_1S_1 and $\{a,b\} = \{580,600\}$ for T_1S_1

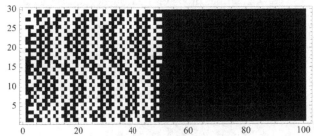

Figure 24. Successful stabilization of CML (30×100 - 30 pining sites, 100 iterations) in T_1S_1 pattern - stabilization after 52 iterations is visible.

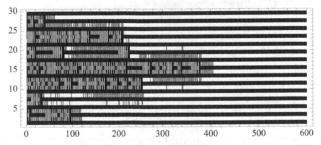

Figure 25. CML T_1S_2 in configuration 30×600 – stabilization after 400 iterations is visible.

4.3. Experimental results

All simulations were done in the framework of four case studies A, B, C and D. In all numerical case studies both CML regimes T_1S_1 and T_1S_2 were compared to show how the complexity of both regimes can influence the number of cost function evaluations etc. The method of evolutionary deterministic chaos control described here is relatively simple, easy to implement and easy to use. Based on its principles and its possible universality it can be stated that evolutionary deterministic chaos control is capable of solving this class of CML deterministic chaos control problems. The main aim of this part was to show how various CML control problems were solved by means of evolutionary algorithms. Evolutionary deterministic chaos control was used here in four basic comparative simulations. Each comparative simulation was repeated 100 times and all results (see [13]) were used to create graphs for performance evaluation of evolutionary deterministic chaos control. They were chosen to show that evolutionary deterministic chaos control can be regarded as a blackboxĺ method and that it can be implemented using arbitrary evolutionary algorithms.

5. Conclusions

In this chapter selected applications of simulated annealing were briefly mentioned, such as: evolutionary identification of bifurcations, synthesis of chaotic systems and evolutionary control of spatiotemporal CML systems. All experiments mentioned here are a part of a more extended set of experiments, so we recommend that interested readers read our original sources for a full description. It has been numerically demonstrated that SA is still a useful algorithm, capable of solving various problems from engineering as well as from theory.

Acknowledgement

This work was supported by the Development of human resources in research and development of latest soft computing methods and their application in practice project, reg. no. CZ.1.07/2.3.00/20.0072 funded by Operational Programme Education for Competitiveness, co-financed by ESF and state budget of the Czech Republic.

Author details

Ivan Zelinka and Lenka Skanderova
Department of Computer Science, Faculty of computer science,17. listopadu 15, 708 33 Ostrava-Poruba, VSB-TUO Ostrava, Czech Republic

6. References

[1] Gilmore R., Catastrophe Theory for Scientists and Engineers,John Wiley and Sons, 1993
[2] Rössler O (1979) An equation for hyperchaos. Phys. Lett. A, 71:155
[3] Arnold V.(1991). The Theory of Singularities and Its Applications, Accademia Nazionale Dei Lincei, Pisa, Italy, 1991
[4] Poston T, Stewart I.(1977). Catastrophe Theory and its Applications, 842-844, IEEE Press, New York, USA,1977
[5] Hilborn R.(1994). Chaos and Nonlinear Dynamics,Oxford University Press,1994
[6] Price K., Storn R. et al.(1994). Differential Evolution - A Practical Approach to Global Optimization, Springer-Verlag, 2005
[7] Zelinka I. (2004). SOMA - Self Organizing Migrating Algorithm, In: *New Optimization Techniques in Engineering*,Onwubolu, Babu B., (Ed.), 167-218, Springer-Verlag, New York, 2004

[8] Davis L. (1996). Handbook of Genetic Algorithms, Van Nostrand Reinhold, Berlin, 1996

[9] Zelinka I., Davendra D., Senkerik R., Jasek R., Oplatkova Z. (1996). Evolutionary Techniques And Its Possibility To Identify Catastrophic Events, *In Proceeding of the 5th Global Conference on Power and Optimization*, 983-44483-49, Dubai, UAE, June 1-3 2011

[10] Zelinka I., Davendra D., Senkerik R., Jasek R.(2011). Evolutionary Techniques And Its Possibility To Identify Catastrophic Events - An Extended Study, *Matousek Radek: Mendel 2011 -17th International Conference on SoftComputing*, pp. 73-79, ISBN 978-80-214-4302-0, Brno University of Technology, 2011a

[11] Ivan Zelinka, Roman Senkerik, Eduard Navratil (2006). Investigation On Realtime Deterministic Chaos Control By Means Of Evolutionary Algorithms, , *Proceeding of the Chaos 06*, June 22-24 2006, Reims, France

[12] Ivan Zelinka, Roman Senkerik, Eduard Navratil (2009). Evolutionary Identification of Chaotic System, *Proceeding of the Chaos 09*, June 22-24 2009, London.

[13] Zelinka I, Celikovsky S, Richter H and Chen G., (2010). Evolutionary Algorithms and Chaotic Systems, pp.550, Springer, Germany, 2010

[14] Cerny V., Thermodynamical approach to the traveling salesman problem: An efficient simulation algorithm, J. Opt. Theory Appl., 45, 1, 41-51, 1985

[15] Goldberg, David E.(1989). *Genetic Algorithms in Search, Optimization, and Machine Learning*, Addison-Wesley Publishing Company Inc.

[16] Kirkpatrick, S., Gelatt Jr., C.D., Vecchi, M.P. (1983).*Optimization by Simulated Annealing*, Vol. 220, No. 4598, 1983, 671–680.

[17] Metropolis, A., Rosenbluth, W., Rosenbluth, M.N., Teller, H., Teller, E. *Equation of State Calculations by Fast Computing Machines The Journal of Chemical Physics*, Vol. 21, No. 6, 1953, 1087–1092.

[18] Price K.(1999). An Introduction to Differential Evolution, In: *New Ideas in Optimization*, D. Corne, M. Dorigo and F. Glover,(Ed.), p. 79-108, McGraw-Hill, London, UK.

[19] Zelinka, Ivan (2004). Self Organizing Migrating Algorithm, In: *New Optimization Techniques in Engineering*, G. C. Onwubolu, B.V. Babu, (Ed.), Springer-Verlag.

[20] Hargis, PJ et al (1994). The Gaseous Electronics Conference Radiofrequency Reference Cell – A Defined Parallel-Plate Radiofrequency System For Experimental And Theoretical-Studies Of Plasma-Processing Discharges, *Review of Scientific Instruments*, 65(1) pp. 140-154, 1994

[21] Lorenz E.N. Deterministic nonperiodic flow, Journal of the Atmospheric Sciences, 20 (2), 130–141, 1963

[22] Stewart I. The Lorenz attractor exists, Nature, 406, 948–949, 2000

[23] May R. Simple mathematical model with very complicated dynamics, Nature, 261, 45-67, 1976

[24] Gilmore R., Lefranc M. The Topology of Chaos: Alice in Stretch and Squeezeland (Wiley-Interscience, New York), 2002

[25] Schuster H. G., Handbook of Chaos Control (Wiley-VCH, New York), 1999

[26] Zelinka I., Nolle L., Plasma reactor optimizing using differential evolution, in Differential Evolution: A Practical Approach to Global Optimization, Eds.: Price K.V., Lampinen J., Storn R. (Springer-Verlag, New York), 499-512, 2005

[27] Nolle L., Zelinka I., Hopgood A. A., Goodyear A., Comparison of an self organizing migration algorithm with simulated annealing and differential evolution for automated waveform tuning, Advances in Engineering Software, 36 (10), 645-653, 2005

[28] Schuster H. G., Handbook of Chaos Control (Wiley-VCH, New York), 1999

[29] Controlling Chaos and Bifurcations in Engineering Systems (CRC Press, Boca Raton), 2000

[30] Richter H., Reinschke K. J., Optimization of local control of chaos by an evolutionary algorithm, Physica D, 144, 309-334, 2000

[31] Richter H., Reinschke Kurt J., Optimization of local control of chaos by an evolutionary algorithm. Physica D 144 (2000), 309-334. 2000

[32] Richter H., An evolutionary algorithm for controlling chaos: The use of multi-objective fitness functions. In: Parallel Problem Solving from Nature-PPSN VII. (Eds.: Merelo GuervÃşs, J.J.; Panagiotis, A.; Beyer, H.G.; FernÃąndez Villacanas, J.L.; Schwefel, H.P.), Lecture Notes in Computer Science, Vol. 2439, Springer-Verlag, Berlin Heidelberg New York, 2002, 308-317, 2002

[33] Zelinka I., Investigation on realtime deterministic chaos control by means of evolutionary algorithms, Proc. First IFAC Conference on Analysis and Control of Chaotic Systems, Reims, France, 211-217, 2006

[34] Nolle, L., Goodyear, A., Hopgood, A.A., Picton, P.D., Braithwaite, N.StJ.: On Step Width Adaptation in Simulated Annealing for Continuous Parameter Optimisation, Reusch, B. (Ed): Computational Intelligence - Theory and Applications, Lecture Notes in Computer Science, Vol. 2206, Springer, 2001, pp 589-598

[35] Nolle L., Zelinka I., Hopgood A. A., Goodyear A., Comparison of an self organizing migration algorithm with simulated annealing and differential evolution for automated waveform tuning, Advances in Engineering Software, 36 (10), 645-653, 2005

[36] Zelinka I., Nolle L., Plasma reactor optimizing using differential evolution, in Differential Evolution: A Practical Approach to Global Optimization, Eds.: Price K.V., Lampinen J., Storn R. (Springer-Verlag, New York), 499-512, 2006

[37] Zelinka I., Investigation on Evolutionary Deterministic Chaos Control, IFAC, Prague 2005a

[38] Zelinka Ivan, Investigation on Evolutionary Deterministic Chaos Control – Extended Study, In: 19th International Conference on Simulation and Modeling, (ECMS 2005), Riga, Latvia, in June 1-4, 2005

[39] Zelinka I., Senkerik R., Navratil E., Investigation on Evolutionary Optimitazion of Chaos Control, CHAOS, SOLITONS, FRACTALS, doi:10.1016/j.chaos.2007.07.045, 2007

[40] Hu G., Xie F., Xiao J., Yang J., Qu Z., Control of patterns and spatiotemporal chaos and its application, in Handbook of Chaos Control, Ed.: Schuster H. G. (Wiley VCH, New York), 2005

[41] Zelinka, I., Real-time deterministic chaos control by means of selected evolutionary algorithms Engineering Applications of Artificial Intelligence (2008), doi:10.1016/j.engappai.2008.07.008

[42] Zelinka I., Davendra D., Senkerik R., Jasek R., Oplatkova Z., Analytical Programming - a Novel Approach for Evolutionary Synthesis of Symbolic Structures, Evolutionary Algorithms, Prof. Eisuke Kita (Ed.), ISBN: 978-953-307-171-8, InTech 2011

[43] Zelinka I., Davendra D., Senkerik R., Jasek R. Evolutionary Techniques And Its Possibility To Identify Catastrophic Events – An Extended Study. In Matousek Radek: Mendel 2011 -17th International Conference on SoftComputing. Brno: Brno University of Technology. 2011. ISBN 978-80-214-4302-0. p. 73-79.

[44] Alligood K, Sauer T, Yorke J, Chaos - an introduction to dynamical systems. Springer. New York

Optimization Design of Nonlinear Optical Frequency Conversion Devices Using Simulated Annealing Algorithm

Yan Zhang

Additional information is available at the end of the chapter

1. Introduction

Laser has become to be a fundamental light source in modern communication, scientific research, and industrial applications. More and more laser frequencies are required for various applications. However, common laser crystals can provide only some fixed frequencies which cannot satisfy various requirement. Nonlinear optical process presents an alternative approach for generating rich laser frequencies. The traditional nonlinear optical processes usually require the so called phase-matching condition [1, 2], which requires the nonlinear optical crystals with birefringence. The phase-matching condition raises a restriction of the choice of natural birefringence materials in the applications of frequency conversion. Quasi-phase-matching method uses periodic modulation of the nonlinear property of a crystal to compensate the mismatch between the wave vectors of the interaction light beams [3]. This method allows utilization of the large component of the nonlinear susceptibility tensor, which is usually inaccessible with the common phase matching. Periodic optical superlattice provides a reciprocal vector to compensate the phase mismatch between the interacting light beams. Thus, only one nonlinear process can be performed in the periodic optical superlattice. This idea can be naturedly expended to the aperiodic optical supperlattice which can provide a series of reciprocal vectors. The reciprocal vectors can be preset for special nonlinear process. The key problem is how to design different aperiodic optical supperlattice for matching the specified nonlinear optical process with high conversion efficiency.

In this chapter, the simulated annealing (SA) method is used to successfully design nonlinear optical frequency conversion devices for achieving different nonlinear optical processes, for example, multiple second harmonics generation and coupled third harmonic generation in the aperiodic optical superlattice, multiple wavelengths parametric amplification, multiple wavelengths second harmonics generation and coupled third harmonic generation in the defective nonlinear photonic crystals. The simulation results demonstrate that the SA method is an effective algorithm for nonlinear optical frequency conversion devices design. The designed devices can archive the preset goal well.

2. Design of aperiodic optical supperlattice

Unlike the periodic optical supperlattice, the aperiodic optical superlattice can provide more spatial Fourier components of structure, therefore, some coupled parametric processes may be realized in this kind of devices. Firstly, the optimal design problem of the aperiodic optical superlattice is described in the real-space representation. Then several model designs are carried out to demonstrate the effectiveness of the present design method. The $LiTaO_3$ is selected as basic crystal for polarizing. The direction of polarization vectors in successive domain are opposite, thus are the signs of the nonlinear optical coefficients. However, the width of each individual domain is no longer equal and should be determined by the specified nonlinear optical processes.

2.1. Design method

We use the second harmonic generation (SHG) process for a single wavelength as an example. Assume that a laser beam with frequency $\omega_1 = \omega$ is perpendicularly incident on the surface of an aperiodic optical superlattice. In order to use the largest nonlinear coefficient d_{33}, let the propagation and polarization directions of the input light are along the x and z axes, respectively. Two optical fields are involved in the SHG process. one is the fundamental wave with $\omega_1 = \omega$ and other is the second harmonic wave with $\omega_2 = 2\omega$. Under the slowing-wave and small-signal approximations, the conversion efficiency η_{SHG} from the fundamental wave to second harmonic wave can be written as:

$$\eta_{SHG} = \frac{I_{2\omega}}{I_\omega} = \frac{8\pi^2 |d_{33}|^2 I_\omega L^2}{c\varepsilon_0 \lambda^2 n_{2\omega} n_\omega^2} \left| \frac{1}{L} \int_0^L e^{i(k_{2\omega} - 2k_\omega)x} \tilde{d}(x) dx \right|^2, \tag{1}$$

where $k_\omega = n_\omega \omega / c$ ($k_{2\omega} = n_{2\omega} 2\omega / c$) is the wave number of the fundamental (second harmonic) wave, c is the speed of light in vacuum, n_ω ($n_{2\omega}$) is the refractive index of crystal at the fundamental (second harmonic) wavelength, ε_0 is the permittivity of vacuum, and L is the total length of the sample. I_ω ($I_{2\omega}$) is the intensity of the fundamental (second harmonic) wave beam, and $\tilde{d}(x)$ only takes binary values of 1 or -1 which depends on the polarization direction. The coherence length $l_c^{(s)}(\lambda)$ for the SHG is defined as:

$$l_c^{(s)}(\lambda) = \frac{2\pi}{\Delta k} = \frac{2\pi}{k_{2\omega} - 2k_\omega} = \frac{\lambda}{2(n_{2\omega} - n_\omega)}. \tag{2}$$

Thus Equation 1 can be rewritten as

$$\eta_{SHG} = C_s C^2(\lambda) \xi_{eff}^{(s)2}(s), \tag{3}$$

with

$$C_s = \frac{8\pi^2 |d_{33}|^2 I_\omega L^2}{c\varepsilon_0}, \tag{4}$$

$$C(\lambda) = \frac{1}{\lambda \sqrt{n_{2\omega} n_\omega}}, \tag{5}$$

and

$$\xi_{eff}^{(s)}(\lambda) = \left| \frac{1}{L} \int_0^L e^{i(2\pi x / l_c^{(s)}(\lambda))} \tilde{d}(x) dx \right|, \tag{6}$$

the parameter $\zeta_{eff}^{(s)}(\lambda)$ depends on the polarization direction of each domain.

Assume that the thickness of the each domain of the aperiodic optical superlattice is Δx, thus the number of blocks in the sample is $N = L/\Delta x$. The position of each domain is $x_q = q\Delta x$ for $q = 0, 1, 2, ... (N-1)$. Equation 6 can be evaluated as

$$\zeta_{eff}^{(s)}(\lambda) = \frac{1}{N\Delta x} \left| \sum_{q=0}^{N-1} \tilde{d}(x_q) \int_{x_q}^{x_q+\Delta x} e^{i(2\pi x/l_c^{(s)}(\lambda))} dx \right|$$

$$= \left| sinc\left[\frac{\Delta x}{l_c^{(s)}(\lambda)} \right] \right| \left| \left\{ \frac{1}{N} \sum_{q=0}^{N-1} \tilde{d}(x_q) e^{i[2\pi(q+0.5)\Delta x/l_c^{(s)}(\lambda)]} \right\} \right|, \qquad (7)$$

where $sinc(x) = sin(\pi x)/(\pi x)$. It can be seen that $\zeta_{eff}^{(s)}(\lambda)$ has two contributions: one belongs to the unit block and depends on the Δx and the coherence length $l_c^{(s)}(\lambda)$; the other is caused by the interference effect among the blocks and depends on the configuration of domains and the polarization direction of each block.

The optimization design of the aperiodic optical superlattice for the SHG can be ascribed as a search for the maximum of $\zeta_{eff}^{(s)}(\lambda)$ with respect to $\tilde{d}(q\Delta x)$. The first factor in Equation 7 has its maximum value $2/[\pi(2m+1)]$ when $\Delta x = [(2m+1)/2]l_c^{(s)}(\lambda)$. The second factor has its maximum value of 1 in the case of the periodic structure with a period of $a = 2\Delta x = l_c^{(s)}(\lambda)$, $d(x_q)$ takes opposite sign between two consecutive blocks. In this case, the phase lagging factor perfectly matches the reversal of the domain orientation between two adjacent blocks and the ideal constructive interference emerges. However, in the case of the aperiodic structure, it is quite difficult to find a solution and can be solved with the SA algorithm.

In order to demonstrate the effectiveness of the SA algorithm for design of aperiodic optical superlattices, a simple example of a single wavelength SHG is considered here. The parameters are chosen as follows: the wavelegth of the incident beam is $\lambda = 1.064\mu m$, the thickness of the unit block is $\Delta x = l_c^{(s)}(\lambda)/2 = 3.8713\mu m$, and the number of blocks is 2142. Thus the total length of sample is $L = 8298.8\mu m$. The refractive indexes of material at corresponding wavelengths are evaluated by the Sellmeier equation [4]. The objective function in the SA algorithm is chosen as

$$E = |\zeta^0 - \zeta_{eff}^{(s)}(\lambda)|, \qquad (8)$$

where ζ^0 is a preset value in guiding the SA procedure. Fig. 1 sketches a flowchart of the SA algorithm for constructing aperiodic optical superlattice. As shown in Fig. 1, the initial temperature and dropping rate are selected at the beginning of program, a random sign modulation $\tilde{d}(x_i)$ is substituted into Equation 8 to calculate the initial object function E_0. A new object function E_1 is calculated with changing the sign of a unit block in $\tilde{d}(x_i)$ and the difference $\Delta E = E_1 - E_0$ is obtained. A random number $p, 0 \leq p \leq 1$, is generated by the computer. If p satisfies $p \leq exp(-\Delta E/T)$, this change will be accepted and E_0 will be replaced by E_1, else the sign of this unit block will be retrieved and E_0 does not change. After test all of blocks, this procedure will be repeated with a new temperature $T = T \times \Delta T$ until no sign changes in the $\tilde{d}(x)$. Thus, the stable modulation left is the optimal one.

Finally, a perfect periodical structure with a pari of antiparallel domains for each unit block and with a period of $a = 2\Delta x = l_c^{(s)}$ as expected can be obtained. The reduced effective nonlinear coefficient $\zeta_{eff}^{(s)}$ reaches its theoretical maximum value of $2/\pi = 0.6366$. This means that the SA algorithm is appropriate for dealing with the above mentioned inverse source problem.

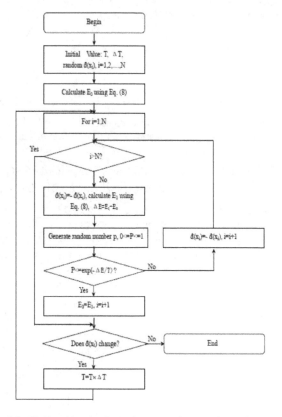

Figure 1. Flowchart of the SA algorithm for designing aperiodic optical superlattice.

2.2. Multiple wavelength SHG

A particular design of the aperiodic optical supperlattice is carried out. It is expected that it can implement multiple wavelength SHG with an identical effective nonlinear coefficient $\zeta_{eff}^{(s)}(\lambda_\alpha) = \zeta^0$ with ζ^0 is a constant. The thickness of each layer $\Delta x = 3.0 \mu m$ for matching the state of the art of microfabrication in practice. The objective function in the SA algorithm is set as

$$E = \sum_\alpha [|\zeta^0 - \zeta_{eff}^{(s)}(\lambda_\alpha)|] + \beta[\max\{\zeta_{eff}^{(s)}(\lambda_\alpha)\} - \min\{\zeta_{eff}^{(s)}(\lambda_\alpha)\}], \qquad (9)$$

where the function $\max\{...\}$ $(\min\{...\})$ manifests to take their maximum (minimum) value among all the quantities including into $\{...\}$. β is an adjustable parameter taking a value of $0.3 - 3$. Five wavelengths are $0.972\mu m$, $1.082\mu m$, $1.283\mu m$, $1.364\mu m$, and $1.568\mu m$. Other parameters are selected as: the total length of the sample $L = 8295\mu m$, the number of blocks $N = 2765$, and the wavelength sampling interval is $1nm$.

The obtained results are shown in Fig. 2. The wavelength is scanned with a interval of $0.05nm$ which is much small than that in the design procedure. There exist six strong peaks with almost identical peak value. Five of them are located at the expected wavelengths. One strong peak with an unexpected wavelength $\lambda = 0.981\mu m$ appears very close to the expected wavelength $\lambda = 0.972\mu m$. There are also some stray peaks appearing in the lower wavelength regions and small dense oscillation structures as a background. The average value of $\xi_{eff}^{(s)}(\lambda_\alpha)$ for preset five peaks is 0.1927 and the nonuniformity is 3.18×10^{-4}.

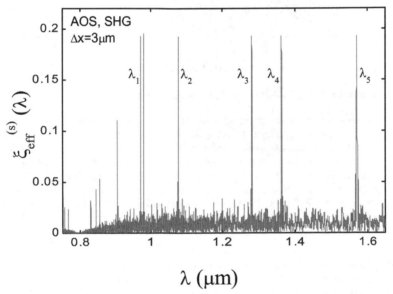

Figure 2. Calculated results for the constructed aperiodic optical superlattice that implements multiple wavelengths SHG with an identical nonlinear optical coefficient.

In order to further reveal the characteristic of the SHG in the constructed aperiodic optical superlattic, the plot of the variation of $\xi_{eff}^{(s)}(\lambda_\alpha)$ with the optical propagating distance x from the imping surface of incident light is shown in Fig. 3. It can be obviously seen that all curves exhibit nearly linearly increasing behavior with a nearly identical slope, which hints that the arrangement of domains is relatively favorable to the SHG process. The individual contribution is accumulated with each in the constructive interference state.

2.3. Coupled third harmonic generation for multiple wavelengths

Third harmonic generation (THG) has a wide application as a mean to extend coherent light sources to the short wavelengths. THG can be directly created using a third-order

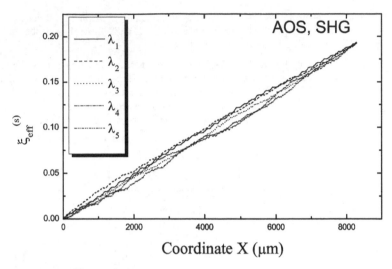

Figure 3. Variation of $\xi_{eff}^{(s)}(\lambda_\alpha)$ with the optical propagating distance x.

nonlinear process, however, this method is of little practical importance because of intrinsic weak third-order optical nonlinearity. An efficient THG can be achieved by cascading two second-order nonlinear process. Two nonlinear optical crystal are involved: the first one is for SGH and the second one for sum frequency generation. THG can also be generated form the coupled parametric processess with high efficiency. The coupled THG (CTHG) is raised from the coupling effect of two nonlinear optical precesses: one is the SHG and the other is a sum frequency process. This two processes couple with each other in a single crystal. This coupling leads to a continuous energy transfer from the fundamental to the second, and then to the third harmonic fields. Thus, a direct third harmonic wave can be generated with high efficiency.

The THG process can be analyzed by solving the coupled nonlinear equations that describe interaction of these three fields: E_ω, $E_{2\omega}$, and $E_{3\omega}$ in the aperiodic optical superlattice. Under the small signal approximation, the third harmonic wave conversion efficiency is expressed by

$$\eta_{THG} = \frac{I_{3\omega}}{I_\omega} = \frac{144\pi^4|d_{33}|^4 I_\omega^2 L^4}{c^2\epsilon_0^2\lambda^4 n_{3\omega}n_{2\omega}^2 n_\omega^3}\left|\frac{2}{L^2}\int_0^L e^{i(k_{3\omega}-k_{2\omega}-k_\omega)x}\tilde{d}(x)\int_0^x e^{i(k_{2\omega}-2k_\omega\zeta}\tilde{d}(\zeta)d\zeta dx\right|^2. \quad (10)$$

The coherence length $l_c^{(t)}(\lambda)$ for the CTHG is defined as

$$l_c^{(t)}(\lambda) = \frac{2\pi}{k_{3\omega} - k_{2\omega} - k_\omega} = \frac{\lambda}{(3n_{3\omega} - 2n_{2\omega} - n_\omega)}. \quad (11)$$

Thus, Equation 10 can be rewritten as

$$\eta_{THG} = C_t C'^2(\lambda)(\xi_{eff}^{(ct)}(\lambda))^2, \quad (12)$$

with

$$C_t = \frac{144\pi^4 |d_{33}|^4 I_\omega^2 L^4}{c^2 \epsilon_0^2}, \tag{13}$$

$$C'(\lambda) = \frac{1}{\lambda^2 n_\omega^{3/2} n_{2\omega} \sqrt{n_{3\omega}}}, \tag{14}$$

and

$$\xi_{eff}^{(ct)}(\lambda) = \left| \frac{2}{L^2} \int_0^L e^{i[2\pi x / l_c^{(t)}(\lambda)]} \tilde{d}(x) dx \int_0^x e^{i[2\pi \zeta / l_c^{(s)}(\lambda)]} \tilde{d}(\zeta) d\zeta \right|. \tag{15}$$

The variable $\xi_{eff}^{(ct)}(\lambda)$ is the reduced coupled effective nonlinear coefficient for the CTHG.

Assuming that the thickness of unit block is Δx, the number of the blocks in sample is $N = L/\Delta x$. The position of blocks is coordinated with $x_q = q\Delta x$, for $q = 0, 1, 2, 3 ... (N-1)$. Equation 15 will be rewritten as

$$
\begin{aligned}
\xi_{eff}^{(ct)}(\lambda) &= \left| \frac{2}{(N\Delta x)^2} \sum_{q=0}^{N-1} \tilde{d}(x_q) \int_{x_q}^{x_q + \Delta x} dx e^{i[2\pi x / l_c^{(t)}(\lambda)]} \sum_{p=0}^{q} \tilde{d}(x_p) \int_{x_p}^{x_p + \Delta x} d\zeta e^{i[2\pi\zeta / l_c^{(s)}(\lambda)]} \right| \\
&= 2 \left| \left[\frac{1}{\Delta x} \int_0^{\Delta x} dx e^{i[2\pi x / l_c^{(t)}(\lambda)]} \right] \left[\frac{1}{\Delta x} \int_0^{\Delta x} d\zeta e^{i[2\pi\zeta / l_c^{(s)}(\lambda)]} \right] \right. \\
&\quad \left. \times \left\{ \frac{1}{N} \sum_{q=0}^{N-1} \tilde{d}(x_q) e^{i[2\pi x_q / l_c^{(t)}(\lambda)]} \left[\frac{1}{N} \sum_{p=0}^{q-1} \tilde{d}(x_p) e^{i[2\pi x_p / l_c^{(s)}(\lambda)]} \right] \right\} + \Delta u \right| \\
&= 2 \left| \left\{ sinc\left[\frac{\pi \Delta x}{l_c^{(t)}(\lambda)} \right] sinc\left[\frac{\pi \Delta x}{l_c^{(s)}(\lambda)} \right] \right\} \right. \\
&\quad \left. \times \left\{ \frac{1}{N^2} \sum_{q=0}^{N-1} \tilde{d}(x_q) e^{i[2\pi(q+0.5)\Delta x / l_c^{(t)}(\lambda)]} \left[\sum_{p=0}^{q-1} \tilde{d}(x_p) e^{i[2\pi(p+0.5)\Delta x / l_c^{(s)}(\lambda)]} \right] \right\} + \Delta u \right|,
\end{aligned}
\tag{16}
$$

with

$$
\begin{aligned}
\Delta u &= \frac{2}{L^2} \sum_{q=0}^{N-1} \tilde{d}(x_q) \int_{x_q}^{x_{q+1}} dx e^{i[2\pi x_q / l_c^{(t)}(\lambda)]} \int_{x_q}^{x} d\zeta e^{i[2\pi\zeta / l_c^{(s)}(\lambda)]} \\
&= \frac{1}{N^2} \left(\frac{l_c^{(s)}(\lambda)}{i\pi \Delta x} \right) \left\{ e^{\frac{i\pi\Delta x}{l_c^{(s)}(\lambda)} + \frac{i\pi\Delta x}{l_c^{(t)}(\lambda)}} sinc\left[\frac{\Delta x}{l_c^{(s)}(\lambda)} + \frac{\Delta x}{l_c^{(t)}(\lambda)} \right] - e^{\frac{i\pi\Delta x}{l_c^{(t)}(\lambda)}} sinc\left[\frac{\Delta x}{l_c^{(t)}(\lambda)} \right] \right\} \\
&\quad \times \sum_{q=0}^{N-1} e^{i[2\pi x_q (1/l_c^{(s)}(\lambda) + 1/l_c^{(t)}(\lambda))]}
\end{aligned}
\tag{17}
$$

From Equation 16, it can been found that $\xi_{eff}^{(ct)}(\lambda)$ has the contributions from two factors: one factor (double *sinc* functions) belongs to unit block and strongly depends on Δx and the coherence length $l_c^{(t,s)}(\lambda)$; the other factor which is included inside the second curly braces reflects the interference effect among the blocks in sample, depending on the arrangement of domains and the phase lagging from one block to other block. Δu contributes to a small correction.

A model design of the AOS that achieves the coupled THG is carried out. The parameters used in the design are : $\Delta x = 3\mu m$, $L = 8067\mu m$, $N = 2689$, and $\lambda = 1.570\mu m$. Fig. 4 displays the calculated results. The wavelength is scanned with an interval of $0.1nm$. There exists only one strong sharp peak at the preset wavelength of $\lambda = 1.570\mu m$ with $\xi_{eff}^{(ct)} = 0.1811$. It can be found that the designed structure performs the preset goal well.

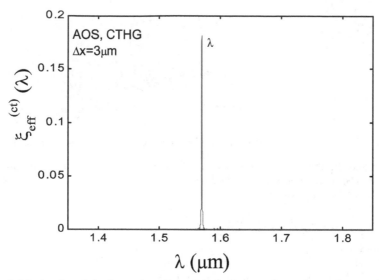

Figure 4. Calculated result for the constructed aperiodic optical superlattice that implements the CTHG.

The same method can be used to construct aperiodic optical superlattic that implements multiple wavelengths CTHG with identical effective nonlinear coefficient. The relevant parameters are: $\lambda_\alpha = [1.40, 1.60, 1.80]\ \mu m$, $\Delta x = 3\mu m$, $L = 8067\mu m$, and $N = 2689$. The dependence of $\xi_{eff}^{(ct)}(\lambda)$ on the wavelength is depicted in Fig. 5. The behavior of $\xi_{eff}^{(ct)}(\lambda)$ exhibits fairly good uniformity. The coupled effective nonlinear coefficient is almost identical for three different wavelengths and the average value is 0.04792.

2.4. Multiple wavelengths parametric amplification

Parametric generation provides unique possibility of generating widely tunable radiation from a single pump light source, so it has attracted extensive interest since parametric amplification was theoretically predicted in 1960's [5]. To derive the mathematical expressions for parametric amplification in a aperiodic optical superlattice, the related formulas of optical parametric process in a homogeneous nonlinear medium should be briefly described here. Consider three optical plane waves with the frequencies ω_1, ω_2, and ω_3 ($\omega_3 = \omega_2 + \omega_1$), the equations governing the propagation of electromagnetic waves are written as

$$\begin{aligned}
\frac{dE_1}{dx} &= -\frac{\sigma_1}{2}\sqrt{\frac{\mu}{\epsilon_1}}E_1 - \frac{i\omega_1}{2}\sqrt{\frac{\mu}{\epsilon_1}}d_{33}E_3E_2^*e^{-i\Delta kx} \\
\frac{dE_2^*}{dx} &= -\frac{\sigma_2}{2}\sqrt{\frac{\mu}{\epsilon_2}}E_2^* + \frac{i\omega_2}{2}\sqrt{\frac{\mu}{\epsilon_2}}d_{33}E_1E_3^*e^{i\Delta kx} \\
\frac{dE_3}{dx} &= -\frac{\sigma_3}{2}\sqrt{\frac{\mu}{\epsilon_3}}E_3 - \frac{i\omega_3}{2}\sqrt{\frac{\mu}{\epsilon_3}}d_{33}E_1E_2e^{i\Delta kx},
\end{aligned} \tag{18}$$

where $\Delta k = k_3 - k_1 - k_2$, and σ_i (ϵ_i) is the loss coefficient (permittivity of crystal) for ω_i ($i = 1, 2, 3$); μ is the magnetic permeability in vacuum. It is noted that these equations are coupled to each other via the nonlinear coefficient d_{33}.

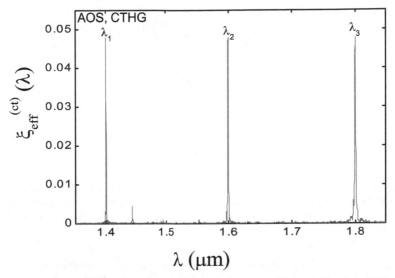

Figure 5. Calculated result for the constructed aperiodic optical superlattice that implements the coupled THG for three wavelength with an identical nonlinear coefficient.

Introducing a new field variable

$$A_i = \sqrt{\frac{n_i}{\omega_i}} E_i, \quad i = 1, 2, 3,$$ (19)

with n_i is the refraction index of crystal at $\omega_i (i = 1, 2, 3)$ and assuming the loss coefficients are negligible small, we can rewrite the first two equations in Equation 18 as

$$\frac{dA_1}{dx} = -\frac{ig}{2} A_2^* e^{i(\Delta k)x}$$
$$\frac{dA_2^*}{dx} = +\frac{ig}{2} A_1 e^{i(\Delta k)x},$$ (20)

where

$$g = \sqrt{\left(\frac{\mu}{\epsilon_0}\right) \frac{\omega_1 \omega_2}{n_1 n_2}} d_{33} E_3(0),$$

where ϵ_0 is permittivity of vacuum. In this derivation, we have used the approximation of small signal. In addition, we assume that $\omega_1 |A_1(x)|^2$ and $\omega_2 |A_2(x)|^2$ both remain small compared with $\omega_3 |A_3(0)|^2$ throughout the interaction region, thus $A_3(x)$ can be regarded as a constant. As the meaningful quantity is the relative phase between A_1 and A_3, therefore, we can set $A_3(0)$ to be real. Therefore, the relationship between the field variables $A_1(x)$, $A_2(x)$ and $A_1(x_0)$, $A_2(x_0)$ in homogeneous medium can be expressed as follows:

$$\begin{pmatrix} A_1(x) \\ A_2^*(x) \end{pmatrix} = \begin{pmatrix} M_{11} & M_{12} \\ M_{21} & M_{22} \end{pmatrix} \begin{pmatrix} A_1(x_0) \\ A_2^*(x_0) \end{pmatrix},$$ (21)

where

$$M_{11} = e^{-i(\Delta k/2)(x-x_0)}\left[\cosh(b(x-x_0)) + \frac{i(\Delta k)}{2b}\sinh(b(x-x_0))\right],$$

$$M_{12} = e^{-i(\Delta k/2)(x-x_0)}e^{-i\Delta k x_0}\left[-i\frac{g}{2b}\sinh(b(x-x_0))\right],$$

$$M_{21} = M_{12}^*,$$

$$M_{22} = M_{11}^*,$$

and

$$b = 0.5\sqrt{g^2 - (\Delta k)^2}. \tag{22}$$

Equations 21 and 22 tell that only when b is a real number, the signal and idler lights can be amplified. It requires that g must be greater than Δk. If the wavelengths of the pump and signal lights are selected as $1.064\mu m$ and $1.78\mu m$, respectively, Δk has the value of $0.20\mu m^{-1}$. Even considering the largest nonlinear coefficient $d_{33} = 21.6pm/V$ of $LiNbO_3$, it also requires the intensity of pump light being larger than $1.35 \times 10^{17}W/m^2$, which is impossible in practical applications.

For the aperiodic optical superlattice with block thickness of Δx, the coordinate of each blocks can be denoted by $x_q = q\Delta x$, for $q = 0,1,2,3....N$, N is the total number of blocks in sample. Since d_{33} for each unit block remains constant, therefore, Equations 21 and 22 are still valid within each block. By using the transfer matrix method, the total transfer matrix can be established by cascading individual matrix associated with each block in sequence. For instance, the transfer matrix for the $(q+1)$th block from its left interface at x_q to its right interface at x_{q+1} can be expressed as

$$\begin{pmatrix} A_1(x_{q+1}) \\ A_2^*(x_{q+1}) \end{pmatrix} = \begin{pmatrix} M_{11} & M_{12} \\ M_{21} & M_{22} \end{pmatrix}\begin{pmatrix} A_1(x_q) \\ A_2^*(x_q) \end{pmatrix} = M(x_q \to x_{q+1})\begin{pmatrix} A_1(x_q) \\ A_2^*(x_q) \end{pmatrix} \tag{23}$$

where

$$M_{11} = e^{-i(\Delta k/2)\Delta x_q}\left[\cosh(b(x_q)\Delta x_q)) + \frac{i(\Delta k)}{2b(x_q)}\sinh(b(x_q)\Delta x_q))\right],$$

$$M_{12} = e^{-i(\Delta k/2)\Delta x_q}e^{-i\Delta k x_q}\left[-i\frac{g(x_q)}{2b(x_q)}\sinh(b(x_q)\Delta x_q))\right],$$

$$M_{21} = M_{12}^*,$$

$$M_{22} = M_{11}^*,$$

and

$$\Delta x_q = x_{q+1} - x_q. \tag{24}$$

Finally, the total transfer matrix reads

$$\begin{pmatrix} A_1(x_N) \\ A_2^*(x_N) \end{pmatrix} = \begin{pmatrix} M_{11}^{tot} & M_{12}^{tot} \\ M_{21}^{tot} & M_{22}^{tot} \end{pmatrix}\begin{pmatrix} A_1(x_0) \\ A_2^*(x_0) \end{pmatrix} = M^{tot}(x_0 \to x_N)\begin{pmatrix} A_1(x_0) \\ A_2^*(x_0) \end{pmatrix},$$

where

$$M^{tot}(x_0 \to x_N) = \Pi_{q=0}^{N-1}M(x_q \to x_{q+1}). \tag{25}$$

The initial conditions are known as $A_1(0)$ and $A_2^*(0)$ at $x_0 = 0$. In the general case, the initial idler wave $A_2(0)$ is considered as zero, so after signal wave passes through the aperiodic optical superlattice once, it is amplified by $G = M_{11}^{tot}$ times, therefore, G is the so-called amplification coefficient of the signal wave.

In the case of aperiodic optical superlattice, $\tilde{d}(x_q)$ varies with x_q, so g is a function of x_q as

$$g(x_q) = \sqrt{\left(\frac{\mu}{\epsilon_0}\right) \frac{\omega_1 \omega_2}{n_1 n_2}} |d_{33}| \tilde{d}(x_q) E_3(0). \tag{26}$$

Owing to $\tilde{d}^2(x_q) = 1$, the sign modulation of $\tilde{d}(x_q)$ does not bring any effect on b. However, $g(x_q)$ appearing in the transfer matrix is feeling to this sign modulation alone. Consequently, it is expected that the modulated structure may bring some benefits due to considerable effect of the sign modulation of $\tilde{d}(x_q)$ on parametric amplification process. In the case of multiple wavelengths parametric amplification, the situation becomes much more complicated, and it belongs to solving an inverse source problem.

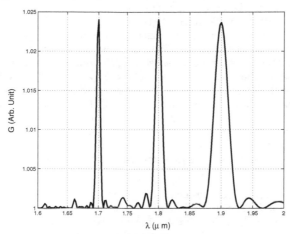

Figure 6. Calculated result for the constructed aperiodic optical superlattice that implements the parametric amplification for three wavelengths with an identical amplification coefficient.

The optimization design of aperiodic optical superlattice served as parametric amplifier for multiple wavelengths with identical amplification coefficient $G(\lambda_\alpha)$ is carried out. Three signal wavelengths λ_α are selected as $1.70\mu m$, $1.80\mu m$, and $1.90\mu m$. The pump intensity is $I_p = 10^{10} W/m^2$. Considering the practical technique for poling and dispersion of crystal, thickness of unit block $\Delta x = 8\mu m$ is selected in the simulation. The objective function for the SA algorithm is chosen as

$$E = \sum_\alpha |G_0 - G(\lambda_\alpha)| + \beta [max\{G(\lambda_\alpha)\} - min\{G(\lambda_\alpha)\}], \tag{27}$$

where β is a adjustable parameter taking a value of $0.3 \sim 3$. In multiple wavelengths parameter amplification, there is a trade-off between the amplification coefficients and uniformity, adjusting the value of β can balance them. Figure 6 exhibits the calculated amplification coefficient as a function of wavelength for signal light. There exist three strong expected peaks and some small dense oscillation as background, satellite peaks are quite low. The amplifier coefficients are 1.0240, 1.0240, and 1.0237 for signal wavelengths $1.7\mu m$, $1.8\mu m$, and $1.9\mu m$, respectively. The average value $< G(\lambda_\alpha) >$ is 1.0239 and the maximal relative deviation is $\Delta G = [max\{G(\lambda_\alpha)\} - min\{G(\lambda_\alpha)\}]/ < G(\lambda_\alpha) >= 2.9 \times 10^{-4}$. These data show that the constructed aperiodic optical superlattice can meet the predefined requirement well.

3. Design of photonic crystal devices

Photonic crystals have attracted extensive attentions in the past decades. Two remarkable characters of the photonic crystals are photonic band gaps (PBGs) and defect states [6]. Based on these two characters, many devices can be designed.

3.1. Photonic crystal device for multiple wavelengths filtering

By inserting photonic quantum–wells (PQWs) into an ideal photonic crystal, a series of the discrete defect states may be created and they provide the function of multiple channeled filtering. Many researches have been reported on how to generate the defect states. However, the frequencies of the defect states cannot be changed with freedom. In practice, the favorable design of optical multiple channeled filters need to pass arbitrarily preassigned frequencies. In this section, the issue of designing the specific PQWs which have the preassigned filtering channels is discussed. The aperiodic PQWs (APQWs) are sandwiched by two finite-length ideal photonic crystals, which consist of two alternately stacked layers A and B with different dielectric constants of ε_A and ε_B, respectively. Their thicknesses are denoted by d_A and d_B, respectively, and $a = d_A + d_B$ is the lattice constant of the one-dimensional (1D) photonic crystal. The APQWs are composed of two different alternately stacked basic constituent layers with the dielectric constants of ε_C and ε_D. However, the thickness of each individual layer may not be equal and the individual layer thickness is determined by the merits of the desirable filters.

The transmission spectrum of designed APQW structures is calculated by using the transfer-matrix method. The transfer-matrix in each individual layer can be obtained by solving the Maxwell equations with a combination of boundary conditions. For a normally incident EM plane wave with the TE polarization, the transfer-matrix for the j-th layer is given by

$$\widehat{M}_j = \widehat{G}_{j+1}^{-1}\widehat{G}_j\widehat{P}_j, \tag{28}$$

where $j \in \{1, 2, ..., N\}$ for N number of layers. $\widehat{G}_j$ is the transfer matrix. The propagating matrix $\widehat{P}_j$ reads

$$\widehat{P}_1 = \begin{pmatrix} 1 & 0 \\ 0 & 1 \end{pmatrix}, \quad j = 1 \tag{29}$$

for air at the most left-hand side of the sample and

$$\widehat{P}_j = \begin{pmatrix} \exp(ik_jd_j) & 0 \\ 0 & \exp(-ik_jd_j) \end{pmatrix}, \quad j = 2, 3, 4... \tag{30}$$

for the jth layer in sample. $\hat{G}_j$ reads

$$\hat{G}_j = \begin{pmatrix} \dfrac{1}{\sqrt{\varepsilon_j}} & \dfrac{1}{-\sqrt{\varepsilon_j}} \end{pmatrix}, \tag{31}$$

where d_j denotes the thickness of the j-th layer, $k_j = 2\pi\sqrt{\varepsilon_j}/\lambda$, ε_j is the dielectric constant of the j-th layer; λ the wavelength of the incident light wave in vacuum. Thus, the total transfer matrix can be obtained by multiplying all individual transfer matrixes in sequence. The transmission and reflection coefficients of EM waves of the sample can be calculated from

$$\begin{pmatrix} t_n \\ r_n \end{pmatrix} = \prod_j \hat{M}_j \begin{pmatrix} t_1 \\ r_1 \end{pmatrix}, \tag{32}$$

for instance, the transmission probability is given by

$$T = \sqrt{\frac{\varepsilon_n}{\varepsilon_1}} \left| \frac{t_n}{t_1} \right|^2. \tag{33}$$

For the wave which is not normal incident or TM mode, the similar approach can be used to obtain the transmission probability.

To design the APQW for producing specified defect states located at the preset frequencies $\omega_\alpha^{(0)}$ within a given range of $[\omega_a \quad \omega_b]$, a perfect PC should be selected to serve as the prototype photonic crystal, into which the APQW is implanted. It is required that the chosen prototype PC should have an appropriate PBG located at this frequency range and with a certain width, not narrower than the range of $[\omega_a \quad \omega_b]$. After determining this prototype PC, the APQW structure is determined by using the SA algorithm. The objective function is defined as

$$O = \sum_\alpha \sum_s |\omega_\alpha^{(o)} - \omega_\alpha^{(s)}|, \quad \omega_\alpha^{(o)}, \omega_\alpha^{(s)} \in [\omega_{\alpha-1}, \quad \omega_\alpha], \quad \alpha = 1,2,3.... \tag{34}$$

with

$$\omega_0 (= \omega_a) < \omega_1^o < \omega_1 < .... < \omega_{\alpha-1} < \omega_\alpha^o < \omega_\alpha (= \omega_b), \tag{35}$$

where $\omega_\alpha^{(s)}$ denotes the frequencies of the defect states appearing in $[\omega_{\alpha-1}, \omega_\alpha]$, which are generated in every routed configuration of the APQW during the SA routine. ω_α denote a series of the frequencies to partition the whole region of $[\omega_a, \omega_b]$ into several subregions. In each subregion, only one of the preassigned confined states appears. For instance, $\omega_\alpha^{(o)}$ is located in the subregion of $[\omega_{\alpha-1}, \omega_\alpha]$. In the SA routine, more than one defect states may occur in one subregion, thus, s may be larger than 1, therefore, the sum over s should be take into account. The optimal design of the APQWs corresponds to a search for the minimum of O. The sandwiched part in the sample is divided into n unit blocks with the thickness δd; the dielectric constant of each individual block is chosen as one of the binary of ε_C and ε_D, decided by the SA algorithm.

An APQW is design for achieving two channeled filtering in a given range of $[0.352 \quad 0.506](2\pi c/a)$, c is the speed of light in the vacuum. The dielectric constants are selected as $\varepsilon_A = \varepsilon_C = 13.0$ and $\varepsilon_B = \varepsilon_D = 1.0$. The thicknesses of the constituent layers A and B in the prototype PC are set to be $d_A = d_B = 0.5a$, thus, the second PBG of the prototype PC just is located at $[0.352 \quad 0.506](2\pi c/a)$. In the following calculations, five AB layers, $(AB)_5$, on either side of the APQWs are employed. The sandwiched part is divided into $n = 100$ blocks and the thickness of the basic block $\delta d = 0.02a$ is selected. Two filtering frequencies are preassigned as $\omega_1^{(o)} = 0.420(2\pi c/a)$ and $\omega_2^{(o)} = 0.480(2\pi c/a)$. The transmission spectrum of the designed sample is displayed in Fig. 7. The frequency increment in the scan is taken as $\delta\omega = 1.0 \times 10^{-5}(2\pi c/a)$ to ensure that any unwanted extra stray frequency peak does not occur. Two dashed vertical lines remark the positions of the second PBG of the prototype $(AB)_5$ photonic crystal. It is evident that there exist only two expected defect states in the desired frequency range. The frequencies of the defect states accord exactly with the preset values. Their transmittances are 0.90 and 0.86 for $\omega_1 = 0.420(2\pi c/a)$ and $\omega_2 = 0.480(2\pi c/a)$, respectively.

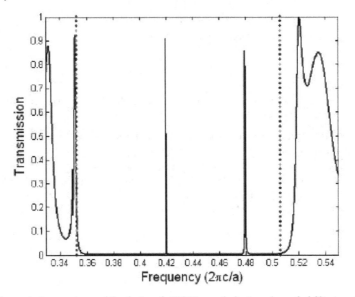

Figure 7. Transmission spectrum of the designed APQW sample for two channeled filtering at the preset frequencies of $\omega_1^{(o)} = 0.420$ and $\omega_2^{(o)} = 0.480(2\pi c/a)$.

3.2. Photonic crystal device for multiple wavelengths' second harmonic generation

When a defect is introduced into a perfect photonic crystal, the defect mode will appear in the band gap. Furthermore, the light with the frequency corresponding to the defect mode will be located around the defect layer; the intensity of the located wave has been improved 3-4 orders comparing with the intensity of the incident wave. Therefore, if a nonlinear material is used as the defect medium, the nonlinear effect can be greatly enhanced. It was found that when the frequency of the fundamental wave (FW) was tuned to the defect state, the SHG can be greatly enhanced. Due to the strong localization, low group velocity, and spatial phase locking in the PC, the giant enhancement of SHG for each FW has been achieved.

For simplicity, a one-dimensional layer structure is used as the sample. The incident wave is normally impinged upon the surface of the sample. For the $l-th$ layer, the electric field $E_l^{(1)}$ ($E_2^{(1)}$) of the FW (SHG), neglecting the pump power depletion, satisfies the following equations.

$$\left[\frac{d^2}{dz^2} + k_l^{(1)2}\right] E_l^{(1)}(z) = 0, \tag{36}$$

$$\left[\frac{d^2}{dz^2} + k_l^{(2)2}\right] E_l^{(2)}(z) = -k_{20}^{(2)2}\chi^l(z)E_l^{(1)2}(z), \tag{37}$$

where $k_l^{(1)} = n_l^{(1)}k_{10}$, $k_l^{(2)} = n_l^{(2)}k_{20}$, $k_{10} = \omega/c$, $k_{20} = 2\omega/c$, ω is the frequency of the FW, $n_l^{(1)}$ ($n_l^{(2)}$) is the refractive index of the $l-th$ layer for the wavelength of FW (SHG), c is the velocity of the light in vacuum and χ^l is the nonlinear optical coefficient of the $l-th$ layer. The solution of Equation 36 has the form

$$E_l^{(1)}(z) = A_l^{(1)}e^{ik_l^{(1)}(z-z_{l-1})} + B_l^{(1)}e^{-ik_l^{(1)}(z-z_{l-1})}, \tag{38}$$

where $A_l^{(1)}$ and $B_l^{(1)}$ represent the amplitudes of forward and backward FW at interface, respectively. Utilizing the continuous condition at each interface, the transfer matrix method, and the initial conditions ($A_l^{(1)} = 1$ and $B_N^{(1)} = 0$), the electric field of the FW in each layer can be obtained. N is the total number of layers in the sample.

Similarly, the SHG electric field in the $l-th$ layer of photonic crystal can be expressed as

$$E_l^{(2)}(z) = A_l^{(2)}e^{ik_l^{(2)}(z-z_{l-1})} + B_l^{(1)}e^{-ik_l^{(1)}(z-z_{l-1})} + C_{21}e^{i2k_l^{(1)}(z-z_{l-1})} + C_{22}e^{-i2k_l^{(1)}(z-z_{l-1})}$$
$$- \frac{2k_{20}^2\chi_l}{k_l^{(2)2}} A_l^{(1)}B_l^{(1)}, \tag{39}$$

$A_l^{(2)}$ and $B_l^{(2)}$ represent the amplitudes of the forward and backward SHGs at interface, respectively. C_{21} and C_{22} can be obtained as

$$C_{21} = \frac{-k_{20}^2\chi_l A_l^{(1)2}}{k_l^{(2)2} - 4k_l^{(1)2}},$$

$$C_{22} = \frac{-k_{20}^2\chi_l B_l^{(1)2}}{k_l^{(2)2} - 4k_l^{(1)2}}. \tag{40}$$

Using the initial conditions $A_1^{(2)} = 0$, $B_N^{(2)} = 0$, the electric field of the SHG at each interface can be derived. The conversion efficiencies of the forward and backward SHG waves are defined respectively as follows

$$\eta_{forth}^{(2)} = \frac{n_N^{(2)}|A_N^{(2)}|^2}{n_1^{(1)}|A_1^{(1)}|^2}, \eta_{back}^{(2)} = \frac{|B_1^{(2)}|^2}{|A_1^{(1)}|^2}. \tag{41}$$

As an example, the photonic crystal structure that can implement multiple wavelengths SHG is designed. The PQWs gives localized states at the frequencies of the FW and SHG,

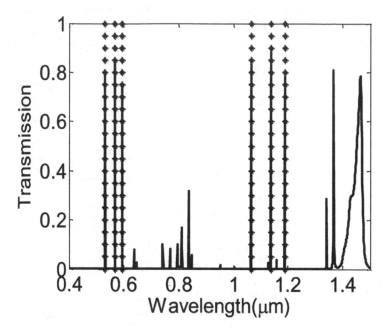

Figure 8. Transmission spectrum of the designed photonic quantum well structure. The dash lines indicate $\lambda_{1,1} = 1.064\mu m$, $\lambda_{1,2} = 1.136\mu m$, $\lambda_{1,3} = 1.188\mu m$, $\lambda_{2,1} = 0.532\mu m$, $\lambda_{2,2} = 0.568\mu m$, and $\lambda_{2,3} = 0.594\mu m$.

respectively. The preset wavelengths of FWs are $\lambda_{1,1}^o = 1.064\mu m$, $\lambda_{1,2}^o = 1.136\mu m$, and $\lambda_{1,3}^o = 1.188\mu m$, and the wavelengths of the corresponding second harmonics are $\lambda_{2,1}^o = 0.532\mu m$, $\lambda_{2,2}^o = 0.568\mu m$, and $\lambda_{2,3}^o = 0.594\mu m$, respectively. The conversion efficiencies for three FWs are required to be nearly equal. The periodic structure $(AB)_5$ is selected as the prototype photonic crystal. A and B are $LiNbO_3$ and air, respectively. The widths of the A and B layers are selected as $d_A = 0.1814\mu m$ and $d_B = 0.1330\mu m$, respectively. This prototype photonic crystal has two band gaps $[0.916\mu m \quad 1.314\mu m]$ and $[0.482\mu m \quad 0.612\mu m]$. The FWs and SHGs are located in the two band gaps, respectively. Then a aperiodic structure is designed and insert into the prototype photonic crystals. The thickness of C and D unit cell is $d_C = d_D = 0.04\mu m$, the number of unit cells is 300. However, each cell is selected from C or D which is determined by the SA algorithm with an objective function as

$$O = \sum_{\alpha} \sum_{s} \sum_{k} \left[|\lambda_{\alpha,s}^o - \lambda_{\alpha,s}^k| + \beta_1 |\eta^0 - \eta_{1,s}^{(k)}| \right] + \beta_2 |max(\{\eta_{1,s}^{(k)}\}) - min(\{\eta_{1,s}^{(k)}\})| \qquad (42)$$

where

$$\lambda_{1,s}^o, \lambda_{1,s}^{(k)} \in [\lambda_{1,s-1}, \lambda_{1,s}] \in [\lambda_a, \lambda_b],$$
$$\lambda_{2,s}^o, \lambda_{2,s}^{(k)} \in [\lambda_{2,s-1}, \lambda_{2,s}] \in [\lambda_c, \lambda_d],$$
$$\alpha = 1, 2 \qquad s = 1, 2, 3, \ldots,$$

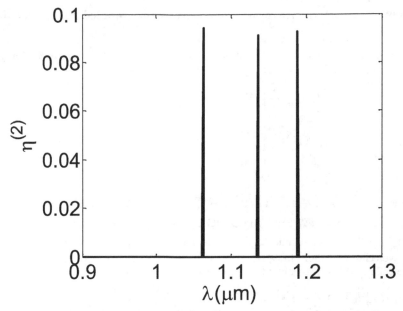

Figure 9. Wavelength dependence of the conversion efficiency of the photonic quantum well structure
for the forward SHG.

with

$$\lambda_{1,0}(=\lambda_a) < \lambda_{1,1}^o < \lambda_{1,1} < \lambda_{1,2}^o < \lambda_{1,2} < \ldots < \lambda_{1,s}^o < \lambda_{1,s}(=\lambda_b);$$
$$\lambda_{2,0}(=\lambda_c) < \lambda_{2,1}^o < \lambda_{2,1} < \lambda_{2,2}^o < \lambda_{2,2} < \ldots < \lambda_{2,s}^o < \lambda_{2,s}(=\lambda_d).$$

β_1 and β_2 are two adjustable constants. $\lambda_{a,s}^{(k)}$ and $\eta_{1,s}^k$ denote the wavelengths of the defected
states and corresponding conversion efficiencies generated from every transit structure during
the SA process. s is the number of the FW to be designed and it was selected as $s = 3$ in this
work. The PQW structure is designed by the SA.

Figure 8 presents the transmission spectrum of the designed photonic quantum well structure.
The band structure of the PC $(AB)_{10}$ is almost unchanged. The wavelengths designed appear
at $\lambda_{1,1} = 1.064\mu m$, $\lambda_{1,2} = 1.136\mu m$, $\lambda_{1,3} = 1.188\mu m$, $\lambda_{2,1} = 0.532\mu m$, $\lambda_{2,2} = 0.568\mu m$, and
$\lambda_{2,3} = 0.594\mu m$ respectively. They agree with the required wavelengths quite well.

The properties of the SHG for this structure is also investigated. The largest nonlinear
coefficient d_{33} of $LiNbO_3$ is used for achieving high conversion efficiency. The intensity
of the incident FW is selected as $0.021GW/m^2$ for each wavelength. The wavelength
dependence of the SHG is shown in Fig. 9. Only three expected wavelengths appear. The
conversion efficiencies of the forward SHGs are $\eta_1 = 0.0943$, $\eta_2 = 0.0912$, and $\eta_3 = 0.0926$,
respectively. The conversion efficiencies have been enhanced nearly 10^3 time comparing
with the periodically poled lithium niobate structure with identical length. The conversion
efficiencies of the forward SHGs are nearly identical, which correspond to the designed
aim well. Comparing with the structure with only the FW located at the defect state, the
conversion efficiencies have also been mightily enhanced.

3.3. Photonic crystal device for multiple wavelengths' coupled third harmonic generation

For the coupled third harmonic generation, the electric field $E_l^{(1)}$ ($E_l^{(2)}$, $E_l^{(3)}$) of the FW (SHG, CTHG) for the $l - th$ layer must satisfy the following equations:

$$\left[\frac{d^2}{dz^2} + k_l^{(1)2} \right] E_l^{(1)}(z) = 0, \tag{43}$$

$$\left[\frac{d^2}{dz^2} + k_l^{(2)2} \right] E_l^{(2)}(z) = -k_{20}^{(2)2} \chi_l(z) E_l^{(1)2}(z), \tag{44}$$

$$\left[\frac{d^2}{dz^2} + k_l^{(3)2} \right] E_l^{(3)}(z) = -2k_{30}^{(2)2} \chi_l(z) E_l^{(1)}(z) E_l^{(2)}(z), \tag{45}$$

where $k_l^{(1)} = n_l^{(1)} k_{10}$, $k_l^{(2)} = n_L^{(2)} k_{20}$, $k_l^{(3)} = n_L^{(3)} k_{30}$, $k_{10} = \omega/c$, $k_{20} = 2\omega/c$, and $k_{30} = 3\omega/c$ are wave vectors of the FW, SHG, and CTHG, respectively. ω is the frequency of the FW, $n_l^{(1)}$ ($n_l^{(2)}$, $n_l^{(3)}$) is the refractive index of the $l - th$ layer for the wavelength of FW (SHG, CTHG), c is the velocity of the light in vacuum and χ^l is the nonlinear optical coefficient of the $l - th$ layer. Similarly, the expression of CTHG electric field in the $l - th$ layer is

$$E_l^{(3)}(z) = A_l^{(3)} e^{ik_l^{(3)}(z-z_{l-1})} + B_l^{(3)} e^{-ik_l^{(3)}(z-z_{l-1})} + C_{31} e^{i[k_l^{(1)}+k_l^{(2)}](z-z_{l-1})} + C_{32} e^{-i[k_l^{(1)}+k_l^{(2)}](z-z_{l-1})}$$
$$+ D_{31} e^{i[k_l^{(1)}-k_l^{(2)}](z-z_{l-1})} + D_{32} e^{-i[k_l^{(1)}-k_l^{(2)}](z-z_{l-1})} + E_{31} e^{i3k_l^{(1)}(z-z_{l-1})}$$
$$+ E_{32} e^{-i3k_l^{(1)}(z-z_{l-1})} + F_{31} e^{ik_l^{(1)}(z-z_{l-1})} + F_{32} e^{-ik_l^{(1)}(z-z_{l-1})}, \tag{46}$$

and all parameters in this equation can be expressed as

$$
\begin{aligned}
C_{31} &= \frac{-k_{30}^2 \chi_l A_l^{(1)} A_l^{(2)}}{k_l^{(3)2} - (k_l^{(1)}+k_l^{(2)})^2}, & C_{32} &= \frac{-k_{30}^2 \chi_l B_l^{(1)} B_l^{(2)}}{k_l^{(3)2} - (k_l^{(1)}+k_l^{(2)})^2}, \\
D_{31} &= \frac{-k_{30}^2 \chi_l A_l^{(1)} B_l^{(2)}}{k_l^{(3)2} - (k_l^{(1)}-k_l^{(2)})^2}, & D_{32} &= \frac{-k_{30}^2 \chi_l A_l^{(2)} B_l^{(1)}}{k_l^{(3)2} - (k_l^{(1)}-k_l^{(2)})^2}, \\
E_{31} &= \frac{-k_{30}^2 \chi_l A_l^{(1)} C_{2l}}{k_l^{(3)2} - 9k_l^{(1)2}}, & E_{32} &= \frac{-k_{30}^2 \chi_l B_l^{(1)} C_{22}}{k_l^{(3)2} - 9k_l^{(1)2}}, \\
F_{31} &= \frac{-k_{30}^2 \chi_l B_l^{(1)} C_{2l}}{k_l^{(3)2} - k_l^{(1)2}} + \frac{2k_{30}^2 k_{20}^2 \chi_l^{(2)} \chi_l A_l^{(1)2} B_l^{(1)}}{k_l^{(2)2} (k_l^{(3)2} - k_l^{(1)2})}, \\
F_{32} &= \frac{-k_{30}^2 \chi_l A_l^{(1)} C_{22}}{k_l^{(3)2} - k_l^{(1)2}} + \frac{2k_{30}^2 k_{20}^2 \chi_l^{(2)} \chi_l B_l^{(1)2} A_l^{(1)}}{k_l^{(2)2} (k_l^{(3)2} - k_l^{(1)2})}.
\end{aligned}
\tag{47}
$$

By using the initial conditions $A_1^{(2)} = 0$, $B_N^{(2)} = 0$, $A_1^{(3)} = 0$, and $B_N^{(3)} = 0$, the electric fields of CTHG at each interface can be obtained. Therefore, the conversion efficiencies of the forward and backward waves are defined respectively as

$$\eta_{forth}^{(3)} = \frac{n_N^{(3)} |A_N^{(3)}|^2}{n_1^{(3)} |A_1^{(1)}|^2}, \quad \eta_{back}^{(3)} = \frac{|B_1^{(3)}|^2}{|A_1^{(1)}|^2}. \tag{48}$$

Similarly, a prototype photonic crystal $(AB)_{10}$ is designed. The thicknesses of A and B layers are $d_A = 0.2557\mu m$ and $d_B = 0.1875\mu m$, respectively. Thus this photonic crystal has three band gaps as $[\lambda_a = 1.283\mu m, \lambda_b = 1.835\mu m]$, $[\lambda_c = 0.667\mu m, \lambda_d = 0.848\mu m]$, and $[\lambda_e = 0.477\mu m, \lambda_f = 0.533\mu m]$. The double wavelengths CTHG is considered here, the preset wavelengths are $\lambda_{1,1}^O = 1.458\mu m$, $\lambda_{1,2}^O = 1.578\mu m$, $\lambda_{2,1}^O = 0.729\mu m$, $\lambda_{2,2}^O = 0.789\mu m$, $\lambda_{3,1}^O = 0.486\mu m$, and $\lambda_{3,2}^O = 0.526\mu m$, respectively. The object function in this case is similar with that for multiple wavelengths SHG. The transmission spectrum of the designed structure is shown in Fig. 10. The peak wavelengths appear at $\lambda_{1,1} = 1.458\mu m$, $\lambda_{1,2} = 1.578\mu m$, $\lambda_{2,1} = 0.729\mu m$, $\lambda_{2,2} = 0.789\mu m$, $\lambda_{3,1} = 0.486\mu m$, and $\lambda_{3,2} = 0.526\mu m$, respectively. They agree well with the required wavelengths. Figure 11 presents the dependence of conversion

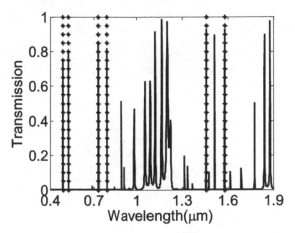

Figure 10. Transmission spectrum of the designed photonic quantum well structure for double wavelengths CTHG. The dashed lines represent $\lambda_{1,1} = 1.458\mu m$, $\lambda_{1,2} = 1.578\mu m$, $\lambda_{2,1} = 0.729\mu m$, $\lambda_{2,2} = 0.789\mu m$, $\lambda_{3,1} = 0.486\mu m$, and $\lambda_{3,2} = 0.526\mu m$, respectively.

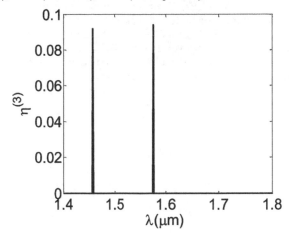

Figure 11. Conversion efficiency of the forward CTHG.

efficiency of the CTHG on the wavelength of FW of the designed structure. Only for the two preset wavelengths, the conversion efficiency is quite high. The conversion efficiencies are $\eta_{1,1} = 0.0917$ for $\lambda_{1,1} = 1.458\mu m$ and $\eta_{1,2} = 0.0938$ for $\lambda_{1,2} = 1.578\mu m$, the conversion efficiencies are nearly identical which corresponds to the required aim well.

4. Conclusion

In a conclusion, the SA algorithm is employed to design nonlinear frequency conversion devices. The basic design method is explained in detail. Some devices include multiple second harmonics generation devices, multiple coupled third harmonics generation devices, multiple channeled photonic crystal filters, multiple second harmonics photonic crystal devices, and multiple coupled third harmonics photonic crystal devices are designed using the proposed method. The designed devices can achieved preset goals well. It is expected that this new proposed method can provide a novel approach for nonlinear conversion devices design.

Author details

Yan Zhang
Beijing Key Lab for Terahertz Spectroscopy and Imaging
Key Laboratory of Terahertz Optoelectronics, Ministry of Education
Department of Physics, Capital Normal University, Beijing, 100048 China

5. References

[1] Yariv, A. & Yeh, A. (1984). *Optical Wave in Crystal*, Wiley, New York.

[2] Shen, Y. R. (1984). *The Principles of Nonlinear Optics*, Wiley, New York.

[3] Bloembergen, N. & Sievers, A. J. Nonlinear optical properties of periodic laminar structures, *Appl. Phys. Lett.*, Vol. 17 (No. 11) 483-485.

[4] Meyn, J. P. & Fejer, M. M. (1997). Tunable ultraviolet radiation by second-harmonic generation in periodically poled lithium tantalate, *Opt. Lett.*, Vol. 22 (No. 16) 1214-1216.

[5] Giordmaine, J. A. & Miller R. C. Tunable coherent parametric oscillation in $LiNbO_3$ at optical frequencies, *Phys. Rev. Lett.* Vol. 14 (No. 24) 973-976.

[6] Yablonobitch E. (1987). Inhibited spontaneous emission in solid-state physics and electronics, *Phys. Rev. Lett.* Vol. 58 (No. 20) 2059-2062.

Chapter 6

Simulated Quenching for Cancellation of Non-Linear Multi-Antennas Coupling

Igor Arambasic, Javier Casajus Quiros and Ivana Raos

Additional information is available at the end of the chapter

1. Introduction

Multiple antennas are a must in today's mobile device providing high data rates and/or large communication range. At the same time, as mobile terminal volume is not enlarged, the level of electronic interferences inside mobile terminals is increased. When observing the flow of data through the terminal energy dissipation of many electronic components interlaced with numerous data metallic wires is detected. Apart from dissipation, all these components also capture some energy dissipated from another source. This undesirable transfer of energy between physical mediums, like metallic wires or circuit segments, is known as coupling. It is likely to occur either in a place where no energy dissipation protection is available due to the lack of space, or where economic electronic elements are used in order to decrease the costs of the product. The interior of mobile receiver terminal fulfils both assumptions and coupling results in an irreducible error floor urging the development of coupling cancellation methods.

In this chapter coupling cancellation module, based on two simulated quenching (SQ) methods, is presented and analyzed. The development of these methods was stimulated by Simulated Annealing (SA) approach which can statistically guarantee finding an optimal solution, as shown in [12], if sufficient number of iterations is available. Since standard SA approach is time-consuming, we decided to ignore physical analogy. Hence, two SQ methods evolved: standard SQ which focuses on precision and Improved Fast SQ where search progress is accelerated on the cost of the decoupling precision.

2. System description

2.1. Non-linear coupling model

Coupling is commonly defined as undesirable transfer of energy between physical mediums (like metallic wires or optical fibers) or circuit segments. Inside multi-antennas mobile terminal the data received at the antennas is affected on its path both by direct distortion imperfections and coupling as modeled in Figure 1.

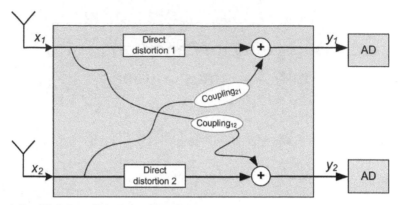

Figure 1. Simplified direct distortion and coupling

In most practical cases the reasonable assumption for the coupling functions is to model them as polynomials and limit them to third order nonlinear behavior which is consistent with the analog electronic elements and follows the nonlinear behavior experienced in many radio frequency (RF) front ends [1]. Hence, if no direct distortion is present, the input of two AD converters can be described mathematically as:

$$y_1 = x_1 + (c_{11}x_2 + c_{12}x_2^2 + c_{13}x_2^3)$$
$$y_2 = x_2 + (c_{21}x_1 + c_{22}x_1^2 + c_{23}x_1^3)$$

(1)

where x_1 and x_2 are the signals received on the corresponding antennas, and y_1, y_2 the signals at the input of AD converter. Parameters c_{ij} corresponding to the coupling of the jth order ($j = 1..3$) experienced on the ith ($i = 1, 2$) input of AD converter signals. These elements describe energy absorption/dissipation that the signals are experiencing when passing through RF front-end. Hence, the direct coupling function is either described mathematically with three parameters (c_1, c_2, c_3) or as $[C_1, C_2, C_3]$ in [dB] describing the physical process of coupling power. The relation between interference amplitude in the coupling function and the interference power at physical level is analyzed in [1] and described as:

$$C_{ij} = 10log\frac{c_{ij}^2 P_{j0}}{P_i}[dB] \iff c_{ij}^2 = \frac{P_i}{P_{j0}}10^{C_{ij}/10}$$

(2)

with P_i the power of the received signal at input i, P_{j0} normalized power of the interference of the jth order and C_{ij} the coupling parameter expressed in [dB] for the ith antenna and j^{th} coupling order. In Table 1 the unit power of three interference orders for different constellations is given. These numbers can be used for simulation purposes when the power of transmitted signal is normalized to 1.

The influence of coupling, depending on the system performance, can be divided in 3 levels: strong, moderate and weak. The strict definition of these three levels can not be made as it depends on the constellation type. However, the borders can graphically be seen in Figure 2 where the presented curve shows theoretical performance of the corresponding system without coupling. Thus when referred to strong coupling, we are referring to coupling

	P_{10}, P_i	P_{20}	P_{30}
Binary	2.00	6.00	20.00
QPSK	2.00	6.00	20.00
8-PSK	2.00	6.00	20.00
16QAM	2.00	7.92	39.20
64QAM	2.00	7.92	39.20

Table 1. The unit power of three interference orders for different constellations

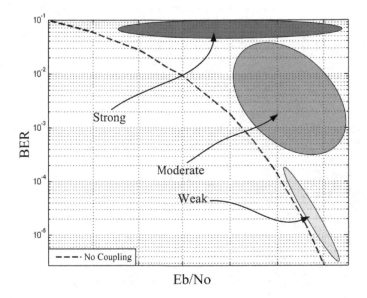

Figure 2. Coupling strength classification depending on the lost system performance

that almost completely destroys the received signal and whose system performance almost shows flat line. Moderate coupling level follows the theoretical curve, but the system performance exhibits slow improvement, while the weak coupling system follows closely the ideal theoretical curve but the system performance is still visibly deteriorated. In the following, search for the decoupling function is mainly made for strong and medium coupling levels as they are more demanding cases.

2.2. Coupling cancellation module

The coupling cancellation is performed with nonlinear software decoupling module located at the output of analog-to-digital (AD) converter as shown in Fig. 3. The advantage of this position is that it deals directly with sampled physical data avoiding any dependency on specific signal type. Inside the module, cancellation is achieved by determining the inverse coupling function.

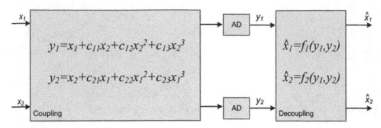

Figure 3. Coupling cancellation module positioned at the output of AD converters

Taking into account that the signals at the output of decoupling module, $\hat{x}_1$ and $\hat{x}_2$, should theoretically be equal to x_1 and x_2, the inverse functions take the form of:

$$\hat{x}_1 = y_1 - c_{11}\hat{x}_2 - c_{12}\hat{x}_2^2 - c_{13}\hat{x}_2^3$$
$$\hat{x}_2 = y_2 - c_{21}\hat{x}_1 - c_{22}\hat{x}_1^2 - c_{23}\hat{x}_1^3 \tag{3}$$

Assuming that all distortion parameters c_{ij} are a priori known, a problem of two nonlinear equations with two unknown variables is presented. By extracting $\hat{x}_2$ the problem is reduced to single variable and can be described as a nonlinear problem of the ninth order:

$$\sum_{i=0}^{i=9} k_i \hat{x}_1^i = 0 \tag{4}$$

with:

$$k_0 = y_1 - c_{11}y_2 - c_{12}y_2^2 - c_{13}y_2^3$$

$$k_1 = c_{11}c_{21} + 2c_{12}c_{21}y_2 + 3c_{13}c_{21}y_2^2 - 1$$

$$k_2 = c_{11}c_{22} - c_{12}c_{21}^2 + 2c_{12}c_{22}y_2 - 3c_{13}c_{21}^2y_2 + 3c_{13}c_{22}y_2^2$$

$$k_3 = c_{11}c_{23} - 2c_{12}c_{21}c_{22} + 2c_{12}c_{23}y_2 + c_{13}c_{21}^3 - 6c_{13}c_{21}c_{22}y_2 + 3c_{13}c_{23}y_2^2$$

$$k_4 = -2c_{12}c_{21}c_{23} - c_{12}c_{22}^2 + 3c_{13}c_{21}^2c_{22} - 3c_{13}c_{22}^2y_2 - 6c_{21}c_{23}c_{13}y_2 \tag{5}$$

$$k_5 = -2c_{12}c_{22}c_{23} + 3c_{13}c_{21}c_{22}^2 + 3c_{13}c_{21}^2c_{23} - 6c_{13}c_{22}c_{23}y_2$$

$$k_6 = -c_{12}c_{23}^2 + 6c_{13}c_{21}c_{22}c_{23} + c_{13}c_{22}^3 - 3c_{13}c_{23}^2y_2$$

$$k_7 = 3c_{13}c_{21}c_{23}^2 + 3c_{13}c_{22}^2c_{23} \qquad k_8 = 3c_{13}c_{22}c_{23}^2 \qquad k_9 = c_{13}c_{23}^3$$

It is shown in [1] that the existence of one analytically expressed inverse function supporting the range of all input pairs (x_1, x_2) is extremely low and depends on all involved parameters $(x_1, x_2, c_{11}, c_{12}, c_{13}, c_{21}, c_{22}, c_{23})$, together with the signal constellation definition which determines the root space. Consequently mathematical surface approximation in combination with calibration process is proposed. This approach is based on finding a surface that matches a series of constraints by minimizing the distance between reference and re-constructed or inverse surface. In other words, a set of predefined points, denominated calibration data, are available to the observed process (in our case coupling) forming the reference surface. This reference surface is then used as basis for building the approximated inverse surface.

With the introduction of the fitting surface approach the solution to the inverse coupling problem can be divided into two steps: calibration process and point-to-point real-time decoupling. Once all decoupling surface design parameters are defined, the decoupling, based on eq. 9, is implemented inside coupling cancellation module on all incoming pair of signals achieving signal enhancement with very low processing demands.

In order to develop a surface fitting algorithm four important parameters should be defined, namely:

- calibration data
- mathematical surface model
- cost function
- parameter search algorithm

2.2.1. Calibration data

The calibration process includes the transmission of the calibration data used for the reference surface construction and the search for the inverse surface based on some search optimized algorithm. The calibration data should be well defined covering the whole direct function domain. For discrete signal coupling systems, the calibration points would correspond to the constellation specific points of the two antennas. In other words the whole domain of two 16 QAM constellations is covered with at least 256 (16×16) data points, while 64 QAM constellation requires a minimum of 4096 (64×64) points as the influence of all point combinations should be analyzed. The required number of calibration points is analyzed in detail in [1]. All the results presented in this chapter correspond to 2000 calibration symbols.

2.2.2. Mathematical surface model

Low-order polynomials tend to be smooth and high order polynomial curves like the one of the ninth degree, tend to be "lumpy" with several local minimum and maximums making the surface approximation severe. Having in mind that complex curves can be formed without higher order multiplications, a model based on a sum of two independent higher order polynomials with one simple linear multiplication is proposed in [3]:

$$\hat{x}_1 = \sum_{i=1}^{i \leq N_1} a_i y_1^i + \sum_{j=1}^{j \leq N_2} b_j y_2^j + k_1 y_1 y_2 + k_2 \tag{6}$$

where N_1 and N_2 represent the degrees of freedom of variables y_1 and y_2 respectively, while variables a_i, b_j, k_1, k_2 are the decoupling coefficients that are to be found with surface approximation search.

This surface function is simple and offers a unique solution to each input pair. The ranks of polynomials, controlled with (N_1, N_2), are determined as a trade off between the acceptable system performance and the required computational power. In [2], the approximation with 20 coefficients for the coupling cancellation fitting surface is proven to be accurate enough.

Hence, $(N_1, N_2) = (9,9)$ is selected for describing the mathematical surface model. In order to be able to adopt the surface search method to general decoupling problem, the data, on which the search is carried out, is restrained to $\langle -1, 1 \rangle$. This is achieved by implementing the normalization according to the maximum received symbol level taking into account all calibration symbols on both antennas, as shown in the following equation:

$$y_{1k}^N = \frac{y_{1k}}{Max(|y_{1k}|,|y_{2k}|)}$$
$$k = 1..N \tag{7}$$
$$y_{12k}^N = \frac{y_{12k}}{Max(|y_{1k}|,|y_{2k}|)}$$

where y_{1k}^N and y_{2k}^N are the k-th normalized received symbols on the corresponding antennas, $Max(|y_{1k}|,|y_{2k}|)$ is the maximum received absolute value level, and N is the number of calibration signals. Eventually, since the approximation surface is constructed based on the normalized levels, the true value of reconstructed symbol is obtained by expanding the reconstructed normalized symbol $\hat{x}_{1k}^N$ to the received dynamic range:

$$\hat{x}_{1k} = \hat{x}_{1k}^N Max(|y_{1k}|,|y_{2k}|) \tag{8}$$

Hence, the decoupling approximation surface is defined as:

$$\hat{x}_{1k} = Max(|y_{1k}|,|y_{2k}|) \left\{ \sum_{i=1}^{i \leq N_1} a_i \left(y_{1k}^N \right)^i + \sum_{j=1}^{j \leq N_2} b_j \left(y_{2k}^N \right)^j + k_1 y_{1k}^N y_{2k}^N + k_2 \right\} \tag{9}$$

This way, the processing load of the decoupling process is basically concentrated on the approximation fitting surface parameter search.

2.2.3. Cost function

The objective of surface search consists in finding the decoupling coefficients that minimize the cost function. The calculation of cost function has to be carried out for each new candidate and presents the most demanding part of the decoupling processing load. The cost function typically implemented for the search of approximate inverse function is root mean square, also known as the quadratic mean:

$$Q_j = \sqrt{\frac{1}{N} \sum_{i=1}^{N} \left(x_{ji} - \hat{x}_{ji} \right)^2} \tag{10}$$

where N is the number of symbols used, x_{ji} is the sent i^{th} calibration symbol on j^{th} antenna, and $\hat{x}_{ji}$ its corresponding value calculated using the coefficients of new surface candidate according to eq. 9. The set of decoupling coefficients displaying minimum Q_j value are then used in decoupling module as the inverse coupling surface function.

2.2.4. Parameter search algorithm

SA methods are chosen as starting point since this approach can statistically guarantee finding an optimal solution, although no estimate can be made on the number of trials needed to reach it. The name and inspiration come from the annealing in metallurgy, as the technique mimics the nature of the metal which is heated and than cooled slowly in order to reach its absolute minimum energy state.

During the last few decades a number of variations of original SA algorithm have been published. The comparison of different SA algorithms, with other mostly heuristic algorithms can be find in [4, 6–10, 13, 18]. Regardless of different variations, any algorithm based on physical SA has proven to be an effective global optimization method because of several important features:

- it can process the cost functions with arbitrary degrees of nonlinearities and discontinuities, as no restriction on the form of the cost function exists
- it can statistically guarantee finding an optimal solution
- it can be implemented easily when convergence speed is not relevant

The basic assumption of the SA class of approaches is that sometimes, in order to avoid the trap of local minimum, intermediate points that lead to worse minimum solution are accepted. The fact is that classical SA search is very slow when compared to other heuristic methods and is often avoided as more importance is given to speed than to precision. Hence, the original SA algorithm is rarely used, but it is worth mentioning some of the known SA enhancements like Quantum Annealing (QA), Simulated Quenching (SQ), Mean Field Annealing (MFA), Fast Simulated Annealing (FSA), Parallel Recombinative Simulated Annealing (PRSA) or Adaptive Simulated Annealing (ASA) that have been proposed in numerous articles [5, 7, 14–16]. In contrast to the original SA approach these methods have been characterized as fast search algorithms. Eventually, inspired by SA algorithms two SQ approaches, which do not follow physical analogy, are put forward for parameter search algorithms. The first one offers high precision but requires large number of iterations to reach it, while inside the second one the search progress is accelerated on the cost of the decoupling precision. Still, the decoupling results are kept at high level which make the precision loss acceptable compared to the speed gain.

3. Simulated quenching applied to nonlinear decoupling problem

The functioning of the classical SQ method can be described using the pseudo code, divided into initialization and the simulated annealing part as presented in Figure 4.

Inside the first section the temperature factor T is set to the initial temperature (T_0). The temporary minimum of the cost function (Q_{min}) is calculated for the initial set of decoupling coefficients ($Coef_0$). These values are then appointed to actual state configuration. Afterwards, the algorithm enters the search loop until allowed processing time measured in number of iterations is exceeded ($Iter > I_{MAX}$). The selection of new coefficients (neighbors) is done inside the $New\_Candidate$ function, and then the cost function for the set of selected coefficients is calculated (Q_{new}). If the cost function ($Cost$) of the new neighbor presents lower value than temporary minimum cost function (Q_{min}), the perturbation is accepted. The new cost function value (Q_{new}) becomes the new minimum and the corresponding set of the coefficients is stored in $Coef_{min}$. In case of higher cost function value the perturbation is accepted only if the randomly selected number between zero and one is smaller than the $Trans\_Prob$ function of the actual temperature T. However, in this case only the actual position is updated and the global minimum cost configuration is left unchanged. The search at one temperature level is limited

```
Coef_min=Coef_0
Q_min=Cost_Func (Coef_min)
Coef_act=Coef_min
Q_act=Q_min
T=T_0=1
Iter=0
k=set_k( )

While (Iter<I_MAX)
        for  1 to N_VCPL

                Iter++
                Coef_new= New_Candidate(Coef_act)
                Q_new= Cost (Coef_new)

                if (Q_new<Q_min)
                        Q_min=Q_new
                        Q_act=Q_new
                        Coef_min=Coef_new
                        Coef_act=Coef_new
                else
                        if random(0-1)<Trans_Prob(k,T,ΔQ)
                                Q_act=Q_new
                                Coef_act=Coef_new
                        end if
                end if
        end for
        T=Ann_Schedule(T)
end while
```

Figure 4. Pseudo code of SQ applied to Nonlinear Decoupling Problem

with a number of visited candidates per level defined with N_{VCPL} parameter. Afterwards, the temperature T is decreased according to the annealing schedule function (*Ann_Schedule*) and the quest is continued.

According to the formulation of SQ algorithm when applying the SQ method to a decoupling problem, one must specify:

- the state space or the coefficient resolution
  - symbol precision (Res_{symb})
  - coefficient precision (Res_{coef})
- the initial coefficients values or the starting point ($Coef_0$)
- the neighbor selection method (*New_Candidate*)
  - coefficient maximum displacement (R_0)
- the form of the cost function (*Cost_Func*) - already defined with Equation 10.
- the probability transition function (*Trans_Prob*)
  - initial (maximum) probability of the acceptance of the worse move (p_{max})
- the annealing schedule function (*Ann_Schedule*)
  - time reduction factor (α)
  - number of visited candidates per temperature level (N_{VCPL})

- maximum allowed number of iterations (I_{MAX})
- minimum probability of worse move during the search (p_{min})

3.1. Tuning of SQ parameters

The choice of SQ parameters can have a significant impact on the method effectiveness. Unfortunately, there is no selection good enough for all problems, and there is no general way of finding the best set of parameters for a given problem. However, some more generic parameters (e.g. the annealing schedule or probability transition function) can be set based on the experience of other authors like [8, 9, 11, 13, 14, 16]. This way, preliminary SQ search executions are over-dimensioned favoring precision over speed and are used for tuning correctly the search parameters. The empirical tuning of SQ parameters is done for 64QAM signals. The results are based on 2000 calibration symbols transmitted under SNR of 100dB. This way the analysis is concentrated primarily on coupling rather than on noise effects. Since SQ search carries probability factor each presented simulation is in fact executed ten times, and the figures present the averaged values.

3.1.1. The state space

This parameter is defined with the number of design variables, their discrete domain resolution and the overall symbol precision. Starting from a analog domain the search coefficients are transformed into discrete domain by setting the distance between two sample points. For example, by setting the resolution to 0.1 the coefficients can only obtain resolution multiples values like $0.2, -0.1, 0.8$ etc. By setting the resolution to more dense value, like 0.0001, exactly 1000 times more possible candidates are available for each coefficient inside the SQ search. Expanding the solution search area naturally leads to better solution precision, but at the expense of processing time. Apart from the coefficients resolution, the state space also defines the resolution of the received and decoupled symbols which depend on the transmission system requirements and implemented A/D converter. We propose to set $Res_{symb} = 0.00001$ and apply the same resolution on decoupling symbols, that is, $Res_{coef} = 0.00001$.

3.1.2. Coefficients initial values

The initial assumption is that no coupling takes place, and the signal arrives without any distortion. Consequently, the signals that suffered larger distortions will require longer search time as their solution is located far from the starting point. This way the algorithm favors the solutions of smaller coupling which is expected to occur more frequently under realistic conditions. By using the decoupling model in accordance to eq. 9, all coefficients are set to zero, except a_1 which is set to one:

$$Coef_0 : \begin{cases} a = [1,0,0,0,0,0,0,0,0] \\ b = [0,0,0,0,0,0,0,0,0] \\ k = \qquad [0,0] \end{cases} \tag{11}$$

In fact, to make the indexing simpler, the coefficients are expressed as 20 dimensional vector where first nine elements correspond to coefficients $a_i, i = 1,..,9$, second nine elements correspond to $b_i, i = 1,..,9$, and the last two correspond to k_1 and k_2.

3.1.3. Probability transition function

The key SA feature that prevents the system of becoming stuck in a local minimum is its probability to move to the new state even when this new state has worse characteristics than the current one. The probability of making the transition from the current state to a candidate new state is a function of the energies of the two states, and of a global time varying parameter T denominated as temperature. Even though the algorithm is open to the use of any probability function (p), the new configurations are usually accepted or rejected according to the Boltzmann probability distribution, k_B is the Boltzmann constant that relates temperature to energy. When SA problem is not related directly to the physical energy this constant is replaced with problem specific constant K and modified Boltzmann probability function is used accordingly:

$$p(\Delta E) = e^{-\frac{\Delta E}{k_B T}} \longleftrightarrow p(\Delta Q) = e^{-\frac{\Delta Q}{KT}} = e^{-\frac{Q_{new}-Q_{act}}{KT}} \tag{12}$$

where Q_{new} and Q_{act} are the cost function values associated with the actual and new candidate state respectively, and ΔQ their difference. However for a given ΔQ the transition probability is not constant throughout the annealing process as it also depends on the actual temperature. By setting the initial temperature T_0 to high values the probability of search wandering is increased. For example, if $\Delta Q = 0.1$ and initial temperature $KT_0 = 1$ the perturbation will be accepted if the random variable falls between $\langle 0, 0.9 \rangle$ which correspond to 90%, while for $\Delta Q = 0.1$ and initial temperature $KT_0 = 0.1$ this probability falls to 36%. As the temperature is constantly decreased according to the annealing schedule, the probability of worse move tends to zero. This is in accordance with the physical simulated annealing where no wondering around is possible at low temperatures.

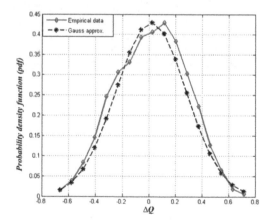

Figure 5. Approximation of the consecutive cost function differences with Gauss function

The selection of problem specific constant K depends on the initial probability of uphill movement acceptance defined as p_0 which should be guaranteed for wide range of energy differences. In order to define this energy level we approximated the cost differences of the two consecutive surfaces (ΔQ) with Gaussian probability function, as it fits the actual empirical data. This is shown in Figure 5 where 2000 differences are calculated with maximum allowed individual coefficient displacement of $R_0 = 0.05$. By approximating ΔQ distribution with Gaussian-like probability density function, three standard deviations ($\sigma_{\Delta Q}$) represent 99.7% of all possible cost function differences and as p_0 can be created according to this value as:

$$p_0 = p_{max} = e^{-\frac{3\sigma_{\Delta Q}}{KT_0}} \tag{13}$$

with $T_0 = 1$, K is obtained as:

$$K = -\frac{3\sigma_{\Delta Q}}{\ln(p_{max})} \tag{14}$$

By setting the initial probability of uphill movement close to one, the initial search wander is allowed regardless of the energy difference between two candidates. This slows down the search usually without any solution precision gained. Hence, the initial probability level is generally set to $p_{max} = 50\%$ and numerical value of K is calculated in set_K function before algorithm enters SQ search loop. Inside the set_K function the approximation of Gauss distribution is obtained by implementing the actual neighbor selection method on 2000 new candidates.

3.1.4. Annealing schedule function

The annealing schedule function has no strict definition, as the function only restricts to uphill surface exploration at the beginning, and then gradually restraining the search wondering favoring the movement in the direction of better solution only. Inside physical simulated annealing the probability of acceptance of uphill movement is directly related to temperature, but in mathematical interpretations the initial temperature level has lost its significance, and thus it is set to $T_0 = 1$ in order to simplify the calculation process. Consequently, modified Boltzmann constant K is calculated accordingly. A popular choice for the annealing function is the exponential schedule, where the temperature level, denoted as T or T_L , is decreased by a fixed factor α:

$$T_L = \alpha T_{L-1}; \; T_0 = 1, \; 0 < \alpha < 1, \; L = 1,2,3... \tag{15}$$

where T_L and T_{L-1} are the new and the actual temperature respectively, and index L stands for the number of temperature level changes.

In order to define the annealing schedule both, temperature reduction factor α and number of visited candidates per level N_{VCPL} have to be determined. In theory, when keeping N_{VCPL} constant, the search is done more thoroughly if the temperature is decreased slower and better solution precision is achieved. Additionally, if (α) is constant, and N_{VCPL} is increased, each level is scanned in more detail and, again, better results are expected. However, when both factor are set in favor of precision the search is extremely slowed down and the precision improvement might not justify the processing load.

These two parameters are established empirically. In Figure 6 the dependence of the cost function minimum on the number of visited points per level is shown, with bars of different colors corresponding to different temperature reduction factors. The simulations are done for moderate coupling distortion of [-10,-12,-12] dB and maximum allowed displacement set to $R_0 = 0.05$. It is seen that as α approaches 1 the probability of finding the better solution increases, and as a result minimum cost function moves away from its starting value. However, if N_{VCPL} is low, e.g. $N_{VCPL} = 2$ no significant progress is made even with $\alpha = 0.995$. This is due to the scan space around the actual minimum which is always kept narrow and so

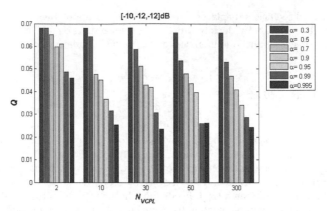

Figure 6. Q as a function of N_{VCPL} and α for [-10,-12,-12] dB coupling distortion

the search is easily stacked in the local minimum. According to empirical decoupling results, the number of visited points per level starts producing good results with $N_{VCPL} \geq 10$.

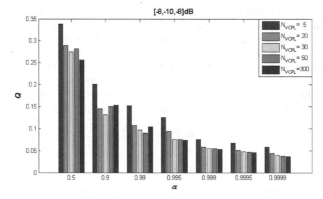

Figure 7. Q as a function of α and N_{VCPL} for [-8,-10,-8] dB coupling distortion

The cost performance as a function of temperature reduction factor is shown in Figure 7 where bars of different colors correspond to different N_{VCPL} levels. For α between 0.5 and 0.95 the search progress presents low consistency as the cost function minimum experienced big differences between two realizations of the same SQ search. It shows that the temperature reduction is reduced too quickly and that the final precision is still not guaranteed as search robustness is not achieved. This statement is confirmed in Figure 7 by comparing the Q function obtained with different N_{VCPL} for this α range. For $\alpha = 0.9$ better precision is achieved with $N_{VCPL} = 30$ than with $N_{VCPL} = 300$. Hence in order to avoid the uncertainty, temperature reduction factor should be between 0.95 and 1 since this area shows signs of consistency with theoretical background (precision is increased with the increase of either N_{VCPL} or α). According to the presented simulation results, the SQ search is adopted adequately to inverse coupling approximation with the number of visited candidates per level set to $N_{VCPL} = 30$, and temperature reduction factor set to $\alpha = 0.995$.

3.1.5. Neighbor selection method

When selecting new candidates (neighbors), it must be possible to move from the initial state to a *good enough* state by relatively short path while at the same time allowing the search to scan the area but never loosing the good path from the sight. The selection of the new candidate set ($Coef_{new}$) can be described as:

$$Coef_{new}(i) = \xi_i R_0 + Coef_{act}(i); \; i = 1, ..., 20 \tag{16}$$

where ξ_i is the randomly chosen number between -1 and 1, and R_0 defines maximum allowed coefficient displacement. If R_0 is large, the SQ search can easily explore wide search area, but needs more iterations to reach the optimal solution as the algorithm is easily distracted and moved away from the good path. If R_0 is small, the algorithm can get stuck in local minimum and conclude the search far from the optimal solution.

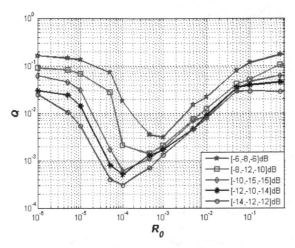

Figure 8. Q in dependence of R_0 under different coupling conditions

The behavior of cost function with respect to R_0 under different coupling conditions is presented in Figure 8 as this parameter is retrieved empirically. The conducted search is based on classical SQ algorithm with $N_{VCPL} = 30$ and $\alpha = 0.995$. The figure can be divided into three clearly distinguished areas. The left side, with R_0 lower than 10^{-5} corresponds to algorithm where no wandering around is allowed. The search progress is slow and any encountered local minimum is presented as the final solution. The optimal solution is only found if the search is executed close to it. On the right side of the figure with R_0 values larger than 0.5, wandering is allowed during the whole search process and as a consequence no clear search path is established. The search tends to move too quickly and without any exploration around the actual position. As search is randomly wandering around, finding the optimal solution in this area is highly uncertain. The central part of the image coincides with the meaningful SQ search where wandering around and detail space exploration are in balance. Here, the search method does follow some path and the traps of local minimums are successfully avoided. Based on the presented Q values, we propose to set maximum allowed displacement to $R_0 = 0.0005$.

3.1.6. Maximum number of iterations (I_{MAX})

The strength of SQ method lies in its ability to statistically deliver a true global minimum. However, as mentioned, one of the drawbacks of this method is its slow delivery of the ideal solution once the global minimum area is located. As no indication of time required for reaching the optimal solution is available, the search process is typically suspended after the allowed search time is spent or the cost function has reached the desired level of precision.

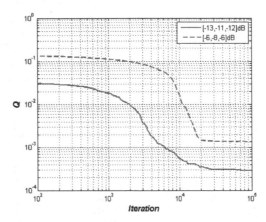

Figure 9. Q in dependence of the number of iterations under two different coupling levels

In Figure 9, Q is depicted as a function of the number of iterations under two different coupling conditions. Both Q functions experience three different segments which correspond to surface wandering at the beginning, almost downhill movement in the middle, and error floor at the end. In both cases error floor is reached after around 20000 iterations and it would make sense to use this number as maximum number of permitted iterations. Still, if we take into account that surface with Q level smaller than 0.005 produce gratifying decoupling results, in this cases the search can be stopped after 4000 and 12000 iterations respectively. The process of establishing the satisfying level of cost function (Q_{suff}) is explained in [1] where relation between BER and the corresponding quadratic mean square cost function level is analyzed. In the end we propose to set maximum number of iterations to 16000 and use it in combination with satisfying cost function level to control the search execution.

3.2. SQ example

The SQ search is conducted under moderate coupling conditions of [-10,-12,-10] dB using the SQ search parameters adopted to nonlinear decoupling problem gathered inside Table 2. The table consist of two columns with standard values based on theoretical assumptions occupying the left column, and values based on empirical decoupling analysis in the right column.

The behavior of adopted SQ search algorithm is shown in Figure 10, where cost function is presented in dependence of number of iterations for 10 different SQ search executions. The image shows that the search path in first 500 iterations is similar in all ten instance. The curves then start to spread, and are grouped again at the end. Nevertheless, the cost

Standard Values	Values based on Empirical Decoupling Analysis
$Res_{symb} = 0.00001$	$N_{VCPL} = 30$
$Res_{coeff} = 0.00001$	$\alpha = 0.995$
$Coef_0(i) = \begin{cases} 1, & i = 1 \\ 0, & i = 2,...,20 \end{cases}$	$R_0 = 0.0005$
$Q = \sqrt{\frac{1}{N} \sum_{i=1}^{N} (x_{1i} - \hat{x}_{1i})^2}$	$Q_{suff} = 0.005$
$Coef_{new}(i) = \xi_i R_0 + Coef_{act}(i)$ $i = 1..20; \xi_i \in \langle -1, 1 \rangle$	$I_{MAX} = 16000$
$p(\Delta Q) = e^{-\frac{\Delta Q}{kT}}$ $k = -\frac{3\sigma_{\Delta Q}}{ln(p_{max})}$	
$T_L = \alpha T_{L-1}$ $T_0 = 1, \alpha < 1, L = 1,2,3...$	
$p_{max} = 50\%$ $p_{min} = 0.1\%$	

Table 2. Set of SQ search parameters after empirical analysis

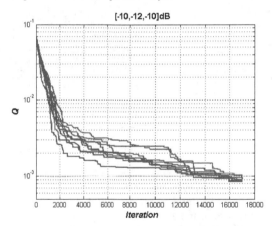

Figure 10. Ten instances of adopted SQ search algorithm under moderate coupling

function solutions are kept in the same orders of magnitude throughout the entire search process. The small differences between the temporary cost function progress and stable final solution precision confirms that the SQ parameters have been selected adequately. The search successfully avoids local minimum traps and follows the correct search path. Furthermore, since BER performance enters saturation for $Q < 0.005$ the presented search can be stopped at 4000 iterations preserving the decoupling precision.

Even though the obtained cost function value is similar for all ten instances of conducted SQ search, the presented decoupling coefficients numerically offer completely different solutions. Two different sets of 20 decoupling coefficients, obtained as a result of two execution of classical SQ algorithm under the same coupling conditions, are presented in Figure 11. The difference between the cost functions in this case is almost zero as surface cost functions are

a₁	a₂	a₃	a₄	a₅	a₆	a₇	a₈	a₉
1,00840	0,00468	0,00433	0,00218	0,00245	-0,02087	0,00018	0,01541	-0,00384
b₁	b₂	b₃	b₄	b₅	b₆	b₇	b₈	b₉
-0,09903	-0,01802	-0,01042	-0,00752	0,00664	0,02397	-0,01103	-0,01454	0,00752
k₁	k₂							
0,00237	0,00002							

a₁	a₂	a₃	a₄	a₅	a₆	a₇	a₈	a₉
1,01160	-0,00424	0,00040	0,00448	-0,01285	0,01531	0,01581	-0,01373	-0,00417
b₁	b₂	b₃	b₄	b₅	b₆	b₇	b₈	b₉
-0,10036	-0,01088	-0,00315	-0,00896	-0,01443	-0,00261	0,01502	0,00645	-0,00351
k₁	k₂							
0,00298	-0,00001							

Figure 11. Two sets of decoupling coefficients for [-10,-12,-10]dB coupling environment

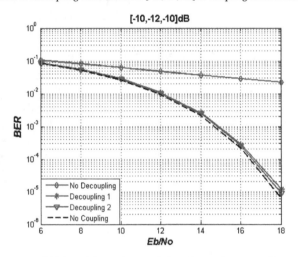

Figure 12. Performance of SQ based decoupling module under moderate coupling

$Q_a = 0.0009$ and $Q_b = 0.0008$ respectively. This points out that the constructed inverse coupling surfaces are similar. However, they are based on different building material as for example a_7 is very close to zero in first solution while in second one is $a_7 = 0.015$. On the other hand a_5 and b_3 show opposite behavior, as they present higher importance in second than in first solution. Furthermore, the amplitudes of decoupling coefficients don't exhibit the tendency of reduction as the exponential order is increased. For example, $a_8 \gg a_3$ or $b_7 \gg b_3$ indicating that the surface simplification based on simple reduction of the order of polynomials might not achieve the same decoupling efficiency.

The system performance of decoupling module based on the obtained coefficients traces almost the same curve inside E_b/N_0 -BER graph as shown in Figure 12. The entire description of system used for transmission simulations is found in [1]. The upper curve on the image presents the system behavior under coupling of [-10,-12,-10] dB and without decoupling module. The lowest curve shows the theoretical system performance without any distortion and only with additive white Gaussian noise (AWGN). The two curves in the middle show that the system performance with the decoupling module is very close to the theoretical system performance This confirms that the cost function and inverse surface model are both selected adequately and that SQ search produces accurate results.

4. Improved Fast Simulate Quenching (IFSQ)

The proposed Improved Fast SQ (IFSQ) approach applies changes to three vital parts of SQ method:

- annealing schedule
- probability transition function
- maximum allowed displacement.

The IFSQ implements the annealing schedule function according to Boltzman function while the probability transition function corresponds to Caucy distribution. The novel part of IFSQ approach is also to keep the maximum allowed displacement factor a function of temperature.

All enhanced SA methods labeled as fast are based on steeper annealing schedule function when compared to traditional SA approach. Previously described SQ approach is based on the exponential annealing schedule function where the temperature level is decreased by a fixed factor during the entire search process. However, it makes sense to decrease the temperature more rapidly at the beginning when wandering is desirable, and than reduce the temperature carefully towards the end when SQ turns into a greedy search algorithm. This is precisely the effect achieved with the following annealing schedule function used in IFSQ approach:

$$T_L = \frac{T_\alpha}{ln(L+1)}; \quad L = 1, 2, 3..$$ (17)

where L is the actual temperature level and T_α is the temperature constant. The numerical value of T_α is actually irrelevant to performance of IFSQ search. In real physical process this factor controls the initial temperature and as such influences the probability of uphill movement during the search since probability is directly related to temperature with Boltzmann constant k_B. As decoupling problem is not related directly to the physical energy k_B is replaced with problem specific constant k_c which is adjusted according to the initial temperature level. In order to easily compare the SQ to IFSQ search T_α is chosen to equal the initial temperature level of SQ search algorithm:

$$T_1^{SQ} = T_1^{IFSQ}$$
$$\alpha T_0 = \frac{T_\alpha}{ln(2)} \quad \Rightarrow \quad T_\alpha = \alpha ln(2)$$ (18)

with $T_0 = 1$ and $\alpha = 0.995$ which corresponds to the temperature reduction factor of the adjusted SQ search. As a result, the initial temperature level of IFSQ method is set to $T_\alpha = 0.69$.

The difference between SQ and IFSQ annealing schedules based on adjusted parameters is seen in Figure 13. As can be seen the temperature level of the SQ algorithm is kept high during the first ten levels. At this time, IFSQ temperature is decreased to less then 30% of the initial temperature and shortly afterwards starts to decrease slowly, while SQ temperature decrease now gets steeper. At the end, IFSQ keeps temperature almost constant allowing the thorough search of actual neighbor space. On the other hand, SQ search turns into a greedy algorithm without any uphill excursions allowing only perturbations which lead to better solution. In short, when compared to SQ method IFSQ annealing schedule is steeper at the beginning and

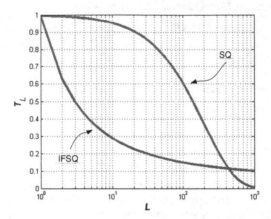

Figure 13. Comparison of standard SQ and IFSQ annealing schedule functions

kept at higher level towards the end of the search which allows higher convergence speed at start up, and better analysis of close neighborhood area at lower temperature levels.

The second important difference between SQ and IFSQ approach is the choice of the probability of uphill movement. The SQ method is based on Boltzmann probability density function with the drawback in its thin tail, which makes the configurations with substantial cost function difference rather unreachable under small number of iterations. It was noted in [17] that Cauchy distribution, which has a fatter body than Boltzmann distribution, permits easier access to larger set of candidates without any significant algorithm convergence loss. The authors define modified Cauchy distribution, which is also used in IFSQ, as:

$$p(\Delta Q) = \frac{T_L}{\left(\Delta Q^2 + k_c T_L^2\right)^{(D+1)/2}} \tag{19}$$

where k_c relates T_L to ΔQ and D defines the degrees of freedom. According to eq. 9 parameter D is equal to 20 while modified Cauchy distribution constant k_c is chosen to ensure maximum probability of transition (p_{max}) at first temperature level T_1 to be satisfied for 99% of all possible cost function differences. Since ΔQ follows the Gaussian distribution 99% of all possible numerical values of ΔQ matches three standard deviations $\sigma_{\Delta Q}$ of the corresponding distribution. Hence, p_{max} can be expressed as:

$$p_{max} = \frac{T_1}{\left(\left(3\sigma_{\Delta Q}\right)^2 + k_c T_1^2\right)^{(D+1)/2}} \tag{20}$$

By extracting k_c the following statement is obtained:

$$k_c = \sqrt{\frac{1}{T_1^2}\left(\sqrt[(D+1)/2]{\frac{T_1}{p_{max}}} - \left(3\sigma_{\Delta Q}\right)^2\right)} \tag{21}$$

The difference between these two probability transition approaches are seen easily in Figure 14 where transition probability functions of SQ and IFSQ approach are presented.

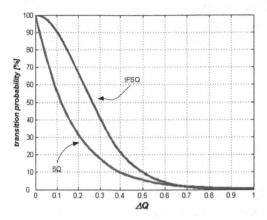

Figure 14. Transition probability functions of SQ and IFSQ approach

As expected the probability function based on modified Cauchy distribution is fatter than the one based on Boltzmann function allowing uphill movements with more ease. The advantage of IFSQ probability transition function lies inside area which covers ΔQ from 0.1 to 0.6. With $\Delta Q = 0.2$, for example, transition probability of IFSQ marks approximately 65%, while SQ is limited to approximately 32%. B including this middle class of ΔQ values more often into the search path, search robustness is increased but convergence speed doesn't suffer substantial loss.

The depth of exploration depends not only on the transition probability function but also on the annealing schedule and maximum displacement factor R_0. The annealing schedule function of IFSQ is very steep at the beginning, suppressing the initial deep exploration rather fast and keeping the rest of the search concentrated on small energy differences around the actual point. Thus, so called deep exploration which easily permits uphill movements is available only at the beginning. Still, these initial search opportunities can not be exploited if R_0 factor is small as only small part of the potential search space can be reached for the analysis. Small maximum displacement factor is adequate choice for the advanced search status when global minimum area is well located, and extense search is required in order to find the best solution. By keeping R_0 constant during the entire search process, as in SQ approach, two opposite search requirement can not be met and consequently R_0 is chosen as their compromise. This is changed in IFSQ approach maximum displacement factor is set to high value covering whole search space at the beginning, and it is gradually decreased as the search advances. The dependence is made according to the:

$$R_0(L) = \delta R_0(L-1), R_0(0) = r, L = 1, 2, \ldots \tag{22}$$

where L stands for the corresponding temperature level, δ is the search space reduction factor, and r the initial maximum allowed displacement. The numerical values of δ and r are determined through empirical analysis. Additionally, since IFSQ approach is not oriented only on precision, the maximum number of iterations is not limited to probability, but the search is stopped if in five consecutive temperature levels no cost function improvement is obtained.

4.1. Tuning of IFSQ parameters

The parameters describing IFSQ approach can be divided into the ones inherited from the SQ method and the ones developed for the decoupling solution which correspond to three new IFSQ parameters that have to be set empirically (r, δ, N_{VCPL}).

The inherited SQ factors are set to the numerical values obtained in previous SQ analysis while three new IFSQ factors have to be set empirically (r, δ, N_{VCPL}). When determining the correct level of the unknown parameters, the parameters that are still not analyzed are over-dimensioned which guarantees the correct functioning of IFSQ search at the cost of execution time. The first set of simulations focuses on adequate pair of parameters for maximum allowed displacement definition (r, δ). Afterwards, the obtained pair is used for analyzing the appropriate number of visited candidates per temperature level (N_{VCPL}).

4.1.1. Search space reduction factor and initial maximum allowed displacement

Since probability transition function in IFSQ presents high values for all energy differences, it can be stated that IFSQ favors the wide search space exploration during the entire search process. However, the depth of exploration depends not only on the transition probability function but also on the annealing schedule and maximum displacement factor R_0. The annealing schedule function of IFSQ is very steep at the beginning, suppressing the deep exploration rather fast and keeping the rest of the search concentrated on small energy differences around the actual point.

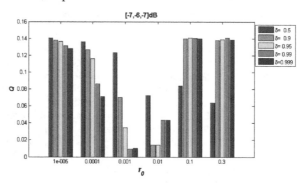

Figure 15. IFSQ search based on different sets of (r, δ) factors under strong coupling

If the starting search space is large, and the reduction factor very close to one, the search will progress rather slowly. In this case the probability of worse movement decreases and even enters the downhill search but the search space is kept large all the time. As a consequence five consecutive temperature levels without the reduction of cost function occur far before the global minimum area is located. This is confirmed in Figure 15, where the precision of IFSQ search based on different sets of (r, δ) factors under strong coupling is presented. As is seen in the right image side, when the starting search space is set to $r_0 = 0.1$ or $r_0 = 0.3$ the algorithm presents poor precision for all space reduction factors except for $\delta = 0.5$. Still, with reduction factor of 50% the search is easily drown into saturation as clear tendency path can hardly be established at such fast pace.

If the starting search space is too small, the search progress cannot move far from the starting point and the obtained solution results depend largely on the coupling strength. Under strong coupling the starting search space corresponding to $r_0 = 10^{-5}$ and $r_0 = 10^{-4}$ represents the selection of narrow starting search space. The obtained cost function precision is generally low, but as the reduction factor gets closer to one, it is increased in both cases. This is logical as if the small search space is additionally reduced at fast pace the algorithm is easily left without any new candidates and no progress can be made.

Consequently, two starting search spaces, in the middle of the image, built around $r_0 = 0.001$ and $r_0 = 0.01$ offer the adequate selection. In fact the best precision under strong coupling is reached with the following four pair of factors: $(0.001, 0.99)$, $(0.001, 0.999)$, $(0.01, 0.90)$ and $(0.01, 0.95)$. The pairs are in accordance with the theoretical expectations as they ratify that in vicinity of adequate set of parameters smaller search space requires lower reduction factor to obtain the same precision level.

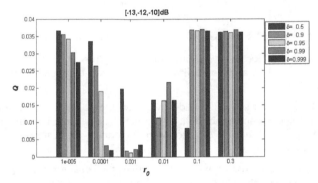

Figure 16. IFSQ search based on different sets of (r, δ) factors under moderate coupling

The same analysis is repeated for system under moderate coupling of [13,-12,-10] dB in Figure 16. The behavior of algorithm is similar and the potentially adequate set of parameters is found in the central part of the image. However, in this case the best values are moved slightly to the left since the coupling strength is lower and the the ideal solution is located closer to the initial search point. Comparing the results obtained at two different coupling levels, the only pair of parameters appearing in both is $r_0 = 0.001$ and $\delta = 0.99$. Hence, these values are used as adequate parameters for IFSQ search adopted to nonlinear decoupling problem.

4.1.2. Number of visited points per level

The number of visited candidates per temperature level defines the number of energy configurations analyzed between two temperature changes. If this number is large, the search space is analyzed in detail which produces stable results but consumes a lot of the processing time. Nevertheless, if the number of visited configurations is small, the search progress is made based on unreliable data which leads to poor cost function results.

The performance of IFSQ search method based on different N_{VCPL} number under strong coupling conditions of [-8,-6,-6] dB is depicted in Figure 17. As expected, when N_{VCPL} number is small, like for $N_{VCPL} = 5$ or $N_{VCPL} = 3$, the search is easily drown into a blind ally.

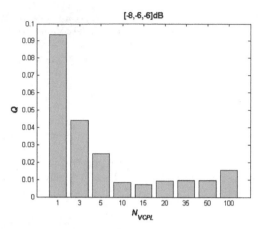

Figure 17. Cost function of IFSQ search with different N_{VCPL} factor under [-8,-6,-6] dB coupling

Local minimum area is located well, but as all temperature levels are spent fast, no uphill movements are available, and no additional progress can be made despite the additional number of iterations.

On the other hand, if number of visited candidates is large and the temperature reduction function is not smooth enough the search can get stacked while in wandering phase and can only offer local minimum as final solution. Eventually the best precision under strong coupling is reached with $N_{VCPL} = 10$ and $N_{VCPL} = 15$.

When the analysis is centered on moderate coupling the behavior of IFSQ method changes very little and the adequate selection of visited number of candidates per level lies between 5 and 15. Since strong coupling conditions discard $N_{VCPL} = 5$ as too small, and moderate coupling exhibits slightly better results with $N_{VCPL} = 10$ than with $N_{VCPL} = 15$, the adequate parameter adjusted to the nonlinear coupling problem is set to $N_{VCPL} = 10$.

4.2. IFSQ example

The parameters of IFSQ algorithm are adjusted to nonlinear coupling problem through empirical analysis based on different set of simulations. The adopted set of IFSQ search parameters is presented in Table 3. The table consists of two columns with inherited SQ values in the left column, and new IFSQ functions and parameters values based on empirical analysis in the right one.

The behavior of IFSQ algorithm applied to coupling of [-10,-12,-12]dB is shown in Figure18, where cost function is presented in dependence of number of iterations for 10 instances of IFSQ search under same operating conditions.

Unlike SQ search which produced 10 closely related curves, the IFSQ curves are spread over wider area as the search progresses due to the higher influence of probability since precision is sacrificed in favor of smaller number of iterations.

Furthermore, the IFSQ cost function is also based on quadratic mean square function for which it has been demonstrated in [1] that smaller Q is not transformed into any significant

Inherited SQ Values	New IFSQ Functions
$Res_{symb} = 0.00001$	$T_L = \frac{T_\alpha}{ln(L+1)}$ $T_\alpha = 0.69, L = 1,2,3...$
$Res_{coeff} = 0.00001$	$p(\Delta Q) = \frac{T_L}{\left(\Delta Q^2 + k_c T_L^2\right)^{(D+1)/2}}$
$Coef_0(i) = \begin{cases} 1, & i = 1 \\ 0, & i = 2,...,20 \end{cases}$	$k_c = \sqrt{\frac{1}{T_1^2}\left(\sqrt[(D+1)/2]{\frac{T_1}{p_{max}}} - \left(3\sigma_{\Delta Q}\right)^2\right)}$
$Coef_{new}(i) = \xi_i R_0 + Coef_{act}(i)$ $i = 1..20; \xi_i \in \langle-1,1\rangle$	$R_0(L) = \delta R_0(L-1)$ $R_0(0) = r, L = 1,2,...$
$Q = \sqrt{\frac{1}{N}\sum_{i=1}^{N} (x_{1i} - \hat{x}_{1i})^2}$	$r = 0.001$ $\delta = 0.99$
$p_{max} = 50\%$	$N_{VCPL} = 10$
	$Q_{suff} = 0.005$

Table 3. Theoretic set of IFSQ search parameters after empirical analysis

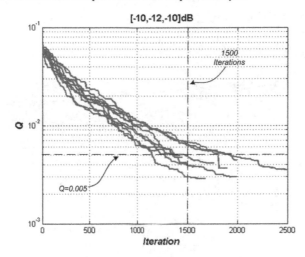

Figure 18. Ten instances of adjusted IFSQ search under moderate coupling

BER enhancement for $Q<0.005$. Since IFSQ is not oriented only on precision of search can be stopped when the cost function reaches Q limit. This occurs on average for 1500 number of iterations as shown in Figure 19 where the corresponding cost function value after 1500 iteration is presented for all ten search instances. The average of all ten executions is located at $\bar{Q} = 0.0056$ which indicates that the search under moderate coupling can be suspended when 1500 iterations are surpassed. When compared with 4000 iterations that is required to SQ approach to reach $Q=0.005$, this presents the reduction of processing load of approximately 37%. When compared to the SQ approach which is not suspended at some cost function limit, the processing gain is even higher as it is reduced from approximately 16000 iterations to 1500 corresponding to reduction of more than 90%. Eventually, if after 1500 iterations the quality of the result is far from $Q=0.005$ the search can easily be repeated with the consequent slight reduce of the processing load gain.

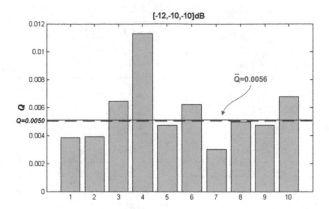

Figure 19. The precision of IFSQ search after 1500 iterations

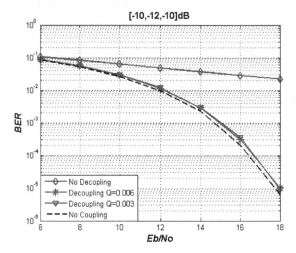

Figure 20. Performance of IFSQ based decoupling module under moderate coupling

The reduction of permitted number of iterations to 1500 is verified in Figure 20 where the performance of IFSQ decoupling module under moderate coupling conditions is presented. The first curve on the image presents the behavior of system without the decoupling module under coupling of [-10,-12,-10] dB. The lowest curve shows the theoretical system performance with only AWGN. Two curves in the middle present two decoupling module instances based on IFSQ approach stopped after 1500 iterations. Actually, the coefficients used for generating this two curves correspond to the seventh and tenth IFSQ execution depicted in Figure 19. Regardless of the numerical difference of cost functions, the performance of both decoupling modules is very similar. Since the search is abandoned when cost function reaches sufficient Q value defined with $Q_{suff} = 0.005$ the performance of decoupling module does not follow the theoretical transmission curve as close as is the SQ approach.

5. Conclusion

The effect of coupling are minimized with the software module positioned at the output of analog-to-digital converter and before any further digital signal processing. Inside the module, signal reconstruction based on the approximation of inverse nonlinear coupling is achieved. The generation of inverse coupling function is based on fitting surface approach which can be divided into two steps: calibration process and point-to-point real-time decoupling. Inside calibration process inverse nonlinear coupling surface is build based on function formed with 20 degrees of freedom. Inspired by SA class of approaches, two SQ algorithms are proposed for locating the optimal inverse function parameters.

Even though classical SQ method can not be used under real time conditions it provides the upper limit of the decoupling precision module and is used for tuning the required system parameters like for example calibration data size. It is intended only for proof of concept and precision reference to other two decoupling search approaches. Eventually actually confirms the adequate selection of the surface model and proves the concept of decoupling software module. The performance of decoupling module based on the SQ search method shows stable behavior and excellent decoupling results.

The proposed Improved Fast SQ search method is included in decoupling module as the fast version of the previously developed SQ search. It follows the same search logic as the SQ algorithm with the difference in the annealing schedule which is much steeper, the initial search space is wider and the probability of uphill movement is higher at the beginning. This way the search is carried out more thoroughly in the initial stage, allowing stepper search progress sooner than in the original SQ approach. Furthermore, since the search space is reduced according to the exponential function, the maximum allowed displacement is reduced with temperature, and as consequence the search concentrates more on small space around the global minimum area. The performance of IFSQ decoupling module, based on 1500 iterations, shows good decoupling results, with slightly lower BER level when compared to the standard SQ search. Nevertheless, the required number of iterations is reduced by more than 90% which justifies the precision loss. The approach requires less processing power than SQ, and as such might be used in mobile phones inside the decoupling module.

With the introduction of normalization, the search domain is well defined between $\langle -1, 1 \rangle$, and the search depth is easily controlled with symbol resolution factor. This proposal allows the adaptation of implemented search methods to general decoupling problem offering at the same time constant precision and efficient optimization of search process with no restrictions on the physical coupling source nor signal constellation.

Acknowledgments

This work has been carried out in the frame of Spanish MCIN project TEC2009-14219-C03-01.

Author details

Igor Arambasic, Javier Casajus Quiros and Ivana Raos
ETSI Telecomunicacion, Universidad Politecnica de Madrid, Spain

6. References

[1] Arambasic, I. [2008]. *RF Front-End Non-Linear Coupling Cancellation*, PhD thesis, Escuela Técnica Superior de Ingenieros de Telecomunicación.

[2] Arambasic, I., Quiros, F. J. C. & Raos, I. [2007a]. Efficient rf front-end non-linear multi antenna coupling cancellation techniques, *PIMRC 2007. IEEE 18th International Symposium on Personal, Indoor and Mobile Radio Communications, 2007* pp. 1 – 5.

[3] Arambasic, I., Quiros, F. J. C. & Raos, I. [2007b]. Improvement of multiple antennas diversity systems through receiver nonlinear coupling cancellation, *2007. International Waveform Diversity and Design Conference* pp. 102 – 106.

[4] Drago, G., Manella, A., Nervi, M., Repetto, M. & Secondo, G. [1992]. A combined strategy for optimization in non linear magnetic problems using simulated annealing and search techniques, *IEEE Transactions on Magnetics* 28(2): 1541–1544.

[5] Finnerty, S. & Sen, S. [2004]. Simulated annealing based classification, *Sixth International Conference on Tools with Artificial Intelligence, 1994. Proceedings.* (Nov): 824 – 827.

[6] Forrest, S. [1996]. Genetic algorithms, *Computing Surveys* 28: 77–80.

[7] Ingber, L. [1989]. Very fast simulated re-annealing, *Lester Ingber Papers 89vfsr*, Lester Ingber. available at http://ideas.repec.org/p/lei/ingber/89vfsr.html.

[8] Ingber, L. [1993]. Simulated annealing: Practice versus theory, *Mathl. Comput. Modelling* 18(11): 29–57.

[9] Ingber, L. [1996]. Adaptive simulated annealing (asa): Lessons learned, *Lester Ingber Papers 96as*, Lester Ingber. available at http://ideas.repec.org/p/lei/ingber/96as.html.

[10] Ingber, L. & Rosen, B. [1992]. Genetic algorithms and very fast simulated reannealing: a comparison, *Mathematical and Computer Modelling* pp. 87–100.

[11] Johnson, D. S., Aragon, C. R., McGeoch, L. & Schevon, C. [1989]. Optimization by simulated annealing: An experimental evaluation, *Operations Research* pp. 865–892.

[12] Kirkpatric, S., Galett, C. D. & Vecchi, M. P. [1983]. Optimisation by simulated annealing, *Science* 220(4598): 621–680.

[13] Li, Y., Yao, J. & Yao, D. [2002]. An efficient composite simulated annealing algorithm for global optimization, *IEEE 2002 International Conference on Communications, Circuits and Systems and West Sino Expositions* 21: 1165– 1169.

[14] Mendonca, P. & Caloba, L. [1997]. New simulated annealing algorithms, *Proceedings of 1997 IEEE International Symposium on Circuits and Systems, 1997. ISCAS '97.* 3: 1668 – 1671.

[15] Renyuan, T., Shiyou, Y., Yan, L., Geng, W. & Tiemin, M. [1996]. Combined strategy of improved simulated annealing and genetic algorithm for inverse problem, *IEEE Transactions on Magnetics* 32: 1326 – 1329.

[16] Rosen, B. [1992]. Function optimization based on advanced simulated annealing, *Workshop on Physics and Computation, 1992* pp. 289–293.

[17] Szu, H. H. & Hartley, R. L. [1987]. Nonconvex optimization by fast simulated annealing, *Proceedings of the IEEE* 75(11): 1538 – 1540.

[18] van Laarhoven, P. J. M. & Aarts, E. [1987]. *Simulated Annealing: Theory and Applications*, D. Reidel.

Chapter 7

Simulated Annealing and Multiuser Scheduling in Mobile Communication Networks

Raymond Kwan, M. E. Aydin and Cyril Leung

Additional information is available at the end of the chapter

1. Introduction

Adaptive modulation and coding (AMC) is an effective way for improving the spectral efficiency in wireless communication systems. By increasing the size of the modulation scheme constellation, the spectral efficiency can be improved, generally at the cost of a degraded error rate. A similar trade-off is possible by using a higher rate channel code. By an appropriate combination of the modulation order and channel code rate, we can design a set of modulation and coding schemes (MCSs), from which an MCS is selected in an adaptive fashion in each transmission-time interval (TTI) in order to maximize system throughput under different channel conditions. The use of AMC yields a rich variety of scheduling strategies [25]; [12]. In practice, a commonly encountered constraint is that the probability of erroneous decoding of a Transmission Block should not exceed some threshold value [11].

Multiple orthogonal channelization codes (multicodes) can be used to transmit data to a single user, thereby increasing the per-user bit rate and the granularity of adaptation [11, 16]. In Wideband Code-Division Multiple Access (WCDMA), the channelization codes are often referred to as Orthogonal Variable Spreading Factor (OVSF) codes. The number of OVSF codes per base station (BS) is quite limited due to the orthogonality constraint [11] and thus OVSF codes and transmit power are scarce resources. Fig. 1 shows the number of OVSF codes as a function of the spreading factor for WCDMA. Note that a lower value of spreading factor corresponds to a higher bit rate and vice versa. According to Fig. 1, if a spreading factor of 2 is needed, the system can allocate at most two such OVSF codes. On the other hand, if a spreading factor of 4 is required, a total of 4 such codes can be allocated. In High Speed Downlink Packet Access (HSDPA), a fixed spreading factor of 16 has been specified, thereby limiting the number of OVSF codes to 16[1].

The allocation of the number of OVSF codes (or multicodes) and the MCS level for each user depends on the strength of the received signal at the user, which, in turn, depends on 1) the quality of the wireless channel, and 2) the level of the transmit power to the respective user.

---

[1] In principle, 16 OVSF codes can be used. However, one code is allocated for other purposes such as signalling. Thus, a maximum of 15 codes can be allocated for data traffic [11].

As shown in Fig. 2, if the spreading factor and the number of OVSF codes are fixed, one way to increase the user bit rate is to increase the MCS level. As each MCS level is associated with a specific signal quality requirement, the highest MCS level that can be allocated depends on the channel quality at the user receiver, which is stochastic by nature. Thus, at a given channel quality at the receiver, the MCS level can be increased by increasing the transmit power to the user. Another way to increase the user bit rate at a fixed spreading factor is to fix the MCS level while increasing the number of OVSF codes allocated to the respective user, as shown in Fig. 3. In order to achieve a given signal quality requirement for each OVSF code, a higher power level is required to be allocated to this user. Thus, the general problem of HSDPA resource allocation boils down to the joint allocation of user-specific MCS, number of OVSF codes, and power level over all users connected to a given base station, subject to the constraints of code and power resources as shown in Fig.4. It is important to note that this allocation is done very rapidly (on the order of two or more milliseconds) in order to exploit the channel diversity of the users. HSDPA is based on a shared channel concept, in which multiple users share the channel in a time-multiplexed fashion, and the process of resource allocation is performed at regular time intervals. Note that in HSDPA, as shown in Fig. 5, the shared channel is a dual to the dedicated channel in which the bit rate for each user is kept constant over a relatively long time period by appropriate closed-loop power control.

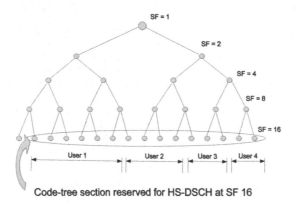

Figure 1. Orthogonal Variable Spreading Factor (OVSF) code tree.

For simplicity, the downlink transmit power is normally held constant (or slowly changing)[2] in HSDPA [11]. A number of scheduling algorithms have been proposed for HSDPA [7]. The most commonly encountered ones are (1) round-robin in which users are allocated resources in turn, regardless of channel conditions (2) Max C/I in which resources are allocated to the user with the best channel condition (3) proportional fair in which resources are assigned to the user with the *relatively* best channel condition. Other schedulers include minimum bit rate (MBR), MBR with proportional fairness and minimum delay (MD).

In exploiting multiuser diversity, a common way to achieve the best network throughput is to assign resources to a user with the largest signal-to-noise ratio (SNR) among all backlogged

---

[2] In some cases, the specification stipulates a slight power reduction for a mobile with an exceptionally good channel quality [22].

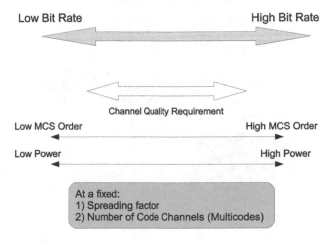

Figure 2. Bit rate and channel quality requirement trade-off for HSDPA.

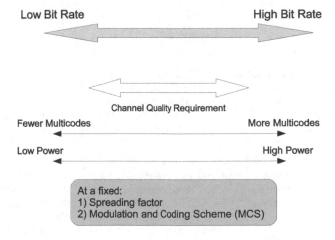

Figure 3. Bit rate and channel quality requirement trade-off for HSDPA.

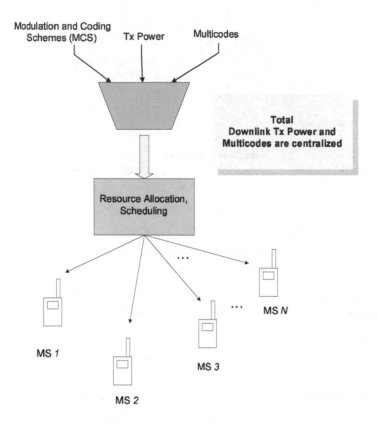

Figure 4. Resource allocation in HSDPA.

users (i.e. users with data to send) at the beginning of each scheduling period [5]. However, due to limited mobile capability, a user might not be able to utilize all the radio resources available at the BS. Thus, transmission to multiple users during a scheduling period may be more resource efficient. In [2, 15], the problem of downlink multiuser scheduling subject to limited code and power constraints is addressed. It is assumed in [15] that the exact path-loss and received interference power at every TTI for each user are fed back to the BS. This would require a large bandwidth overhead.

In this chapter, the problem of optimal (maximum aggregate throughput) multiuser scheduling in HSDPA is addressed[3]. The MCSs, numbers of multicodes and power levels for all users are jointly optimized at each scheduling period, given that only limited CSI information, as specified in the HSDPA standard [22], is fed back to the BS. This problem corresponds to a general resource allocation formulation for HSDPA, as compared to those in the existing literature, where resources are typically not allocated jointly among users for simplicity. Due to the inherent complexity, an integer programming formulation is proposed for the above problem. Due to the complexity of obtaining an optimal solution, an

---

[3] The materials presented here are mostly based on the contents in [14].

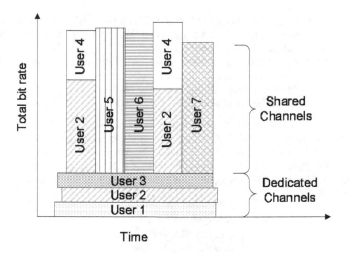

Figure 5. Resource allocation for shared and dedicated channels.

evolutionary simulated annealing (ESA) approach is explored. It is shown that ESA can provide a near-optimum performance with significantly reduced complexity.

2. System model

In a communication system, the quality of the channel is often quantified by the Signal to Interference and Noise Ratio (SINR), which is defined as the ratio of the received signal power relative to the power contribution from interference and noise. A better channel quality is represented by a higher received signal power and a smaller interference and noise power.

We consider downlink transmissions from a BS to a number of mobile users. Let P_i denote the downlink transmit power to user i, h_i denote the link gain from the BS to user i, and I_i be the total received interference and noise power at user i. The received SINR for user i is then given by

$$\gamma_i = \frac{h_i P_i}{I_i}, \; i = 1, \ldots, N,$$ (1)

where N is the number of users and

$$\sum_{i=1}^{N} P_i \leq P_T$$ (2)

where P_T is the total HSDPA power constraint. Ideally, the user would measure the received SINR, and report its value back to the BS. Upon receiving the SINR value for this user, the BS would decide what MCS and the number of multicodes that the user can be allocated, taking into account all the resource constraints that the BS has. However, if each user i were to send back its exact SINR value γ_i to the BS, the required feedback channel bandwidth would be impractically large. As specified in [22], the channel quality information fed back by a mobile, also known as the *channel quality indicator* (CQI), can only take on a finite number of non-negative integer values $\{0, 1, \ldots, K\}$. According to [22], the CQI is provided by the mobile via the High Speed Dedicated Physical Control Channel (HS-DPCCH). Each CQI value maps directly to a maximum bit rate[4] that a mobile can support, based on the channel quality and mobile capability [23], while ensuring that the block error rate (BLER) does not exceed 10%. Finally, upon receiving the CQIs from all the users, the BS decides on the most appropriate combination of MCS and number of multicodes for each user.

Although the mapping between the CQI and the SINR is not specified in [22], it has been discussed in various proposals [18]; [13]. In [8], a mapping is proposed in which the system throughput is maximized while the BLER constraint is relaxed. Let $\tilde{\gamma}_i = 10 \log_{10}(\gamma_i)$ be the received SINR value, in dB, for user i and let q_i be the CQI value that user i reports back to the BS via HS-DPCCH. The mapping between q_i and $\tilde{\gamma}_i$ can generally be expressed as a piece-wise linear function [6, 8, 18]

$$
q_i = \begin{cases} 0 & \tilde{\gamma}_i \leq t_{i,0} \\ \lfloor c_{i,1}\tilde{\gamma}_i + c_{i,2} \rfloor & t_{i,0} < \tilde{\gamma}_i \leq t_{i,1} \\ q_{i,max} & \tilde{\gamma}_i > t_{i,1} \end{cases} \tag{3}
$$

where the terms $\{c_{i,1}, c_{i,2}, t_{i,0}, t_{i,1}\}$ are model and mobile capability dependent constants, and $\lfloor . \rfloor$ denotes the floor function. Due to the quantization operation implied in (3), $\tilde{\gamma}_i$ cannot generally be recovered exactly from the value of q_i alone. It should be noted that the region $t_{i,0} < \tilde{\gamma}_i \leq t_{i,1}$ is the operating region for the purpose of link adaptation. This region should be chosen large enough to accommodate the SINR variations encountered in most practical scenarios [11], i.e. the probability that $\tilde{\gamma}_i$ falls outside this region should be quite small. As part of our proposed procedure, $\tilde{\gamma}_i$ is approximated as

$$
\tilde{\gamma}_i^{\dagger} = \tilde{\gamma}_i^{(l)} + \left(\tilde{\gamma}_i^{(u)} - \tilde{\gamma}_i^{(l)} \right) \xi, \tag{4}
$$

where

$$
\tilde{\gamma}_i^{(l)} = \frac{q_i - c_{i,2}}{c_{i,1}}, \tag{5}
$$

$$
\tilde{\gamma}_i^{(u)} = \frac{q_i + 1 - c_{i,2}}{c_{i,1}}, \tag{6}
$$

and ξ is a uniformly distributed random variable, i.e. $\xi \sim U(0, 1)$. In a more conservative design, the value of ξ could be set to 0. Note that this approximation assumes that $\tilde{\gamma}_i$ is uniformly distributed between $\tilde{\gamma}_i^{(l)}$ and $\tilde{\gamma}_i^{(u)}$ for a given value of q_i.

For $q_i = 0$ and $q_i = q_{i,max}$, $\tilde{\gamma}_i$ could be approximated as $t_{i,0}$ and $t_{i,1}$ respectively, or more generally as $t_{i,0} - \xi_{i,0}$ and $t_{i,1} + \xi_{i,1}$ respectively, with $\xi_{i,0}$ and $\xi_{i,1}$ following some pre-defined probability distributions. Finally, the estimated value of γ_i is given by $\hat{\gamma}_i = 10^{\tilde{\gamma}_i^{\dagger}/10}$. We refer to the mapping from SINR to q_i in (3) as the *forward mapping*, and the approximation of SINR based on the received value of q_i in (4) as the *reverse mapping*.

---

[4] In this chapter, the bit rate refers to the transport block size, i.e. the maximum number of radio link control (RLC) protocol data bit (PDU) bits that a transport block can carry, divided by the duration of a TTI, i.e. 2 ms [11].

3. Joint optimal scheduling

Note that the value of the channel quality, q_i, reported by user i indicates the rate index that is associated with the maximum bit rate that the user can be supported by the BS, and is related jointly to a required number of OVSF codes (multicodes) and MCS. The number of multicodes and MCS assigned to each user as well as the estimated SINR values of the users determine the transmit power required by the BS. Since the number of multicodes and transmit power are limited, the BS might not be able to simultaneously satisfy the bit rate requests for all users as indicated by $\{q_i, i = 1, \ldots, N\}$. Therefore, for a set $\{q_i, i = 1, \ldots, N\}$, the BS must calculate a set of *modified* CQIs, $\{J_i, i = 1, \ldots, N\}$, for all users by taking into account the transmit power and number of multicodes constraints.

From the *forward* and *reverse* mappings in (3) and (4), the modified CQIs are chosen as

$$J_i = \min\left(\max\left(\eta_i(\tilde{\gamma}_i^\dagger, \phi_i), 0\right), q_{i,max}\right), i = 1, \ldots, N \tag{7}$$

where ϕ_i is the power adjustment factor for user i, i.e. $\hat{\gamma}_i \mapsto \phi_i \hat{\gamma}_i$, and

$$\eta_i(\tilde{\gamma}_i^\dagger, \phi_i) = \lfloor c_{i,1}\left(\tilde{\gamma}_i^\dagger + 10\log_{10}\phi_i\right) + c_{i,2}\rfloor, \tag{8}$$

$$0 \le \phi_i \le 10^{\left(\frac{q_{i,max}-(c_{i,1}\tilde{\gamma}_i^\dagger + c_{i,2})}{10c_{i,1}}\right)}. \tag{9}$$

Fig. 6 summarizes the conversion process from the received CQI, q_i, to the final assigned rate index, J_i.

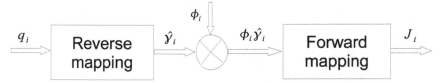

Figure 6. The conversion process from the received CQI, q_i, from the mobile to the assigned rate index J_i at the base station. ([14]©IET)

The multiuser joint optimal scheduling problem **P1** can be expressed as

$$\mathbf{P1}: \quad \max_{\mathbf{A}, \underline{\phi}} \sum_{i=1}^{N} \sum_{j=0}^{J_i} a_{i,j} r_{i,j} \tag{10}$$

subject to (7)-(9) and

$$\sum_{j=0}^{J_i} a_{i,j} = 1, \ \forall i, \tag{11}$$

$$\sum_{i=1}^{N} \sum_{j=0}^{J_i} a_{i,j} n_{i,j} \le N_{max}, \tag{12}$$

$$a_{i,j} \in \{0,1\}, \tag{13}$$

$$\sum_{i=1}^{N} \phi_i \le N. \tag{14}$$

In (10), J_i is the maximum allowable CQI value for user i and $r_{i,j}$ denotes the achievable bit rate for user i and CQI value j [22]; the decision variable $a_{i,j}$ is equal to 1 if rate index j is assigned to user i; otherwise, $a_{i,j} = 0$. In (12), N_{max} is the maximum number of multicodes available for HSDPA at the BS and $n_{i,j}$ is the required number of multicodes for user i and CQI value j [22]. Depending on multicode availability, the assigned combination of MCS and the number of multicodes may correspond to a bit rate that is smaller than that permitted by J_i. The constraint in (14) can be obtained by substituting $P_i = \phi_i P_T / N$ into (2). The objective in the optimization problem **P1** is to choose $\mathbf{A} = \{a_{i,j}\}$ and $\phi = \{\phi_i\}$ at each TTI so as to maximize the sum bit rate for all users, subject to (7)-(9) and (11)-(14).

4. Linearization

It is important to note that the quantity J_i, which appears in the upper summation index in (10), is itself a function of the decision variable ϕ_i. On the other hand, ϕ_i is related to J_i via a non-linear relationship (9). Thus, the problem **P1** is not a standard linear integer programming problem. As such a problem is highly non-linear, a global optimal solution is very difficult to obtain. To solve problem **P1** with linear integer programming methods, the problem needs to be appropriately transformed into a linear problem by introducing additional auxiliary variables. The first step is to re-formulate the model as follows:

$$\mathbf{P1'}: \quad \max_{\mathbf{A},\phi} \sum_{i=1}^{N} \sum_{j=0}^{q_{i,max}} b_{i,j} a_{i,j} r_{i,j} \tag{15}$$

subject to

$$\sum_{j=0}^{q_{i,max}} b_{i,j} a_{i,j} = 1, \ \forall i, \tag{16}$$

$$\sum_{i=1}^{N} \sum_{j=0}^{q_{i,max}} b_{i,j} a_{i,j} n_{i,j} \leq N_{max}, \tag{17}$$

together with (7)-(9),(13)-(14), where the new variable $b_{i,j}$

$$b_{i,j} = \begin{cases} 0, j > J_i \\ 1, j \leq J_i \end{cases} \tag{18}$$

is introduced to limit the rate index j to no higher than J_i.

After the above re-formulation, Problem **P1'** is still non-linear due to terms involving the product $a_{i,j} b_{i,j}$, and the presence of the floor function $\lfloor . \rfloor$ and the logarithm in (7). Subsequent linearlization of Problem **P1'**, involves introducing a new decision variable $m_{i,j} = a_{i,j} b_{i,j}$ and re-writing the problem as follows:

$$\mathbf{P1''}: \quad \max_{\mathbf{A},\mathbf{B},\phi} \sum_{i=1}^{N} \sum_{j=0}^{q_{i,max}} m_{i,j} r_{i,j} \tag{19}$$

subject to

$$\sum_{j=0}^{q_{i,max}} m_{i,j} = 1, \ \forall i, \tag{20}$$

$$\sum_{i=1}^{N} \sum_{j=0}^{q_{i,max}} m_{i,j} n_{i,j} = \ \leq N_{max}, \tag{21}$$

$$m_{i,j} \leq b_{i,j}, \ \forall i,j \tag{22}$$

$$m_{i,j} \leq a_{i,j} M, \ \forall i,j \tag{23}$$

$$m_{i,j} \geq b_{i,j} - (1 - a_{i,j}) M, \ \forall i,j \tag{24}$$

$$e_{i,j} - \phi_i \leq (1 - \omega_{i,j}) M, \ \forall i,j, \tag{25}$$

$$\phi_i - e_{i,j+1} \leq (1 - \omega_{i,j}) M, \ \forall i,j, \tag{26}$$

$$J_i = \sum_{j=0}^{q_{i,max}} j \omega_{i,j}, \forall i, \tag{27}$$

$$j - J_i \leq (1 - b_{i,j}) M, \ \forall i,j \tag{28}$$

$$J_i + 1 - j \leq b_{i,j} M, \ \forall i,j \tag{29}$$

$$\sum_{j=0}^{q_{i,max}} \omega_{i,j} = 1 \tag{30}$$

$$b_{i,j}, a_{i,j}, m_{i,j}, \omega_{i,j} \in \{0,1\} \tag{31}$$

together with (14), where

$$e_{i,j} = \begin{cases} -M & \text{if } j = 0 \\ 10^{\left(\frac{j - (c_{i,1} \hat{\tau}_i^{\dagger} + c_{i,2})}{10 c_{i,1}}\right)} & \text{if } 1 \leq j \leq q_{i,max} \\ M & \text{if } j = q_{i,max} + 1, \end{cases} \tag{32}$$

and M is a large number. In this new formulation, constraints (22)-(24) model the product $a_{i,j} b_{i,j}$, while (25)-(27) models the floor and the max functions in (7) and the constraint in (9). The constraints (28)-(30) are used to linearize the expression defined in (18). Note that the introduction of auxiliary variables increases the size of the model, and, thereby, increases the complexity of the problem. The linearized Problem **P1″** was solved using a commercial optimization software package implementing the branch-and-bound method [19]. An alternative method to solve Problem **P1** is to use meta-heuristics and is discussed in Section 5.

5. Simulated annealing

Meta-heuristic approaches attract much attention with their success in solving hard combinatorial and optimization problems. One of these successful approaches is Simulated annealing (SA) [24], which is proven to be a powerful meta-heuristic approach used for optimization in many combinatorial problems. In SA, a probabilistic decision making process is typically involved, in which a control parameter, often known as temperature τ, is used to control the probability of accepting a poorer solution in the neighborhood of the current solution. The idea is to provide the possibility of reaching a better solution by diversifying the search within search space, redirecting the search in a new neighborhood when the chance of discovering a better solution within the old neighborhood is not high. The algorithm explores the solution space through a simulated cooling process from a given initial (hot) temperature to a final (frozen) temperature. At a higher temperature, the probability of selecting the poorer solution is higher, and thereby allowing the search to be more extensive within the solution space. However, as the temperature decreases, the search becomes more confined in the region near the desirable solution within the solution space, and thereby providing a refinement to the existing solution. Essentially, the search is conducted through two nested loops; the outer one decreases the temperature using a particular cooling schedule, while the inner one repeats the search at the same temperature. Within the inner loop, a sequence of solutions are obtained by manipulating the current solution. Each solution is the result of one iteration.

Let x_n be the solution at iteration n, and $x_n' = N(x_n)$, where $N(x_n)$ is some neighbor function of x_n. The next solution in the search process is a probabilistic function of x_n, and is given by [24]

$$x_{n+1} = \begin{cases} x_n', & \text{if } s(x_n') > s(x_n) \\ x_n', & \text{if } r < e^{-\Delta s / \tau_k} \\ x_n, & \text{otherwise} \end{cases} , \tag{33}$$

where τ_k corresponds to the kth temperature level, $s(\cdot)$ is the objective function to be maximized, $\Delta s = s(x_n) - s(x_n')$, and r is the outcome of a random variable which is uniformly distributed in [0,1]. This method for choosing a new solution is commonly referred to as the Metropolis rule [24]. The motivation is to diversify the search process, thereby reducing the possibility of locally optimal solutions. As the temperature decreases, so does the probability of accepting a worse solution.

SA has become a basis which inspires different algorithmic variations for solving a large variety of optimization problems. *Evolutionary* Simulated Annealing (ESA) is one of these recently developed population-based SA algorithm enhanced with evolutionary operators [3]. Instead of manipulating a single solution, ESA makes use of a population of solutions in order to combine the advantages of both SA and population-based approaches. A single instance of SA is devised to act as an evolutionary operator and is invoked successively starting at a fixed initial temperature each time. Each invocation of SA is commonly referred to as a *generation*. ESA evolves the population of solutions with the SA operator alongside the selection and replacement operators *generation-by-generation*. The idea is to decrease the temperature during each SA operation and raise it back to the fixed initial value whenever the SA operator is invoked. These artificially induced fluctuations in temperature allows the solution space to be explored more thoroughly, ad thereby reducing the possibility of being trapped in local optima. Recently, a comprehensive study on implementing ESA for facility location problems has been reported in [26].

In this chapter, we propose to use the ESA algorithm to solve the multiuser scheduling problem as outlined in (7)-(14) due to its ability to cope with the highly non-linear nature of the problem. Our ESA implementation consists of two components - an initial solution, and an SA operator. The SA operator is invoked once per generation for G generations. For each SA operation, a search is conducted over N_τ different temperatures. Starting with an initial temperature τ_{hot}, the k-th temperature level is given by

$$\tau_k = \tau_{hot}\theta^{k-1}, k = 1, 2, \ldots, N_\tau, \tag{34}$$

where $\theta \in (0,1)$ is the cooling coefficient. The N_τ-th temperature level is also referred to as the frozen temperature τ_{frozen}. Note that the combined use of (33) and (34) corresponds to a variant of simulated annealing known as the *Simulated Quenching* (SQ) [9].

In the proposed scheme, each temperature level is associated with U iterations. For each iteration, a user i is randomly selected, resulting in a solution to the problem of the form

$$x_n = (\phi_1, \ldots, \phi_i, \ldots, \phi_N, \mathbf{a}_1, \ldots, \mathbf{a}_i, \ldots, \mathbf{a}_N), \tag{35}$$

at iteration $n \in \{1, \ldots, U\}$, where $\mathbf{a}_i = (a_{i,1}, a_{i,2}, \ldots, a_{i,J_i})$.

By applying function $f(.)$ to the current value of ϕ_i, new solutions can be generated. Each new value, ϕ_i', is obtained by applying the function $f(.)$ successively until ϕ_i' satisfies (9) and (14). Once a suitable ϕ_i' is available, the corresponding J_i is then obtained using (7). Subsequently, the value of a_{i,J_i} is set to 1 while the remaining elements are set to 0, i.e. $\mathbf{a}_i = \{\overbrace{0,0,\ldots,1}^{J_i+1}\}$. If constraint (12) is violated, $\mathbf{a}_i$ is cyclically shifted to the left by one position, i.e. $\mathbf{a}_i = \{\overbrace{0,0,\ldots,1,0}^{J_i+1}\}$. This process is repeated until (12) is satisfied, resulting in an updated vector $\mathbf{a}_i'$. Subsequently, the new solution is given by

$$x_n' = (\phi_1, \ldots, \phi_i', \ldots, \phi_N, \mathbf{a}_1, \ldots, \mathbf{a}_i', \ldots \mathbf{a}_N). \tag{36}$$

The computational complexity of ESA in terms of the number, N, of users at given values of G and N_τ is discussed as follows. The number of iterations, U, of solutions explored at each temperature is chosen to be N. Thus, the time required to check whether a solution x_n' in (36) satisfies constraints (12) and (14) has a complexity of $\mathcal{O}(N)$. Subsequently, due to the fact that the time to verify these constraints grows linearly with N, the complexity of ESA is $\mathcal{O}(N^2)$.

As both SA and ESA are heuristic algorithms, solutions obtained by these methods may not necessarily be optimal, but are generally close to optimal. The "temperature" parameter determines trade-off between the speed of convergence towards the optimal value, and how far the solution is relative to that of the optimal. Generally, a higher temperature allows the optimal value to be approached faster, while a lower temperature provides improved fine-tuning, and thereby improving the solution quality. ESA converges faster than conventional SA since the search is diversified by periodically re-increasing the temperature. As with any heuristic algorithm, a detailed convergence study requires the determination of appropriate parameter values through experimentation.

6. Simulation results

A number of different simulation cases were used to illustrate the effectiveness of ESA for the multiuser HSDPA resource allocation problem. The first case involves $N = 2$ users, and the following values $t_{i,0} = -4.5$, $t_{i,1} = 25.5$, $c_{i,1} = 1$, $d_{i,1} = 4.5$, and $q_{i,max} = 30$ for $i = 1,2$ are used for the parameters in (3). These values are obtained from [18], assuming that the mobiles are of category 10 (i.e. have a wide CQI range) as defined in [22]. Values for $n_{i,j}$ and $r_{i,j}$ are obtained from [22]. The fading channel following the general Nakagami model [21] is assumed so that $\{\gamma_i, i = 1,2\}$ in (1) are outcomes of Gamma distributed random variables

$\{\Gamma_i, i = 1, 2\}$ with pdfs given by

$$f_{\Gamma_i}(\gamma) = \begin{cases} \left(\frac{\alpha_i}{\overline{\Gamma}_i}\right)^{\alpha_i} \frac{\gamma^{\alpha_i-1}}{\Gamma(\alpha_i)} \exp\left(\frac{-\alpha_i\gamma}{\overline{\Gamma}_i}\right) & \gamma \geq 0 \\ 0 & \gamma < 0 \end{cases}, \tag{37}$$

where $\Gamma(.)$ is the Gamma function, α_i is the fading figure, and $\overline{\Gamma}_i$ is the mean of Γ_i. The parameter values are listed in Table 1. Let $\boldsymbol{\Gamma} = \{\Gamma_1 \ \Gamma_2\}$, and let the aggregate transport block size (TBS), T, per TTI be

Scenario	User i	$\overline{\Gamma}_i$ (in dB)	α_i
I	1	5	6.5
	2	6	3
II	1	12	6.5
	2	10	3
III	1	17	6.5
	2	16	3

Table 1. List of parameter values used ([14]©IET)

$$T = \sum_{i=1}^{N} \sum_{j=0}^{J_i} a_{i,j} r_{i,j}. \tag{38}$$

The performance improvements of the proposed Joint Global Optimum (JGO) and ESA approaches, as discussed in sections 4 and 5 respectively, are compared to that of a simple greedy (SG) algorithm. The idea behind the SG algorithm is to allocate resources to users in decreasing order of their estimated SINR values, $\hat{\gamma}_i$. In other words, the user with the highest $\hat{\gamma}$ is first allocated as much resources as it can possibly use. Subsequently, remaining resources that can be productively used are then assigned to the user with the next highest $\hat{\gamma}$. This allocation of resources continues until resources are exhausted.

Fig. 7 shows the cumulative distribution function (CDF) of T for the three different scenarios in Table 1. The results in this figure are obtained based on two thousand channel realizations. It can be seen that ESA can achieve a performance that is close to the optimal. A summary of the average performance, i.e. $E_{\Gamma}[T]$, for all three schemes is presented in Table 2. It can be seen that both JGO and ESA can provide a good throughput improvement over SG.

The second study involves the comparison of performance among the three algorithms by increasing the number of users from 2 to 5. The average computation times per TTI required by JGO, ESA, and SG on a personal computer with an Intel Core™ 2 Duo T5500 processor are plotted as a function of the number of users in Fig. 8. As expected, SG is the fastest and JGO is the slowest. The running for ESA is about 0.1 s per TTI and increases slowly with the number of users. With the use of parallel dedicated processors at the BS, ESA becomes a viable alternative to SG. Fig. 9 shows the average computation time, normalized to the 2-user case, as a function of the number of users; the average is taken over only twenty channel realizations due to the long simulations times needed for JGO. The following parameter values are used: $\alpha_1 = \alpha_2 = \ldots = \alpha_N = 5$ and $\overline{\Gamma}_1 = \overline{\Gamma}_2 = \ldots = \overline{\Gamma}_N = 8.45$ dB. It can be seen clearly that even though JGO provides a globally optimal solution, the complexity increases very rapidly with

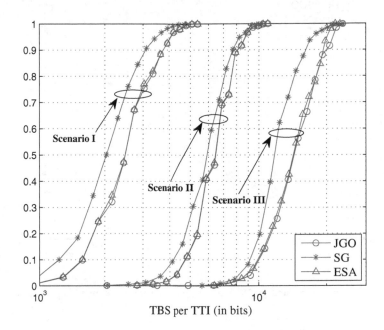

Figure 7. CDF of the aggregate bit rate in TBS per TTI. ([14]©IET)

Scenario	Scheme	ATBS/TTI (kbits)	Gain (%)
	SG	2.151	0
I	ESA	2.588	20.03
	JGO	2.591	20.42
	SG	6.031	0
II	ESA	6.492	7.64
	JGO	6.507	7.88
	SG	12.472	0
III	ESA	14.587	16.95
	JGO	14.944	19.82

Table 2. Average rate (in TBS per TTI) for the three different algorithms under the three scenarios. ([14]©IET)

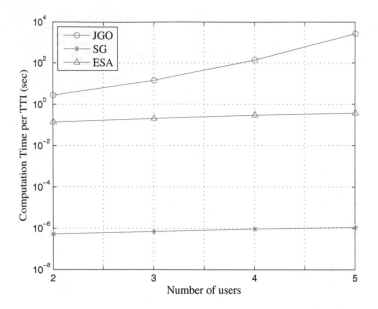

Figure 8. Average computation time per TTI as a function of the number of users. ([14]©IET)

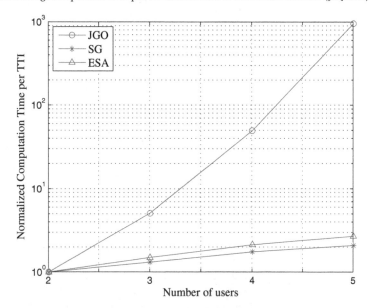

Figure 9. Average computation time per TTI, normalized to the 2-user case, as a function of the number of users. ([14]©IET)

the number of users. On the other hand, ESA offers a very similar performance at a much reduced complexity.

Fig. 10 shows the CDFs of T for SG and ESA for different numbers of users. As in Fig. 9, $\alpha_1 = \alpha_2 = \ldots = \alpha_N = 5$ and $\bar{\Gamma}_1 = \bar{\Gamma}_2 = \ldots = \bar{\Gamma}_N = 8.45$ dB. The CDF curves for JGO are not shown due to the excessively long running times but are expected to be close to those for ESA. Table 3 shows the average aggregate TBS per TTI values for SG and ESA. It can be seen that the performance improvement of ESA over SG increases with the number of users.

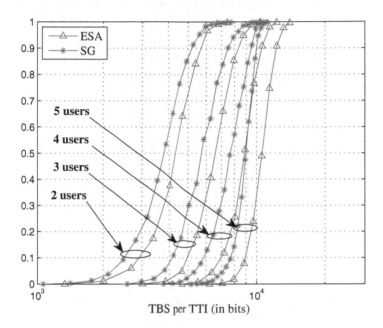

Figure 10. CDF of the aggregate bit rate in TBS per TTI for SG and ESA with different number of users. ([14]©IET)

No. of Users	Scheme	ATBS/TTI (kbits)	Gain (%)
2	ESA	4.324	12.21
	SG	3.853	0
3	ESA	6.676	14.75
	SG	5.818	0
4	ESA	8.865	15.41
	SG	7.681	0
5	ESA	10.651	20.00
	SG	8.877	0

Table 3. Average rates (in TBS per TTI) for the ESA and SG algorithms with different number of users. For each user, $\alpha = 5$ and $\bar{\Gamma} = 8.45$ dB. ([14]©IET)

The CDFs of T for ESA, SG, max C/I, and Round Robin (RR) with five users are plotted in Fig. 11. Note that max C/I is a special case of SG in which, for each TTI, resources are allocated only to the user with the best channel condition. On the other hand, RR refers to a base-line scheduling scheme, whereby each user is scheduled one at a time in a round robin fashion. Under such a scheme, the respective channel quality of the users are not used during the scheduling. The corresponding values of $E_T[T]$ for ESA, SG, max C/I, and RR are 10.6, 8.8, 2.8, and 1.9 bits per TTI respectively. The prominent steps in the CDFs for RR and max C/I are due to the coarse quantization resulting from allocation of resources to only one user in each TTI. It can be seen that RR has the lowest bit rate as it does not take into account user channel conditions.

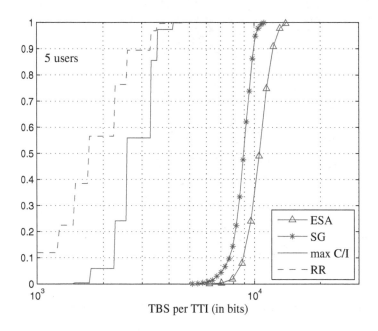

Figure 11. CDF of the aggregate bit rate in TBS per TTI for ESA, max C/I, and Round Robin (RR) with five users. ([14]©IET)

7. Conclusion

In this chapter, the issue of allocating resources to multiple users simultaneously in HSDPA has been examined via a number of optimization methods. The problem formulation based on the channel feedback scheme specified in the WCDMA standard has been presented. Simulation results have shown that both the global optimal and the simulated annealing-based methods can provide a substantial throughput improvement over a more simple greedy algorithm. It has been observed that the method based on simulated annealing can achieve a bit rate that is very close to that of the global optimal, with a much lower computational complexity. The advantage of simulated annealing-based method relative to the simple greedy method increases with the number of users. In this chapter, it was assumed that the user SINR values, on which the channel quality indicators are based, can be accurately estimated. One research direction would be to study the performance degradation due to noisy SIR estimates and methods in reducing this degradation. Another potential study item is to investigate the benefits and trade-offs of other heuristic optimization methods for the same problem.

Acknowledgement

This work was supported in part by the Natural Sciences and Engineering Research Council (NSERC) of Canada under Grant OGP0001731, by the UBC PMC-Sierra Professorship in Networking and Communications and by a Marie Curie International Incoming Fellowship PIIF-GA-2008-221380.

Author details

Raymond Kwan and M. E. Aydin
University of Bedfordshire, United Kingdom

Cyril Leung
University of British Columbia, Canada

8. References

[1] Abedi, S. [2005]. Efficient Radio Resource Management for Wireless Multimedia Communications: A Multidimensional QoS-Based Packet Scheduler, *IEEE Transactions on Wireless Communications* 4(6): 2811 – 2822.

[2] Aniba, G. & Aissa, S. [2005]. Resource Allocation in HSDPA using Best-Users Selection Under Code Constraints, *Proc. of IEEE Vehicular Technology Conference, Spring*, Vol. 1, pp. 319 – 323.

[3] Aydin, M. E. & Fogarty, T. C. [2004]. A Distributed Evolutionary Simulated Annealing Algorithm for Combinatorial Optimisation Problems , *Journal of Heuristics* 10(3): 269 – 292.

[4] Baum, K. L., Kostas, T. A., Sartori, P. J. & Classon, B. K. [2003]. Performance Characteristics of Cellular Systems with Different Link Adaptation Strategies, *IEEE Transactions on Vehicular Technology* 52(6): 1497 – 1507.

[5] Bedekar, A., Borst, S. C., Ramanan, K., Whiting, P. A. & Yeh, E. M. [1999]. Downlink Scheduling in CDMA Data Network, *Proc. of IEEE Global Telecommunications Conference, GLOBECOM '99*, Vol. 5, pp. 2653–2657.

[6] Brouwer, F., de Bruin, I., Silva, J. C., Souto, N., Cercas, F. & Correia, A. [2004]. Usage of Link-Level Performance Indicators for HSDPA Network-Level Simulation in E-UMTS, *Proc. of International Symposium on Spread Spectrum Techniques and Applications (ISSSTA)*, Sydney, Australia.

[7] Dahlman, E., Parkvall, S., Sköld, J. & Beming, P. [2007]. *3G HSPA and LTE for Mobile Broadband*, Academic Press.

[8] Freudenthaler, K., Springer, A. & Wehinger, J. [2007]. Novel SINR-to-CQI Mapping Maximizing the Throughput in HSDPA, *Proc. of IEEE Wireless Communications and Networking Conference (WCNC)*, Hong Kong, China.

[9]   H.A. Oliveira, J., Ingber, L., Petraglia, A., Petraglia, M., Machado, M. & Petraglia, M. [2012]. *Stochastic global optimization and its applications with fuzzy adaptive simulated annealing*, Springer.

[10] Haleem, M. A. & Chandramouli, R. [2005]. Adaptive Downlink Scheduling and Rate Selection: A Cross-Layer Design, *IEEE Journal on Selected Areas in Communications* 23(6): 1287 – 1297.

[11] Holma, H. & Toskala, A. (eds) [2006]. *HSDPA/HSUPA For UMTS High Speed Radio Access for Mobile Communications*, John Wiley & Sons.

[12] Jeon, W. S., Jeong, D. G. & Kim, B. [2004]. Packet Scheduler for Mobile Internet Services using High Speed Downlink Packet Access, *IEEE Transactions on Wireless Communications* 3(5): 1789 – 1801.

[13] Ko, K., Lee, D., Lee, M. & Lee, H. [2006]. Novel SIR to Channel-Quality Indicator (CQI) mapping method for HSDPA System, *Proc. of IEEE Vehicular Technology Conference (VTC)*, Montreal, Canada.

[14] Kwan, R., Aydin, M. E., Leung, C. & Zhang, J. [2009]. Multiuser Scheduling in High Speed Downlink Packet Access, *IET Communications* 3(8): 1363 – 1370.

[15] Kwan, R. & Leung, C. [2007]. Downlink Scheduling Schemes for CDMA Networks with Adaptive Modulation and Coding and Multicodes, *IEEE Transactions on Wireless Communications* 6(10): 3668 – 3677.

[16] Lee, S. J., Lee, H. W. & Sung, D. K. [1999]. Capacities of Single-Code and Multicode DS-CDMA Systems Accommodating Multiclass Service, *IEEE Trans. on Vehicular Technology* 48(2): 376 –384.

[17] Liu, Q., Zhou, S. & Giannakis, G. B. [2005]. Cross-Layer Scheduling with Prescribed QoS Guarantees in Adaptive Wireless Networks, *IEEE Journal on Selected Areas in Communications* 23(5): 1056 – 1066.

[18] Motorola & Nokia [2002]. Revised CQI Proposal, *Technical Report R1-02-0675*, 3GPP RAN WG1.

[19] Rardin, R. [1998]. *Optimization in Operations Research*, Prentice Hall, Upper Saddle River, NJ.

[20] Rhee, J.-H., Holtzman, J. M. & Kim, D. K. [2004]. Performance Analysis of the Adaptive EXP/PF Channel Scheduler in an AMC/TDM System, *IEEE Communications Letters* 8(8): 497 – 499.

[21] Simon, M. K. & Alouini, M.-S. [2000]. *Digital Communication over Fading Channels: A Unified Approach to Performance Analysis*, John Wiley & Sons.

[22] *Universal Mobile Telecommunications Systems (UMTS); Physical Layer Procedures (FDD)* [2007]. *Technical Specification 3GPP TS25.214*, 3rd Generation Partnership Project.

[23] *Universal Mobile Telecommunications Systems (UMTS); UE Radio Access Capabilities* [2007]. *Technical Specification 3GPP TS25.306*, 3rd Generation Partnership Project.

[24] Van Laarhoven, P. J. M. & Aarts, E. H. [1987]. *Simulated Annealing: Theory and Applications*, Kluwer Academic Publishers, New York.

[25] Yang, J., Khandani, A. K. & Tin, N. [2005]. Statistical Decision Making in Adaptive Modulation and Coding for 3G Wireless System, *IEEE Transactions on Vehicular Technology* 54(6): 2006 – 2073.

[26] Yigit, V., Aydin, M. E. & Turkbey, O. [2006]. Solving large-scale uncapacitated facility location problems with evolutionary simulated annealing , *International Journal of Production Research* 44(22): 4773 – 4791.

[27] Zerlin, B., Ivrlac, M., Utschick, W., Nossek, J., Viering, I. & Klein, A. [2005]. Joint Optimization of Radio Parameters in HSDPA, *Proc. of IEEE Vehicular Technology Conference, Spring*, Vol. 1, pp. 295 – 299.

Chapter 8

Application of Simulated Annealing in Water Resources Management: Optimal Solution of Groundwater Contamination Source Characterization Problem and Monitoring Network Design Problems

Manish Jha and Bithin Datta

Additional information is available at the end of the chapter

1. Introduction

Estimating various characteristics of an unknown groundwater pollutant source can be formulated as an optimization problem using linked simulation-optimization. Meta-heuristics based optimization algorithms such as Simulated Annealing (SA), Genetic Algorithm (GA), Tabu Search etc. are now being accepted as reliable, faster and simpler ways to solve this optimization problem. In this chapter we discuss the suitability of a variant of traditional Simulated Annealing (SA) known as the Adaptive Simulated Annealing (ASA) in solving unknown groundwater pollutant source characterization problem. Growing anthropogenic activities and improper management of their impacts on groundwater quality has resulted in widespread contamination of groundwater worldwide. Coupled with ever increasing water demand leading to increased reliance on groundwater, it has resulted in a widespread recognition of public health risk posed by contaminated groundwater. This has triggered massive efforts for better management of groundwater quality in general and remediation of contaminated aquifers in particular. The sources of contamination in groundwater are often hidden and inaccessible. Characteristics of these pollutant sources such as their location, periods of activity and contaminant release history are often unknown. Groundwater contaminant source identification problem aims at estimating various characteristics of an unknown groundwater pollutant source using measured contaminant concentrations at a number of monitoring locations over a period of time. It has been widely accepted that for any remediation strategy to work efficiently, it is very important to know the pollutant source characteristic. A detailed account of different categories of source identification problems and various approaches to solve them has been presented in Pinder [26].

Typically, groundwater contamination is first detected by one or more arbitrarily located well or monitoring location. Unknown Groundwater source identification problem specifically attempts to ascertain the following source characteristics:

1. Source Type (point, areal etc.)
2. Spatial location and extent of the source
3. Release pattern (slug, continuous, intermittent etc.)
4. Point of time when the source first became active (start time)
5. Contaminant flux released as a function of time elapsed since start time (release history)

Source type is often obvious. In some cases, information on groundwater contaminant source location may be available from preliminary investigations. If an exhaustive record of pollutant inventory and industrial activities of the area is available, it may be possible to infer start time. Release history of the source, however, is difficult to ascertain as the source is not physically accessible for measurements and hence it is unlikely that any accurate temporal record of contaminant fluxes released from the source exists.

Release history reconstruction problem is one of the most widely studied groundwater source identification problems. Ascertaining release history of the contaminant sources from available contaminant concentration measurements is an inverse problem as it requires solving groundwater flow and transport equations backwards in time and space. The process of solving this inverse problem is essentially the process of finding various unknown characteristics of source using observed information about the transport media and the effects caused by the source. In such circumstances, a solution cannot be guaranteed, especially when observed information is sparse. Even if the solution exists, it may not be unique. This is because different combinations of various source characteristics can produce the same effect at a monitoring location. Moreover, the solution of this problem is highly sensitive to measurement errors either in the observation data or model parameters and hence this problem has been classified as an ill-posed inverse problem[33] . When this inverse problem has to be solved by using inaccurate values of media parameters such as hydraulic conductivity and porosity and contaminant concentration observed at arbitrarily placed monitoring wells, it becomes even more challenging to obtain a reliable solution.

Methods proposed in the past to solve this ill-posed inverse problem can be broadly classified as optimization approaches, analytical solutions, deterministic direct methods and probabilistic and geo-statistical simulation approaches. A detailed review of these methodologies can be found in Atmadja & Bagtzoglou [2]; Michalak & Kitanidis [25]; Bagtzoglou & Atmadja [3] and Sun et al. [31, 32]. The most effective of all suggested methods seems to be those based on optimization or probabilistic and geo-statistical simulation. Of the optimization methods, linked simulation-optimization approaches have been established as one of the most efficient methods. In this approach, a numerical groundwater flow and transport simulation model is linked to the optimization model. All the linked simulation-optimization approaches aim at solving a minimization problem with an objective function representing the difference in measured concentration and simulated concentration at various monitoring locations. The optimization model generates candidate solutions for various source characteristics. This is used as an input for the simulation model to generate estimated contaminant concentration observations at designated monitoring locations. The optimization algorithm then calculates the value of objective function by calculating the difference in contaminant concentrations estimated by simulation model and actual observed values at the same monitoring locations over a period of time. Over a number of iterations, the optimization algorithm minimizes the objective function value. Most prominent approaches in this category are linear programming with response matrix approach [9], nonlinear optimization with embedding technique [21–23], artificial neural network approach [28–30], constrained robust least square approach [31, 32], classical optimization based approach [5–7], genetic algorithm based approach [1, 24, 27] etc.

In recent past, heuristic global search approaches such as Genetic Algorithm [12], Harmony Search, Tabu Search, Ant-Colony Optimization, Simulated Annealing[19] have developed rapidly and have been applied to a wide range of optimization problems. One of the major reasons for their popularity is the fact that these optimization methods do not easily get trapped in the local optima, thereby maximizing the probability of achieving a global optimal solution. Genetic algorithm (GA) and its variants, in particular, have been widely applied for solving unknown pollutant source identification. [11, 24, 27]. Genetic Algorithms are computational optimization algorithms that simulate the laws of natural genetics and natural selection and use it to search for the optimal solution.

Apart from GA or its variants, Simulated Annealing has also been used in solving inverse problems in groundwater management. Simulated annealing is inspired by the physical process of annealing in metallurgy which involves heating and controlled cooling of a material to reduce defects in crystal structure. The atoms are excited by heat and they become agitated while getting into higher energy states. The slow cooling allows a better chance for these atoms to achieve lower energy states than the ones they started with. In simulated annealing, a current solution may be replaced by a random "neighborhood" solution chosen with a probability that depends on the difference between corresponding function values and on a global parameter T (called temperature) that is gradually decreased in the process. Implementations of simulated annealing has been relatively limited because the traditional simulated annealing algorithm is reported to converge slower compared with GA or its variants. However, faster variants of simulated annealing have been developed and one of the most promising variants in terms of convergence speed is Adaptive Simulated Annealing (ASA) [14, 15]. The ASA code was first developed in 1987 as Very Fast Simulated Re-annealing (VFSR) [13]. Ingber & Rosen [16] showed that VFSR is at least an order of magnitude superior to Genetic Algorithms in convergence speed and is more likely to find the global optima during a time limited search.

Linked simulation-optimization based approaches are computationally intensive as the simulation model has to be run many thousands of times before an acceptable solution is produced. This has been a deterrent to any desktop based implementation of the simulation-optimization approach. Faster convergence can reduce the computational burden significantly and thereby enhance the possibility of a desktop based implementation of linked simulation-optimization approach. This paper investigates the applicability of ASA to unknown groundwater contaminant source release history reconstruction problem and compares its performance to genetic algorithm based solution. The performance evaluation of competing simulation-optimization approaches are based on a realistic scenario of missing measurement data, where contaminant concentration measurements are available a few years after the sources have ceased to exist. Apart from the convergence speed, the two algorithms are compared for their ability to produce accurate source release histories with moderately erroneous data and with uncertainty in estimation of hydro-geological parameters.

One of the most important factors that affects the execution time and accuracy of solutions generated by linked simulation-optimization approaches is the choice of observation locations. Poorly chosen contaminant observation locations often produce misleading results and hence it becomes important that after the initial estimation of the contaminant sources, a monitoring network is designed and implemented. In this study we use a monitoring network designed specifically to enhance the efficiency of source identification. However, a detailed discussion of the methodology used for monitoring network design is beyond the scope of this book.

2. Methodology

The linked simulation-optimization approach consists of two parts. An optimization algorithm generates the candidate solutions corresponding to various unknown groundwater source characteristics. The candidate solutions are used as input in the numerical groundwater transport simulation model to generate the concentration of contaminant in the study area. The generated concentration at designated monitoring locations is matched to the observed values of contaminant concentrations at various time intervals at the same locations. The difference between simulated and observed concentration is used to calculate the objective function value which is utilized by the optimization algorithm to improve the candidate solution. The process continues until an optimal solution is obtained. A detailed schematic representation of this process of using SA as the optimization algorithm in a linked simulation-optimization model is presented in Figure 1. The classical simulated annealing (SA) algorithm has many associated guiding parameters such as the initial parameter temperature, annealing schedule, acceptance probability function, goal function etc. Effective application of the classical simulated annealing to a particular optimization problem normally involves a lot of trials and adjustments to achieve ideal values for all or most of these parameters. ASA, which is a variant of classical SA, helps overcome this difficulty to a certain extent by automating the adjustments of parameters controlling temperature schedule and random step selection thereby making the algorithm less sensitive to user defined parameters compared with classical SA. This additional ability of ASA combined with inherent ability of classical SA to find the global optimal solution even when multiple local optimums exists, makes it a natural choice for solving the groundwater pollutant source identification problem.

2.1. Governing equations

The three-dimensional transport of contaminants in groundwater can be represented by the following partial differential equation [17]

$$\frac{\partial C}{\partial t} = D_{ij}\frac{\partial}{\partial x_i}\left(\frac{\partial C}{\partial x_j}\right) - \frac{\partial}{\partial x_i}\left(\vartheta_i C\right) + \frac{q_s}{\theta}C_s + \sum_{k=1}^{N} R_k \tag{1}$$

Where

C is the concentration of contaminants dissolved in groundwater, ML^{-3};
t is time, T;
x_i, x_j is the distance along the respective Cartesian coordinate axis, L;

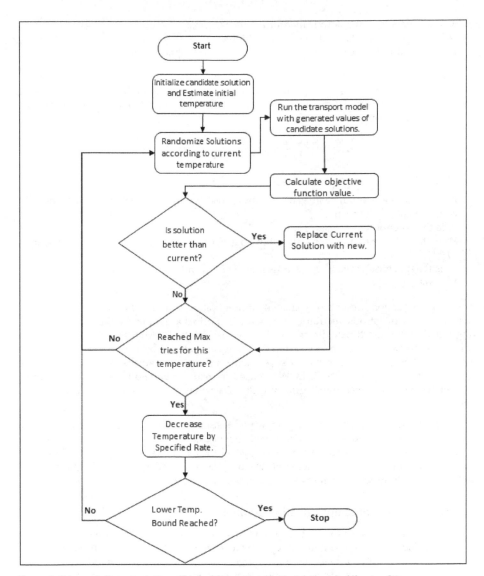

Figure 1. Schematic Representation of Linked Simulation-Optimization Model using SA

D_{ij} is the hydrodynamic dispersion coefficient, $L^2 T^{-1}$;

ϑ_i is the seepage or linear pore water velocity, LT^{-1};

q_s is the volumetric flux of water per unit volume of aquifer representing sources (positive) and sinks (negative), T^{-1};

C_s is the concentration of the sources or sinks, ML^{-3};

θ is the porosity of the porous medium, dimensionless;

N is the number of chemical species considered;

$\sum_{k=1}^{N} R_k$ is the chemical reaction term for each of the N species considered, $ML^{-3}T^{-1}$.

In order to solve this transport equation, linear pore water velocity needs to be known for the study area. Hence, it becomes necessary to first calculate the hydraulic head distribution using a groundwater flow simulation model. The partial differential equation for groundwater flow is given by the following equation:

$$\frac{\partial}{\partial x}\left(K_{xx}\frac{\partial h}{\partial x}\right) + \frac{\partial}{\partial x}\left(K_{yy}\frac{\partial h}{\partial y}\right) + \frac{\partial}{\partial x}\left(K_{zz}\frac{\partial h}{\partial z}\right) + W = S_s\frac{\partial h}{\partial t} \tag{2}$$

Where

K_{xx}, K_{yy}, and K_{zz} are the values of hydraulic conductivity (LT^{-1}) along the x, y and z co-ordinate axes respectively;

H is the potentiometric head (L);

W is the volumetric flux per unit volume representing sources and/or sinks of water (T^{-1});

S_s is the specific storage of the porous media (L^{-1}); and

t is time (T).

The flow equation describes transient groundwater flow in three dimensions in a homogeneous anisotropic medium, provided the principal axes of hydraulic conductivity are aligned with the co-ordinate directions. A computer code called MODFLOW is used to solve this groundwater flow equation. MODFLOW was developed by United States Geological Survey (USGS) and is one of the most popular computer programs being used to simulate groundwater flow today. MODFLOW is based on modular finite-difference method which discretizes the study area into a grid of cells. The potentiometric head is calculated at the center of each cell.

To solve the three dimensional ground water transport equation, another computer code called MT3DMS is used. This is also a very popular computer program developed by the USGS and uses modular finite-difference just like MODFLOW. The transport simulation model (MT3DMS) utilizes flow field generated by the flow model (MODFLOW) to compute the velocity field used by the transport simulation model. [34]

2.2. Formulation of the optimization problem

It is assumed in this study that information on a set of potential source locations are available. The objective of simulation-optimization method then reduces to regenerating the source release histories at these potential source locations. Spatial and temporal contaminant concentration(C) is known at specific monitoring locations at various point of time. Candidate source fluxes are generated by the optimization algorithm. These values are used for forward transport simulations in MT3DMS. The difference between simulated and observed contaminant concentrations are then used to calculate the objective function. The objective function for this optimization problem is defined as:

$$MinimizeF1 = \sum_{k=1}^{nk} \sum_{iob=1}^{nob} \left(cest_{iob}^k - cobs_{iob}^k\right)^2 . w_{iob}^k \tag{3}$$

Where,

$cest^k_{iob}$ = Concentration estimated by the identification model at observation well location iob and at the end of time period k.

nk = Total number of concentration observation time periods;

nob= Total number of observation wells;

$cobs^k_{iob}$ = Observed concentration at well iob and at the end of time period k;

w^k_{iob} = Weight corresponding to observation location iob, and the time period k.

The weight w^k_{iob} can be defined as follows:

$$w^k_{iob} = \frac{1}{(cobs^k_{iob} + n)^2} \tag{4}$$

Where n is a constant, sufficiently large, so that errors at low concentrations do not dominate the solution [18]. It is possible to include other forms of this weight.

2.3. Optimization algorithms

Of the various simulated annealing implementations, it is evident in literature that the adaptive simulated annealing algorithm converges faster [16] while maintaining the reliability of results and hence it was preferred over traditional Boltzmann annealing implementation [19]. Its application to the unknown pollutant source identification has been limited but it is potentially a good alternative because its convergence curve is steep, thereby producing better results when execution time is limited.

Currently, the most widely used optimization algorithm for solving groundwater source identification problem using linked simulation-optimization model is Genetic Algorithm and its variants. The effectiveness of ASA in solving this problem is compared against the effectiveness of GA. Genetic algorithms (GAs) are population based search strategies which are popular for many difficult to solve optimization problems including inverse problems. GAs emulate the natural evolutionary process in a population where the fittest survive and reproduce [12]. GA-based search performs well because of its ability to combine aspects of solutions from different parts of the search space. Real coded genetic algorithm was used with a population size of 100, crossover probability of 0.85 and a mutation probability of 0.05. The values were chosen based on a series of numerical experiments.

3. Performance evaluation

In order to evaluate the performance of two different optimization algorithms involving comparison of solutions obtained, it is vital to first ensure that only one solution exists. In other words, a unique solution has to be guaranteed. This is possible only under the following idealized assumptions [33]:

1. The numerical models used for simulation of groundwater flow and transport are able to provide exact solution of the governing equations in forward runs.

2. All the model parameters and concentration measurements are known without any associated errors.

3. The unknown parameter is piecewise constant.

The first assumption is valid for cases where grid size and time step used in the numerical solution tends to zero. However since the groundwater simulation models used in this study have been proven to be stable and convergent, this assumption approximately holds. The second assumption however, cannot hold in real life scenarios. Hence it becomes necessary to use synthetically generated observation values initially which can be considered free of measurement errors. The third condition is implemented by assuming that the unknown fluxes are constant in every stress period. In such conditions it approximately resembles a well posed problem. Therefore these evaluations are initially carried out for synthetic data (simulated data) with known parameter values. There is another related issue of unique solutions. Whenever numerical simulation and optimization models are used, the convergence of the solutions may be another issue related to unique solutions. These issues are discussed in [4]. In this study the use of synthetic observation data, with known hydro-geologic parameter values reduces the ill-posed nature of the problem. The uniqueness of the solution cannot be guaranteed. However, sufficient iterations were allowed to ensure convergence to the optimal solution. Performance of the source identification methodology is evaluated using synthetic data from a three dimensional aquifer study area. The synthetic contaminant concentration data is obtained by solving the numerical flow and transport simulation models.

3.1. Simulating errors in concentration measurement data

Once the global optimal solution has been obtained for the idealistic assumption, the performance evaluation of developed methodology can take into account the effects of contaminant concentration measurement errors as well as uncertainty associated with the determination of hydro-geological parameters. To test the performance for realistic scenarios, concentration measurement errors are incorporated by introducing varied amounts of synthetically generated statistical noise in the simulated concentration values. The perturbed simulated concentrations represents erroneous measurements and is defined as follows:

$$C_{pert} = C_{ns} + S_{ud} \times a \times C_{ns} \tag{5}$$

Where,

C_{pert} = Perturbed Concentration values

C_{ns} = Simulated Concentration

S_{ud} = a uniform random number between -1 and +1

a = a fraction between 0 and 1.0.

3.2. Performance evaluation criteria

The execution time of the algorithms is compared based on convergence curves which represent the value of objective function achieved versus time. To compare the ability of competing linked simulation-optimization approaches to produce accurate source histories, the errors in estimating source fluxes accurately is also used as a performance criterion. Normalized absolute error of estimation (NAEE) is used as the measure of errors in estimation of the sources. It can be represented as:

$$NAEE(\%) = \frac{\sum_{i=1}^{S} \sum_{j=1}^{N} \left| \left(q_i^j \right)_{est} - \left(q_i^j \right)_{act} \right|}{\sum_{i=1}^{S} \sum_{j=1}^{N} \left(q_i^j \right)_{act}} \times 100 \qquad (6)$$

Where,

NAEE = Normalized Absolute Error of Estimation

S = Number of Sources = 2 in this case.

N= number of transport stress periods = 5 in this case.

$\left(q_i^j \right)_{act}$ = Actual source flux for source number i in stress period j

$\left(q_i^j \right)_{est}$ = Estimated source flux for source number i in stress period j

4. Discussion of solution results

The developed methodology was applied to a hypothetical illustrative study area with synthetically generated concentration measurements over space and time. Advantage of using a hypothetical study area lies in the fact that unknown data errors do not distort the performance evaluation of the methodology. This helps in understanding the drawbacks of developed methodology and improving it further.

4.1. Study area

The hypothetical study area is a heterogeneous aquifer measuring 2100m x 1500m x 30m and consisting of three unconfined layers as shown in Figure 2.

The East and west boundaries are constant head boundaries, whereas north and south boundaries are no flow boundaries. There are two sources (S1 and S2) of contamination. S1 is located in the top layer and S2 in middle layer. Five monitoring location (M1 through M5) are located in the first layer as shown in Figure 3. A grid size of 30m x 30m x 10m is used for finite difference based numerical calculation of groundwater flow and transport equations. Transport time step used for MT3DMS is 36.5 days. Other model parameters are listed in Table 1. Only a conservative contaminant is considered. There are two point sources of contaminants. One in the top layer and another one in the middle layer. A time horizon of 16 years is considered. Entire time horizon is divided into 5 different stress periods. The first four stress periods are each 1.5 years long and the final stress period is of 10 years duration. Sources are assumed to be active only in the first four stress periods or in the initial 6 years. Original source fluxes are presented in Table 2. It is assumed that groundwater contamination is detected at five different locations in the study area at the

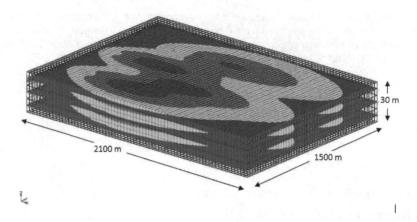

Figure 2. Illustrative Study Area

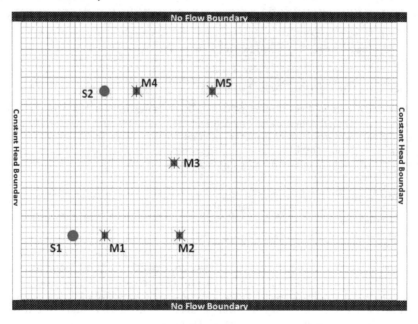

Figure 3. Top View of Study Area Showing Sources and Monitoring Locations

end of 8 th year, that is two years after the sources had ceased to exist. The observation wells are monitored for a period of 8 years starting from year 9 at an interval of 36.5 days. Observed contaminant concentration measurements at the designated monitoring locations are generated using MT3DMS as transport simulation model followed by perturbation as per Equation 5.

Parameter	Values
Length of Study Area (m)	2100
Width of Study Area (m)	1500
Saturated thickness, b(m)	30
Grid spacing in x-direction, Δx (m)	30
Grid spacing in y-direction, Δy (m)	30
Grid Spacing in z-direction, Δz (m) 10	
Hydraulic conductivity in x-direction, K_{xx} (m/day)	12
Hydraulic conductivity in y-direction, K_{yy} (m/day)	8
Vertical Anisotropy	5
Hydraulic Gradient (m/m)	0.002
Effective porosity, θ	0.3
Longitudinal dispersivity, α_L (m)	18
Transverse dispersivity, α_T (m)	4
Initial contaminant concentration (mg/l)	0.00

Table 1. Model Parameters

Sources	Layer	Row	Column	Contaminant Flux (g/sec)	
				Stress Period 1 1.5 years	6.000
				Stress Period 2 1.5 years	4.000
Source 1	1	12	15	Stress Period 3 1.5 years	8.000
				Stress Period 4 1.5 years	5.000
				Stress Period 5 10 years	0.000
				Stress Period 1 1.5 years	7.000
				Stress Period 2 1.5 years	9.000
Source 2	2	38	9	Stress Period 3 1.5 years	6.000
				Stress Period 4 1.5 years	7.300
				Stress Period 5 10 years	0.000

Table 2. Original Source Fluxes

4.2. Release history estimation with error free data

A set of error free observation data is generated. These observations are then used to evaluate the developed linked simulation-optimization methodology based on both GA and ASA. Input parameters used for GA and ASA are presented in Table 3. Every iteration of ASA based method uses one run of the groundwater transport simulation model (MT3DMS) whereas every generation of GA based method uses 100 (population size) runs of the same simulation model. Irrespective of the method, one run of the groundwater transport simulation model takes 4.281 sec to run on a Dell Optiplex®running an Intel®Core™2 Duo Processor at 2.93GHz. The execution time for one transport simulation run is however dependent on the computing platform. In order to keep the comparison independent of computing platform, both the methods were compared based on number of transport simulation runs which is directly proportional to the execution time. Both the methods were used to estimate source release histories using the error free data. In order to verify the convergence of each optimization method, time of run was made practically unconstrained. It was found that eventually both the optimization algorithms were able to achieve an objective function value very close to zero and identified the release history accurately. The objective function convergence profile as well as estimated fluxes were plotted at the end of 40,000 simulation runs of the groundwater transport model. Minimum value of objective function achieved is plotted against number of runs of the transport simulation model. The estimated flux values for both the sources in each stress period is also plotted against actual source fluxes. Convergence profile and source flux estimates are shown in Figure 4. Convergence profile

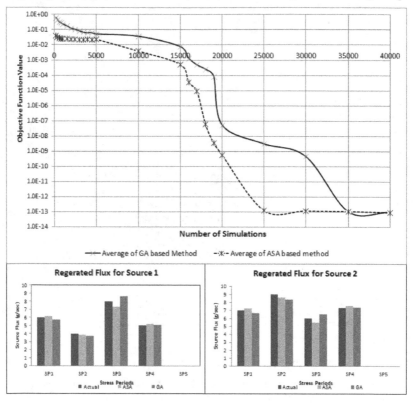

Figure 4. Convergence Profile and Estimated Release History with Error Free Data

shows that the objective function value for source identification model converges to a value very close to zero with about 5,000 simulation runs. However, further convergence is accelerated when using ASA algorithm. From these results, it can be concluded that the developed methodology is able to achieve optimal solution for an ideal error free scenario which resembles a well-posed problem.

4.3. Release history estimation with erroneous data

Five sets of erroneous observation data are generated with the formulation described in Equation 5. The value of fraction 'a' is specified as 0.1. These erroneous observations are used to reconstruct the release histories of contaminant sources. Linked simulation optimization method using ASA is compared with the one using GA as the optimization algorithm. Parameters used for both the optimization algorithms is presented in Table 3. Unlike the case with error free measurement data, in this case both the methods were used

Parameters of ASA	Parameters of GA	
Accepted to generated ratio 1.00E-06	Mutation Strategy: Polynomial Mutation Variable Boundaries : Rigid	
Cost Precision 1.00E-15	Population size	80
Maximum Cost Repeat 5	Total no. of generations	600
Temperature Ratio Scale 1.00E-05	Cross over probability	0.8
Temp. Anneal Scale 100	Mutation probability	0.05

Table 3. Parameters used in Optimization Algorithms

to reconstruct source release histories using the erroneous data with a limit on execution time. In order to make the comparison consistent by ensuring same number of simulation runs in the ASA and GA based methodologies, the number of simulation runs are restricted to 40,000. This restriction was based on the fact that increasing the number of simulation runs even to 80,000 resulted in very little improvement in the objective function value. Minimum value of objective function achieved is averaged over five solutions and is plotted against number of runs of the transport simulation model. The plot is presented in Figure 5. This

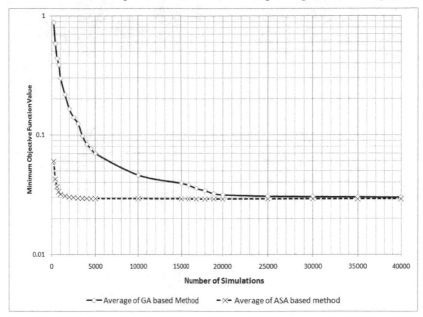

Figure 5. Convergence Plot

plot clearly shows that ASA based method converges much faster in the beginning and the GA based method is able to achieve comparable objective function values only after a much larger simulation runs. Because of the erroneous measurement data this problem may be ill-posed and the solution may not be unique. Therefore, lower objective function values do not always mean accurate reconstruction of the release histories.

In order to test the effectiveness of the competing methods based on accuracy of solutions produced, reconstructed release histories were compared to the actual release history after every set of 10,000 transport simulation runs. The results are shown in Figure 6. It can be seen that ASA based method is more efficient compared to GA based method after 10,000 and 20,000 simulation runs. However, as the execution time increases further with increase in number of simulation runs, the release histories produced by both methods become similar. This is also confirmed from the calculated values of NAEE presented in Table 4. As the execution time increases, the NAEE of ASA based method appears to increase only slightly. This could be due to statistical variation in the five different solutions and may be attributed to the input data error. Averaging over larger number of solutions may modify this inference. NAEE of GA based method consistently improves. However, the NAEE values obtained using ASA is still better in comparison.

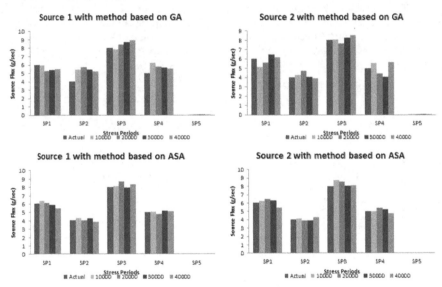

Figure 6. Reconstructed Release Histories using the competing methods

No. Of Simulation Runs	NAEE (%)	
	GA	ASA
10000	6.86	4.25
20000	6.53	4.18
30000	5.82	3.83
40000	4.26	3.62

Table 4. Normalized Absolute Error of Estimation

5. Application of simulated annealing for monitoring network design

Monitoring network design in the context of groundwater quality management essentially means specifying the spatial location of monitoring wells and frequency of sampling. Since this is one of the most cost intensive part of most contaminated groundwater remediation problems, an efficient and cost effective design of monitoring network is essential. Monitoring of groundwater quality may be necessitated by a variety of objectives such as:

1. Unknown groundwater source characterization

2. Compliance monitoring for limiting the effects of groundwater contamination

3. Better aquifer characterization

4. Hydro-geological parameter estimation

Irrespective of the various objectives, the problem of monitoring network design can be formulated as an optimization problem [8, 20]. While designing a monitoring network for estimating unknown groundwater source characteristics, the objective of optimization can be to maximize the reliability of estimated source characteristics or to minimize the total number of monitoring locations in the network or both. Compliance monitoring is aimed at minimizing the area of contamination when the contamination is first detected at monitoring network or maximizing the probability of detection of contaminant in groundwater. Often, only the average values of hydro-geological parameters of the aquifer are known. This results in uncertainty in the modeling results. In order to better characterize an aquifer, spatial distribution of hydro-geological properties should be specified. This objective can be achieved by sampling hydro-geologic parameter at sufficient locations such that the interpolated values can represent actual hydrological parameters accurately. The objective of optimization in this case is to find the minimum number of samples required to accurately represent a population of random hydro-geological parameter values. In all such cases, Adaptive Simulated Annealing can be efficiently used as the tool for optimization. Our attempts to develop classical simulated annealing algorithm for optimal design of a dedicated monitoring network for enhancing the efficiency of source identification was successful to a large extent. However, the mixed integer nature of the decision variables in a monitoring network design problem makes the application of classical simulated annealing algorithm a bit constraining. Adaptive Simulated Annealing is more suitable to solve this monitoring network design problems.

6. Suitability and sensitivity of adaptive simulated annealing

In the application discussed here, Simulated Annealing is utilized for finding the global minimum of a cost function that characterizes large and complex systems such as transport of pollutants in groundwater.Simulated Annealing, as an algorithm, is very efficient in solving non-convex optimization problems by ensuring that it does not always move downhill on a complex non-convex search space and hence avoids getting trapped in local minimum. Simulated annealing also differs significantly from conventional iterative optimization algorithms in that gross features of the final state of the system are seen at higher temperatures whereas the finer details of the state appear at lower temperatures [10]. The fact that simualted annealing ensures a global optimal solution enhances its suitability for solving ill-posed inverse problems in general and the problem of unknown groundwater pollutant source characterization in particular.

Its ease of use and remarkable efficiency in handling complex objective functions and constraints has made simulated annealing an attractive choice for solving a wide range of complex optimization problems. However, the slow convergence and hence long time of execution of standard Boltzmann-type simulated annealing has been a constraint. Adaptive Simulated Annealing removes that constraint by making the annealing schedules decrease exponentially in annealing-time, thereby making the convergence much faster. A major difference between ASA and traditional Boltzamnn Annealing algorithms is that the ergodic sampling takes place in terms of n parameters and the cost function. In ASA the exponential annealing schedules permit resources to be spent adaptively on re-annealing and on pacing the convergence in all dimensions, ensuring ample global searching in the first phases of search and ample quick convergence in the final phases[15].

Another major advantages of using Adaptive Simulated Annealing is also the fact that the parameters of algorithm are adjusted adaptively and hence the solutions do not vary widely if parameter values are changed within reasonable limits. This is in contrast with Genetic Algorithm where even minor changes to parameters such as mutation probability, cross over probability or population size causes a significant difference in the solutions.

7. Conclusion

A linked simulation-optimization method for source identification was developed based on adaptive simulated annealing. It was applied to an illustrative study area. The results obtained were compared with those obtained using genetic algorithm, a more commonly used optimization approach. It is evident from the limited numerical experiments that adaptive simulated annealing algorithm based solutions converge to the actual source fluxes faster than genetic algorithm based solutions. This results in substantial saving in computational time. The source fluxes identified by using adaptive simulated annealing are closer to actual fluxes when compared to the results obtained using genetic algorithm, even when the observation data are erroneous and the hydro-geological parameters are uncertain. It can be concluded that adaptive simulated annealing is computationally more efficient for use in simulation-optimization based methods for identification of unknown groundwater pollutant sources, specially in a time constrained environment. Use of ASA has the potential to reduce CPU time required for solution by an order of magnitude. However, with very large number of iterations in the linked simulation-optimization approach, it is possible that the solutions obtained using GA could converge to a marginally better solution compared to that ASA based algorithm. However, it appears that ASA based solutions converge very close to the optimal solution using only a small fraction of iterations required while using GA. The relevance of contaminant monitoring locations is demonstrated. Further studies are required to develop dedicated monitoring networks which can increase the efficiency of source identification.

Author details

Manish Jha and Bithin Datta
James Cook University, Townsville and CRC CARE, Adelaide, Australia

8. References

[1] Aral, M., Guan, J. & Maslia, M. [2001]. Identification of contaminant source location and release history in aquifers, *Journal of hydrologic engineering* 6(3): 225–234.

[2] Atmadja, J. & Bagtzoglou, A. [2001]. State of the art report on mathematical methods for groundwater pollution source identification, *Environmental Forensics* 2(3): 205–214.

[3] Bagtzoglou, A. & Atmadja, J. [2005]. Mathematical methods for hydrologic inversion: The case of pollution source identification, *in* T. Kassim (ed.), *Water Pollution*, Vol. 3 of *The Handbook of Environmental Chemistry*, Springer Berlin / Heidelberg, pp. 65–96. 10.1007/b11442.
URL: *http://dx.doi.org/10.1007/b11442*

[4] Datta, B. [2002]. Discussion of "identification of contaminant source location and release history in aquifers" by Mustafa M. Aral, Jiabao Guan, and Morris L. Maslia, *Journal of Hydrologic Engineering* 7(5): 399–400.

[5] Datta, B., Chakrabarty, D. & Dhar, A. [2009a]. Optimal dynamic monitoring network design and identification of unknown groundwater pollution sources, *Water Resources Management* 23(10): 2031–2049.

[6] Datta, B., Chakrabarty, D. & Dhar, A. [2009b]. Simultaneous identification of unknown groundwater pollution sources and estimation of aquifer parameters, *Journal of Hydrology* 376(1-2): 48–57.

[7] Datta, B., Chakrabarty, D. & Dhar, A. [2011]. Identification of unknown groundwater pollution sources using classical optimization with linked simulation, *Journal of Hydro-Environmental Research* 5(1): 25–36.

[8] Dhar, A. & Datta, B. [2010]. Logic-based design of groundwater monitoring network for redundancy reduction, *Journal of water resources planning and management* 13(1): 88–94.

[9] Gorelick, S., Evans, B. & Remson, I. [1983]. Identifying sources of groundwater pollution: an optimization approach, *Water Resources Research* 19(3): 779–790.

[10] Haykin, S. [1999]. *Neural networks: a comprehensive foundation*, Prentice Hall.

[11] Hilton, A. & Culver, T. [2005]. Groundwater remediation design under uncertainty using genetic algorithms, *Journal of water resources planning and management* 131: 25.

[12] Holland, J. [1975]. Adaptation in natural and artificial systems, *Ann Arbor, MI: University of Michigan Press* 31.

[13] Ingber, L. [1989]. Very fast simulated re-annealing, *Mathematical and Computer Modelling* 12(8): 967–973.

[14] Ingber, L. [1993]. Adaptive simulated annealing (asa), *Global optimization C-code, Caltech Alumni Association, Pasadena, CA* .

[15] Ingber, L. [1996]. Adaptive simulated annealing (asa): Lessons learned, *Control and Cybernetics* 25: 33–54.

[16] Ingber, L. & Rosen, B. [1992]. Genetic algorithms and very fast simulated reannealing: A comparison, *Mathematical and Computer Modelling* 16(11): 87–100.

[17] Javandel, I., Doughty, C. & Tsang, C. [1984]. *Groundwater transport: Handbook of mathematical models*, DOE/SF/00098-T8, American Geophysical Union, Washington, DC; Lawrence Berkeley Lab., CA (USA).

[18] Keidser, A. & Rosbjerg, D. [1991]. A comparison of 4 inverse approaches to groundwater-flow and transport parameter-identification, *Water Resources Research* 27(9): 2219–2232.

[19] Kirkpatrick, S. [1984]. Optimization by simulated annealing - quantitative studies, *Journal of Statistical Physics* 34(5-6): 975–986.

[20] Loaiciga, H. [1989]. An optimization approach for groundwater quality monitoring network design, *Water Resources Research* 25(8): 1771–1782.

[21] Mahar, P. & Datta, B. [1997]. Optimal monitoring network and ground-water-pollution source identification, *Journal of water resources planning and management* 123(4): 199–207.

[22] Mahar, P. S. & Datta, B. [2000]. Identification of pollution sources in transient groundwater systems, *Water Resources Management* 14(3): 209–227.

[23] Mahar, P. S. & Datta, B. [2001]. Optimal identification of ground-water pollution sources and parameter estimation, *Journal of Water Resources Planning and Management-Asce* 127(1): 20–29.

[24] Mahinthakumar, G. & Sayeed, M. [2005]. Hybrid genetic algorithmï£¡local search methods for solving groundwater source identification inverse problems, *Journal of water resources planning and management* 131: 45.

[25] Michalak, A. M. & Kitanidis, P. K. [2004]. Estimation of historical groundwater contaminant distribution using the adjoint state method applied to geostatistical inverse modeling, *Water Resour. Res.* 40(8): W08302.

[26] Pinder, G. [2009]. Optimal search strategy for the definition of a dnapl source, *Technical report*, Defense Technical Information Center, United States of America.

[27] Singh, R. & Datta, B. [2006]. Identification of groundwater pollution sources using ga-based linked simulation optimization model, *Journal of hydrologic engineering* 11: 101.

[28] Singh, R. & Datta, B. [2007]. Artificial neural network modeling for identification of unknown pollution sources in groundwater with partially missing concentration observation data, *Water Resources Management* 21: 557–572.

[29] Singh, R., Datta, B. & Jain, A. [2004]. Identification of unknown groundwater pollution sources using artificial neural networks, *Journal of water resources planning and management* 130: 506.

[30] Singh, R. M. & Datta, B. [2004]. Groundwater pollution source identification and simultaneous parameter estimation using pattern matching by artificial neural network, *Environmental Forensics* 5(3): 143–153.

[31] Sun, A. Y., Painter, S. L. & Wittmeyer, G. W. [2006a]. A constrained robust least squares approach for contaminant release history identification, *Water Resour. Res.* 42(4): W04414.

[32] Sun, A. Y., Painter, S. L. & Wittmeyer, G. W. [2006b]. A robust approach for iterative contaminant source location and release history recovery, *Journal of Contaminant Hydrology* 88(3-4): 181–196.

[33] Sun, N.-Z. [1994]. *Inverse Problems in Groundwater Modeling*, Kluwer Academic Publishers, pp. 12–37.

[34] Zheng, C., Wang, P. P., Zheng, C. & Wang, P. P. [1999]. Mt3dms: A modular three-dimensional multi-species transport model for simulation of advection, dispersion, and chemical reactions of contaminants in ground-water systems. documentation and user's guide, *Contract Report SERDP-99-1, U.S. Army Engineer Research and Development*.

Chapter 9

Simulated Annealing for Fast Motion Estimation Algorithm in H.264/AVC

Zhiru Shi, W.A.C. Fernando and A. Kondoz

Additional information is available at the end of the chapter

1. Introduction

The promising video coding standard, H.264/AVC [1], is developed by the Join Video Team of ITU-T Video Coding Experts Group (VCEG) and ISO/IEC Moving Picture Experts Group (MPEG). By utilizing several new techniques, such as advanced intra predictions, variable block size ME, integer transformation, in-loop deblocking filter, H.264/AVC has achieved significant compression gain compared with previous video coding standards. It is now widely applied to many types of visual services, for example Digital Multimedia Broadcasting, Mobile Phone, and High Definition (HD) video delivery. In the near future, holography video and Super-HD video are expected to hit consumer market. These kinds of large sized video contents require higher coding efficiency while keeping the encoder complexity within an acceptable level. Therefore, new techniques are needed to reduce the computational complexity so that various real time video encoder and delivery services for the large sized video contents could be feasible.

In particular, Block-Matching Motion Estimation (BMME) with Full Search (FS) algorithm [2] is the main computational burden in H.264/AVC due to exhaustively search all possible blocks within the search window using Lagrangian multiplier. Although FS algorithm can obtain the optimum motion vector (MV) in most cases, it consumes more than 80% of the total computational complexity. Thus, a fast and efficient motion estimation algorithm is required for H.264/AVC. Recently, two major approaches were researched to overcome this problem. One employs fast mode decision algorithms to skip unnecessary block modes in variable block checking process [3, 4]. The other one utilizes Fast Motion Estimation (FME) searching algorithms to reduce unnecessary search points [5-11].

Various algorithms have been proposed to reduce search points for FME Search algorithm. Motion adaptive search (MAS) [5] utilized the motion activity information to adjust the search strategy. In Variable Step Search (VSS) algorithm [6], motion search range is determined by using the degree of correlation between neighbouring motion vectors. A Multi-Path Search (MPS) algorithm [7] has been proposed, in which all the eight neighbours around the origin of the search window were performed to find candidate points. This algorithm has good rate-distortion performance, but its computational complexity reduction is limited. To tackle this drawback, the directional gradient descent search (DGDS) algorithm [8] is developed. It searched on the error surface in eight directions by using directional gradient descent. The search patterns in each stage depend on the minima found in eight directions and thus the global minimum can be traced more efficiently.

The hybrid multi-hexagon-grid search (UMHexagonS) algorithm [9] was adopted in H.264/AVC reference software JM as its significant reduce the computational complexity with only little degradation in rate-distortion performance. UMHexagonS takes advantage of four kinds MV predictions to decided initial search point, i.e. the Median Prediction (MP), the Uplayer Prediction (UP), the Corresponding-block Prediction (CP) and the Neighbouring Reference-picture Prediction (NRP). After selecting the best initial point, it employs the unsymmetrical-cross search pattern and uneven-hexagon-grid search pattern, which are shown in Figure 1 as step2 and setp3-2. In these uneven search patterns, the number of horizontal search points is more than that of vertical points. This is mainly based on a common assumption, that the movement in the horizontal direction is higher than that in vertical direction. However, motion characteristic in each video sequence is unique. Also, the characteristic may change with the time. Therefore, with this horizontal-heavy pattern, UMHexagonS would lose accuracy and waste searching power.

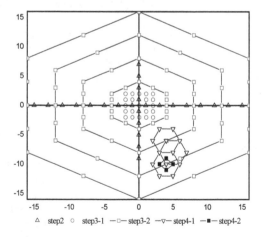

Figure 1. Search process of UMHexagonS algorithm

Predictive Intensive Direction searching (PIDS) algorithm was proposed in [10] to solve the problem caused by uneven search patterns by using a adaptive searching pattern. In PIDS algorithm, the correlation between predicted motion vector and optimal motion vector was investigated. The study revealed that the probability of predicted and optimum motion vector existing in the same directional region is at least 75%. Based on this statement, PIDS algorithm exploited the predicted MV direction to decide the intensive search direction. Thus, the intensive-direction search and coarse-direction search are selected adaptively for different regions. One example of search process of PIDS is depicted in Figure 2. As the uneven search pattern is changing according to the predicted motion vector of each block, it performs more precisely than UMHexagonS and achieves more computation reduction.

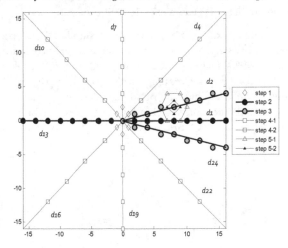

Figure 2. Search pattern of PIDS, example of intensive search in d_1

However, the PIDS algorithm's adaptive intensive search selection is limited in directional regions. With fixed number of search points in each direction, it cannot adjust the search range for different motion scenes. In study [11], a statistic analysis of MV distribution was carried out. A large number of global minima occupy near the search centre especially at the zero MV (0, 0) with a certain percentage of optimal MVs outside the radius of 10 pels. It indicated that most predicted and optimal MVs have high locality correlation. Meanwhile, some irregular MVs can hardly be well predicted due to poor correlation. In this chapter, direction and distance correlation between predicted MV and optimal MV are investigated MV correlation statistics information is calculated for each frame as its motion characteristic. With this information, the intensive and coarse search regions are adaptively changed for each block. The Simulated Annealing concept [12, 13] is employed to control searching process and to adaptively choose the intensive search region. After this Introduction the chapter is organized into five more sections as follows.

Section 2 statistical analyse MV direction and distance correlation characteristic. The block-matching motion estimation is described in this section. Section 3 gives an overview of simulated annealing and simulated quenching algorithm. Based upon analyses, the proposed SAAS algorithm is presented in section 4. The experimental results are given and illustrated in section 5. Finally, section 6 draws the final conclusion.

2. Statistical analysis of MV correlation characteristic

Because of the consistency of object and the consistency of motion, MVs have high correlation in both spatial and temporal domains. Thus MV prediction technique is adopted in H.264/AVC to improve ME efficiency. A predicted motion vector, mv_{pred}, is generated by previously coded neighbourhood motion vectors and MVD, the difference between the current vector and the predicted vector, is encoded and transmitted.

For the regions with smooth motion of a moving background and uniform motion of rigid objects, there normally exist very high correlations between predicted and optimal motion vectors. So that the BMME search algorithm only need to check a few points to obtain optimal position. While for the poor motion vector correlation scenario, like the complex and irregular motion, more candidate points are needed to be checked. Therefore, MV correlation characteristic will affect the searching strategy chosen in the BMME algorithm. In order to adaptively select an appropriate search pattern, MV correlation is statistical analysed in this section.

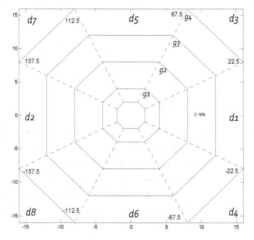

Figure 3. Direction and distance classification of MV correlation $p\left(MVC_{d_i,g_j}\right)$

To sufficient describe MV correlation characteristic, the MV correlation statistics are calculated in two aspects: motion vector directional correlation statistic and motion vector distance correlation statistic. Combining these two correlations together, the search window is divided into 8 direction regions d_i and a group of octagon grids g_j, as illustrated in Figure 3. Normally, the motion content of each video sequence is unique and the scene is changing with time. MVs correlation characteristic is changing with sequences and time. In this case, the analysis of MV correlation is frame based to improve the accuracy. The predicted and optimal motion vectors of previous frame are utilized for current coding frame.

MV directional difference d_{MVD} describes the directional similarity between predicted MV direction d_{pred} and optimal MV direction d_{best}, and is measured in degrees as follows

$$d_{MVD} = d_{best} - d_{pred} \qquad (1)$$

where, $d_{MVD} \in [-180°, 180°]$ is classified into 8 classes, with boundary of $\pm 22.5°$, $\pm 67.5°$, $\pm 112.5°$ and $\pm 157.5°$ as illustrated in Figure 3. The statistical calculation is carried out by exploding the MV directional distribution in these classes. Then the distribution probabilities $p(MVC_{d_i})$ of MV directional correlation are obtained. If MV directional correlation is high, d_{best} locates in forward or backward of d_{pred}, as shown in Figure 4. Class $d_1 \in (-22.5°, 22.5°)$ and Class $d_2 \in (-180°, -157.5°) \cup (157.5°, 180°)$ indicate the forward and backward direction and normally have higher probabilities than other classes.

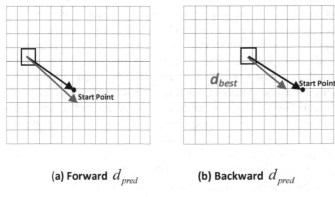

(a) Forward d_{pred} **(b) Backward** d_{pred}

Figure 4. Two situation of d_{best} locating along d_{pred}

MV distance correlation is measured by the distance between global minimum point and searching centre, which is known as the motion vector difference (MVD). Several Octagon grids g_j are utilized to categorise the MV distance correlation, as such circle-approximated pattern is more accurate to describe the MVD distribution. The interval between neighbour octagon grids is 4 pels, which is shown in figure 3. To evaluate the characteristic of MV distance correlation, MV distance correlation probabilities $p(MVC_{g_j})$ are calculated. Considering both directional and distance, MV correlation probabilities $p(MVC_{d_i, g_j})$ for the current coding frame are defined as:

$$p\left(MVC_{d_i, g_j}\right) = p\left(MVC_{d_i}\right) \times p\left(MVC_{g_j}\right) \qquad (2)$$

where $d_i \in (1,8)$ is the directional classes and $g_j \in (1, sr/4)$ is the octagon grids within search range sr. The MV correlation $p(MVC_{d_i, g_j})$ represents the possibility of optimal MV obtained in the class (d_i, g_j).

$p\left(MVC_{g_j}\right)$		g_1 [2,4]	g_2 [4,8]	g_3 [8,12]	g_4[12,16]	g_5[16,20]	g_6[20,24]	g_7[24,28]	g_8[28,32]
		50.85%	40.09%	2.26%	0.10%	0.00%	1.65%	4.94%	0.10%
$d1$	8.03%	4.08	3.22	0.18	0.01	0.00	0.13	0.40	0.01
$d2$	35.72%	18.16	14.32	0.81	0.04	0.00	0.59	1.76	0.04
$d3$	6.79%	3.45	2.72	0.15	0.01	0.00	0.11	0.34	0.01
$d4$	0.41%	0.21	0.16	0.01	0.00	0.00	0.01	0.02	0.00
$d5$	17.81%	9.06	7.14	0.40	0.02	0.00	0.29	0.88	0.02
$d6$	23.93%	12.17	9.59	0.54	0.02	0.00	0.39	1.18	0.02
$d7$	6.28%	3.19	2.52	0.14	0.01	0.00	0.10	0.31	0.01
$d8$	1.03%	0.52	0.41	0.02	0.00	0.00	0.02	0.05	0.00

Table 1. MV correlation probabilities of video sequence coastguard, the 10th frame

One example is given in Table 1, which shows the MV correlation characteristic in the 10th frame of "coastguard" CIF video sequence. For better understanding, the 10th frame of the "coastguard" is given in Figure 5. It can be observed that the fast moving boats bring some fast and irregular motion, while camera panning generates smooth movement on background. According to Table 1, more than 35% of optimal MVs are detected in the directional class d_2. In class d_5 and class d_6, there are also big percentage of optimal MVs appears, which implies the motion of this frame is directional irregular. While the distance correlation suggests that 90% of optimal MVs locate within the radius of 8 pels, which is quite stable when considering distance correlation. Considering both directional and distance correlation, there are only 3 partition regions, i.e. $\left(d_2,g_1\right)$, $\left(d_2,g_2\right)$ and $\left(d_6,g_1\right)$ with more than 10% probabilities to contain the optimal position. In the meanwhile, 21 of 64 regions' MV correlation probabilities are more than 0.1%. This suggests that intensive search is only needed to be performed in these regions. While the rest of regions, it is sufficient to be coarsely searched or even be totally skipped.

Figure 5. The 10th frame of CIF video sequence "coastguard".

Further illustration is demonstrated in Figure 6. The directional division describe the direction difference between the predicted motion vector and the optimal motion vector. The Octagon grid partitions represent the distance difference between two vectors. Such category division is not in image pels domain. It represents the unique motion character of each frame. Direction class d_1 covers $\pm22.5^o$ of direction different between predicted motion vector and optimal motion vector. For each MB, the predicted motion vector determines the initial direction d_1 and then the division pattern is rotated accordingly. As the motion correlation for each frames are different, the division pattern is different among frames. For each macroblock, the predicted MVs are different, so that the search pattern is also adaptively changed.

Based on above satiric analysis, SAAS algorithm is proposed, which provides a more accurate approach to obtain optimal motion vector. Similar to PIDS algorithm, the number of search points in each division is adaptively adjusted. But more computational complexity can be saved as the intensive searching areas are more precisely divided with help of different Octagon grids.

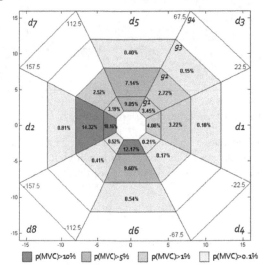

Figure 6. MV correlation statistics of coastguard, the 10th frame

3. Observations of simulated annealing and simulated quenching algorithm

3.1. Simulated annealing algorithm

Simulated annealing (SA) [13] is a probabilistic method for finding the global minimum of an optimization problem. It works by emulating the physical process where liquids are slowly cooled so that the atoms are often able to line themselves up and form a pure crystal.

The crystal can be seemed as the minimum energy state for this system. SA is especially suitable for the large scale problems with the global minimum hidden among several local minimum. The motion estimation is such kind of optimization problem that search for the optimal motion vector with minimum RD cost. However, most fast motion estimation search algorithms look for steepest descent for minimization and go downhill as far as they can go, as shown in Figure 7. Hence, these algorithms are easily trapped into a local minimum.

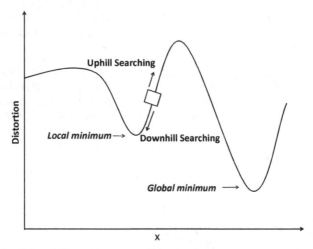

Figure 7. Uphill and downhill searching on rate-distortion surface

Avoiding the disadvantage stated above, SA algorithm can be viewed as a good solution to motion estimation search algorithm, in which occasional uphill moves will help the process escape from local minima. The so-called Boltzmann probability distribution as defined in equation (5),

$$Prob(E) \sim exp(-E/kT) \qquad (3)$$

expresses that a system at temperature T has its energy probabilistically distributed among all different energy states. Even at low temperature, there is a chance for the system to get out of a local energy minimum. Therefore, the system sometimes goes uphill as well as downhill. But lower the temperature, less chances for any significant uphill to take place. The basic elements of simulated annealing are as follows:

- A finite solution space S (set of states).
- An objective function $E(s)$ (analogy of energy) at state s, whose minimization is the goal of the procedure.
- A Neighbourhood structure $N(s)$.
- A nonincreasing function T called cooling schedule, which controls the annealing procedure, and $T(t)$ is called the temperature at time t.

Given the above elements, the process of SA searches for the minimum energy state s_0 is described as follows:

Select an initial solution $s_0 \in S$
Select an initial temperature $t_0 > 0$
Select a decreasing temperature function $T(t)$ as cooling schedule
Repeat
  Repeat
        Randomly generate neighbourhood point $s \in N(s_0)$;
      $\delta = E(s) - E(s_0)$;
      if $\delta < 0$, then $s_0 = s$;

      else, generated randomly c uniformly in the range $(0, 1)$;
        If $c < \exp(-\delta/T(t))$ then $s_0 = s$;
      Until *counter* = *nrep*
      Decrease the temperature t as per annealing schedule $T(t)$
  Until $T(t) < T_{min}$
s_0 is the approximation to the optimal solution.

3.2. Simulated Quenching algorithm

SA solution usually requires a large number of function evaluations to find the global minimum, which cause the speed of process is quite slow. That is the main disadvantage when using in fast motion estimation algorithm. To speed up the algorithm, a Simulated Quenching (SQ) methodology was proposed. Like SA, SQ algorithm also resembles the cooling process of molten metals through annealing. The analogy of the technique remains the same as that of SA except for quick temperature reduction annealing schedule. Thus the cooling rate becomes one of important parameters, which governs the successful working of SQ.

As in fast motion estimation algorithm, video contents and motion character are changing all the time, it's quite difficult to find a unique cooling scheme for such complicated application. In our proposed SAAS algorithm, we adaptive choose annealing schedule according to MV correlation probabilities information. For the frame with steady motion and high MV correlation, larger values of MV correlation probabilities are more easily to distribute in fewer divided regions. In this case, the faster anneal schedule will safely lead to global optimum. While a slower annealing schedule will be choosing when the frame with more irregular motion and MV correlation distribution is flat. The proposed SAAS algorithm with adaptive cooling scheme is specified in next section.

4. Proposed SAAS algorithm

The PIDS algorithm adaptive selects the intensive and coarse search regions in directional partition. However, with fixed number of search points in each direction area, it cannot adjust the search range for different motion scenes. To tackle this drawback, search pattern in SAAS algorithm is no longer restricted to certain directional regions, but is adaptively selected from more specific divided regions based on the MV correlation statistics. Flow chart of the SAAS algorithm is depicted in Figure 8 for better illustration. For each frame, ME search pattern is determined by MV correlation statistics. For each block, 24 directional candidates are employed to determine initial class d_1 as shown in Figure 9. Then, the search window division is carried out based on ME search pattern of the frame. One example of $d_1=c_4$ in the 10th frame of coastguards is demonstrated in Figure 10. In order to avoid trapping into a local minimum, Simulated Annealing based solution methodology is adopted to process the uphill and downhill searches, where MV correlation probabilities are set as the temperature parameter to control the annealing process adaptively.

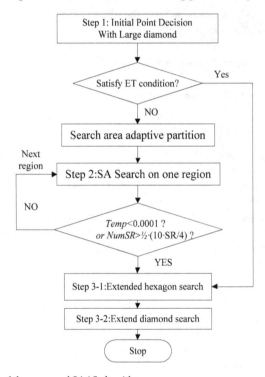

Figure 8. Flow chart of the proposed SAAS algorithm

4.1. Dynamic update of MV correlation probability

In the SAAS algorithm, it is very important to keep MV correlation probabilities accurate. Not only because the MV correlation probabilities is the crucial element for search region partition and annealing schedule, but also motion characteristic of each video sequence is unique and the MV correlation probabilities are changing all the time. A pre-processing step is conducted to reveal the motion correlation characteristic for the each frame.

The MV correlation probabilities $p(MVC_{d_i,g_j})$ are calculated with equation (2) by MV directional and distance correlation probabilities. In order to get more accurate MV correlation characteristic, the first octagon grid is started from 2 pixels to get rid of the points near centre. This is mainly because of the MV directional difference is meaningless when optimal points are close to the centre point. After the calculation, the MV correlation probabilities are sorted by descending order with corresponding region (d_i,g_j), which represents the region in direction d_i and in the g_j grid. A parameter $temp(d_i,g_j)$ that affects the annealing schedule as well as acceptance condition is also assigned by MV correlation probabilities $p(MVC_{d_i,g_j})$.

4.2. Step 1: Initial search point decision

The initial search point is selected from the four prediction models defined in the UMHexagonS. Based on the analysis in the last section, vectors around initial search point have a high probability to be the optimal MV. Therefore, we define large diamond search with 8 searching points around the start search point, which is similar shown in Figure 2 as step1. In contrast to the 25 point rectangular full search in UMHexagonS, this large diamond search reduces the computational requirement without sacrificing its accuracy. The point with the minimum rate-distortion cost is determined as the initial search point.

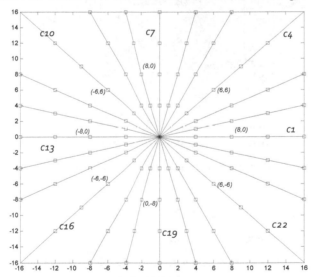

Figure 9. 24 candidate directions for d_1 determination

4.3. Adaptive partition of search area

After obtaining the initial search point, search area need to be divided based on MV correlation probabilities and predicted MV. 24 candidate directions $(c_1, c_2 ..., c_{24})$, 3 times more than PIDS's, are employed which is indicated in Figure 9. The candidate direction c_i with minimum degree difference to d_{pred} is determined as initial search direction d_1. The directional regions with boundary of ±22.5°, ±67.5°, ±112.5° and ±157.5° are spread according to the initial search direction d_1. Then the octagon grids are utilized to divide the search window into regions, where is the search range. Based on that, the search window is adaptively partitioned. The coordinate of each region is represented by (d_i, g_j). Parameter $temp(d_i, g_j)$ are assigned to each region (d_i, g_j) as indexing. One more example is shown in Figure 10, which shows the search window divisions are adjusted when initial direction $d_1=c_4$ in coastguards' 10th frame. Compared to the search window partition in figure 6, when $d_1=c_1$, the whole search pattern is changed as the difference of predicted MV. In next step, the simulated annealing search process will be conducted on different search region $r(d_i, g_j)$ with parameter $temp(d_i, g_j)$ as cooling scheme.

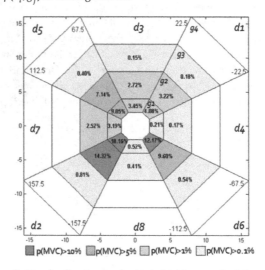

Figure 10. Search area division by directions and grids in SAAS, example of $d_1=c_4$, the 10th frame of coastguard

4.4. Step 2: Simulate annealing search

4.4.1. Objective function and solution space

In order to employ simulated annealing search in BMME algorithm, the SA elements are defined combing the concept of motion estimation in this section. The procedure for optimal MV searching is performed using predicted MV as centre of the search window. To optimally select the least rate-distortion cost, Lagrangian multiplier tool [14] are defined as follow:

$$J(mv, \lambda_M) = SAD(s, c(mv)) + \lambda_M \cdot R(mv - mv_{pred}) \qquad (4)$$

where mv is the candidate motion vector, mv_{pred} is the predicted the motion vector from neighbour blocks. s and c are the source video and the reconstructed video, respectively. SAD represents sum of absolute difference between the block in current frame and the block in the reference frame. $R()$ represents the bits used to encode the motion information computed by a table-lookup and λ_M is the Lagrangian multiplier set according to the quantization parameter (QP), which is given by

$$\lambda_M = \sqrt{0.85 \times 2^{QP/3}} \qquad (5)$$

This rate-constrained function has achieved good RD performance for motion estimation. In SA search step, RD cost function $J(mv, \lambda_M)$ is employed as Objective function E.

$$E = J(mv, \lambda_M) \qquad (6)$$

The divided regions $r(d_i, g_j)$ in search window are denoted as solution space, which is indexed by MV correlation probabilities rather than spatial neighbour region. The order of regions with decreasing MV correlation probabilities for the 10th frame of sequence *coastguard* is shown in Table 2. This mechanism can be seemed as a randomly selection from solution space. Compared to the simple downhill search in continuous space, this scheme intensively searches the regions with higher MV correlations probabilities first. For the regions with lower probabilities, coarse search or early terminal will be applied.

order	MV Correlation Probability %	Region Coordinate	order	MV Correlation Probability %	Region Coordinate
1	18.16	(d_2, g_1)	16	0.81	(d_2, g_3)
2	14.32	(d_2, g_2)	17	0.59	(d_2, g_6)
3	12.17	(d_6, g_1)	18	0.54	(d_6, g_3)
4	9.60	(d_6, g_2)	19	0.52	(d_8, g_1)
5	9.05	(d_5, g_1)	20	0.41	(d_8, g_2)
6	7.14	(d_5, g_2)	21	0.40	(d_5, g_3)
7	4.08	(d_1, g_1)	22	0.40	(d_1, g_7)
8	3.45	(d_3, g_1)	23	0.39	(d_6, g_6)
9	3.22	(d_1, g_2)	24	0.34	(d_3, g_7)
10	3.19	(d_7, g_1)	25	0.31	(d_7, g_7)
11	2.72	(d_3, g_2)	26	0.29	(d_5, g_6)
12	2.52	(d_7, g_2)	27	0.21	(d_4, g_1)
13	1.76	(d_2, g_7)	28	0.18	(d_1, g_3)
14	1.18	(d_6, g_7)	29	0.17	(d_4, g_2)
15	0.88	(d_5, g_7)	30	0.15	(d_3, g_3)

Table 2. Mv search region order in the 10th frame of sequence *coastguard*

4.4.2. Annealing schedule

The annealing schedule is one of crucial parameter for the SA process. If the temperature in the system dropping too fast, the advantage of SA, which converge to the global optimum, is defeated. However the too slow cooling process might affect the efficiency of our fast searching algorithm. Moreover, it quite difficult to set a fixed annealing schedule for the changeable video contents. In SAAS algorithm, the sorted MV correlation probabilities $p(MVC_{d_i,g_j})$ are assigned to corresponding annealing parameters $temp(d_i,g_j)$ for region $r(d_i,g_j)$ to control the annealing schedule.

$$temp(d_i,g_j) = p(MVC_{d_i,g_j}) = p(MVC_{d_i}) \times p(MVC_{g_j}) \tag{7}$$

$temp(d_i,g_j)$ is a set of parameter in pixel domain for particular block, while $p(MVC_{d_i,g_j})$ is a relative parameter in frame level. By using this adaptive annealing schedule, the cooling speed is changing with video content and motion correlation, while governs the successful working of the SA procedure.

To improve the searching efficiency, SAAS performs different number of iterations at different temperature status. Inside each region $r(d_i,g_j)$, mv search is randomly performed along the direction d_i in the range of $[g_{j-1},g_j]$. The number of search points ($NumS(d_i,g_j)$) in division $r(d_i,g_j)$ is determined by a pair of thresholds, $temp\_high$ and $temp\_low$.

$$NumS(d_i,g_j) = \begin{cases} 4, & temp(d_i,g_j) > temp\_high \\ 2, & temp\_low < temp(d_i,g_j) < temp\_high \\ 1, & temp(d_i,g_j) < temp\_low \end{cases} \tag{8}$$

After several experiments with more than 50 different sequences, we empirically determined temp_high = 0.3 and temp_low = 0.15. These thresholds provide satisfying performance on different motion senrou. By utilizing this mechanism, SAAS exploits intensive search in the regions with high MV correlation, and selects fewer search points in less correlation region automatically.

4.4.3. Minimum accepted condition

The minimum accepted condition in SA is based on Boltzmann probability distribution. Referring to equation (3), there is a high probability to perform uphill search when difference of cost function E is smaller and the temperature T is higher. By using Boltzmann concept, SAAS utilizes the following SA Condition.

$$\frac{E(best) - E(r(d_i,g_j))}{E(best)} < \rho \tag{9}$$

Where, is current global minimum and is a threshold controlled by annealing parameter, and is given by:

$$\rho = \frac{-1}{2 \cdot \log\left(temp\left(d_i, g_j\right)\right)} \qquad (10)$$

With ρ, the SA condition is directly proportionate to $temp\left(d_i, g_j\right)$ and inversely proportional to difference of cost function E. If $E(best) > E(r(d_i, g_j))$, region $r\left(d_i, g_j\right)$ is directly identified as the current global optimal. Otherwise, the SA condition still provides occasional upward moves. As ρ is controlled by $temp\left(d_i, g_j\right)$, for the division with lower $temp\left(d_i, g_j\right)$, the chance to conduct upward moves is smaller.

4.4.4. Termination condition

It is impossible to conduct SA search on all search partition, as there are regions partitioned in search window. Moreover, the majority of regions contain low MV correlation probabilities, as shown in Table 1. For these reasons, it is appropriated to limit the total number of search regions (*NumSR*) and have an early termination condition. Two termination conditions are given, one is the temperature status and the other is the number of searched regions.

$$1)\ temp\left(d_i, j\right) < 0.0001$$
$$2)\ NumSR > \frac{1}{2}\left(10 \cdot SR / 4\right) \qquad (11)$$

If one of these termination conditions is satisfied, the SA search will stop and go to the Extended Hexagon Search step which is introduced in UMHexagonS, to refine the local optimum. Otherwise, SA search will proceed to next region by the indexed of the decreasing parameter temp.

4.5. Step 3: Extended hexagon-based search

A large hexagon search pattern and a small diamond search pattern are employed in this step, which is modified from UMHexagonS. The large diamond pattern has six search locations, while the small diamond search pattern has four points. The large hexagon pattern in the step 3-1 is recursively used and its centre recursively moved until the location with the minimum rate-distortion cost lies in the centre of the hexagon. After this, a small diamond pattern in the step 3-2 is recursively utilized until the location with the minimum rate-distortion cost is at the centre of this pattern. Finally, this point is determined as the point of motion vector for the current block. But our Extended Hexagon-based search process is only limited within the one search region $r\left(d_i, g_j\right)$, which contains the optimal MV. Compared to UMHexagonS, this centre basis optimal MV refinement approach can obtain optimal MV with fewer search points.

Sequence	ME TIME (sec)					Average Search Points				
	UMH	PIDS	Gain	SAAS	Gain	UMH	PIDS	Gain	SAAS	Gain
Bus	725.6	618.3	14.79%	558.4	23.04%	30.61	19.43	37.52%	13.15	57.03%
Coastguard	742.5	622.4	16.17%	569.6	23.28%	32.11	19.62	38.90%	13.29	58.62%
Crew	655.5	587.1	10.43%	544.2	16.98%	20.79	14.35	30.99%	10.72	48.45%
Harbour	711.8	580.8	18.40%	554.8	22.04%	33.23	18.12	45.46%	13.09	60.61%
Mobile	648.7	538.7	16.97%	501.5	22.70%	28.85	16.14	44.06%	10.65	63.08%
Stefan	568.8	489.5	13.94%	444.9	21.79%	25.38	15.43	39.22%	9.99	60.63%
Template	597.3	512.2	14.25%	487.5	18.38%	22.40	12.53	44.07%	8.99	59.85%
Average			14.99%		21.17%			40.03%		58.32%

Table 3. Results of proposed SAAS comparing to that of UMHexagonS and PIDS in terms of average search points reduction (%) and motion estimation time reduction (sec) (QP=28)

5. Experimental results

In this section numerous experiments with H.264/AVC reference Joint Model (JM) software version 16.1 were conducted. We compared the proposed SAAS algorithm against the FS, PIDS and UMHexagonS algorithms, in terms of computational complexity (speed measured by ME time and average search points (ASP)) and Rate-distortion performance (PSNR and bit rate). Several commonly used sequences, covering a wide range of motion characteristics, are taken into consideration.

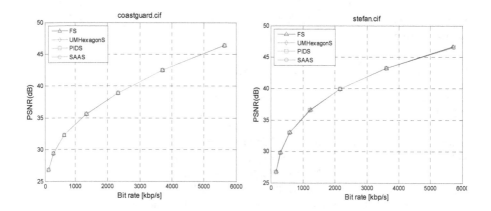

Figure 11. Rate-Distortion performance comparison of FS, UMHexagonS, PIDS and SAAS at various QPs

The group of picture (GOP) structure was IPPP, in which only first frame has been coded as I frame and first P frame has been coded by UMHexagonS. The sequences are tested at 30fps (frames per second). The Content Adaptive Variable Length Coding (CAVLC) entropy coder is used for all the simulations, with 5 reference frames. A search range of 32 and the quantization parameter of 28 are used. The simulation platform in our experiments is done with a PC of 2.44 GHz CPU and 8G RAM.

For complexity comparisons, the proposed algorithm is compared to the hybrid UMHexagonS adopted by the H.264/AVC reference software. Two different measurements are used to calculate the computational efficiency, average search points requirement and encoding time. Results are presented in Table 3. As shown in the Table 3, SAAS needs 48-63% less search points than UMHexagonS and saves average of 21% encoding time. Since it performs more precise search pattern adjustment, SAAS requires average 45% less search points than PIDS.

Sequence	PSNR(dB)				Bit-rate (kb/s)			
	FS	UMH	PIDS	SAAS	FS	UMH	PIDS	SAAS
Bus	35.792	35.786	35.809	35.800	1225.29	1240.05	1262.27	1249.88
	Gain	-0.006	0.017	0.008	Degrade	1.20%	3.02%	2.01%
Coastguard	35.610	35.600	35.602	35.598	1342.64	1344.28	1345.30	1348.56
	Gain	-0.010	-0.008	-0.012	Degrade	0.12%	0.20%	0.44%
Crew	37.895	37.870	37.870	37.869	680.590	672.72	671.94	678.053
	Gain	-0.025	-0.025	-0.026	Degrade	-1.16%	-1.27%	-0.37%
Harbour	35.623	35.627	35.627	35.625	1572.30	1571.14	1569.25	1572.59
	Gain	0.004	0.004	0.002	Degrade	-0.07%	-0.19%	0.02%
Mobile	35.376	35.370	35.377	35.383	1843.16	1843.08	1844.19	1848.52
	Gain	-0.006	0.001	0.007	Degrade	0.00%	0.06%	0.29%
Stefan	36.632	36.607	36.602	36.607	1189.09	1202.54	1206.90	1209.64
	Gain	-0.025	-0.030	-0.025	Degrade	1.13%	1.50%	1.73%
Template	35.608	35.595	35.587	35.585	1159.96	1162.89	1162.81	1164.11
	Gain	-0.013	-0.021	-0.023	Degrade	0.25%	0.24%	0.36%
Average		-0.012	-0.009	-0.010		0.21%	0.51%	0.64%

Table 4. Results of proposed SAAS comparing to that of FS, UMHexagonS and PIDS in terms of PSNR gain (dB) and bit-rate degradation (%) (QP=28)

Considering the large reduction in the computational complexity, the quality degradation is very small. Rate-Distortion performances are presented in Table 4. In all cases, the FS outperforms the others in image quality and bit-rate. Compared to FS, average PSNR degradation of the proposed algorithm is only 0.010. In term of bit-rate, SAAS has a slightly higher degradation than PIDS and UMHexagonS. SAAS has bit-rate decreasing of 0.64% in average. Further information can be obtained in Figure 9, which compares the rate-distortion performance among FS, UMHexagonS, PIDS and SAAS against different QPs (16, 20, 24, 28, 32, 36 and 40). Figure 10 compares the simulation results versus frame number of video sequences *Coastguard*. It is clearly reveal the superiority of SAAS to UMHexagonS in computational reduction, which more than 50% of search points are saved while the PSNR and bit-rate performance are very similar. From the results above, it can be confirmed that the SAAS algorithm has the capability to dramatically reduce the computational burden with negligible degradation in the RD performance.

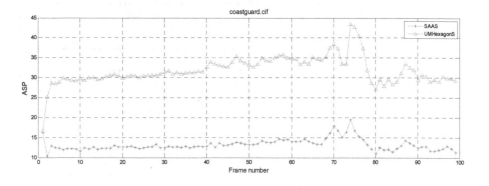

Figure 12. Rate-Distortion performance and complexity cost comparison versus frame

6. Conclusion

This chapter presents a novel fast motion estimation algorithm, Simulated Annealing Adaptive Search algorithm. As mv field has heavy correlation, the proposed algorithm takes the advantage of MV correlation information, which is statistically calculated and plays a significant role in SAAS process. In the SA search step, the search region is adaptively divided and the divisions are searched indexed by MV correlation probabilities in descending order. Furthermore, by utilizing Boltzmann probability concept, the minima acceptation or rejection condition of each SA search is controlled by this correlation information. The experimental results demonstrate that more than 48% of ASP and 21% of ME time can be saved, while maintaining a similar bit-rate without losing the picture quality.

Author details

Zhiru Shi, W.A.C. Fernando and A. Kondoz
I-Lab, CVSSP, University of Surrey, Guildford, United Kingdom

7. References

[1] Joint Video Team of ISO/IEC MPEG & ITU-T VCEG (2004) Text of ISO/IEC 14496 10 Advanced Video Coding 3rd Edition.

[2] Richardson I. E. G. (2003) H. 264 and MPEG-4 video compression. The Atrium, Southern Gate, Chichester, West Sussex, England: John Wiley & Sons.

[3] Jianfeng R, Kehtarnavaz N, and Budagavi M(2008) Computationally efficient mode selection in H.264/AVC video coding. IEEE Trans. Consumer Electronics. 54: 877-886.

[4] Knesebeck M, Nasiopoulos P(2009) An efficient early-termination mode decision algorithm for H.264. IEEE Trans. Consumer Electronics. 55: 1501-1510.

[5] Hosur P. I. (2003) Motion adaptive search for fast motion estimation. IEEE Trans. Consumer Electronics. 49: 1330-1340.

[6] Ki Beom K, Young J, Min-Cheol H(2008) Variable step search fast motion estimation for H.264/AVC video coder IEEE Trans. Consumer Electronics.54: 1281-1286.

[7] Goel S, Bayoumi M. A(2006) Multi-Path Search Algorithm for Block-Based Motion Estimation. IEEE Int. Conf Image Processing. pp. 2373-2376.

[8] Lai-Man P, Ka-Ho N, Kwok-Wai C, Ka-Man W, Uddin Y, Chi-Wang T(2009) Novel Directional Gradient Descent Searches for Fast Block Motion Estimation. IEEE Trans. Circuits and Syst. Video Technol. 19:1189-1195.

[9] Zhibo C, Zhou P, Yun H, Chen Y(2002) Fast integer pel and fractional pel motion estimation. JVT 6th Meeting. JVT-F017.

[10] Zhiru S, Fernando W. A. C, Silva D. V. S. X(2010) A motion estimation algorithm based on Predictive Intensive Direction Search for H.264/AVC. in (ICME) IEEE Int. Conf. Multimedia and Expo. pp. 667-672.

[11] Lin C. C, Lin Y, Hsieh H. J(2009) Multi-direction search algorithm for block motion estimation in H.264/AVC. Image Processing IET 3: 88-99.

[12] Metropolis N, Rosenbluth A. W, Rosenbluth M. N, Teller A. H, Teller E, (1953)Equation of state calculations by fast computing machines. Chemical Physics J. 21:1087.

[13] Kirkpatrick S, Gelatt C. D, Vecchi M. P(1983) Optimization by simulated annealing Science. 220: 671.

[14] Sullivan G. J, Wiegand T(1998) Rate-distortion optimization for video compression. IEEE Magazine Signal Processing 15:74-90.

Multiple Objectives

Chapter 10

A Simulated Annealing Based Approach to Integrated Circuit Layout Design

Yiqiang Sheng and Atsushi Takahashi

Additional information is available at the end of the chapter

1. Introduction

The optimization techniques for integrated circuit (IC) layout design are important. Generally speaking, the basic process of modern hardware engineering includes designing, manufacturing and testing. IC layout is an inevitable stage of designing before manufacturing. There are many applications which are directly related with layout optimization in practice, such as floor plan for very-large-scale integration (VLSI) design, placement for printed circuit board (PCB) design, packing for logistics management, and so on. In this research, we mainly focus on the optimization for three layout problems, which are 2D packing, 3D packing and 2D placement. The 2D/3D packing is to position different modules into a fixed shape, normally rectangular one, with area or volume minimization. The placement can be regarded as the packing problem with interconnect optimization. Since a general placement problem is NP-hard, there are no practical exact algorithms so far to be sure to find optimal solutions. As an alternative to get the optima, heuristics [1-6] are typically used to find near optimal solutions within a given runtime.

As product size keeps shrinking, product lifecycle keeps shortening and product complexity goes up, more electronic components will be integrated into a smaller IC chip or PCB with higher density and shorter time to market. At the same time, multi-objective optimization is common for IC/PCB layout in real product design, so another difficulty is the trade-off between conflicting objectives, such as low power and high performance. Pareto improvement for multiple objectives is one of the biggest challenges we have to face nowadays. The layout problem becomes much harder to find near-optimal or even acceptable solutions with high requirements. In order to improve the best cases and mitigate the worst cases of IC/PCB layout, it becomes increasingly critical and urgent to improve the quality of solution and reduce runtime.

Simulated annealing based algorithm with a good representation for 2D/3D packing is one of the most popular ways to improve the quality of solution. On the one hand, many researches explored different representations [7-12], such as bounded-slice-line grid, sequence pair, FAST sequence pair, Q-sequence, selected sequence pair, etc. In order to code and decode 3D-packing problem, sequence pair for 2D packing is extended to sequence triple and sequence quintuple, and it has been proved that sequence triple could represent the topology of the tractable 3D packing and there are at least one sequence quintuple which can be decoded to a topology as an optimal packing for volume minimization. But the effectiveness to improve solution quality and reduce runtime is quite limited due to huge solution space and complex solution distribution, even if a very good representation is used. The experimental results within a short runtime are still far from near-optimal solutions in real implementation to solve the packing problem. So it is the right time to explore new algorithms in order to solve 2D/3D problem more effectively.

There are many significant shortcomings of traditional heuristics for IC layout optimization. Let us take simulated annealing (SA) and genetic algorithm (GA) as an example. For SA, firstly, some slight modifications of solution are repeated to get a good convergence. Therefore, the global search is inefficient in general. It is disadvantageous to solve the problem with huge solution space, such as VLSI design. Secondly, SA does not use the past experience, including past good solutions and past moves, and it is a big informational waste. To speed up SA, some researchers [4] proposed two-stage SA for VLSI design. But the search speed is still quite slow, and it is not seriously considered to avoid or reduce informational waste. For GA, it evaluates too many candidates in order to get next generations. The evaluation takes too much runtime. Besides GA selects the next generation according to a ranking function, which is not always necessary but takes much time. So it is possible to improve the solution quality or reduce runtime if we can overcome the mentioned shortcomings.

In this research, a simulated annealing based approach [13-14], named mixed simulated annealing (MSA), is proposed to improve solution quality and reduce runtime by overcoming the shortcomings of inefficient global search and informational waste. In mixed simulated annealing, a special crossover operator is designed to use a part of information from past good solutions and get higher improving efficiency, and the solutions gotten by the crossover are much better than random solutions. To evaluate the effectiveness and the reliability of the proposed mixed simulated annealing, we apply it to three mentioned optimization problems, i.e. 2D packing, 2D placement and 3D packing, and get considerable improvement for all three problems. The experimental results show the runtime, the packing ratio of area for 2D packing, the packing ratio of volume for 3D packing and two more objectives (low power and short maximal delay) for 2D placement are improved considerably by using MCNC, ami49_X and ami98_3D benchmarks. For example, the runtime of mixed simulated annealing with sequence quintuple representation is up to 4 times faster than that of 2-stage SA with the same representation, and the packing ratio of volume is improved by up to 12% within 100s runtime.

2. Simulated annealing for integrated circuit layout

Based on the theory of statistical mechanics and the analogy between solid annealing and optimization problem, S. Kirkpatrick, C. D. Gelatt and M. P. Vecchi [1] proposed simulated annealing algorithm in 1983. The annealing is to heat up a solid with a very high temperature and then to cool it down slowly until it reaches or approaches its minimum energy state. Each state of solid represents a feasible solution of problem. The energy of the state is the value of cost function to evaluate the solution. The state with the lowest energy corresponds to the optimal solution with the best value of cost function. SA is a stochastic algorithm with iterative improvement. Each iterative step consists of changing current solution to a new solution, named a move to neighbourhood. The acceptance probability of new solutions depends on the current temperature, which is scheduled from the highest temperature to the lowest temperature. An important point we have to mention here is that, if the physical process is to cool the solid down very quickly, it is known as quenching, instead of annealing. The difference between normal simulated annealing and simulated quenching is the parameter setting of temperature scheduling.

In detail, let S be the solution space with neighbourhood structure. For any solution S belongs to S, we define the cost function $C(S)$, i.e. the total cost function (C_t) for multi-objective placement problem. A non-optimal solution S is defined by local optimum, if it can not reach better solution by moving to any neighbouring solution S'. That is to day, for any neighbour solution (S') of local optimal solution (S), the inequality $C(S) < C(S')$ is always satisfied. The depth $D(S)$ of local optimal solution is defined by the maximum value such that $D(S) + C(S) > C(S')$. The maximum depth of local optimal solution in S is denoted by $d(S)$. Let $X(T_i)$ be a variable of the cost function $C(S)$ at each temperature T_i, where i is 0, 1, 2, ... Let C_{opt} be the minimum cost function. According to [2], the equality $\lim_{i \to \infty} X(T_i) = C_{opt}$ is satisfied with the following conditions: (1) The solution space S is finite and irreducible; (2) There exists an equilibrium distribution for the transition probability matrix; (3) $T_i \geq T_{i+1}$ and $T_i > 0$ for all i; (4) $\lim_{i \to \infty} T_i = 0$; (5) $\sum_{i \in (0, \infty)} [\exp(-d(S)/T_i)] = \infty$.

In real implementation with a given finite runtime, we are using a fast geometric simulated quenching scheduling ($T_{k+1} = qT_k$, $0<q<1$) with repeated inside loop (p times) to enhance the efficiency of standard SA [3] as the following equation.

$$T_i = T_0 \cdot q^{\lfloor i/p \rfloor} \tag{1}$$

where i is the iterative step, T_i is the variable temperature at the ith step, T_0 is the initial temperature when $i = 0$, p is the inside loop number and q the temperature coefficient near but less than 1.

As shown in Figure 1, it is a typical flow chart of SA, which is used for layout optimization in this research. The initial solution is randomly produced or simply follows past layout designs. The temperature scheduling is used to change the current temperature (T). The parameters of the temperature scheduling include the starting temperature T_0, the ending temperature T_e, a temperature coefficient and an inside loop number. One of moving methods is selected with given probabilities, for example, the same probability for each moving method in real experiment (near 33% in the case of three moving methods). A new solution is tried by using the current selected moving method. The new solution is evaluated by a cost function (C) and compared with the old one. The new solution is

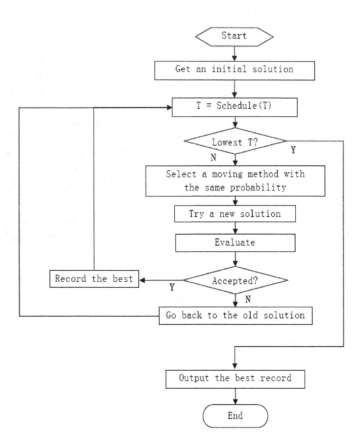

Figure 1. A typical flow chart of simulated annealing

accepted with a calculated acceptance probability $P = \exp[-\Delta C/T]$, which depends on the difference of cost function (ΔC) and the current temperature (T). The probability P is between 0 and 1. The temperature coefficient between 0 and 1 is set to control the speed of temperature reduction. The inside loop number is set to control the repeated moves for each T. If the new solution is improved ($\Delta C < 0$), then $P = 1$, and the best recorder will be implemented: If the new solution is better than the current best, the best record will be replaced. If rejected, the current solution will go back to the old one and continues the next temperature scheduling until reaching the lowest temperature Te. The output is the latest best record. The real implementation of SA algorithm depends on four basic definitions: (1) solution representation, (2) moving methods, (3) cost function, (4) temperature scheduling.

For the solution representation, 2D/3D topology for IC layout is defined by the orthogonal coordinate system, as shown in Figure 2, and is represented by sequence pair for 2D general cases, sequence triple for 3D simple cases or sequence quintuple for 3D general cases. Each

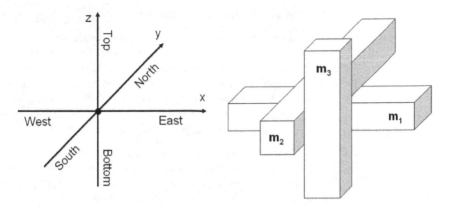

Figure 2. Orthogonal coordinate system and 3D packing topology represented by $\Gamma^1(m_2,m_1,m_3)$, $\Gamma^2(m_1,m_3,m_2)$ and $\Gamma^3(m_1,m_2,m_3)$ according to relative location

layout in 3D general cases is regarded as a set of the relations of relative location between boxes, i.e. "Top-Bottom", "North-South" and "West-East" (TB-, NS- and WE-) relations. The coding and the decoding are based on TB-, NS- and WE- relation corresponding to the order of modules. In Figure 2, box m_2 is on the west of box m_3, i.e. WE-relation, since the x-coordinate of any part of box m_2 is always smaller than or equal to that of any part of box m_3. Similarly box m_1 is on the north of box m_3, i.e. NS-relation, and box m_2 is on the top of box m_1, i.e. TB-relation. The 3D packing can be represented by $\Gamma^1(m_2,m_1,m_3)$, $\Gamma^2(m_1,m_3,m_2)$, and $\Gamma^3(m_1,m_2,m_3)$ according to the coding rule. The detail of representation will be introduced in section 5. The solution space of all mentioned representation is finite, instead of infinite solution space of original layout problem. All solutions decoding by the mentioned representations are feasible.

For the moving methods, let us take 2D placement as example. Three basic moving methods with small changes are designed to change the current solution by using the sequence-pair representation. The "rotation" changes the orientation of a module. The "exchange" exchanges the order of two modules in all sequences. The "move" changes the order of a module in one of sequences. The detail of each moving method will be discussed in section 6 and section 7.

For the cost function in the case of 2D placement, the total value (C_t) includes the dynamic power function (C_p), the maximal delay function (C_d) and the bounding area function (C_a). The estimation for each cost function will be discussed in section 8.

For the temperature scheduling, the starting temperature T_0, the ending temperature T_e, a temperature coefficient and an inside loop number are set according to the size of module number and the requirement of solution quality. As a reference, a set of parameters in our experiment is set as follows: $T_0 = 100000$, $T_e = 10$, Inside loop number $p = 500$, Temperature coefficient $q = 0.98$.

3. How to improve traditional simulated annealing

There are at least two shortcomings which impact the search speed of traditional SA. (1) Inefficient global search: In order to assure a final convergence effectively, the moving methods with relatively small changes should be used, so the global search within a short runtime is quite limited. Even using higher temperature, it is still slow to explore the huge search space of layout problem. (2) Informational waste: It does not use the information of past experience, including past solutions and past moves. It is quite possible to get a very good configuration of past solutions at the beginning but to lose it at last.

First of all, to overcome the shortcoming of inefficient global search, a two-stage algorithm is considered as follows. The first stage is named rough search, and the second stage is named focusing search. The rough search tends to big changes, such as crossover from genetic algorithm, to improve global search ability, while the focusing search tends to small changes, such as exchange, move and rotation, to get final convergence and reach better near-optimal solution.

Secondly, to overcome the shortcoming of informational waste, a special crossover operator from genetic algorithm, which reuses the information of past solutions, is considered. Comparing with random operator, the crossover operator has a search direction, which is based on the configuration from past good solutions, by use a part of configuration of the current best to reduce the informational waste. Besides, a guide with the probabilities to select running method adaptively according to the short-term improving speed is also considered.

In real implementation of 2-stage SA, the temperature scheduling of the second stage is same with that of the first stage using a geometric scheduling ($T_{k+1} = qT_k$, $0<q<1$) with repeated inside loop (p times) as the equation (1). The only difference is the parameter setting. In the second stage, T'_i (instead of T_i in the first stage) is the variable temperature at the ith step in the second stage, T'_0 (instead of T_0) is the initial temperature of the second stage, p' (instead of p) is the inside loop number of the second stage and q' (instead of q) the temperature coefficient of the second stage. The detailed temperature scheduling setting depends on the requirement of runtime. As a reference, two sets of the parameters are set separately as follows: $T_0 = 100000$, $T_e = 100$, $p = 1000$, $q = 0.98$, $T'_0 = 1000$, $T'_e = 1$, $p' = 1000$, $q' = 0.98$. For different benchmarks, the inside loop number can be increased from 1000 to 2000, 5000, etc. Also the temperature coefficient can be closer to 1, such as 0.99, 0.995, etc. The parameter setting with a given runtime is adjusted by selecting the initial temperature, the final temperature, the temperature coefficient and the inside loop number.

4. Mixed simulated annealing

By overcoming the mentioned shortcoming, we proposed a mixed simulated annealing (MSA) to speed up traditional simulated annealing (SA) and 2-stage SA. The basic idea is to improve the global search ability and to speed up the search process by a special crossover operator, which uses the information of past solutions. Just like SA and 2-stage SA, MSA is an iterative improvement method and a stochastic algorithm. The main difference between 2-stage SA and MSA is the special crossover operator to use a part of configuration of the current best and to reduce the informational waste. Although we can get a rough solution by producing solutions randomly, it is with low improving efficiency. The proposed crossover operator has a search direction, which is based on the configuration from past good solutions, to get high improving efficiency.

The intuitive comparison shows several intuitive advantage of MSA comparing with traditional SA and 2-stage SA. For global search ability, 2-stage SA is better than traditional SA due to big changes in the first stage, and MSA is even better than 2-stage SA due to the crossover operator and even bigger changes in the first stage. Traditional SA and 2-stage SA do not use past experience, while MSA is using past good solutions by using the crossover operator.

5. Application to integrated circuit layout optimization

The detailed IC design process includes system specification, architectural design, functional design, logic design, circuit design, layout design and verification. The layout is near the last stage of IC design, and it is a critical stage of electronic product development. As one of the key steps of IC layout, the placement has big impact on the overall quality of IC chip.

5.1. Problem definition

Let us start with the formulation of 3D placement. Let $M = \{m_1, m_2, ..., m_n\}$ denote the modules or blocks to be placed, where n is the number of modules. Each m_i, where $1 \leq i \leq n$, has height h_i, length l_i and width w_i. The packing volume is defined by the minimum bounding rectangular parallelepiped including all modules. For the placement, we need to optimize the interconnect networks. Let $N = \{n_1, n_2, ..., n_l\}$ be the set of interconnect nets between modules, where l is total net number. Let len_i denote the estimated wire length of each net n_i, $1 \leq i \leq l$. Let P_i denote the estimated dynamic power, i.e. the interconnect power of net n_i. Let $(x_i, y_i, z_i, r_{x-i}, r_{y-i}, r_{z-i})$ be the location and rotation on 3D orthogonal coordinate system for each module m_i, $1 \leq i \leq k$, where (x_i, y_i, z_i) means the coordinates of the below-rear-left corner of module m_i, and $(r_{x-i}, r_{y-i}, r_{z-i})$ denotes the rotation (0, 1) of m_i on yz-, zx- and xy-plane. $r_{z-i} = 1$ is the normal state of modules, while $r_{z-i} = 0$ is rotated by 90 degree.

In short, The input is a set of modules $M = \{m_1, m_2, ...\}$ with height, length and width $\{(h_1, l_1, w_1), (h_2, l_2, w_2), ...\}$ and a net list $N = \{n_1, n_2, ...\}$. The constraint is no overlap between m_i and m_j, where $i \neq j$. The output is a set of location and rotation for each module $\{(x_1, y_1, z_1, r_{x-1}, r_{y-1}, r_{z-1}), (x_2, y_2, z_2, r_{x-2}, r_{y-2}, r_{z-2}), ...\}$ such that: (1) Minimize the power consumption; (2) Minimize the maximal delay; (3) Minimize the volume of bounding box.

The 3D-packing problem is a special case of 3D placement with no consideration of power and delay. The 2D placement problem is regarded as a special case of 3D placement with z=0, as shown in Figure 3. The 2D-packing problem is a special case of 3D packing with z=0. All of the mentioned three problems are formulated so far.

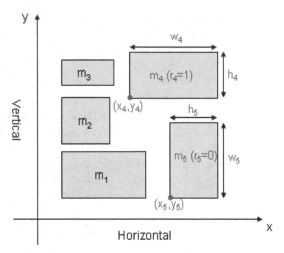

Figure 3. 2D placement as a special case of 3D placement

5.2. Problem representation

The original packing or placement is with infinite solution space. The coding and decoding method is generally needed to connect the problem and its representation. The solution space of a good representation should be finite. And the solutions after a good representation should be feasible and be better to include at least one optimal solution. Sequence quintuple can be used to represent a general 3D-packing topology, but the solution space of sequence quintuple is quite large. Furthermore, sequence quintuple representation is simplified to sequence triple representation, which can be decoded to a relatively simple 3D topology. In the case of 2D-packing topology, sequence pair, which can be simplified from sequence triple, is used to represent a general 2D packing in this research. As an example, the coding from Figure 3 to Figure 6 can be gotten by using the coding-decoding transition method in Figure 4 and Figure 5, which are based on North-South and West-East relation corresponding to the order of modules in sequence pair as follows.

In order to get a positive sequence $\Gamma+$, each West-South corner of module connects to the West-South corner of the whole layout, and each East-North corner of module connects to the East-North corner of the whole layout without any intersection as shown in Figure 4. We can get a sequence $(m_3, m_2, m_4, m_1, m_5)$ corresponding to $(0,1,2,3,4)$ from left side (i.e. two red points in Figure 4) to right side (i.e. two blue points in Figure 4). The positive sequence $\Gamma+$ is changed from the West-North corner to the East-South corner, i.e. from 0 to n-1 in $\Gamma+$, where n is the total number of modules. By using this coding method, we can get the whole sequence $\Gamma+$ as shown in Figure 5, which is $\Gamma+ (m_3, m_2, m_4, m_1, m_5)$. Similarly, in order to get $\Gamma-$, each West-North corner of module connects to the West-North corner of the whole layout, and each East-South corner of module connects to the East-South corner of the whole layout

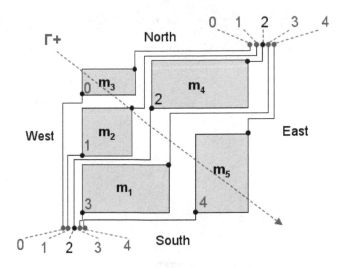

Figure 4. Coding-decoding transition method to get Γ+ (*m₃,m₂,m₄,m₁,m₅*) using the West-South and East-North corners of module to connect with those corners of layout

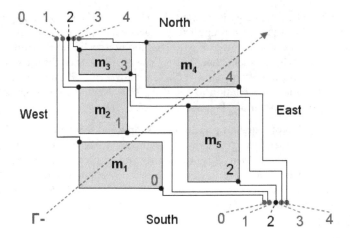

Figure 5. Coding-decoding transition method to get Γ- (*m₁,m₂, m₅,m₃,m₄*) using the West-North and East-South corners of module to connect with those corners of layout

without any intersection. As shown in Figure 5, we can get (*m₁,m₂, m₅,m₃,m₄*) as Γ- using the same method to get Γ+. The negative sequence Γ- is changed from the West-South corner to the East-North corner, i.e. from 0 to *n*-1 in Γ-. So far, we get the coding of a general 2D-packing topology based on North-South and West-East relation corresponding to the order of modules in sequence pair, as shown in Figure 6.

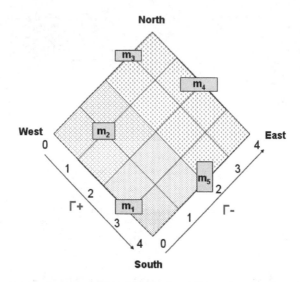

Figure 6. Intuitive image using slant grid (0,1,2,3,4) for Γ^+ and Γ^- to explain the relation between solution representation and 2D-packing topology

Generally, a 3D-packing topology is defined by the orthogonal coordinate system (x, y, z) in sequence triple and sequence quintuple representations. It is regarded as a set of the relations of relative location between boxes, i.e. "Top-Bottom", "North-South" and "West-East" (TB-, NS- and WE-) relations. Let $(m_i\ T\ m_j)$ denote that m_i is on the top of m_j. Similarly, $(m_i\ N\ m_j)$ and $(m_i\ W\ m_j)$ denote NS- and WE-relations. The rule of symmetry to be followed is that $(m_i\ T\ m_j)$ is the same relation as $(m_j\ B\ m_i)$. That is to say, the topology should be reversely decoded if the order of labeling is reversed.

We define the notation of sequence pair, sequence triple and sequence quintuple as follows. Let $(\Gamma^i[0], \Gamma^i[1], ..., \Gamma^i[n-1])$ be the components of Γ^i. Let $F^i(m_j)$ be the order of m_j in sequences Γ^i. For example, if $\Gamma^i[l]$ is m_j, then $F^i(m_j) = l$. So the order of m_j can be represented by $(F^1(m_j), F^2(m_j), ...)$. In general, let $A+B$ be the sequence which is the concatenation of A and B, and $A-B$ be the sequence obtained from A by removing all the elements in B, where A and B are sequences. Let us denote $A[i, j]$, where $i<j$, as the sequence $(A[i], A[i+1], ..., A[j])$, where $A = (A[0], A[1], ..., A[n-1])$.

In case of sequence pair, the two sequences generate a finite solution space which includes at least one optimal solution of 2D packing for area optimization by decoding. Sequence pair defines $(m_i\ W\ m_j)$ when

$$F^1(m_i) < F^1(m_j) \text{ and } F^2(m_i) < F^2(m_j)$$

It defines $(m_i\ N\ m_j)$ when

$$F^1(m_i) < F^1(m_j) \text{ and } F^2(m_i) > F^2(m_j)$$

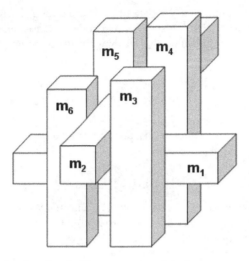

Figure 7. A 3D-packing topology decoded from sequence quintuple

For a given packing with n modules, the solution space is $(n!)^2$. If the rotation of the module is not fixed, then the solution space will increase to $(n!)^2 2^n$.

In case of sequence triple, it consists of three independent sequences Γ^i, where $1 \leq i \leq 3$. The coding and the decoding are based on TB-, NS- and WE- relation corresponding to the order of modules. sequence triple defines $(m_i \ W \ m_j)$ when

$$F^2(m_i) > F^2(m_j) \text{ and } F^3(m_i) < F^3(m_j).$$

It defines $(m_i \ N \ m_j)$ when

$$F^1(m_i) < F^1(m_j), F^2(m_i) < F^2(m_j)$$
$$\text{and } F^3(m_i) < F^3(m_j)$$

It defines $(m_i \ T \ m_j)$ when

$$F^1(m_i) < F^1(m_j), F^2(m_i) > F^2(m_j)$$
$$\text{and } F^3(m_i) > F^3(m_j)$$

For a given packing with n modules, the solution space is $(n!)^3$. If the rotation of the module is not fixed, then the solution space will increase to $(n!)^3 2^{3n}$.

However, sequence triple does not cover all kinds of topology of 3D packing. As shown in Figure 7, $(m_4 \ N \ m_1)$ and $(m_1 \ N \ m_6)$ lead to $(m_4 \ N \ m_6)$. At the same time, $(m_6 \ W \ m_2)$ and $(m_2 \ W \ m_4)$ lead to $(m_4 \ W \ m_6)$. The pair (m_4, m_6) is conflicting with the rule of uniqueness, i.e. each pair of modules should be assigned with a unique topology. That means the packing can not be represented by sequence triple. As a result, the topology with the minimum volume might not be covered by sequence triple.

In case of sequence quintuple, it consists of five sequences Γ^{i}, where $1 \leq i \leq 5$. Sequence quintuple generates a finite solution space which includes at least one optimal solution of 3D packing for volume optimization by decoding. sequence quintuple defines $(m_i \ W \ m_j)$ when

$$F^1(m_i) < F^1(m_j) \text{ and } F^2(m_i) < F^2(m_j)$$

It defines $(m_i \ N \ m_j)$ when

$$F^3(m_i) < F^3(m_j) \text{ and } F^4(m_i) < F^4(m_j)$$

It defines $(m_i \ T \ m_j)$ when

$$F^5(m_i) < F^5(m_j)$$

where m_i and m_j is overlapping in the projected xy-plane after WE- and NS- decoding. For a given packing with n modules, the solution space is $(n!)^5$. If the rotation of the module is not fixed, then the solution space will increase to $(n!)^5 2^{3n}$.

6. Moving methods for SA, 2-stage SA and MSA

According to section 5.2, we design the following moving methods. First of all, three basic moving methods, which are named by rotation, exchange and move, are used in the focusing search. Based on the basic methods, the group rotation and the group exchange are also used as two of moving methods in the rough search. They are repeatedly used the rotation and exchange operator with a given number. The groups are randomly selected modules for rotation or pairs of modules for exchange.

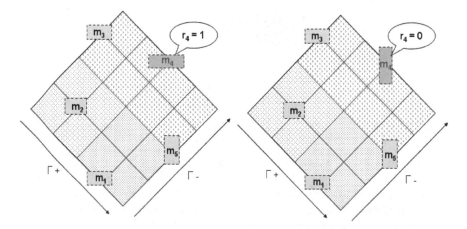

Figure 8. An example of layout before and after "rotation" in focusing search

In detail, the rotation changes the orientation of a module. When a rotation is applied to module m_i, r_i is changed to $1 - r_i$. As an example shown in Figure 8, if a rotation is applied to module m_4, r_4 is changed to $1 - r_4$. With respect to 3D packing, r_i is randomly selected from r_{x-i}, r_{y-i}, and r_{z-i}.

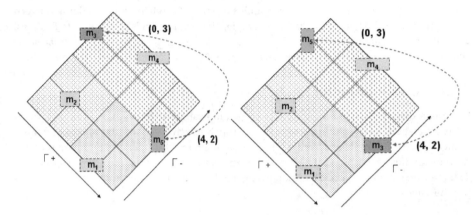

Figure 9. An example of layout before and after "exchange" in focusing search

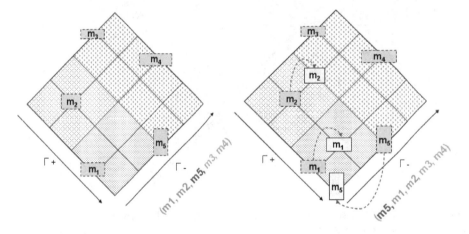

Figure 10. An example of layout before and after "move" in focusing search

The exchange moving method exchanges the order of two modules in Γ^i, where Γ^i corresponds to all sequences, i.e. the sequence pair (Γ^+, Γ^-), the sequence triple $(\Gamma^1, \Gamma^2, \Gamma^3)$ or the sequence quintuple $(\Gamma^1, \Gamma^2, \Gamma^3, \Gamma^4, \Gamma^5)$. When an exchange is applied to module m_i and m_j with sequence triple representation, $F^1(m_i)$, $F^2(m_i)$, $F^3(m_i)$, $F^1(m_j)$, $F^2(m_j)$ and $F^3(m_j)$ are changed to $F^1(m_j)$, $F^2(m_j)$, $F^3(m_j)$, $F^1(m_i)$, $F^2(m_i)$ and $F^3(m_i)$, respectively. In the case of sequence pair, $F_+(m_i)$, $F_-(m_i)$, $F_+(m_j)$, and $F_-(m_j)$ are changed to $F_+(m_j)$, $F_-(m_j)$, $F_+(m_i)$, and $F_-(m_i)$, respectively. For example, if the modules m_3 and the module m_5 are operated by the exchange in Figure 9, then $(F_+(m_5), F_-(m_5))$ is changed from $(4, 2)$ to $(0, 3)$, and $(F_+(m_3), F_-(m_3))$ is changed from $(0, 3)$ to $(4, 2)$.

The move changes the order of a module in Γ^i. When a move is applied to module m_i in Γ^i, $F^i(m_i)$ is changed to another value, say j, and the orders of modules whose order is between $F^i(m_i)$ and j are shifted accordingly. For example, , if the operation is to move m_5 to $F_-(m_5) = 0$ in Γ^-, the move will lead to $F_-(m_1) = F_-(m_1) + 1$ and $F_-(m_2) = F_-(m_2) + 1$, i.e.$\Gamma^-(m_1, m_2, m_5, m_3, m_4)$ is changed to $\Gamma^-(m_5, m_1, m_2, m_3, m_4)$ as shown in Figure 10.

7. Crossover operator for MSA

Besides, a special crossover operator is designed to generate a new solution from the current solution and the best solution so far in the rough search based on the representation in section 5.2. The margin and centre of the new solution (child) inherit the margin of the current solution (father) and the reversed centre of the best solution (mother), respectively. The reason to reverse the best solution is to get a different solution even two given solutions are the same solution.

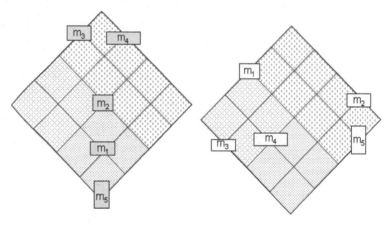

Figure 11. An example of two layouts before the crossover operator: the current layout (F: father) and the best layout so far (M: mother)

For the detail of crossover, two sequences Γ^+ and Γ^- are selected randomly from $(\Gamma^1, \Gamma^2, \Gamma^3)$ or $(\Gamma^1, \Gamma^2, \Gamma^3, \Gamma^4, \Gamma^5)$ for 3D packing. Let us denote the father as (Γ_f^+, Γ_f^-) which is selected from the current solution. The mother (Γ_m^+, Γ_m^-) is from the best solution so far. A number i is an integer randomly produced between 1 and $k/2-1$. The child of sequence pair (Γ_c^+, Γ_c^-) is given by $\Gamma_f^+[0, i] + \Gamma'_m^+ + \Gamma_f^+[(k-i-1), k-1]$ and $\Gamma_f^-[0, i] + \Gamma'_m^- + \Gamma_f^-[(k-i-1), k-1]$, where Γ'_m^+ and Γ'_m^- are the inverse of $\Gamma_m^+ - \Gamma_f^+[0, i] - \Gamma_f^+[(k-i-1), k-1]$ and the inverse of $\Gamma_m^- - \Gamma_f^-[0, i] - \Gamma_f^-[(k-i-1), k-1]$, respectively.

To make it clearer, let us take an example to explain the crossover operator. As shown in Figure 11, the left layout is represented by $\Gamma^+(m_3,m_4,m_2,m_1,m_5)$ and $\Gamma^-(m_5,m_1,m_2,m_3,m_4)$ as the father, which is the capital "F" in Figure 12. The right one is $\Gamma^+(m_1,m_3,m_4,m_2,m_5)$ and $\Gamma^-(m_3,m_4,m_1,m_5,m_2)$ as the mother, which is the reversed capital "M" in Figure 12. If we assume the i be 1, the child will be the layout $\Gamma^+(m_3,m_2,m_4,m_1,m_5)$ and $\Gamma^-(m_5,m_2,m_1,m_3,m_4)$ as the right layout of Figure 12, where $\Gamma^+(m_3, ..., m_5)$ and $\Gamma^-(m_5, ..., m_4)$ are from the father as the margin of left picture of Figure 12, and $\Gamma^+(...,m_2,m_4,m_1,...)$ and $\Gamma^-(...,m_2,m_1,m_3,...)$ are from mother with an inverse order as the centre of left picture of Figure 12.

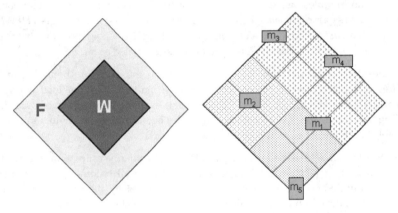

Figure 12. The layout (child) after the crossover operator between the current layout (F: father) and the best layout so far (M: mother) with an inverse order

8. Objectives and cost function

To solve multi-objective problem, we are using the total cost function, which includes area of bounding rectangle for 2D case, volume of bounding box for 3D case, interconnect power and maximal delay. Especially, the interconnect power and the maximal delay are two typical conflicting objectives, which need to experiment carefully to satisfy the requirements in real product design.

For the multi-objective optimization of 2D placement in this research, three different objectives are defined by one formula as follow.

$$C_t = \alpha \cdot C_p + \beta \cdot C_d + \gamma \cdot C_a \tag{2}$$

where $\alpha+\beta+\gamma=1$, and C_t is the total cost function, which includes the power function C_p, the delay function C_d and the area function C_a. And α, β, γ can be user-defined. As mentioned, C_p and C_d are normally conflicting in real implementation. That is to say, good C_p may lead to bad C_d, so we have to consider the trade-off between C_p and C_d using a lot of random values of α and β.

For power estimation, the dynamic power of a net n_i is proportional to $C(i)$, $V_{dd}(i)^2$, $f(i)$ and $S(i)$, where $C(i)$ is the capacitance of a net, $V_{dd}(i)$ is the voltage of power supply, $f(i)$ is the clock frequency, and $S(i)$ is switching probability of the net. Normally $C(i)$ is proportional to the length of net, so let Len_i represent its value. In case of no information, let us assume that $V_{dd}(i)$ and $f(i)$ are same for each net and $S(i)$ is randomly defined from 0 to 1. So the interconnect power is simplified as the function of Len_i and $S(i)$.

For performance estimation, the maximal delay among all nets is used. The delay is defined by the wire length of nets. To get the wire length estimation for each net, the half perimeter wire length ($HPWL$) is used for the approximation of wire length. Given any net n_i, connected with modules $\{m_1, m_2, ..., m_s\}$, $HPWL$ is half perimeter of the minimum bounding box for all centres of module m_i, where i is an integer from 1 to s. In case of $r_i=1$, $HPWL[n_i]$ is given by $max[x_i + h_i/2] - min[x_i + h_i/2] + max[y_i + w_i/2] - min[y_i + w_i/2]$. So $HPWL[n_i]$ is gotten from (h_i, w_i, n_i), (x_i, y_i, r_i). The power and the delay are estimated so far.

For the objective of 2D packing, the area estimation is the minimum bounding rectangle including all modules, which is the total height H multiplied by the total width W. In practical implementation, we use a relative value as the cost function of area, i.e. the bounding area divided by the area of total modules, because any value with unit would not be scalable to use the experiments by diverse benchmarks.

For the objective of 3D packing, instead of 2D case, the volume estimation is given by the minimum bounding rectangular parallelepiped including all modules, which is the total height H multiplied by the total width W and multiplied by the total length L. In real implementation, the cost function is also using the relative value of volume.

9. Experiment and comparison

To evaluate the effectiveness and reliability of the proposed MSA in practice, a set of experiments was implemented, comparing with traditional SA and 2-stage SA. In the case of 2D packing and placement, we are using ami49_X and MCNC benchmarks. The ami49_X is produced by duplicating ami49 circuit X times. In the case of 3D packing, ami98_3D benchmark is produced by inheriting the height and width of 2D ami49_2 benchmark and randomly getting the length between the given minimum and maximum dimensions. The implementation for 3D packing is to compare MSA with the mentioned 2-stage SA. MSA is implemented in Python environment on 2.16GHz PC with 3.00GB memory. For a fair comparison, SA and 2-stage SA is also implemented at the same machine. The maximum runtime is within 14,400s (4 hours) each time.

For area optimization of 2D packing, let γ be 1 and $\alpha+\beta$ be 0 in the cost function. As shown in Table 1, the best, average and worst cases among 50 trials are gotten. The comparison of solution quality and runtime between SA and MSA is gotten. MSA reduced near 21% runtime with better solution quality. As shown in Table 2, a near log-linear trend of average improvement rates from SA to MSA is gotten. That means MSA should be more suitable for the placement with a larger number of modules.

For interconnect optimization of 2D placement, let γ be 0 and $\alpha+\beta$ be 1 in the cost function. The experiment is using ami49_X benchmarks. To get the figures, α is randomly produced from 0.1 to 0.9. 240 solutions are tested for comparison. For all tested ami49_X with X from 1 to 12, block number from 49 to 588, and net number from 408 to 4896, the improved results are gotten. Figure 13 shows that MSA obtains at least 13% Pareto improvement with the constraint of less than 108.2% maximal delay. To get the worst cases, we tested more 120 solutions with α given by 0.1, 0.3, 0.5, 0.7, and 0.9. As shown in Figure 14, MSA got near 6% worst-case mitigation on average for the interconnect power with no degradation of maximal delay.

Benchmarks	Best (mm²)	Average (mm²)	Worst (mm²)	Runtime (s)
apte	47.08	47.36	47.67	3.2
xerox	19.80	20.50	21.21	1.5
hp	9.03	9.17	9.34	2.3
ami33	1.18	1.23	1.29	17
ami49	36.91	37.79	38.83	37
ami49_2	73.58	75.48	77.38	142
ami49_4	147.3	151.1	155.8	547

Table 1. Area optimization by MSA for 2D packing

Benchmarks	Solution(mm²)		Runtime (s)		Improvement (%)	
	SA	MSA	SA	MSA	Solution	Runtime
apte	47.38	47.36	4.1	3.2	0.04%	22%
xerox	20.51	20.50	1.9	1.5	0.05%	21%
hp	9.18	9.17	2.7	2.3	0.11%	15%
ami33	1.24	1.23	22	17	0.52%	23%
ami49	37.96	37.79	45	37	0.48%	18%
ami49_2	75.98	75.48	194	142	0.71%	27%
ami49_4	152.2	151.0	720	547	0.88%	24%

Table 2. Average improvement of area for 2D packing

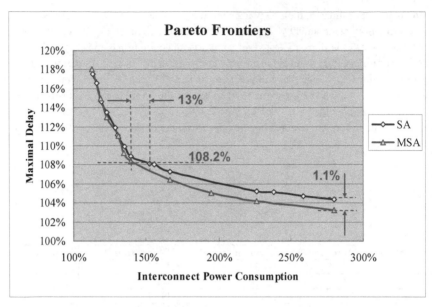

Figure 13. Pareto frontiers and its improvement by MSA for 2D placement (sequence pair)

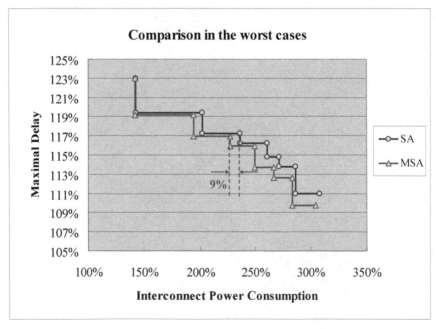

Figure 14. Worst-case mitigation by MSA for 2D placement (sequence pair)

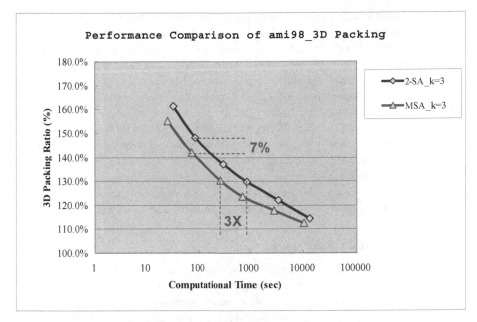

Figure 15. Performance improvement by MSA for 3D packing (sequence triple)

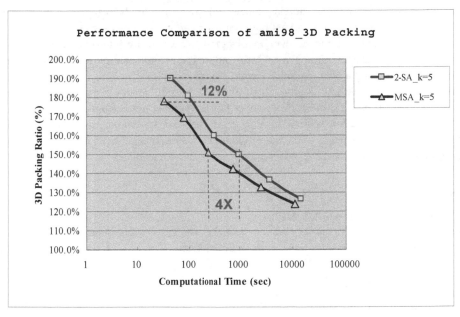

Figure 16. Performance improvement by MSA for 3D packing (sequence quintuple)

For volume optimization of 3D packing, we compare the computational performance of volume ratio using 2-stage SA and MSA. The results show considerable improvement from 2-stage SA to MSA. The improvement of packing ratio is between 2% and 7% for sequence triple representation. The improvement for runtime is up to 3 times, as shown in Figure 15. With regard to sequence quintuple representation, the experiment also shows the improvement from 2-stage SA to MSA. The improvement of packing ratio is between 3% and 12%. The improvement for runtime is up to 4 times with the sequence quintuple representation, as shown in Figure 16. The packing ratio of volume is improved by near 7% with less than 100s runtime, if we select MSA with sequence triple representation, instead of 2-stage SA with the same representation. The packing ratio of volume is improved by near 12% with less than 100s runtime, if we select MSA with sequence quintuple representation, instead of 2-stage SA with the same representation. In short, the overall solution quality and the runtime of MSA algorithm are better than these of 2-stage SA algorithm.

10. Conclusion and future work

In summary, the optimization techniques for integrated circuit (IC) layout design with large solution space are facing big challenges to get better solution quality with less runtime. In this research, a new simulated annealing based approach, named mixed simulated annealing (MSA), is proposed to solve three typical layout design problems, which are 2D packing, 2D placement and 3D packing, by using sequence pair, sequence triple and sequence quintuple representations. A new crossover operator is designed to reuse the information of past solutions and get high improving efficiency. Based on experiment, MSA improved both the best and the worst cases of 2D placement for interconnect power and maximal delay. For area minimization, MSA reduced computational runtime with the better solution quality, and a near log-linear trend of average improvement rates from SA to MSA is gotten for both solution quality and runtime. The overall quality of packing by MSA is normally better than the published results. For the volume minimization of 3D packing, MSA improved the solution quality (up to 12% better) and the computational time (up to 4 times faster). For the future work, the proposed MSA has potential to be extended to more general problems, such as 2D/3D packing or placement with rectilinear boxes.

Author details

Yiqiang Sheng and Atsushi Takahashi
Department of Communications and Integrated Systems, Graduate School of Science and Engineering, Tokyo Institute of Technology, Tokyo, Japan

Acknowledgement

The authors would like to thank Prof. Kunihiro Fujiyoshi at Tokyo University of Agriculture and Technology, to thank Prof. Shuichi Ueno, Dr. Tayu, Mr. Shinoda, Mr. Inoue and Mr.

Zhao at Tokyo Institute of Technology, and to thank Mr. Yamada, Mr. Ando and Mr. Ukon at Osaka University for their discussion, comment and support.

11. References

[1] S. Kirkpatrick, C. D. Gelatt and M. P. Vecchi, "Optimization by Simulated Annealing," *Science*, vol. 220, no. 4598, pages 671–680, 1983.

[2] B. Hajek, "Cooling schedules for optimal annealing," Mathematics of Operations Research, vol. 13, no. 2, pages 311–329, 1988.

[3] L. Ingber, "Simulated Annealing: Practice versus Theory," *Mathematical Computer Modelling*, vol.18, no.11, pages 29–57, 1993.

[4] J. Varanelli and J. Cohoon, "A two-stage simulated annealing methodology," *Fifth Great Lakes Symposium on VLSI*, pages 50-53, 1995.

[5] Y. Sheng, A. Takahashi and S. Ueno, "A Stochastic Optimization Method to Solve General Placement Problem Effectively," *Proceedings of Information Processing Society of Japan (IPSJ) DA Symposium*, vol. 2011, no.5, pages 27-32, 2011.

[6] Y. Sheng, A. Takahashi and S. Ueno, "RRA-Based Multi-Objective Optimization to Mitigate the Worst Cases of Placement," *The IEEE 9th International Conference on ASIC*, pages 357-360, 2011.

[7] S. Nakatake, K. Fujiyoshi, H. Murata, and Y. Kajitani, "Module placement on BSG-structure and IC layout applications," *Proceedings of International Conference on CAD*, pages 484-491, 1996.

[8] H. Murata, K. Fujiyoshi, S. Nakatake and Y. Kajitani, "VLSI module placement based on rectangle-packing by the sequence-pair," *IEEE Transactions on Computer-Aided Design of Integrated Circuits and Systems*, vol. 15, no. 12, pages 1518-1524, 1996.

[9] X. Tang and D. F. Wong, "FAST-SP: a fast algorithm for block placement based on sequence pair," *Proceedings of IEEE Asia South Pacific Design Automation Conference*, pages 521-526, 2001.

[10] C. Zhuang, K. Sakanushi, L. Jin and Y. Kajitani, "An enhanced Q-sequence augmented with empty-room-insertion and parenthesis trees," *Proceedings of Design, Automation and Test in Europe Conference and Exhibition*, pages 61-68, 2002.

[11] C. Kodama and K. Fujiyoshi, "Selected sequence-pair: an efficient decodable packing representation in linear time using sequence-pair," *Proceedings of IEEE Asia South Pacific Design Automation Conference*, pages 331-337, 2003.

[12] H. Yamazaki, K. Sakanushi, S. Nakatake and Y. Kajitani, "The 3D-Packing by Meta Data Structure and Packing Heuristics," *IEICE Transaction on Fundamentals of Electronics*, Communications and Computer Sciences, vol. E83-A, no. 4, pages 639-645, 2000.

[13] Y. Sheng, A. Takahashi and S. Ueno, "An Improved Simulated Annealing for 3D Packing with Sequence Triple and Quintuple Representations," *IEICE Technical Report on VLSI Design Technologies*, Vol.111, No.324, pp.209-214, 2011.

[14] Y. Sheng, A. Takahashi and S. Ueno, "2-Stage Simulated Annealing with Crossover Operator for 3D-Packing Volume Minimization," *Proceedings of the 17th Workshop on Synthesis And System Integration of Mixed Information technologies (SASIMI)*, pages 227-232, 2012.

Chapter 11

Design and Identification Problems of Rotor Bearing Systems Using the Simulated Annealing Algorithm

Fran Sérgio Lobato, Elaine Gomes Assis,
Valder Steffen Jr and Antônio José da Silva Neto

Additional information is available at the end of the chapter

1. Introduction

The study of rotating machinery appears in the context of machines and structures due to the significant number of phenomena typical to their operation that impact their dynamic behavior and maintenance. Consequently, rotor bearing systems face numerous problems that affect a wide variety of machines, e.g., compressors, pumps, motors, centrifuge machines, large and small turbines. This type of machine finds various applications in the industry, such as, automotive, aerospace and power generation. In most applications an unpredictable stoppage can lead to considerable financial losses and risks. Therefore, there is an evident need for the complete modelling of rotating systems, including the components of the interface between fixed and moveable parts, such as the hydrodynamic bearings. Bench-scale experimental analyses provide more complete models of the main components of the rotor, with strong emphasis on the modelling of the bearings of rotary machines, since they constitute the rotor-foundation structure connecting elements.

The machinery parameters are needed to study the dynamic behavior of the system, namely the Campbell diagram, stability analysis, critical speeds, excitation responses, control and health monitoring. The determination of unknown parameters in rotating machinery is a difficult task. To overcome this difficulty, the use of optimization techniques to solve the inverse problem represents an important alternative approach.

In the literature, various works have been proposed to determine unknown parameters of dynamic systems. Edwards et al. [1] presented a procedure to determine unbalance and support parameters simultaneously based on the least-squares method. Xu et al. [2] proposed a rotor balancing method by using optimization techniques, which does not need trial weights. Assis and Steffen [3] developed strategies in order to use optimization techniques for determining the parameters of gyroscopic systems and they commented about the difficulties that arise in using classical optimization algorithms due to their difficulty in avoiding local minima. The properties of the supports located at the ends of the rotor were considered as variables in the optimization procedure. An inverse problem was developed by using a hybrid cascade-type optimization scheme considering a single unbalance distribution. Castro et al. [4] proposed an optimization method based on genetic algorithms to tune displacements of the rotor supported by hydrodynamic bearings. Castro et al. [5] applied a hybrid algorithm based on genetic algorithm and simulated annealing to tune the orbits of the rotary system in the critical region. In this search algorithm, the genetic algorithm is applied in order to make an approximation of the optimal result, while the simulated annealing refines this result. Tiwari and Chakravarthy [6] presented an identification algorithm for simultaneous estimation of the residual unbalances and the bearing dynamic parameters by using the impulse response measurements for multi-degree-of-freedom flexible rotor-bearing systems. Kim et al. [7] presented a bearing parameter identification of rotor–bearing system using clustering-based hybrid evolutionary algorithm. Castro et al. [8] applied multi-objective genetic algorithm to identify unbalance parameters. Nauclér and Söderstöm [9] consider the problem of unbalance estimation of rotating machinery based on the development of a novel method which takes disturbances into account, leading to a nonlinear estimator. More recently, Saldarriaga et al. [10] proposed a methodology for the experimental determination of the unbalance distribution on highly flexible rotating machinery using Genetic Algorithms. Modal analysis techniques were previously performed to obtain an initial guess for the unknown parameters. A pseudo-random optimization-based approach was used first to identify the parameters of the system in such a way that a reliable rotor model was obtained. Satisfactory results encouraged the use of the proposed approach in the industrial context. Sudhakar and Sekhar [11] proposed a method dedicated to fault identification in a rotor bearing system by minimizing the difference between equivalent loads estimated in the system due to the fault and theoretical fault model loads. This method has a limitation since the error found in the identified fault parameters increases when decreasing the number of measured experimental data.

In this context, the present chapter discusses the possibility of using the Simulated Annealing algorithm (SA) for the identification of unknown parameters of a rotor model from the unbalanced response of the system. Basically, the SA algorithm exploits the analogy between the search for a minimum in the optimization problem and the process of gradual cooling of a metal in a crystalline structure of minimal energy. A desirable characteristic of a minimum search method is the ability to avoid the convergence to a local optimal point, e.g., in terms of the physical process of annealing a meta-stable structure is obtained in the end. Thus, the paradigm of SA is to offer means of escaping from local optima through the analysis of the neighbourhood of the current solution, which can assume, within a given probability, worse solutions, but makes the finding of a new path to the global optimum possible. Metropolis et al. [12] presented an algorithm that simulates the evolution of a crystalline structure in the liquid state up to its thermal equilibrium.

Metropolis' algorithm can be used to generate sequences of configurations in a combinatorial optimization problem. SA is seen as a sequence of Metropolis algorithms, executed with a decreasing sequence of the control parameter. The temperature (control parameter) is continually reduced after a certain number of neighbourhood searches in the current state.

It is worth mentioning that although the SA is a powerful and important optimization tool, often it is not applied according to strict adherence to sufficiency conditions, permitting the researcher to truly claim that the optimal solution has been (statistically) found. According to Ingber [13], the reason typically given is simply that many variants of this technique are considered to be too consuming of resources to be applied in such strict fashion. There exist faster variants of SA canonical, but these apparently are not as quite easily coded and so they are not widely used. Many modifications of SA are really quenching, and should aptly be called simulated quenching (SQ).

In the present contribution, the canonical SA, e.g., based on the algorithm proposed by Kirkpatrick et al. [14] to include a temperature schedule for efficient searching, is used for the design and identification of rotor bearing systems. The goal for the first problem presented is to increase the difference between two critical speeds of a rotor-bearing system that was previously modelled by using the finite element method. In this case, the design variables are the parameters of the rotor-bearing system. To solve this multi-criteria optimization problem a methodology based on a combination of SA, non-dominated sorting strategy and crowding distance operator for guaranteeing convergence and diversity of potential candidates in the population is proposed. The second problem studied is related to the identification of unknown parameters of flexible rotor-bearing systems, modelled mathematically by using the finite element method. The difference between the unbalance experimental responses of the rotor and the simulated unbalance responses (obtained by using the mathematical model) is used to write the objective function to be minimized, so that the damping and stiffness parameters are found. For illustration purposes, the *experimental* (synthetic) data used were generated by using the solution of the direct problem to which artificial noise was added.

This chapter is organized as follows. The rotor bearing formulation is revisited in Section 4. In Sections 5 and 6 the main characteristics of the SA and multi-objective optimization are briefly presented, respectively. The Multi-objective Optimization Simulated Annealing (MOSA) proposed in this work is described in Section 7. The results and discussion are presented in Section 8. Finally, the conclusions and suggestions for future work complete the chapter.

2. Rotor bearing modelling

The mathematical model used to calculate the unbalance forces, natural frequencies and vibration mode shapes is obtained by using the Finite Element Method. The discrete rotor model is composed of symmetric rigid disc elements, symmetric Timoshenko beam elements, nonsymmetric coupling elements, and nonsymmetric viscous damped bearings, as presented in Figure 1.

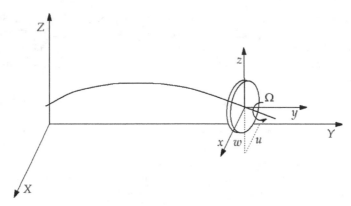

Figure 1. Rotor references frames.

Two reference systems are considered, namely the inertial frame (X,Y,Z) and the frame (x,y,z) that is fixed to the disk [3]. By using the Lagrange's equations in steady-state conditions, the rotor model is represented by the following matrix differential equation [15]:

$$M\ddot{q} + C\dot{q} + Kq = F_1 + F_2 \sin(\Omega t) + F_3 \cos(\Omega t) + F_4 \sin(a\Omega t) + F_5 \cos(a\,\Omega t) \qquad (1)$$

where q is the N order generalized coordinate displacement vector; K is the stiffness matrix which takes into account the symmetric matrices of the beam and the nonsymmetric matrices of the bearings; C is the matrix containing the antisymmetric matrices due to gyroscopic effects and the nonsymmetric matrices due to bearings viscous damping; F_1 is the constant body force such as gravity; F_2 and F_3 are the forces due to unbalance; F_4 and F_5 are the forces due to the nonsynchronous effect; and a is a constant.

3. Simulated annealing

SA resembles the cooling process of molten metal through annealing (slow cooling process). At high temperature (T), the atoms in the molten metal can move freely with respect to each other, but as the temperature is reduced, the movement of the atoms gets restricted. The atoms start to get arranged and finally form crystals having the minimum possible energy which depends on the cooling rate. If the temperature is reduced at a very fast rate, the crystalline state may not be achieved at all and, instead, the system may end up in a polycrystalline state, which may have a higher energy state than the crystalline state. Therefore, in order to achieve the absolute minimum energy state, the temperature should be reduced at a slow rate [16].

From the optimization point of view, this physical process is analogous to the determination of near-global or global optimum solutions. The energy of the atoms represents the objective function and the final ground state corresponds to the global minimum of the objective function. The analogy between the physical system and the optimization problem is shown in Table 1 [17].

Physical system	Optimization problem
State	Feasible Solution
Energy	Cost Function
Ground state	Optimal solution
Rapid quenching	Local search
Careful annealing	Simulated annealing

Table 1. Analogy between simulated annealing and optimization.

The basic steps of canonical SA are presented in Figure 2 and described in the following subsections [18].

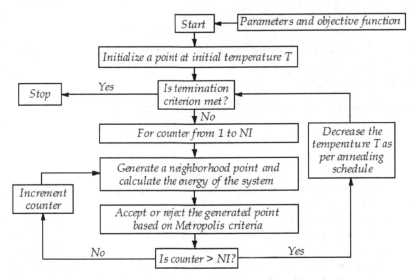

Figure 2. Simulated Annealing algorithm flowchart (*NI* is the number of iterations).

3.1. Initial population

In this iterative technique, an initial guess is randomly generated according to the design space. It should be emphasized that other forms of generating the initial population can be used to initialize the optimization process.

3.2. Initial temperature

The control of the 'temperature' parameter must be carefully defined since it controls the acceptance rule defined by the Boltzmann distribution. T has to be large enough to enable the algorithm to move off a local minimum but small enough not to move off a global minimum. According to Chibante et al. [18], the value of T should be defined in an application based approach (*ad-hoc*) since it is related with the magnitude of the objective function value.

3.3. Perturbation mechanism

This operator permits the creation of new solutions from the current one. In other words it deals with the exploration of the neighbourhood of the current solution by adding small changes to the current solution.

A solution s is defined as a vector $s = (x_1, ..., x_n)$ representing a point in the search space. A new solution is generated by using a vector $\sigma = (\sigma_1, ..., \sigma_n)$ of standard deviations to create a perturbation from the current solution. A neighbour solution is then produced from the present solution by:

$$x_{i+1} = x_i + N(0,\sigma_i)$$ (2)

where $N(0,\sigma_i)$ is a random Gaussian number with zero mean and σ_i standard deviation.

3.4. Temperature update

The most common cooling schedule is the geometric rule for temperature variation:

$$T_{i+1} = \exp\left(\frac{\log\left(stop_{temp}/start_{temp} \right)}{n_{temp} - 1} \right) T_i$$ (3)

where $stop_{temp}$ and $start_{temp}$ are the final temperature (standard deviation) and the initial temperature, respectively, and n_{temp} is the number of temperatures considered. However, other schedules have been proposed in the literature [19]. Another parameter is the number of iterations for each temperature, which is often related with the size of the search space or with the size of the neighbourhood. This number of iterations can even be constant or, alternatively, can be defined as a function of the temperature or based on a feedback from the process [18].

3.5. Termination criterion

Among the several strategies proposed for the termination of the algorithm, we can cite some very common approaches: the maximum number of iterations; the minimum temperature value; the minimum value of the objective function; the minimum value of the acceptance rate and the maximum computational time.

4. Multi-objective optimization

Real-world design problems involve the simultaneous optimization of two or more (often conflicting) objectives, known as multi-objective optimization problems (MOOP). The solution of such problems is different from the one of the single-objective optimization problems. The main difference is that MOOP normally have not one but a set of solutions, which should be equally satisfactory [20,21].

Traditionally, the treatment of such problems is done by transforming the original MOOP into a scalar single-objective problem. Several studies dealing with multi-objective optimization techniques have been reported over the past decades, based on the Kuhn-Tucker's criterion. These techniques follow the preference-based approach in which a relative preference vector is used to rank multiple objectives. Classical searching and optimization methods use a point-to-point approach, in which the solution is successively modified so that the outcome of the classical optimization method is a single optimized solution. However, Evolutionary Algorithms (EA) can find multiple optimal solutions in one single simulation run due to their population-based search approach. Thus, EA are ideally suited for multi-objective optimization problems.

When dealing with MOOP, the notion of optimality needs to be extended. The most common one in the current literature is that originally proposed by Edgeworth [22] and later generalized by Pareto [23]. This notion is called Edgeworth-Pareto optimality, or simply Pareto optimality, and refers to finding good tradeoffs among all the objectives. This definition leads to a set of solutions that is known as the Pareto optimal set, whose corresponding elements are called non-dominated or non-inferior. The concept of optimality in the single objective context is not directly applicable in MOOPs. For this reason a classification of the solutions is introduced in terms of Pareto optimality, according to the following definitions [20]:

- **Definition 1** - The Multi-objective Optimization Problem (MOOP) can be defined as:

$$f(x) = \left(f_1(x), f_2(x), ..., f_m(x) \right), \ m = 1, ..., M \tag{4}$$

subject to

$$h(x) = \left(h_1(x), h_2(x), ..., h_i(x) \right), \ i = 1, ..., H \tag{5}$$

$$g(x) = \left(g_1(x), g_2(x), ..., g_j(x) \right), \ j = 1, ..., J \tag{6}$$

$$x = \left(x_1, x_2, ..., x_n \right), \ n = 1, ..., N, \ x \in X \tag{7}$$

where x is the vector of design (or decision) variables, f is the vector of objective functions and X is denoted as the design (or decision) space. The constraints h and g (≥ 0) determine the feasible region.

- **Definition 2** - Pareto Dominance: for any two decision vectors u and v, u is said to dominate v, if u is not worse than v in all objectives and u is strictly better than v in at least one objective.
- **Definition 3** - Pareto Optimality: when the set P is the entire search space, or $P = S$, the resulting non-dominated set P' is called the Pareto-optimal set. Like global and local

optimal solutions in the case of single-objective optimization, there could be global and local Pareto-optimal sets in multi-objective optimization.

In the multi-objective context, various Multiple-Objective Evolutionary Algorithms (MOEAs) can be found. This group of algorithms conjugates the basic concepts of dominance described above with the general characteristics of evolutionary algorithms. Basically, the main features of these MOEAs are [20,21]:

- **Mechanism of adaptation assignment in terms of dominance** - between a non-dominated solution and a dominated one, the algorithm will favour the non-dominated solution. Moreover, when both solutions are equivalent in dominance, the one located in a less crowded area will be favoured. Finally, the extreme points (e.g. the solutions that have the best value in one particular objective) of the non-dominated population are preserved and their adaptation is better than any other non-dominated point, to allow for maximum front expansion.
- **Incorporation of elitism** - the elitism is commonly implemented using a previously stored secondary population of non-dominated solutions. When performing recombination (selection-crossover-mutation), parents are taken from this file in order to produce the offspring.

In the literature, various multi-objective algorithms based on SA have been proposed. Basically, the first extensions were proposed by Serafini [24,25] and by Ululgu and Teghem [26], where various ways of defining the probability in the multi-objective framework and how they affect the performance of SA based multi-objective algorithms. Czyzak et al. [27] combined mono-criterion SA and genetic algorithm to provide efficient solutions for multi-criteria shortest path problem. Ulungu et al. [28] designed a MOSA (Multi-objective Optimization Simulated Annealing) algorithm and tested its performance using multi-objective combinatorial optimization problems. Suppapitnarm et al. [29] used the neighbourhood perturbation method to create a new point around an old point using MOSA. In this algorithm, the single objective SA is modified to give a set of non-dominated solutions by using archiving of solutions generated earlier, and using a sorting procedure (based on non-dominance and crowding). Kasat et al. [30] used the concept of jumping genes in natural genetics to modify the binary-coded non-dominated sorting genetic algorithm (NSGA-II) to give NSGA-II-JG. Smith et al. [31] compared the candidate to the current solution according to the cardinalities of their dominant subsets in the file. Marcoulaki and Papazoglou [32] proposed a new multiple objective optimization approach by using a Monte Carlo-based algorithm stemmed from SA. Since the expected result in a multiple objective optimization task is usually a set of Pareto-optimal solutions, the optimization problem states assumed here are themselves sets of solutions.

5. Multi-objective optimization simulated annealing – MOSA

Due to the success obtained by the SA in different science and engineering applications, their extension to the multi-objective context is desirable. In this work, the Multi-objective

Optimization Simulated Annealing (MOSA) algorithm is proposed. This approach is based on the classical SA associated with the so-called Fast Non-Dominated Sorting operator and has the following structure:

- An initial population of size NP is randomly generated;
- All dominated solutions are removed from the population through the operator Fast Non-Dominated Sorting. In this way, the population is sorted into non-dominated fronts μ_j (sets of vectors that are non-dominated with respect to each other) [20,21];
- Following, SA is applied to generate the new population (potential candidates to solve the MOOP);
- If the number of individuals of the population is larger than a number defined by the user, it is truncated according to the Crowding Distance criterion [20,21].

The steps presented are repeated until a determined stopping criterion is reached. The operators used in the MOSA are described below.

5.1. Fast non-dominated sorting

The so-called Fast Non-Dominated Sorting operator was proposed by Deb et al. [21] in order to sort a population of size N according to the level of non-domination. Each solution must be compared with every other solution in the population to find if the solution is dominated. This requires O(MN) comparisons for each solution, where M is the number of objective functions. When this process is continued to find the members of the first non-dominated class for all population members, the total complexity is O(MN²). At this point, all individuals in the first non-dominated front are found. In order to obtain the individuals in the next front, the solutions of the first front are temporarily discarded and the above procedure is repeated. In the worst case, the task of obtaining the second front also requires O(MN²) computations. The procedure is repeated so that subsequent fronts are found.

5.2. Crowding distance operator

This operator describes the density of solutions surrounding a vector. To compute the Crowding Distance for a set of population members the vectors are sorted according to their objective function value for each objective function. To the vectors with the smallest or largest values, an infinite Crowding Distance (or an arbitrarily large number for practical purposes) is assigned. For all other vectors, the Crowding Distance ($dist_{x_i}$) is calculated according to [20,21]:

$$dist_{x_i} = \sum_{j=1}^{m} \frac{f_{j,i+1} - f_{j,i-1}}{\left| f_{j\max} - f_{j\min} \right|} \tag{8}$$

where f_j corresponds to the j-th objective function and m equals the number of objective functions. This operator is important to avoid many points close together in the Pareto's Front and to promote the diversity in terms of space objectives [21].

5.3. Consideration of constraints

In this work, the treatment of constraints is made through the Static Penalization Method, proposed by Castro [33]. This approach consists in assigning limit values to each objective function to play the role of penalization parameters. According to Castro [33], it is guaranteed that any non-dominated solution dominates any solution that violates at least one of the constraints. In the same way, any solution that violates only one constraint will dominate any solution that presents two constraint violations, and so on. For a constrained problem the vector containing the objective functions to be accounted for, is given by:

$$f(x) \equiv f(x) + r_p n_{viol} \tag{9}$$

where $f(x)$ it is the vector of objective functions, r_p it is the vector of penalty parameters that depends on the type of problem considered, and n_{viol} is the number of violated constraints.

6. Applications

6.1. Rotor-dynamics design

Modern design of rotor-bearing systems usually aims at increasing power output and improved overall efficiency. The demanding requirements placed on modern rotating machines, such as turbines, electric motors, electrical generators, compressors, turbo-pumps, have introduced a need for higher speeds and lower vibration levels [34]. This problem can be formulated as a multi-objective problem aiming at minimizing, for instance, the total weight of the shaft, the transmitted forces at the bearings and the positions of the critical speeds [35]. In this context, the present application considers the maximization of the difference between the 6th and 5th critical speeds for the system whose finite element model is composed of rigid disks with seventeen elements, two bearings and two additional masses, as shown in Figure 3.

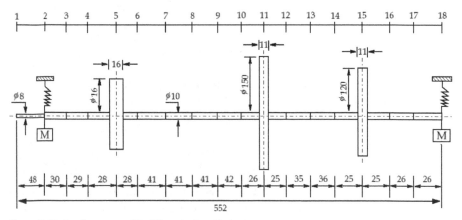

Figure 3. Finite element model of the rotor-bearing system.

The material used for the shaft and disks is the steel-1020 (density = 7800 Kg/m³, Elasticity modulus = 2.1E11 N/m² and Poisson coefficient = 0.3). The shaft geometry is so that the diameter and length are 10 mm and 552 mm, respectively. The geometric characteristics of the disks are presented in Table 2.

Disc	Mass (Kg)	Moment of Inertia (Kg m²)	External Diameter (mm)	Thickness (mm)
1	0.818	0.0008	90	16.0
2	1.600	0.0045	150	11.2
3	0.981	0.0018	120	10.6

Table 2. Geometric characteristics of the disks.

Mathematically, the optimization problem can be formulated as:

$$\min f_1(x) = \left(ROT_{\text{inf}} - a_1 v_c(5) \right)^2 \tag{10}$$

$$\min f_2(x) = \left(v_c(6) - a_2 ROT_{\text{sup}} \right)^2 \tag{11}$$

where v_c is the critical speeds vector, ROT_i are the permissible rotations (i=inf or sup), a_1=1.3 and a_2=1.3.

For evaluating the methodology proposed in this work, some practical points regarding the application of this procedure should be emphasized:

1. The design variables are the following: radius of bar elements (x_i), where the design space is given by: 0.4 mm $\leq x_i \leq$ 0.8 mm.
2. ROT_{inf} = 1400 Hz and ROT_{inf} = 1900 Hz.
3. To solve the optimization problem the following heuristics are used:
    *   Non-dominated Sorting Genetic Algorithm (NSGAII) parameters [20,36]: population size (50), crossover probability (0.8), mutation probability (0.01). For the considered parameters, the number of objective function evaluations is 12550.
    *   Multi-objective Optimization Differential Evolution (MODE) parameters [37]: population size (50), perturbation rate (0.8), crossover probability (0.8), DE/rand/1/bin strategy for the generation of potential candidates, reduction rate (0.9) and number of pseudo-curves (10). For the considered parameters, the number of objective function evaluations is 15050.
    *   Multi-objective Optimization Simulated Annealing (MOSA) parameters [14]: population size (50), initial temperature (5.0), cooling rate (0.75), number of temperatures (20), number of times the procedure is repeated before the temperature is reduced (25), and tolerance (10⁻⁶). For the considered parameters, the number of objective function evaluations is 12550.
4. Stopping criterion: maximum number of generations (250).

5. Each algorithm was run 20 times by using 20 different seeds for the random generation of the initial population.
6. Objective Function (OFA) is the best value of objective function considering the first objective proposed. Objective Function (OFB) is the best value of objective function considering the second objective function. Objective Function (OFc) is calculated using the origin of the coordinated axes as a reference, e.g., the point (0,0) is used to obtain the distance between this point and each one of the solution points along the Pareto's Front. Thus, the smallest distance obtained was defined as the choice criterion.

Figure 4 shows the Pareto's Front obtained by NSGA II, MODE and MOSA algorithms.

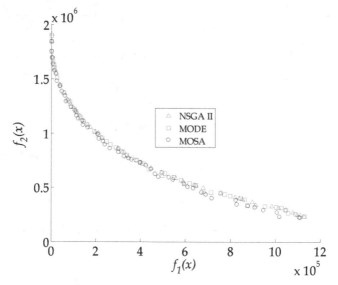

Figure 4. Pareto's Front.

In this figure it is possible to observe that all evolutionary algorithms are able to obtain, satisfactorily, the Pareto's Front for a similar number of objective function evaluations.

Table 3 present some points of Pareto's Front obtained by the MOSA algorithm by considering the criteria specified earlier.

6.2. Identification

As mentioned earlier, the identification of unknown parameters in rotating machinery is a difficult task and optimization techniques represent an important alternative for this goal [3,38,39]. The machine parameters are needed to perform the dynamic analysis and prediction of rotor-bearing systems: Campbell diagram, stability, critical speeds, excitation responses [15]. Another important aspect is when one desires to tune a finite element model to match experimental data generated by tests of an actual rotor system [10].

	OF$_A$	OF$_B$	OF$_C$
x_1 (mm)	0.55186	0.40015	0.50692
x_2 (mm)	0.49994	0.42153	0.52587
x_3 (mm)	0.53139	0.40623	0.50733
x_4 (mm)	0.79128	0.40000	0.50851
x_5 (mm)	0.49810	0.40000	0.50726
x_6 (mm)	0.55709	0.40000	0.50025
x_7 (mm)	0.41059	0.40000	0.50811
x_8 (mm)	0.71018	0.40000	0.50683
x_9 (mm)	0.57777	0.40151	0.50713
x_{10} (mm)	0.44676	0.41028	0.50192
x_{11} (mm)	0.79883	0.40000	0.49997
x_{12} (mm)	0.67159	0.40000	0.50671
x_{13} (mm)	0.57684	0.40000	0.50592
x_{14} (mm)	0.46109	0.40000	0.51012
x_{15} (mm)	0.52452	0.40000	0.50257
x_{16} (mm)	0.61355	0.40399	0.50747
x_{17} (mm)	0.57261	0.40281	0.50533
f_1 (Hz^2)	0.00364	1110741.5	479693.69
f_2 (Hz^2)	1842938.0	225219.04	602024.24

Table 3. Results obtained using MOSA (all the algorithms were executed 20 times so that average values were calculated).

Furthermore, identification procedures try to establish an unequivocal relation in between the damage and specific mechanical parameters, based on a suitable model and can be used to fault detection and machinery diagnosis as in Seibold and Fritzen [40]. On a simple manner parameter identification of rotor-bearing systems can be performed as follows: *i*) the frequency response function (or unbalance response) is measured for different operation speeds; *ii*) the design variables (unknown parameters) are initialized; *iii*) and an error function between experimental and simulated data is minimized.

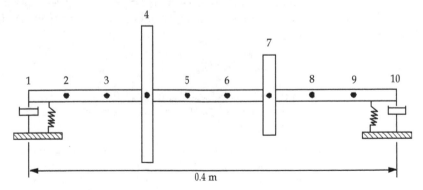

Figure 5. Rotor system finite element model.

In this application, a simple flexible rotor containing two disks and two bearings is studied. The Figure 5 shows the finite element model of the system with 10 nodes, 2 disks and two bearings.

The characteristics of bearing and disks are given in Table 4. It can be observed that damping parameters are also taken into account in this application.

Bearing	Stiffness(N/m)			Damping (Nm/s)		
	k_{xx}	k_{zz}	k_{xz}	c_{xx}	c_{zz}	c_{xz}
A=B	1E06	2E06	1E04	1E03	2E03	1E02
Disk	External Diameter (m)			Thickness (m)		
1	0.5			0.005		
2	0.3			0.005		

Table 4. Parameters of bearings and disks.

The goal of this application is to identify the unknown parameters of the rotor-bearing system, e.g., the stiffness and damping parameters. For this purpose the following steps are established:

1. The objective function consists in the determination of the stiffness and damping values through the minimization of the difference between the experimental and calculated values given by the solution of the direct problem. To mimic real experimental data, sets of synthetic experimental data were generated from eq. (12):

$$\theta_i^{exp} = \theta_i^{cal}\left(Z_{exact}\right) + \kappa\lambda \tag{12}$$

were θ represents the calculated values of the unbalance response by using known values of the physical properties Z_{exact} (k_{xx}, k_{zz}, k_{xz}, c_{xx}, c_{zz}, c_{xz}). In real applications these values are not available (they can be obtained through the solution of the corresponding inverse problem). κ simulate the standard deviation of the measurement errors, and λ is a pseudo-random number from the interval [-1, 1].

$$\theta_i^{exp} = \theta_i^{cal}\left(Z_{exact}\right) + \kappa\lambda \tag{13}$$

In order to examine the accuracy of the inverse problem approach for the estimation of the physical parameters, the influence of noise (κ =0.02, e.g., corresponding to 5% error) was compared to the case without noise (κ =0).

The design variables considered to generate the synthetic experimental data are presented in Table 5. The following ranges for the design space are considered: 5.0E05 N/m ≤ k_{xx} ≤ 1.2E07 N/m, 1.0E06 N/m ≤ k_{zz} ≤ 2.4E07 N/m, 5.0E03 N/m ≤ k_{xz} ≤ 1.2E05 N/m, 5.0E02 Nm/s ≤ c_{xx} ≤ 1.2E04 Nm/s, 1E03 Nm/s ≤ c_{zz} ≤ 2.4E04 Nm/s, 1E01 Nm/s ≤ c_{xz} ≤ 1.2E03 Nm/s.

2. To solve the optimization problem the following heuristics are used:
    - Genetic Algorithm (GA) parameters [41]: population size (50), type of selection (normal geometric in the range [0 0.08]), type of crossover Arithmetic, 2), type of mutation (non-uniform [2 100 3]).
    - Differential Evolution (DE) parameters [42]: population size (25), perturbation rate and crossover probability both equal to 0.8 and DE/rand/1/bin strategy.
    - Particle Swarm Optimization (PS) parameters [43]: population size (25), maximum velocity (100), upper limits (2.0), and a linearly decreasing inertia weight starting at 0.7 and ending at 0.4 was used.
    - Simulated Annealing (SA) parameters [14]: initial design (generated randomly in the design space), initial temperature (5.0), cooling rate (0.75), number of temperatures (20), number of times the procedure is repeated before the temperature is reduced (25), and tolerance (10^{-6}).
3. Stopping criterion: maximum number of objective function evaluations equal to 5000.
4. Each algorithm was run 20 times by using 20 different seeds for the random generation of the initial population.

Table 5 presents the results obtained by the algorithms considered (pristine condition and noisy data).

Considering $\kappa=0$ (see Table 5), all the optimization strategies were able to estimate the parameters satisfactorily as shown by the values obtained for the objective function. However, the SA algorithm shows to be very competitive, in averege, with the smallest standard deviation of the objective function. When noise is taken into account ($\kappa=0.002$, e.g., error corresponding to 5%), all the algorithms were able to obtain good estimates, as presented in Figure 6.

	Error	k_{xx} (N/m)	k_{zz} (N/m)	k_{xz} (N/m)	c_{xx} (Nm/s)	c_{zz} (Nm/s)	c_{xz} (Nm/s)	OF
SA	0 %	984674.3	1802257.4	24197.8	1157.4	1953.4	168.4	4.38
	5 %	962861.5	1817105.5	18378.3	1046.6	2843.4	35.8	7.01
GA	0 %	998204.7	2030908.5	3589.1	1078.8	2068.1	149.7	4.42
	5 %	986445.7	2114381.8	8695.9	1010.5	2164.4	25.8	07.11
DE	0 %	1000380.9	2005635.1	17449.8	1102.4	2092.8	183.7	4.35
	5 %	970336.4	1964371.6	46943.8	1037.2	2347.5	84.5	6.96
PS	0 %	987254.1	2098581.6	57858.5	1079.1	1425.6	119.8	4.40
	5 %	990895.2	2042193.6	15630.8	1118.9	1937.8	189.7	7.09

Table 5. Estimation Results.

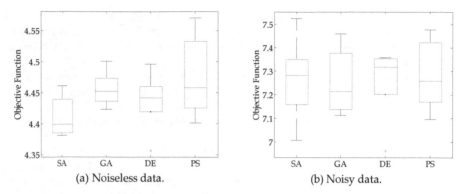

(a) Noiseless data.   (b) Noisy data.

Figure 6. Boxplots showing the influence of different optimizaion strategies to solve the inverse problem.

7. Conclusions

In the present contribution, the mono and multi-objective algorithms based on Simulated Annealing were used in the design and identification of rotor bearing systems. For illustration purposes, two simple test-cases were studied by using the proposed methodology. The goal for the first application was to increase the difference between two critical speeds of the rotor-bearing system through the formulation of a multi-objective problem, where the radii of bar elements were taken as design variables. To solve this multi-objective problem the Multi-objective Optimization Simulated Annealing (MOSA) algorithm was proposed. This evolutionary strategy is based on the Simulated Annealing algorithm associated with the non-dominated sorting and crowding distance operators. The second application consists in the identification of unknown parameters of flexible rotor-bearing systems. The objective function was defined as the difference between the unbalance experimental responses of the rotor and the simulated unbalance responses so that the parameters of damping and stiffness are obtained by an inverse problem approach. The *experimental* (synthetic) data used were generated by using the solution of the direct problem and adding artificial noise. In all applications, the finite element method was used to obtain the mathematical model of the system.

It is important to emphasize that the results obtained in both test-cases are considered satisfactory as compared with those obtained by other evolutionary strategies. In addition, it is possible to conclude that the proposed methodology represents an interesting alternative for design and identification of mechanical systems.

Further research work will be focused on the influence of the optimization parameter values on the solution of the optimization problem. Also, strategies to dynamically update the SA parameters will be evaluated. Finally, the authors will study the performance of the Simulated Quenching algorithm aiming at proposing a hybrid approach involving the Simulated Annealing and Simulated Quenching algorithms.

Author details

Fran Sérgio Lobato, Elaine Gomes Assis and Valder Steffen Jr
Universidade Federal de Uberlândia, Brazil

Antônio José da Silva Neto
Universidade do Estado do Rio de Janeiro, Brazil

Acknowledgement

The authors acknowledge the financial support provided by FAPEMIG and CNPq (INCT-EIE). The fourth author is grateful to the financial support provided by CNPq and FAPERJ.

8. References

[1] Edwards, S., Lees, W., Friswell, M. Experimental Identification of Excitation and Support Parameters of a Flexible-Rotor-Bearing Foundation System for a Single Rundown. Journal of Sound and Vibration; 2000, 232 (5), 963-992.

[2] Xu, B., Qu, L., Sun, R. The Optimization Technique Based Balancing of Flexible Rotors Without Test Runs. Journal of Sound and Vibration; 2000, 238 (5), 877-892.

[3] Assis, E. G., Steffen Jr, V. Inverse problem techniques for the identification of rotor-bearing systems. Inverse Problems in Science and Engineering; 2003, 11 (1), 39-53.

[4] Castro, H. F., Idehara, S. J., Cavalca, K. L., Dias Jr., M. Updating Method Based on Genetic Algorithm Applied to Nonlinear Bearing Model, Proceedings of ImechE 2004, 8th International Conference on Vibrations in Rotating Machinery, Swansea, UK; 2004, 1-10.

[5] Castro, H. F., Cavalca, K. L., Mori, B. D. Journal Bearing Orbits Fitting Method with Hybrid Meta-heuristic Method, Proceedings of the COBEM2005, Ouro Petro, Brazil; 2005, 1-10.

[6] Tiwari, R., Chakravarthy, V. Simultaneous Identification of Residual Unbalances and Bearing Dynamic Parameters from Impulse Responses of Rotor–Bearing Systems. Mechanical Systems and Signal Processing; 2006, 20, 1590-1614.

[7] Kim, Y.-H., Yang, B.-S., Tan, A. C. C. Bearing Parameter Identification of Rotor–Bearing System using Clustering-Based Hybrid Evolutionary Algorithm. Structural and Multidisciplinary Optimization; 2007, 33 (6), 493-506.

[8] Castro, H. F., Cavalca, K. L., Camargo, L. W. F. Multi-objective Genetic Algorithm Application in Unbalance Identification for Rotating Machinery. Proceedings of ImechE 2008 - 9th International Conference on Vibration in Rotating Machinery, London; 2008, 885-897.

[9] Nauclér, O., Söderström, T. Unbalance Estimation using Linear and Nonlinear Regression. Automatica; 2010, 46, 1752-1761.

[10] Saldarriaga, M. V., Steffen Jr, V., Hagopian, J. D., Mahfoud, J. On the Balancing of Flexible Rotating Machines by Using an Inverse Problem Approach, Journal of Vibration and Control; 2011, 17 (7), 1021-1033.

[11] Sudhakar, G. N. D. S., Sekhar, A. S. Identification of Unbalance in a Rotor Bearing System. Journal of Sound and Vibration; 2011, 330, 2299-2313.

[12] Metropolis, N., Rosenbluth, A. W., Rosenbluth, M. N., Teller, A. H. Equation of State Calculations by Fast Computing Machines, Journal of Chemical Physics; 1953, 21 (6), 1087-1092.

[13] Ingber, L. Simulated Annealing: Practice versus Theory, Mathematical Computing Modelling; 1993, 18 (11), 29-57.

[14] Kirkpatrick, S., Gelatt, C. D. Jr., Vecchi, M. P. Optimization by Simulated Annealing. Science; 1983, 220 (4598), 671-680.

[15] Lalanne, M., Ferraris, G. Rotordynamics Prediction in Engineering, John Wiley and Sons; 1998.

[16] Vasan, A., Raju, K. S. Comparative analysis of Simulated Annealing, Simulated Quenching and Genetic Algorithms for optimal reservoir operation, Applied Soft Computing; 2009, 9, 274-281.

[17] Aarts, E., Korst, J. Simulated Annealing and Boltzmann Machines: A Stochastic Approach to Combinatorial Optimization and Neural Computing, Wiley Publishers, ISBN 978-0-471-92146-2, United States of America; 1991.

[18] Chibante, R., Araújo, A., Carvalho, A. Parameter Identification of Power Semiconductor Device Models using Metaheuristics, chapter of book: Simulated Annealing Theory with Applications, edited by Rui Chibante; 2010.

[19] Fouskakis, D., Draper, D. Stochastic Optimization: A Review, International Statistical Review; 2002, 70 (3), 315-349.

[20] Deb, K. Multi-Objective Optimization using Evolutionary Algorithms, John Wiley & Sons, Chichester, UK, ISBN 0-471-87339-X; 2001.

[21] Deb, K., Pratap, A., Agarwal, S., Meyarivan, T. A Fast and Elitist Multi-Objective Genetic Algorithm-NSGA-II, KanGAL Report Number 2000001; 2000.

[22] Edgeworth, F. Y. Mathematical Psychics, P. Keagan, London, England; 1881.

[23] Pareto, V. Manuale di Economia Politica, Societa Editrice Libraria, Milano, Italy; 1906. Translated into English by A. S. Schwier as Manual of Political Economy, Macmillan, New York; 1971.

[24] Serafini, P. Mathematics of Multiobjective Optimization Berlin: CISM Courses and Lectures, Springer Verlag; 1985.

[25] Serafini, P. Simulated Annealing for Multiple Objective Optimization Problems. In Multiple criteria decision making. Expand and enrich the domains of thinking and application. Springer Verlag; 1994, 283.

[26] Ululgu, E. L., Teghem, J. Multiobjective Combinatorial Optimization Problems: A survey. Journal of Multicriteria Decision Analysis; 1994, 3, 83-95.

[27] Czyzak, P., Hapke, M., Jaszkiewicz, A. Application of the Pareto-simulated Annealing to the Multiple Criteria Shortest Path Problem. Tech. Rep., Politechnika Poznanska Instytut Informatyki, Poland; 1994.

[28] Ulungu, L. E., Teghem, J., Fortemps, P. Heuristics for Multiobjective Combinatorial Optimization Problems by Simulated Annealing. In MCDM: theory and applications, Sci-Tech Windsor; 1995.

[29] Suppapitnarm, A., Seffen, K. A., Parks, G. T., Clarkson, P. J. A Simulated Annealing Algorithm for Multiobjective Optimization. Engineering Optimization; 2000, 33, 59-70.

[30] Kasat, R. B., Kunzru, D., Saraf, D. N., Gupta, S. K. Multiobjective Optimization of Industrial FCC Units using Elitist Nondominated Sorting Genetic Algorithm. Industrial & Engineering Chemistry Research; 2002, 41, 4765-4775.

[31] Smith, K. I., Everson, R. M., Fieldsend, J. E. Dominance-based Multi-objective Simulated Annealing, IEEE Transactions on Evolutionary Computation; 2008, 12 (3), 323-342.

[32] Marcoulaki, E. C., Papazoglou, I. A. A Dynamic Screening Algorithm for Multiple Objective Simulated Annealing Optimization. 20th European Symposium on Computer Aided Process Engineering – ESCAPE20; 2010.

[33] Castro, R. E. Multi-objective Optimization of Structures using Genetic Algorithm. PhD Thesis (in portuguese). Federal University of Rio de Janeiro, Brazil; 2001.

[34] Saruhan H. Design Optimization of Rotor-Bearing Systems, Journal of Engineering Sciences; 2003, 9 (3), 319-326.

[35] Shiau, T. N., Chang, J. R. Multi-objective Optimization of Rotor-Bearing System with Critical Speed Constraints, Journal of Engineering for Gas Turbines and Power; 1993, 115 (2), 246-256.

[36] Srinivas, N., Deb, K. Multiobjective Function Optimization using Nondominated Sorting Genetic Algorithms. Evolutionary Computation; 1995, 2, 221-236.

[37] Lobato, F. S. Multi-objective Optimization to Engineering System Design, Thesis, School of Mechanical Engineering, Universidade Federal de Uberlândia, Brazil (in Portuguese); 2008.

[38] Bachschmid, N, Bruni, B., Collina, A. On the Identification of Rotor Bow, Coupling Misalignment and Unbalance in Rotor Systems from Bearing Measurements. Proc. 9th International Congress on Condition Monitoring and Diagnostic Engineering Management (COMADEM 96). Sheffield, UK; 1996.

[39] Chen, J. H., Lee, A. C. Estimation of Linearized Dynamic Characteristics of Bearings Using Synchronous Response, Int. Journal of Mechanical; 1995, 37 (2), 197-219.

[40] Seibold, S., Fritzen, C. P. Identification Procedures as Tools for Fault Diagnosis of Rotating Machinery, Int. Journal of Rotating Machinery; 1995, 1 (3), 267-275.

[41] Houck, C., Joines, J., Kay, M. A Genetic Algorithm for Function Optimization: A MTLAM implementation, NCSU-IE, TR 95–09; 1995.

[42] Price, K., Storn, R. Differential Evolution - A Simple Evolution Strategy for Fast Optimization . Dr. Dobb's Journal; 1997, 22 (4), 18-24.

[43] Kennedy, J., Eberhart, R. C. Particle Swarm Optimization. In Proceeding of IEEE International Conference Neural Networks, Perth, Australia; 1995, 1942-1948.

Chapter 12

Optimum Functionally Gradient Materials for Dental Implant Using Simulated Annealing

Ali Sadollah and Ardeshir Bahreininejad

Additional information is available at the end of the chapter

1. Introduction

Biomaterials should simultaneously satisfy many requirements and possess properties such as non-toxicity, corrosion resistance, thermal conductivity, strength, fatigue durability, biocompatibility and sometimes aesthetics. A single composition with a uniform structure may not satisfy all such requirements. Natural biomaterials often possess the structure of Functionally Graded Materials (FGMs) which enables them to satisfy these requirements. FGMs provide the structure with which synthetic biomaterials should essentially be formed. The size of biomaterial components is relatively small. In the case of dental applications, the components are generally smaller than 20 mm. This substantially reduces the difficulty of fabricating such materials due to a mismatch in thermal expansion which causes micro crack formation during the cooling cycle.

Biomaterials are essential for life and health in certain cases. They have a generally high added value for their size. Thus, biomaterials form one of the most important areas for the application of FGMs. It is an area for which FGMs, at the present time, are sufficiently developed for practical use. The dental implant is used for restoring the function of chewing and biting, and therefore eating, which is the most fundamental activity of human beings required for living. We are living in an era of longer life expectancy and thus, dental care becomes especially important for better quality of life in old age.

Implant may be classified to "implant" as an artificial bone for medical use and "dental implant" as an artificial tooth for dental use. The specified properties are slightly different depending on their use. The implants in orthopaedics are used mostly as structurally enforced artificial bone which is inserted inside the corpus. Medical implants lay more weight on strength, toughness, torque in mechanical properties and the specific problem of tribology and abrasion resistance in artificial joint. Dental implant is usually much smaller and is used to reconstruct the masticatory function when tooth root is completely lost or extracted.

Implant is placed in the jawbone in the manner to penetrate from the inside to the outside of the bone. The function is quite different at the inside of bone, outside and at the boundary. In the inside of jaw bone, bone affinity and stress relaxation are important and in the outside of bone, that is, in oral cavity, the sufficient strength is necessary. In the application of human body implant, FGM is usually composed of Collagen Hydroxyapatite (HAP) and titanium (Watari et al., 2004; Hedia, 2005).

HAP is indeed a principal component in human bones and related tissues. HAP inclusion in forming the dental implant material can bring about an enhanced biocompatibility with the native hosting tissues. The main advantages of using FGM dental implant are: 1) reduction of stress shielding effect on the surrounding bones that usually arises in the presence of fully metallic implants (Hedia, 2005), 2) improvement of biocompatibility with bone tissues (Watari et al., 2004), 3) preventing the thermal-mechanical failure at the interface of HAP coated metallic implants (Wang et al., 2007) and 4) meeting the biomechanical requirements at each region of the bone while enhance the bone remodeling, hereby maintaining the bone's health status (Yang & Xiang, 2007). The latter is more related to volume fraction of FGM. The first three aspects of using FGM implant have been investigated in the previous studies (Watari et al., 2004; Hedia, 2005; Wang et al., 2007).

However, limited knowledge has been available in the effect on bone remodeling due to the use of FGM dental implants. The other issue needs to be systematically studied is how to devise an optimal FGM pattern for dental implant application. It has been widely accepted that a mating mechanical property to the host bone should be made in order to avoid stress shielding (Hedia & Mahmoud, 2004; Hedia et al., 2006) and promote osseointegration and bone remodeling (Chu et al., 2006; Yang & Xiang, 2007). However, there are few reports available which examine whether or not a mating property could result in the best remodeling consequence and ensure a long-term success.

Recently, optimization of FGM dental implant was studied by Lin et al. (2009) using the Response Surface Methodology (RSM) and the results show the incompatibility of properties with each other and the need for using multi-objective algorithms to overcome the problem. Another issue concerns the existing material engineering technology which may not allow us to make such mating pattern for individuals in a cost efficient way. As a result, how to optimally tailor FGM pattern for remodeling is of noteworthy implication in developing FGM implantation.

This chapter aims at extending a more realistic FGM design for dental implantation. Using Simulated Annealing (SA), the multi-objective optimization model was developed to optimize FGM gradient pattern for desirable on-going bone turnover outcome and mechanical responses. SA algorithm has shown great potential for solving optimization problems as they conduct global stochastic search. The multi-objective optimization problem was solved using SA and the results were compared with the RSM.

2. Properties of FGM dental implant

In this study, the configuration of FGM dental implant follows the patterns from literature (Wang et al., 2007; Yang & Xiang, 2007). The material gradient is governed by a power law with parameter m, as in Equation (1). The volume fractions of the two-phase composite FGM dental implant can be calculated from the following equations (Hedia, 2005; Wang et al., 2007; Yang & Xiang, 2007):

$$V_C = \left(\frac{y}{h} \right)^m \tag{1}$$

$$V_m = (1 - V_C) \tag{2}$$

where V_c denotes the volumetric fraction of HAP/Col (ceramic), V_m denotes the volumetric fraction of titanium (metal), m is a constant to define the variation in material composition, y is the vertical position within the implant region and h is the total length of the implant. Fig. 1 shows the schematic view of FGM dental implant with graded material composition used in dentistry.

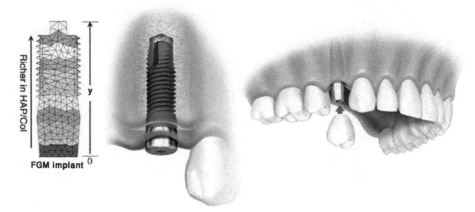

Figure 1. Schematic view of FGM dental implant with graded material composition.

Accordingly, the Young modulus and Poisson ratio can be calculated as (Hedia, 2005):

$$E_0 = E_c \left[\frac{E_c + (E_m - E_c)v_m^{2/3}}{E_c + (E_m - E_c)(v_m^{2/3} - v_m)} \right] \tag{3}$$

$$v = v_m V_m + v_c V_c \tag{4}$$

where E_0 is the equivalent Young modulus at different regions of the implant, E_c is the Young modulus of HAP/Col, E_m is the Young modulus of titanium. v_c and v_m are the Poisson ratios for HAP/Col and titanium, respectively. The HAP/Col and titanium compositions vary according to the relative length of y/h, with respect to the material gradient m, meaning that m governs the variation in the volumetric fraction of the titanium to HAP/Col compositions. Referring to the properties of FGM implant, the values of E_c and E_m are kept within the range of $E_c \gg 1$ GPa and $E_m \gg 110$ GPa, respectively (Hedia, 2005; Wang et al., 2007; Yang & Xiang, 2007).

Fig. 2 demonstrates the variation of mechanical properties including Young's modulus and Poisson's ration for diverse FGM pattern. From Fig. 2, the horizontal axis is the vertical position (y) along FGM dental implant, which is varied from 0 to 10 mm. By observing Fig. 2, $y=0$ mm indicates the region directly connected to the crown, where FGM has the richest content of titanium when $m=10$, while the highest content of collagen HAP is obtained when $m=0.1$. In other words, $m=10$ and $m=0.1$, respectively, give the highest and lowest gradients in the Young modulus and Poisson ratio in the region of the crown's end. Therefore, altering m enables us to tailor the property gradient, thereby providing a means to optimizing the remodeling performance induced by the FGM dental implant.

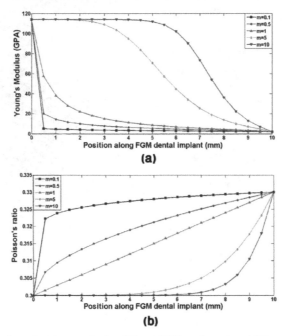

Figure 2. Variation in material properties for different FGM configuration: (a) Young's modulus, (b) Poisson's ration.

3. Bone remodeling calculations

The biomechanical environment changes considerably when using FGM dental implant. Consequently, the bone remodels itself to adapt to the new changes that is imposed on it by minimizing the difference between the new mechanical response and related equilibrium state. Strain energy density is one of the most important mechanical stimuli to explain the bone remodeling (Weinans et al., 1992). The mathematical equations of bone remodeling are given as follows (Huiskes et al., 1987; Weinans, 1992; Turner et al., 1997; Turner, 1998; Lin et al., 2008a, 2008b):

Bone apposition:

$$\frac{\partial \rho}{\partial t} = B(\frac{\eta}{\rho} - (1+\xi)\Xi) \quad if \frac{\eta}{\rho} \succ (1+\xi)\Xi \tag{5}$$

Bone equilibrium:

$$\frac{\partial \rho}{\partial t} = 0 \quad if (1-\xi)\Xi \leq \frac{\eta}{\rho} \leq (1+\xi)\Xi \tag{6}$$

Bone resorption:

$$\frac{\partial \rho}{\partial t} = B(\frac{\eta}{\rho} - (1-\xi)\Xi) \quad if \frac{\eta}{\rho} \prec (1-\xi)\Xi \tag{7}$$

where η denotes the mechanical stimulus (i.e. strain energy density), ρ is the bone density, B is the remodeling constant set to $1gr/cm^3$ (Weinans et al., 1992), Ξ is the remodeling reference value equal to 0.004 J/g (Weinans et al., 1992; Turner, 1998), and ξ is the bandwidth of bone remodeling with an adapted value of 10% (Weinans et al., 1992). After the bone density values are calculated from the remodeling equations, the Young modulus of cortical and cancellous bones (in GPa) can be updated by using the following equations (Rho et al., 1995; O'Mahony et al., 2001):

$$E_{cortical} = -23.93 + 24\rho_{cortical} \tag{8}$$

$$E_{cancellous} = 2.349\rho_{cancellous}^{2.15} \tag{9}$$

Equations (8) and (9) are utilized to update Young modulus after the densities are determined via the remodeling calculations. The internal bone remodeling system is formed using Equation (5) to Equation (9).

4. Design optimization problem

The bone remodeling provides quantitative data of changes in bone densities and the stiffness of dental apparatus. The former indicates how the bones react to the change in biomechanical environment in terms of the variation in bone morphology. The latter indicates how the bone remodeling alters the mechanical response, thereby stabilizing the implant and in turn strengthening the bone. In this research, the changes in bone densities and vertical displacement are taken as the direct measures of on-going performance of implantation.

From the biomechanical point of view, increase in surrounding bone density and decrease in the occlusal displacement indicate the positive sign to a long-term success in dental implantation. Thus, design of FGM gradient parameter (m) is expected to maximize the densities and minimize the displacement, which in a form of multi-objective optimization may be represented as:

$$\begin{cases} \min f_1(m) = \dfrac{1}{D_{cortical}} \\ \min f_2(m) = \dfrac{1}{D_{cancellous}} \\ \min f_3(m) = u(m) \\ subject \;\; to \;\; 0.1 \leq m \leq 10 \end{cases} \tag{10}$$

where f_1, f_2 and f_3 represent the objective functions, $D_{cortical}$ and $D_{cancellous}$ are the densities of cortical and cancellous bones, respectively and $u(m)$ denotes the vertical displacement at the top of artificial crown. The objective functions f_1, f_2 and f_3 represent the condition of FGM dental implant at month 48 (Lin et al., 2009). These polynomial response functions are given as:

$$D_{cortical}(m) = -2e^{-6}m^6 + 8e^{-5}m^5 - 1e^{-3}m^4 + 6.2e^{-3}m^3 - 1.9e^{-2}m^2 + 1.76e^{-2}m + 1.9297 \tag{11}$$

$$D_{cancellous}(m) = 2e^{-6}m^6 - 6e^{-5}m^5 + 6e^{-4}m^4 - 2.6e^{-3}m^3 + 3e^{-3}m^2 - 2.4e^{-3}m + 1.1712 \tag{12}$$

$$u(m) = 7e^{-10}m^6 - 2e^{-8}m^5 - 3e^{-7}m^4 - 2e^{-6}m^3 + 7e^{-6}m^2 - 1e^{-5}m + 4e^{-5} \tag{13}$$

The polynomial response functions were obtained using experimental tests on various quantities of material gradient on the FGM dental implant. Lin et al. (2009) proposed to adopt the RSM to construct the appropriate objective functions for a single design variable problem. Fig. 3 represents the cortical and cancellous densities, and displacement versus material gradient (m). As m increases, the displacement function $u(m)$ is increased as shown in Fig. 3c. The increase in m results in an increase in the cortical density as shown in Fig. 3a. From Fig. 3b, the increase in m results the decrease in the density of cancellous.

The design objectives were to maximize both $D_{cortical}$ and $D_{cancellous}$ in order to determine the best possible material configuration for implant that will give the maximum amount of bone remodeling. At the same time, the objective function f_3 is minimized in order to reduce the downward implant displacement. An ideal situation would be to attain a consistent optimal material gradient, where the maximum bone turnover can be made and the displacement is kept to minimal. To explore such a multi-objective design, first, the two objective optimization problems of either cortical or cancellous densities versus the displacement were formulated as follows:

$$\begin{cases} \min f_1 = \dfrac{1}{D_{cortical}} \\ \min f_3 = \max(u(m)) \\ subject \;\; to \;\; 0.1 \leq m \leq 10 \end{cases} \tag{14}$$

and

$$\begin{cases} \min f_2 = \dfrac{1}{D}_{cancellous} \\ \min f_3 = \max(u(m)) \\ subject \quad to \quad 0.1 \le m \le 10 \end{cases} \tag{15}$$

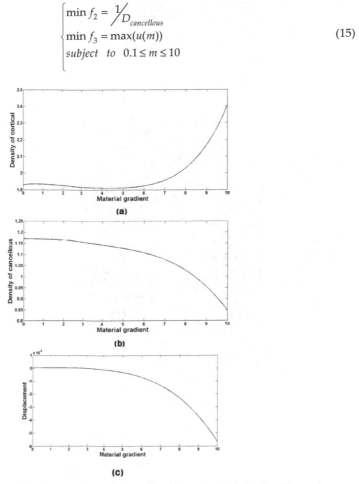

Figure 3. Mass densities and displacement for FGM dental implant: (a) cortical density, (b) cancellous density, (c) displacement (*u*) (The horizontal axis is *m*).

Fig. 4 shows the trend of cortical density function (f_1), cancellous density function (f_2) and the displacement function (f_3). From Figs. 4b and 4c, it is clear that f_2 and f_3 have the same trend and behavior and it is expected to obtain one optimal solution. Based on Fig. 3c, we need to minimize the maximum of displacement in order to obtain the minimum value of displacement. The function f_3 is minimized by multiplying $u(m)$ by -1. In other hand, Figs. 4a and 4c show the different trend and behavior which with increasing *m*, the cortical density function decreases while, the displacement function increase. Therefore, it is anticipated to obtain a range of optimal solutions. The problem investigated in this chapter, is taken from (Lin et al., 2009) where the results were obtained using RSM.

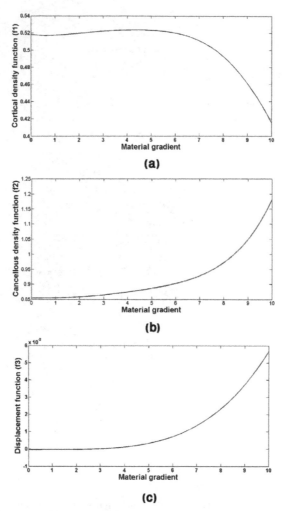

Figure 4. Mass densities and displacement functions for FGM dental implant: (a) cortical density function (f_1), (b) cancellous density function (f_2), (c) displacement function (f_3) (The horizontal axis is m).

5. Multi-objective optimization

The multi-objective optimization has become an important research topic for scientists and researchers. This is mainly due to the multi-objective nature of real life problems. It is difficult to compare results of multi-objective methods to single objective techniques, as there is not a unique optimum in multi-objective optimization as in single objective optimization. Therefore, the best solution in multi-objective terms may need to be decided by the decision maker.

The increasing acceptance of SA for solving multi-objective optimization problems is due to their ability to: 1) find multiple solutions in a single run, 2) work without derivatives, 3) converge speedily to Pareto-optimal solutions with a high degree of accuracy, 4) handle both continuous functions and combinatorial optimization problems with ease and 5) are less susceptible to the shape or continuity of the Pareto front (Suman & Kumar, 2006).

5.1. Pareto-optimal solutions

The concept of the Pareto-optimal solutions was formulated by Vilfredo Pareto in the 19th century (Rouge, 1896). Real life problems require simultaneous optimization of several incommensurable and often conflicting objectives. Usually, there is no single optimal solution. However, there may be a set of alternative solutions. These solutions are optimal in the wider sense that no other solutions in the search space are superior to each other when all the objectives are considered. They are known as Pareto-optimal solutions. When the objectives associated with any pair of non-dominated solutions are compared, it is found that each solution is superior with respect to at least one objective. The set of non-dominated solutions to a multi-objective optimization problem is known as the Pareto-optimal set (Zitzler & Thiele, 1998).

6. Simulated annealing

In 1953, Metropolis developed a method for solving optimization problems that mimics the way thermodynamic systems go from one energy level to another (Metropolis et al., 1953). He thought of this after simulating a heat bath on certain chemicals. This method is called Simulated Annealing (SA). Kirkpatrick et al. (1983) originally thought of using SA on a number of problems. The name and inspiration come from annealing in metallurgy, a technique involving heating and controlled cooling of a material to increase the size of its crystals and reduce their defects. The heat causes the atoms to become free from their initial positions (a local minimum of the internal energy) and wander randomly through states of higher energy.

The system is cooled and as the temperature is reduced the atoms migrate to more ordered states with lower energy. The final degree of order depends on the temperature cooling rate. The slow cooling process is characterized by a general decrease in the energy level for with occasional increase in energy. On the other hand, a fast cooling process, known as quenching, is characterized by a monotonic decrease in energy to an intermediate state of semi-order which is used as temperature schedule in this chapter.

At the final stages of the annealing process, the system's energy reaches a much lower level than in rapid cooling (quenching). Annealing (slow cooling) therefore allows the system to reach lower global energy minimum than is possible using a quick quenching process, equivalent to a local energy minimum.

By analogy with this physical process, each step of the SA algorithm replaces the current solution by a random "nearby" solution, chosen with a probability that depends both on the difference between the corresponding function values and also on a global parameter T (temperature), that is gradually decreased during the process. The dependency is such that the current solution changes almost randomly when T is large, but increasingly "downhill" as T goes to zero (Fleischer, 1995). The allowance for "uphill" moves potentially saves the method from becoming stuck at local optima. Several parameters need to be included in an implementation of SA.

These are summarized by Davidson and Harel (1996):

- The set of configurations, or states, of the system, including an initial configuration (which is often chosen at random).
- A generation rule for new configurations, which is usually obtained by defining the neighborhood of each configuration and choosing the next configuration randomly from the neighborhood of the current one.
- The target, or cost function, to be minimized over the configuration space. (This is the analogue of the energy).
- The cooling schedule of the control parameter, including initial values and rules for when and how to change it (This is the analogue of the temperature and its decreases).
- The termination condition, which is usually based on the time and the values of the cost function and/or the control parameter.

SA is a popular optimization algorithm due to the simplicity of the model and its implementation. However, due to CPU time-consuming nature of standard SA, a fast temperature schedule to fulfill the required conditions is suggested. In fact, simulated annealing algorithm with the fast cooling process is called simulated quenching (SQ) which is used as an optimization method in this chapter to overcome the slow SA optimization process.

7. SA for multi-objective optimization

SA has been used as an optimization method for solving a wide range of combinatorial optimization problems. It has also been adapted for solving multi-objective problems due to its simplicity and capability of producing a desirable Pareto set of solutions. In addition, it is not susceptible to the shape of the Pareto set, since shape may be considered as a concern for mathematical programming techniques.

7.1. The method of Suppapitnarm and Parks (SMOSA)

The concept of archiving the Pareto-optimal solutions for solving multi-objective problems with SA has been used by Suppapitnarm et al. (2000). The Suppapitnarm Multi-Objective Simulated Annealing (SMOSA) enables the search to restart from an archived solution in a solution region, where each of the pair of non-dominated solutions may be superior with respect to at least one objective. Since SA only generates a single solution at a given iteration, an independent archive is required to record all non-dominated solutions found during search. Pioneering work in this area was first performed by Engrand (1997), and was further developed by Suppapitnarm et al. (2000).

7.1.1. Acceptance probability and archiving

A new acceptance probability formulation based on an annealing schedule with multiple temperatures (one for each objective function) was also proposed. The changes in each objective function values are compared with each other directly before archiving. This ensures that the moves to a non-dominated solution are accepted. It does not use any weight vector in the acceptance criteria. Hence, the acceptance probability step is given as:

$$P = \min\left(1, \prod_{i=1}^{N} \exp\left\{-\Delta s_i \middle/ T_i\right\}\right) \tag{16}$$

where $\Delta S=(Z_i(Y)-Z_i(X))$ and N is the number of objective functions, X is the current solution, Y is the generated solution, Z_i is the objective function, and T_i is the annealing temperature. Thus, the overall acceptance probability is the product of individual acceptance probabilities for each objective associated with a temperature T_i .

7.1.2. Annealing schedule

A new annealing schedule is developed to control the lowering of individual temperatures associated with each objective function. If the temperatures are lowered too fast the chance of accepting solutions reduces rapidly and large parts of the search space are never explored. In contrast, if the temperature is reduced too slowly, many redundant solutions which do not lead to non-dominated solutions are accepted and the Pareto-optimal set of solutions develops very slowly. The latter is particularly undesirable if objective function evaluations are expensive and/or if computation time is a important factor.

A statistical record of the values of each of the objective functions (f_i) is maintained. First, the temperatures are lowered after N_{T1} iterations by setting each temperature to the standard deviation (σ) of the accepted values of f_i ($T_i = \sigma_i$). Thereafter, the temperatures based on the quenching schedule are updated after every N_{T2} iterations or N_A acceptances as follows:

$$T_{i(k+1)} = T_{i(k)} \times \alpha \qquad 0 < \alpha_i < 1 \tag{17}$$

where T_i is the temperature, k is the time index of annealing, and α_i is the cooling ratio of each objective function. The suitable values for N_{T1} and N_{T2} were chosen 1000 and 500 iterations, respectively (Suppapitnann, 1998).

7.1.3. Return to base strategy

In order to completely expose the trade-off between objective functions, the random selection of a solution from the archive, from which to recommence search, is systematically controlled using an intelligent return-to-base strategy. After the start of search, a return-to-base is first activated when the basic features of the trade-off between objectives have developed. It seems sensible that this take place when the temperatures are first lowered, i.e., after N_{T1} iterations. Thereafter, the rate of return is, naturally, increased to intensify the search in the trade-off. The number of iterations N_{Bi} to be executed prior to the ith return-to-base after the start of search is updated as given:

$$N_{Bi} = r_B N_{Bi-1} \quad i = 2,3,4,... \tag{18}$$

where r_B is a constant parameter which varies between 0 and +1 and dictates the frequency of return. Recommendation values for r_B and N_{B1} may be chosen as 0.9 and $2N_{T2}$, respectively (Suppapitnann, 1998). In order to fully develop the trade-off, solutions that are more isolated from the rest of the trade-off solution should be favored in returns-to-base. The extreme solutions, those solutions that correspond to minimum values for each objective in the trade-off, also require special consideration. These solutions are almost invariably only just feasible, which makes the design space around them difficult to search.

For these reasons, a base set of candidate solutions was proposed which consists of a number of the most isolated of those solutions currently held in the archive and the M extreme solutions in the archive. Therefore, when a return-to-base is activated, the search diversifies into less well explored regions of the trade-off. To evaluate the degree of isolation for a solution, the following formula was proposed (Suppapitnarm et al., 2000):

$$I(X_j) = \sum_{\substack{i=1 \\ i \neq j}}^{A_s} \sum_{k=1}^{M} \left(\frac{\left| f_k(X_i) - f_k(X_j) \right|}{\left| f_{k\max} - f_{k\min} \right|} \right)^2 \tag{19}$$

where $I(X_j)$ is the normalized value for distance in objective space for the jth solution from all other archived solutions and X_j denotes the jth archived solution. A_s and M are the total number of solutions and extreme solutions stored in the archive, respectively. $f_{k\max}$ and $f_{k\min}$ are the maximum and minimum values for k^{th} objective function (f_k), respectively. Each solution - except for the extreme solutions - is ranked in order to decrease isolation distance, thereby, establishing an ordered set with the most isolated solutions at its top and the least isolated solutions at the bottom.

7.1.4. Step size control

An improvement in SA performance may be gained by varying the maximum allowable step changes in each of the decision variables during perturbation between iterations (Parks, 1990). Hence, the value of each design variable is rescaled to U_{ik} such that it varies between -1 and +1 at its lower and upper bounds, respectively. At the next iteration, $U_{i(k+1)}$ is modified as given:

$$U_{i(k+1)} = U_{ik} + rand \times S_i \tag{20}$$

where $rand$ is a uniformly distributed random number between -1 and +1, and S_i is the maximum (positive) step-size for each design variable. If the solution is accepted, S_i is updated using following equation:

$$S_i = S_i(0.9 + 0.21 \times |rand|) \tag{21}$$

A suitable value for the upper bound for each S_i was set to 0.5 to permit, initially, a wide search around the current position. Accordingly, a lower bound of 0.0001 was chosen for the smallest possible value of each S_i to prevent stagnation during search (Parks, 1990). Therefore, the maximum step change in the design variables is monitored and is varied to reduce violation of the constraints.

7.1.5. The steps and flowchart of the SMOSA

The basic steps involved in the SMOSA algorithm for a problem having N objective functions and n decision variables are as follows (Suman, 2004):

Step 1. Start with a randomly generated initial solution vector, X (an $n \times 1$ vector whose elements are decision variables) and evaluate all objective functions and put it into a Pareto set of solutions.

Step 2. Generate a random perturbation and a new solution vector, Y, in the neighborhood of current solution vector, X, re-evaluate the objective functions and apply a penalty function approach to the corresponding objective functions, if necessary.

Step 3. Compare the generated solution vector with all the solutions in the Pareto set and update the Pareto set, if necessary.

Step 4. If the generated solution vector is archived, assign it as the current solution vector by putting $X=Y$ and go to Step 7.

Step 5. If the generated solution vector is not archived, accept it with the probability using Equation (16). If the generated solution is archived, assign it as the current solution vector by putting $X=Y$ and go to Step 7.

Step 6. If the generated solution vector is not archived, retain the earlier solution vector as the current solution vector and go to Step 7.

Step 7. Periodically, restart with a randomly selected solution from the Pareto set. While periodically restarting with the archived solutions, Suppapitnarm et al. (2000) have recommended biasing towards the extreme ends of the trade-off surface.

Step 8. Reduce the temperature using Equation (17) and annealing schedule.

Step 9. Repeat Steps 2 to 8, until a predefined number of iterations is carried out.

In addition, the flowchart of SMOSA optimizer is illustrated in Fig. 5.

8. Optimization of the two objective functions using SMOSA

An ideal situation would be to attain a consistent optimal material gradient, where the maximum one turnover can be made and the displacement is kept to minimal. The problem described in previous sections was solved by multi-objective SA code written in MATLAB software programming and run on Pentium IV, 2500 GHz and 4 GB RAM. The SMOSA was run 5 times and the obtained averaged results were compared to results obtained from RSM.

The parameters which must be specified before running the algorithm are initial temperature, frozen state represented by the final temperature, cooling ratio (annealing), i.e.

the rate at which the temperature is lowered between two cooling cycles, the randomly generated initial solution, and the lower and upper bounds for design variable (m). Table 1 shows the user parameters used for the SMOSA.

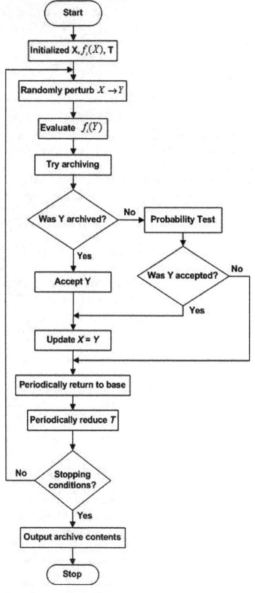

Figure 5. Flowchart of the SMOSA optimizer.

User Parameters	Quantities
Initial temperature for each objective (T_{i0})	100
Final temperature for f_2 and f_3	1e-6
Final temperature for f_1 and f_3	1e-8
Cooling ratio (α_i)	0.98
Lower bound	0.1
Upper bound	10

Table 1. Optimization parameters associated with the SMOSA.

The SMOSA was conducted on two objective functions, f_3 as displacement function and f_1 as cortical density function as in Equation (14). Fig. 6 represents the comparison of Pareto front for two objective functions using SMOSA and RSM (Lin et al., 2009). Comparing Figs. 6a and 6b, the same trend is seen in both figures. It can be seen that the increase in f_1, results in f_3 to decrease and vice versa. Hence, SMOSA confirms the results obtained by RSM. However, the data ranges obtained by SMOSA do not match exactly with the data range obtained by RSM.

The data range given by SMOSA for f_1 is from 0.51688 to 0.51778 as shown in Fig. 6b while, RSM gives values from 0.5169 to 0.5175 for f_1 (see Fig. 6a). Similarly, the data range given by SMOSA for f_3 is from -3.9054e-5 to -3.5907e-5 and for RSM for f_3 is from 3.5205e-5 to 3.603e-5. The date range for cortical density function given by SMOSA is almost 33% more than the range obtained by RSM in micro scale. This shows the efficiency of the SMOSA in providing more data range for cortical density than RSM.

The safety factor (acceptance capability) obtained by SMOSA is 33% higher than the one given by RSM for magnitude of cortical density function. This increasing of data range is interesting for FGM dental implant design and shows that SMOSA has outperformed RSM in cortical density function. SMOSA gives the data range for displacement almost 73% more than the values given by RSM in micro scale. That means SMOSA enables the designer with a wider choice for design.

In general, SMOSA method gives more selection of material gradient (m) for designing of the FGM dental implant but with higher displacement compared to the RSM. The order of quantities (micro-scale) shows the importance of accuracy in the optimization of the FGM implant. Hence, any improvement in quantities may be considerable although such improvements may seem to be negligible.

Fig. 7 illustrates the trend for cortical density and displacement functions with respect to m. By inspecting Fig. 7, the acceptable range for m is from 0.1 to 0.65. The magnitude of f_1 decreases as m increases which means the density of cortical ($D_{cortical}$) increases. In contrast, with the increase in m the quantity of vertical displacement (f_3) increases. This trend shows the non-dominated solution from the Pareto front plot so that the increase in one function results in the decrease of the other function and vice versa. Such data was extracted from the Pareto front depicted in Fig. 6b.

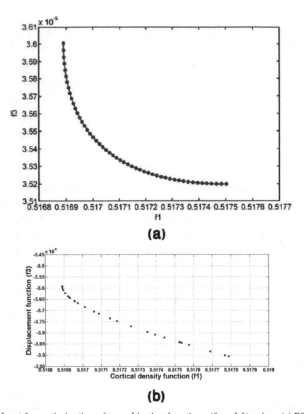

(a)

(b)

Figure 6. Pareto front for optimization of two objective functions (f_3 and f_1) using: (a) RSM, (b) SMOSA.

Fig. 8 demonstrates f_1, f_2 and f_3 with respect to the m. When the temperature is high at the beginning of the optimization process, all invalid moves were accepted by the acceptance probability (P), as shown in Fig. 8. By decreasing the temperature at each iteration, the probability of accepting invalid moves is reduced and therefore, only qualified points and valid moves (so called non-dominated solutions) were accepted.

As a next step, the multi-objective simulated annealing method was applied on other two objective functions as shown in Equation (15). The result indicates the Pareto front is a cluster of points that are gathered in one point representing an optimal solution. Going back to Figs. 4b and 4c for minimizing both objective functions (f_2 and f_3), we expect to have one optimal solution as the two functions have a similar trend to reach the optimal point.

In other words, if one moves from the right side of the Figs. 4b and 4c to the left side, the cancellous density increases while the displacement decreases. This situation may be considered as an optimal state. The optimal material gradient is taken as 0.1 (m=0.1). The values for f_3 and f_2 are equal to -3.9068e-5 and 0.8540, respectively. Hence, the best material gradient for these two objective functions is given when m=0.1.

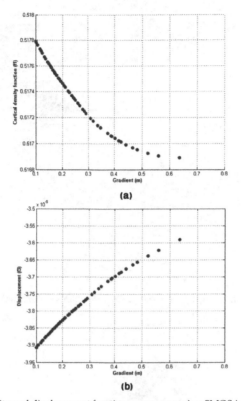

Figure 7. Cortical density and displacement functions versus m using SMOSA for: (a) f_1, (b) f_3.

9. Optimization of the three objective functions using SMOSA

The results obtained from the optimization of two objective functions may not adequately address the full design requirements and therefore, the three objective functions were developed as defined in Equation (10). Fig. 9a shows the Pareto front surface for three objective functions using RSM. Fig. 9b illustrates the 3D plot of the Pareto front for three objective functions (f_1, f_2, and f_3) using SMOSA. From Fig. 9, the good harmony and similarity between the results obtained by SMOSA and RSM are depicted.

Fig. 10 represents various aspects of Fig. 9b. This figure shows the trend for f_1, f_2, and f_3 in terms of the material gradient. The acceptable range for m varies from 0.1 to 0.65 (see Fig. 10). As shown in Fig. 10a, the maximum value for cortical density is obtained for $m=0.63$. In Fig. 10b, the increase in f_2 leads to increase in m, and hence, decrease in the cancellous density. This indicates that for material gradient 0.1 ($m=0.1$) cancellous density has the maximum value. In addition, by observing Fig. 10c, when $m=0.1$, the displacement has the minimum value. Finally, based upon the obtained results, the optimal range for material gradient is almost varying from 0.1 to 0.65 ($0.1 \leq m \leq 0.65$).

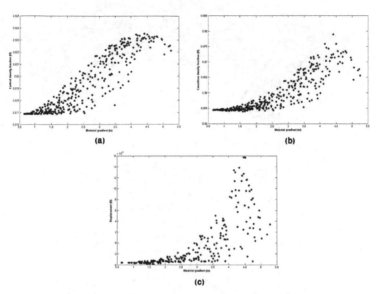

Figure 8. Distribution of mass densities and displacement functions with respect to the m using SMOSA: (a) f_1, (b) f_2, (c) f_3.

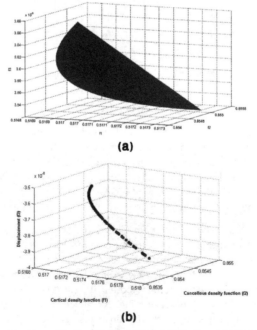

Figure 9. 3D Pareto front for three objective functions $(f_1, f_2$ and $f_3)$ using: (a) RSM, (b) SMOSA.

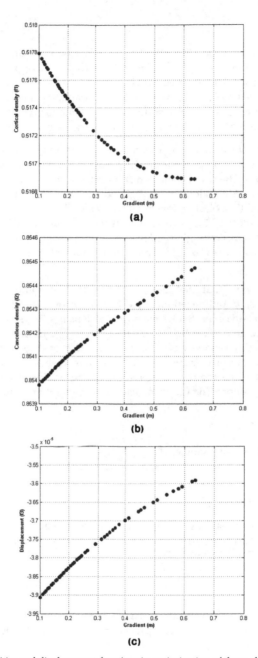

Figure 10. Mass densities and displacement functions in optimization of three objectives in terms of material gradient using SMOSA for: (a) f_1, (b) f_2, (c) f_3.

10. Conclusions

This chapter presents some important findings for Functionally Graded Material (FGM) dental implant design in a power law configuration. This is vital for maintaining the overall health of the bone tissues. The research clearly suggests that, a better performance in bone turnover can be achieved by lowering the FGM dental implant material gradient. However, this will at the same time reduce the stiffness of implantation, consequently placing the bone-implant interface at higher risk of damage during the early healing stage.

The problem may be solved by the multi-objective optimization method. The Pareto front was determined using the Suppapitnarm Multi-Objective Simulated Annealing (SMOSA) optimization procedure. The results obtained from the SMOSA confirm the results obtained by the Response Surface Methodology (RSM), in addition to offering further improvements. The SMOSA optimized the objective functions on a wider data range than RSM and offered better results with respect to the cortical density function (almost 33% more than RSM). SMOSA optimization in this case, gives more selection of material gradient (m) for designing FGM dental implant compared to RSM. The material gradient varies from 0.1 to 0.65 given by SMOSA.

By considering the point that the scale in the FGM dental implant is in micro, the importance of accuracy in optimization of the FGM implant is understood. The design of FGM gradient parameter is expected to maximize the densities (cortical and cancellous) and minimize the displacement and plays a more important role in the design methodology. However, sacrifice may be made when the third criterion of displacement is introduced, which means that an optimal gradient m for bone remodeling may not be the best for stiffness. It is expected that the design methodology can produce more favorably patient specific implant, better improving the immediate and long-term restorative outcomes.

Author details

Ali Sadollah and Ardeshir Bahreininejad*
Faculty of Engineering, University of Malaya, Kuala Lumpur, Malaysia

Acknowledgement

The authors would like to acknowledge for the Ministry of Higher Education of Malaysia and the University of Malaya, Kuala Lumpur, Malaysia for the financial support under UM.TNC2/IPPP/UPGP/628/6/ER013/2011A grant.

11. References

Engrand, P. (1997). A multi-objective approach based on simulated annealing and its application to nuclear fuel management, *5th International Conference on Nuclear Engineering*, Nice, France, pp. 416-423.

---

* Corresponding Author

Chu, C.L., Xue, X.Y., Zhu, J.C. & Yin, Z.D. (2006). In vivo study on biocompatibility and bonding strength of hydroxyapatite-20 vol%Ti composite with bone tissues in the rabbit. *Biomedical Materials and Engineering*, Vol.16, No. 3, pp. 203-213.

Davidson, R. & Harel, D. (1996). Drawing graphs nicely using simulated annealing. ACM Transactions on Graphics, Vol. 15, pp. 301-331.

Fleischer, M. (1995). Simulated annealing: past, present, and future, *Simulation Conference Proceedings IEEE*, pp. 155-161, Arlington, VA, USA, Aug., 2002.

Hedia, H.S. & Mahmoud, N.A. (2004). Design optimization of functionally graded dental implant. *Biomedical Materials and Engineering*, Vol. 14, pp. 133-143.

Hedia, H.S. (2005). Design of functionally graded dental implant in the presence of cancellous bone. *Journal of Biomedical Materials Research-Part B Applied Biomaterials*, Vol. 75, pp. 74-80.

Hedia, H.S., Shabara, M.A.N., El-midany, T.T. & Fouda, N. (2006). Improved design of cementless hip stems using two-dimensional functionally graded materials. *Journal of Biomedical Materials Research - Part B Applied Biomaterials*, Vol. 79, pp. 42-49.

Huiskes, R., Dalstra, M., Vondervenne, R., Grootenboer, H. & Slooff, T.J. (1987). A hypothesis concerning the effect of implant rigidity on adaptive cortical bone remodeling in the femur. *Journal of Biomechanics*, Vol. 20, No. 8, pp. 808-809.

Kirkpatrick, S., C.D. Gellat, Jr. & Vecchi, M.P. (1983). Optimization by simulated annealing. *Science*, Vol. 220, pp. 671-680.

Lin, D., Li, Q., Li, W. & Swain, M.V. (2008a). Dental implant induced bone remodeling and associated algorithms. *Journal of Mechanical Behavior of Biomedical Materials*, Vol. 2, No. 5, pp. 410-432.

Lin, D., Li, Q., Li, W. & Swain, M.V. (2008b). Functionally graded implant and its effect on bone remodeling. *Advance Materials Research*, Vol. 47-50, pp. 1035-1038.

Lin, D., Li, Q., Li, W., Zhou, S. & Swain, M.V. (2009). Design optimization of functionally graded dental implant for bone remodeling. *Composites Part B: Engineering*, Vol. 40, pp. 668-675.

Metropolis, N., Rosenbluth, A.W., Rosenbluth, M., Teller, A.H. & Teller, E. (1953). Equation of state calculations by fast computing machines. *Journal of Chemistry and Physics*, Vol. 21, pp. 1087-1092.

O'Mahony, A.M., Williams, J.L. & Spencer, P. (2001). Anisotropic elasticity of cortical and cancellous bone in the posterior mandible increases peri-implant stress and strain under oblique loading. *Clinic Oral Implants Research*, Vol. 12, No. 6, pp. 648-657.

Parks, G. T. (1990). An intelligent stochastic optimization routine for nuclear fuel cycle design. *Nuclear Technology*, Vol. 89(2), pp. 233-246.

Rho, J.Y., Hobatho, M.C. & Ashman, R.B. (1995). Relations of mechanical-properties to density and Ct numbers in human bone. *Medical Engineering & Physics*, Vol. 17, No. 5, pp. 347-355.

Rouge, F. (1896). *V. Pareto, Cours D'Economie Politique.* volume I and II, Laussane.

Suman, B. (2004). Study of simulated annealing based algorithms for multi-objective optimization of a constrained problem. *Computers & Chemical Engineering*, Vol. 28, pp. 1849-1871.

Suman, B. & Kumar, P. (2006). A survey of simulated annealing as a tool for single and multi-objective optimization. *Journal of the Operational Research Society, Vol. 57, pp. 1143-1160.*

Suppapitnarm, A., Seffen, K.A., Parks, G.T. & Clarkson, P.J. (2000). Simulated annealing: an alternative approach to true multiobjective optimization. *Engineering Optimization,* Vol. 33, pp. 59.

Suppapitnann, A. (1998). A simulated annealing algorithm for multiobjective design optimization. M. Phil, Thesis, University of Cambridge.

Turner, C.H., Anne, V. & Pidaparti, R.M.V. (1997). A uniform strain criterion for trabecular bone adaptation: do continuum level strain gradients drive adaptation?. *Journal of Biomechanics,* Vol. 30, No. 6, pp. 555-563.

Turner, C.H. (1998). Three rules for bone adaptation to mechanical stimuli. *Bone,* Vol. 23, No. 5, pp. 399-407.

Wang, F., Lee, H.P. & Lu, C. (2007). Thermal-mechanical study of functionally graded dental implants with the finite element method. *Journal of Biomedical Materials Research - Part A,* Vol. 80, pp. 146-158.

Watari, F., Yokoyama, A., Omori, M., Hirai, T., Kondo, H., Uo, M. & Kawasaki, T. (2004). Biocompatibility of materials and development to functionally graded implant for bio-medical application. *Composites Science and Technology,* Vol. 64, pp. 893-908.

Weinans, H., Huiskes, R., & Grootenboer, H.J. (1992). The behavior of adaptive bone remodeling simulation models. *Journal of Biomechanics,* Vol. 25, No. 12, pp. 1425–1441.

Yang, J. & Xiang, H.J. (2007). A three-dimensional finite element study on the biomechanical behavior of an FGBM dental implant in surrounding bone. *Journal of Biomechanics,* Vol. 40, pp. 2377-2385.

Zitzler, E. & Thiele, L. (1998). Multiobjective optimization using evolutionary algorithms: a comperative case study. *Parallel Problem Solving from Nature V,* Vol. 1498/1998, pp. 292-301.

Chapter 13

Simulated Annealing to Improve Analog Integrated Circuit Design: Trade-Offs and Implementation Issues

Lucas Compassi Severo, Alessandro Girardi, Alessandro Bof de Oliveira, Fabio N. Kepler and Marcia C. Cera

Additional information is available at the end of the chapter

1. Introduction

The design of analog integrated circuits is complex because it involves several aspects of device modeling, computational methodologies, and human experience. Nowadays, the well-stablished CMOS (Complementary Metal-Oxide-Semiconductor) technology is mandatory in most of the integrated circuits. The basic devices are MOS transistors, whose manufacturing process is well understood and constantly updated in the design of small devices. Detailed knowledge of the devices technology is needed for modeling all aspects of analog design, since there is a strong dependency between the circuit behavior and the manufacturing process.

Contrary to digital circuits, which are composed by millions (or even billions) of transistors with equal dimensions, analog circuits are formed by tens of transistors, but each one with a particular geometric feature and bias operation point. Digital design is characterized by the high degree of automation, in which the designer has low influence on the resulting physical circuit. The quality of the CAD (Computer-Aided Design) tools used for circuit synthesis is much more important than the designer experience. These tools are able to deal with a large number of devices and interconnections. Digital binary circuits have robustness characteristics in which the influence of non-linearities and non-idealities are not a major concern. Furthermore, mathematical models of devices for digital circuits are relaxed and computationally very efficient.

On the other hand, analog design still lacks from design automation. This is a consequence of the problem features and the difficulty of implementing generic tools with high design accuracy. Thus, the complex relations between design objectives and design variables result in a highly non-linear n-dimensional system. Technology dependency limits the design automation, since electrical behavior is directly related to physical implementation. In addition, the large number of different circuit topologies, each one with unique details, makes modeling a very difficult task.

In general, the traditional analog design flow is based on the repetition of manual optimization and SPICE (Simulation Program with Integrated Circuit Emphasis) electrical simulations. For a given specification, a circuit topology is captured in a netlist containing devices and interconnections. Devices sizes, such as transistors width and length, or resistors and capacitors values, are calculated manually. The verification is performed with the aid of SPICE models and technology parameters in order to predict the final performance in silicon. Specific design goals such as dissipated power, voltage gain, or phase margin are achieved by manual calculation and then re-verified in simulation. Once the final performance is met, the design is passed on to a physical design engineer to complete the layout, perform design rule checks, and layout versus schematic verification. The layout engineer passes the extracted physical design information back to the circuit designer to recheck the circuit operation on the electrical level. When physical effects cause the circuit to miss specifications, several more iterations of this circuit-to-layout loop may be required. This process is repeated for each analog block in the circuit, even for making any relatively simple specification change. The amount of time and human resources used can vary, depending on the design complexity and the designer experience. However, even for a large and most skilled design team, the short time-to-market and strict design objectives are key issues of analog designs. Improvements in the analog design automation can save design time and effort.

In this chapter we analyze the Simulated Annealing (SA) meta-heuristic applied to adjust circuit parameters in transistor sizing automation procedure at electrical level. Previous works have been done in the field of analog design automation to enable fast design at the block level. Different strategies and approaches have been proposed during the evolution of analog design automation, such as simulation-based optimization [5, 9, 17], symbolic simulation [10], artificial intelligence [6], manually derived design equations [4, 21], hierarchy and topology selection [11], geometric programming [12, 16] and memetic algorithms [15]. The main difficulty encountered for wide spread usage of these tools is that they require appropriate modeling of both devices (technology dependent) and circuit topologies in order to achieve the design objectives in a reasonable processing time.

Moreover, the option of choosing different circuit topologies is also difficult to implement in a design methodology or tool, since most approaches work with topology-based equations, limiting the application range. The possibility of adding new block topologies must also be included in the methodology, since it is critical to the design. The usage of optimization algorithms combined with design techniques seems to be a good solution when applied to specific applications. This is because a general solution most often proves to have short comings for fully exploiting the capabilities of the analog CMOS technology. The key requirements of an analog synthesis tool are: interactivity with the user, flexibility for multiple topologies and reasonable response time. The interface with an electrical simulator and with a layout editor is also convenient [8].

The remaining of this chapter is organized as follows. Section 2 explains the Simulated Annealing meta-heuristic, its parameters, and functions. Circuit modeling, as well as the parameters and functions involved, are described in Sec. 3. Afterward, Sec. 4 presents a basic circuit used to explain the usage of SA, how the searches occur, and the results achieved. In Sec. 5, Simulated Annealing is used to seek solutions to a more complex circuit, in which we could analyze the impact of SA parameters and functions as a mean to automate circuit design. Finally, Sec. 6 conclude this chapter with our final remarks and future works.

2. Simulated annealing

The Simulated Annealing (SA) is a well known random-search technique that exploits an analogy with the way a metal heat and slowly freezes into a minimum energy crystalline structure, the so called annealing process. In a more general system, like an optimization problem, it is used for searching the minimum value of a cost function, avoiding getting trapped in local minima. The algorithm employs random searches which, besides accepting solutions that decrease (i.e. minimize) the objective cost function, may also accept some that increase it. The latter are called "indirect steps", and are allowed in order to escape from local optima.

The SA algorithm uses a *cooling function* $T(t)$, which maps a time instant t to a temperature T, decreasing T as t increases. At each iteration, new steps are randomly taken, based on a *probabilistic state generation function* $g(X)$, leading to new states in the solution space. In this context X is a vector of d parameters, where d is the dimensionality of the solution space. If a step leads to a state with a worse solution, it is only effectively taken, i.e. the new state is accepted, with a probability less than 1. States with better solutions are always accepted. This probability is given by an *acceptance function* $h(\Delta F)$:

$$h(\Delta F) = \frac{1}{1 + exp(\Delta F / T)} \tag{1}$$

Here, $\Delta F = F_{t+1} - F_t$ represents the variation of the cost function calculated at two consecutive times steps F_{t+1} and F_t.

The algorithm is able to reach an optimal solution on the choice of the *cooling function* and *probabilistic state generation function*. If the temperature in *cooling function* decreases too fast, the search will run faster, but the SA algorithm is not guaranteed to find the global optimum anymore [13]. This may be acceptable if a solution is needed in a small amount of time and the solution space is well-know or presents high dimensionality. This is called Simulated Quenching (SQ) [1], and is useful when an approximate solution is sufficient. There are some common sets of options to choose from when implementing an SA algorithm. They are described below.

2.1. Boltzmann annealing

The Boltzmann annealing is the classical simulated annealing algorithm, using physics principles to choose the *probabilistic state generation function* in order to ensure convergence to a global minimum. It employs a Gaussian distribution for generating new states:

$$g_{Boltz}(X) = \frac{1}{(2\pi T(t))^{d/2}} \exp\left(-\frac{(\Delta X)^2}{2T(t)}\right) \tag{2}$$

Here, $\Delta X = X - X_0$ and d is the number of dimensionality of the search space. The Boltzman *cooling function* is described as:

$$T_{Boltz}(t) = \frac{T_0}{\log(t)} \tag{3}$$

where T_0 is the initial temperature, and t is the time step.

Geman and Geman in the classical paper [7] have proved that using Gaussian distribution to generate new states (Eq. 3) with the Boltzman *cooling function* (Eq. 2) is sufficient to reach global minimum of an optimization function at infinite time.

2.2. Fast annealing

Fast Annealing is a variant of the Boltzmann Annealing [20] that uses as *probabilistic state generation function* the Cauchy distribution:

$$g_{Fast}(X) = \frac{T}{(\Delta X^2 + T(t))^{(d+1)/2}} \tag{4}$$

One advantage of the Cauchy distribution over the Gaussian distribution is its fatter tail. When the temperature decreases, the Cauchy distribution generates new states with a lower dispersion than states generated by a Gaussian distribution. In this way the converge using Cauchy distribution becomes faster.

However, in order to guarantee that the algorithm reaches the global minimum, a special *cooling function* is used:

$$T_{Fast}(t) = \frac{T_0}{t} \tag{5}$$

Where T_0 is the initial temperature, and t is the time step. It is important to show that the *cooling function* used in Boltzmann Annealing (equation 3) decreases more slowly than the *cooling function* used in Fast Annealing (equation 5). This characteristic turns the convergence of Fast annealing faster than Boltzmann annealing.

2.3. Reannealing

The reannealing method [14] raises the temperature periodically after the algorithm accepts a certain number of new states or after a given number of iterations. Then the search is restarted with a new annealing temperature. The reannealing objective is to avoid local minima, which presents interesting results when applied in nonlinear optimization problems.

2.4. Simulated Quenching

Simulated Quenching (SQ) [1], described before, is useful when an approximated solution is sufficient and there is a need of faster execution time. An example of the function that can be used to decrease the temperature faster is the exponential *cooling function* shown below.

$$T_{Exp}(t) = T_0 \cdot 0.95^t \tag{6}$$

Using this *cooling function* with Boltzmann *state generation function* (Eq. 2) or Fast *state generation function* (Eq. 4) will turn the optimization faster, but without convergence guarantee.

3. Circuit modeling

In order to design an analog integrated circuit with Simulated Annealing optimizations it is necessary to develop a cost function describing the analog circuit behavior. There are two ways to analyze a circuit behavior. One is based on simplified equations as cost functions, which represent the circuit. This is the faster alternative, but has low precision and limits the solutions in some regions of circuit operation. The other way is to use an external SPICE electrical simulator to evaluate the circuit with a complete model. This alternative provides better accuracy, but demands more computational power.

In this work the second alternative is used, with the electrical simulation performed by Synopsys HSpice ®. In the optimization procedure of analog integrated circuit design, the heuristic parameters are the MOSFET transistor sizes W (channel width) and L (channel length), voltage and current sources bias, and capacitors and resistor values. The design flow using Simulated Annealing proposed in this chapter is shown in Figure 1 .

The proposed methodology has three specification structures as inputs:

- *Design constraints* that represent all functions of circuit specifications and variable bounds;
- A *technology file* containing simulation model parameters for the MOSFET transistors; and
- *SA Options* for the configuration of the SA heuristic, such as temperature function, annealing function and stop condition.

The methodology starts with the initial solution generation that is provided by random generated numbers according to the variables bounds values. The circuit specifications of the generated solution are then evaluated by the cost function, which uses the external electrical SPICE simulator. Thereafter, the SA temperature parameter is initialized with the value specified in the SA options.

Thereafter, a new solution is generated by the SA state generation function (see Section 2), and evaluated by the cost function by means of electrical simulations. The new solution is compared with the current solution and, if it has a lower cost function value, it replaces the current solution. Otherwise, a random number is generated and compared with a probability parameter: if it is greater, the current solution is replaced by the new solution; if smaller, the new solution is rejected.

Finally, the stopping conditions are verified and, if satisfied, the optimization process ends. If not satisfied, the temperature parameter is reduced by the cooling function and the procedure continues. The stopping conditions usually include a minimum value of temperature, a minimum cost function variation, and a maximum number of iterations.

For analog design automation, a multi-objective cost function is necessary to aggregate different - and sometimes conflicting - circuit specifications. A typical multi-objective cost function can be:

$$f_c(X) = \sum_{i=1}^{n} S_i(X) + \sum_{j=1}^{m} R_j(X) \tag{7}$$

In this function, the first sum represents optimization specifications (design objectives) and the second one the design constraints. $S_i(X)$ is the ith circuit specification value and $R_j(X)$ is the jth constraint function. Both are functions of the vector X of design parameters and are normalized and tuned according to the desired circuit performance.

$R_j(X)$ is a function that is dependent on the specification type: minimum required value ($R_{min}(X)$) or maximum required value ($R_{max}(X)$) [3]. These functions are shown in Fig. 2, where a is the maximum or minimum required value and b is the bound value between acceptable and unacceptable performance values. Acceptable but non-feasible performance values are that points between a and b. They return intermediate values for the constraints functions in order to allow the exploration of disconnect feasible design space regions. These functions return additional cost for the cost function if the performance is outside the desired range. Otherwise, the additional cost is zero.

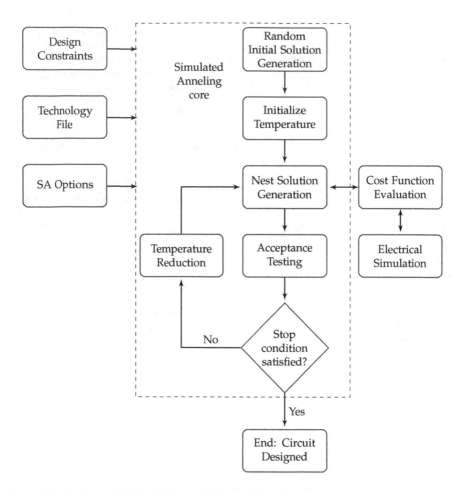

Figure 1. Analog integrated circuit sizing with Simulated Annealing flow.

4. Basic analysis of the search space

This section presents a simple case study, a differential amplifier, to introduce and explain the usage of Simulated Annealing to automate the design of analog integrated circuit. Section 4.1 describes the features of the differential amplifier. Sec. 4.2 explains the modeling of the differential amplifier that allows its simulation and the usage of the SA. Finally, to improve the automation process, some optimization options on SA are applied and their results are discussed in Sec. 4.3 .

4.1. Case study: Differential amplifier

A differential amplifier is a basic analog building block used in general as the input stage of operational amplifiers. Perhaps its simplicity, it is very useful as a first voltage

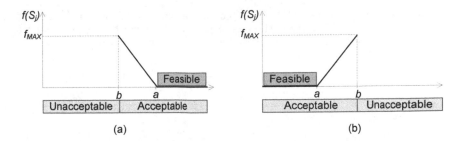

Figure 2. Cost function performance metrics: (a) minimum required value specifications and (b) maximum required value specifications.

amplification stage of many electronic devices and has become the dominant choice in today's high-performance analog and mixed-signal circuits [19]. Ideally, it amplifies the difference between two voltages but does not amplify the common-mode voltages. An implementation of the differential amplifier with CMOS transistors and active load is shown in Fig. 3 . It is composed by a differential pair formed by two input transistors ($M1$ and $M2$), an active current mirror ($M3$ and $M4$) and an ideal tail current source I_{ref}. The output voltage V_{out} depends on the difference between the input voltages V_{in1} and V_{in2}. For a small difference between V_{in1} and V_{in2}, both $M2$ and $M4$ are saturated, providing a high gain. Otherwise, if $|V_{in1} - V_{in2}|$ is large enough, $M1$ or $M2$ will be off and the output will be stuck at $0V$ or at V_{DD}.

The output voltage of the differential amplifier can be expressed in terms of its differential-mode and common-mode input voltages as

$$V_{out} = A_{VD}(V_{in1} - V_{in2}) \pm A_{VC}\left(\frac{V_{in1} + V_{in2}}{2}\right) \tag{8}$$

where A_{VD} is the differential-mode voltage gain and A_{VC} is the common-mode voltage gain. An ideal operational amplifier has an infinite A_{VD} and zero A_{VC}. Although practical implementations try to find an approximation to these values, the implementation of physical circuits insert some non-idealities that limit A_{VD} and A_{VC}.

Another important characteristic of a differential amplifier is the input common-mode range ($ICMR$). We can estimate ICMR by setting $V_{in1} = V_{in2}$ and vary input common-mode voltage (DC component of V_{in1} and V_{in2}) until one of the transistors in the circuit is no longer saturated [2]. The highest common-mode input voltage ($ICMR^+$) is

$$ICMR^+ = V_{DD} - V_{SG3} + V_{TN1} \tag{9}$$

Here, V_{SG3} is the source-voltage of transistor $M3$ and V_{TN1} is the threshold voltage of $M1$. The lowest input voltage at the gate of $M1$ (or $M2$) is found to be

$$ICMR^- = V_{SS} + V_1 + V_{GS2} \tag{10}$$

The voltage at node 1 (V_1) is determined by the physical implementation of the current source I_{ref}, which in general is a single transistor whose drain current is controlled by its gate voltage. V_{GS2} is the gate-source voltage of transistor $M2$.

The small-signal properties of the differential amplifier can be accomplished with the assistance of the simplified model shown in Fig. 4, which ignores body effect. In this figure, gm is the gate transconductance given by the derivative of the drain current in relation to gate-source voltage:

$$gm = \frac{\partial I_D}{\partial V_{GS}} \tag{11}$$

The series resistance rds is the inverse of the output conductance gds and can be estimated in small-signal analysis as

$$\frac{1}{rds} = gds = \frac{\partial I_D}{\partial V_{DS}} \tag{12}$$

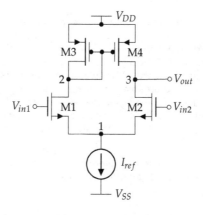

Figure 3. Schematics of a CMOS differential amplifier.

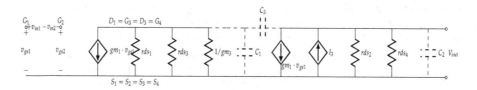

Figure 4. Simplified small-signal model for the CMOS differential amplifier.

The small-signal voltage gain A_{vo}, i.e., the relationship between V_{out} and the differential input voltage $V_{in1} - V_{in2}$, can be estimated in low frequencies by

$$A_{vo} = \frac{gm_1}{gds_2 + gds_4} \tag{13}$$

For higher frequencies, the voltage gain is modified due to the various parasitic capacitors at each node of the circuits, modeled by C_1, C_2 and C_3, which are calculated as follows:

$$C_1 = C_{gd1} + C_{bd1} + C_{bd3} + C_{gs3} + C_{gs4} \tag{14}$$

$$C_2 = C_{bd2} + C_{bd4} + C_{gd2} + C_L \tag{15}$$

$$C_3 = C_{gd4} \tag{16}$$

Considering C_3 approximately zero, the voltage-transfer function can be written as

$$V_{out}(s) \cong \frac{gm_1}{gds_2 + gds_4} \left[\left(\frac{gm_3}{gm_3 + sC_1} \right) V_{gs1}(s) - V_{gs2}(s) \right] \frac{\omega_2}{s + \omega_2} \tag{17}$$

where ω_2 is given as

$$\omega_2 = \frac{gds_2 + gds_4}{C_2} \tag{18}$$

The pole ω_2 determines the cut-off frequency of the amplifier and is also called as ω_{-3dB}. Assuming that

$$\frac{gm_3}{C_1} \gg \frac{gds_2 + gds_4}{C_2} \tag{19}$$

then the frequency response of the differential amplifier reduces to

$$\frac{V_{out}(s)}{V_{in1}(s) - V_{in2}(s)} \cong \left(\frac{gm_1}{gds_2 + gds_4} \right) \left(\frac{\omega_2}{s + \omega_2} \right) \tag{20}$$

This first-order analysis leads to a single pole at the output given by $-(gds_2 + gds_4)/C_2$. Some zeroes occur due to C_{gd1}, C_{gd2} and C_{gd4}, but they can be ignored in this analysis. The gain-bandwidth product (GBW), which is the equal to the unity-gain frequency, can be expressed as

$$GBW = A_{vo} \cdot \omega_{-3dB} \tag{21}$$

The slew-rate (SR) performance of the CMOS differential amplifier depends the value of I_{ref} and the capacitance from the output node to ac ground and is given by

$$SR = \frac{I_{ref}}{C} \tag{22}$$

where C is the total capacitance connected to the output node (approximated by C_2 in our analysis).

Other important specifications for the electrical behavior of the differential amplifier includes power dissipation $P_{diss} = I_{ref} \cdot (V_{DD} - V_{SS})$ and total gate area, calculated as the sum of the product of gate width and lenght of all transistors that compose the circuit:

$$Area = \sum_i W_i \cdot L_i \tag{23}$$

All analog design has a target fabrication technology and a device type, in which the set of transistor model parameters is unique. These parameters determines the electrical characteristics - such as drain current, gate transconductance and output conductance - of the active devices that are part of the circuit. The specifications described before are function of these parameters, together with W and L. Since the parameters are fixed for a given fabrication technology, the designer has as free variables only the gate sizes. Gate sizing is, in effect, the task of analog design.

4.2. Modeling the differential amplifier for automatic synthesis

The modeling of the differential amplifier of Fig. 3 for automatic synthesis is straightforward. Using a simulation-based approach, the circuit specifications are calculated by SPICE electrical simulations. As an example, let us consider the multi-objective design of a differential amplifier that must be optimized in terms of voltage gain A_{v0} and positive input common-mode range $ICMR^+$. Also, there is a list of constraints containing a series of specifications that must be met hardly. Table 1 summarizes the design objectives and constraints for this problem.

Specification	Value
A_v	maximize
$ICMR^+$	maximize
$Area$	$< 120\mu m^2$
PM	$> 70°$
GBW	$> 100MHz$

Table 1. Design specifications and constraints for the differential amplifier of Fig 3 .

The cost function $f_c(X)$ is than formulated as a sum of design specifications and constraints in terms of the vector of the design variables X:

$$f_c(X) = 3 \cdot \frac{ICMR^+(X)}{ICMR^+_{ref}} + \frac{A_{vo}(X)}{A_{vo(ref)}} + R(X) \qquad (24)$$

The specifications are calculated for a given X and normalized by a reference value. In this example, $ICMR^+_{ref} = 1.3V$ and $A_{vo(ref)} = 20dB$. The ponderation of each specification can be implemented with individual weights which indicate the relative importance of the parameter. In this example, we choose a weight of 3 for $ICMR^+$ and 1 for A_{vo}. $R(X)$ is a constraint function which is also a function of X, calculated as follows:

$$R(X) = \frac{R_{max}(Area(X), Area_{ref})}{4} + R_{min}(PM(X), PM_{ref}) + R_{max}(GBW(X), GBW_{ref}) \qquad (25)$$

Here, $R_{max}(S(X), S_{ref})$ and $R_{min}(S(X), S_{ref})$ are constraint functions of maximum and minimum, respectively, in terms of the specification $S(X)$ and the reference value S_{ref}. For example, the constraint of gate area is related to $R_{max}(S(X), S_{ref})$, because it can not be larger than a reference value of $Area_{ref}$. The same occurs for GBW, which can not be smaller than GBW_{ref}, whose constraint is modeled by the function $R_{min}(S(X), S_{ref})$. Both constraint functions insert a penalty value in the cost function $f_c(X)$ if the specification is outside the expected range. Otherwise, they return zero. The following equations show how the constraint functions are implemented:

$$R_{max}(S(X), S_{ref}) = \begin{cases} 0 & \text{if } S(X) \leq S_{ref} \\ \frac{S(X) - S_{ref}}{S_{ref}} & \text{if } S(X) > S_{ref} \end{cases} \qquad (26)$$

$$R_{min}(S(X), S_{ref}) = \begin{cases} 0 & \text{if } S(X) \geq S_{ref} \\ \frac{S(X) - S_{ref}}{S_{ref}} & \text{if } S(X) < S_{ref} \end{cases} \qquad (27)$$

We used in this example the constraint reference values shown in Tab. 1 . In order to simplify the analysis, we consider that all transistors of the circuit are of the same size. It is not a practical approach, since transistor $M1$ must be equal to $M2$, but not necessarily equal to $M3$ and $M4$. However, this simplification allows the 2-D visualization of the problem and can be used to explain design trade-offs and automatic optimal search, providing an intuitive notion of the problem. So, we will consider in this analysis two free variables: $L = L_1 = L_2 = L_3 = L_4$ and $W = W_1 = W_2 = W_3 = W_4$. In this case, $X = [W \; L]$.

The design space for Eq. 24 was fully mapped by electrical simulation varying W and L from $1\mu m$ to $100\mu m$ with a step of $1\mu m$. The target technology node was $0.35\mu m$ $3.3V$ CMOS. Fig. 5 shows the plotted design space as a function of W and L. It is possible to note the highly non-linear nature of the generated function and the existence of a valley in which is localized a minimum value. The optimal solution for this sizing problem, i.e., the minimum value of the design space, is known exactly in this case and is located at $W = 8\mu m$ and $L = 20\mu m$, with the value of -1.9623.

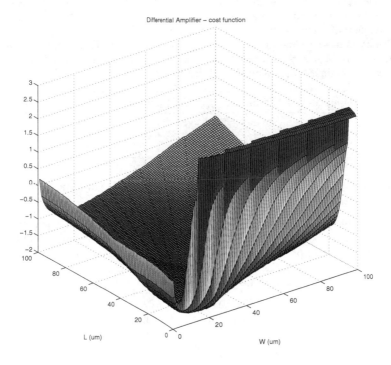

Figure 5. Two-variables design space for a differential amplifier. The minimum is at $W = 8\mu m$ and $L = 20\mu m$, with the value of -1.9623.

4.3. Optimization of a differential amplifier

For the analysis of Simulated Annealing options and the influence over the automatic sizing procedure of analog basic blocks, we will explore different configurations of temperature schedule, state generation function and reannealing for global optimization and further local optimization. Due to the random nature of some parameters of SA, an statistic analysis is needed to understand the search behavior. We performed 1000 optimization runs for each temperature schedule function described before: Boltzman, Exponential and Fast. The state generation function was kept fixed as $g_{Boltz}(X)$ (Eq. 2). Each execution started with a different seed for the random number generator function. The same parameters were used for the three functions, including the same random number vector for a fair comparison. A MATLAB script was implemented and the native SA method (simulannealbnd) was used as the main bound constrained optimization function.

4.3.1. Global optimization

Table 2 shows the mean of the optimal cost function found after 1000 executions of the optimization procedure for each temperature schedule function. The Boltzman schedule achieved the best values, with a mean final cost $\overline{f_c^*}$ of -1.960306, right near the optimal global solution of -1.9623. It means that most of the solutions provided by the procedure with Boltzman are near the global optimum. Exponential and Fast temperature schedules demonstrate worst results in terms of cost. Boltzman result was obtained at expense of a higher execution time and total number of iterators.

Temperature schedule	$\overline{f_c^*}$	Execution time (s)	Iterations
Boltzman	-1.960306	16.32	1777.44
Exponential	-1.834720	9.57	1043.89
Fast	-1.579269	12.99	1416.36

Table 2. Mean values of differential amplifier global optimization procedure for different temperature schedule functions after 1000 executions.

The free variables W and L found by the three temperature schedule functions are shown in Tab. 3. Again, Boltzman demonstrates the best results, with the mean values near the optimal solution. Fast schedule presents the worst results in this configuration.

Temperature schedule	$\overline{W}$ (μm)	$\overline{L}$ (μm)
Boltzman	8.07	20.57
Exponential	11.47	23.00
Fast	34.46	26.32
Optimum value	8.00	20.00

Table 3. Mean W and L values achieved by global optimization procedure of the differential amplifier after 1000 runs for each different temperature schedule function.

Fig. 6 shows a graph comparing the 3 temperature schedules, considering only the optimum solutions obtained in relation to the optimization time. It is possible to notice the very attractive results for Boltzman, which achieved 400 optimum solutions (over a set of 1000 executions) in about 25 seconds of execution time. After this time, the number of optimal solutions does not grow considerably, saturating in 430 at 37 seconds. The same saturation behavior happens with Exponential and Fast temperature schedules, but with a very lower number of optimal solutions and at early execution time.

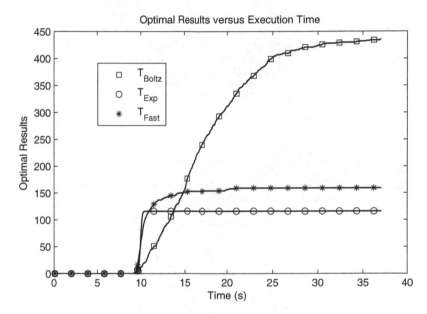

Figure 6. Optimal results versus execution time for the global optimization of a differential amplifier, considering 3 different temperature schedule functions.

4.3.2. Global followed by local optimization

In order to improve the results obtained by global optimization with Simulated Annealing, we apply a local optimization algorithm over the previous set of solutions generated by SA with the three temperature schedule functions. We choose the interior point algorithm [18], which is suitable for linear and non-linear convex design spaces. We suppose that the design space region near the solution provided by the global optimization and evolving the global optimum solution is convex and can be explored by this method. The algorithm was implemented by using the MATLAB native function fmincon. The results can be seen in Tab. 4 . It is clear the improvement obtained by the local optimization. The mean final cost of the 1000 executions for the three temperature schedules are close to the known global optimum of −1.960306. The total execution time (including global followed by local execution times) was increased by about 50%, but it is still in a reasonable value, near 20 seconds.

Temperature schedule	$\overline{f_c^*}$	Execution time (s)
Boltzman	-1.961759	24.40
Exponential	-1.927647	18.51
Fast	-1.786238	22.43

Table 4. Mean values of differential amplifier after local optimization over the results obtained by global optimization shown in Tab. 2.

The mean values found for the free variables after the local search are shown in Tab. 5 . Comparing to the previous values provided by the global optimization, it is possible to note the great improvement of the Exponential temperature schedule, whose mean W and L approached very near to the global optimum.

Temperature schedule	$\overline{W}$ (μm)	$\overline{L}$ (μm)
Boltzman	8.07	19.99
Exponential	9.68	20.30
Fast	20.12	21.59
Optimum value	8.00	20.00

Table 5. Mean W and L values achieved by local optimization procedure of the differential amplifier over the results obtained by global optimization shown in tab. 3.

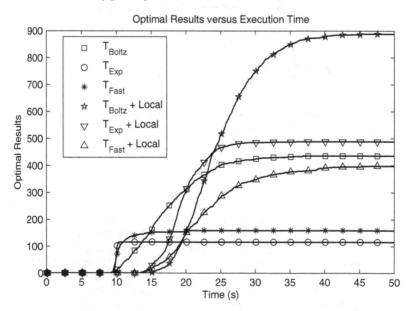

Figure 7. Optimal results versus execution time for the global optimization of a differential amplifier, considering 3 different temperature schedule functions - global and local.

In terms of the number of optimal solutions found over the 1000 executions, the local search also demonstrate an improvement. Fig. 7 shows the results obtained, in which we can see that, for Boltzman schedule, almost 90% of the final solutions are optimal, an improvement of more than 50% over the global optimization. The same occurs for the other temperature schedules.

We can observe the improvement in the number of optimal solutions with local search in Fig. 8, which presents the frequency histogram of the resulting final cost provided by global search (Fig. 8(a)) and global search followed by local search (Fig. 8(b)) for the 3 different temperature schedules. Besides the increase in the number of optimal solutions found, the inclusion of local search after global search also approximated the remaining non-optimal solutions in the direction to the best known value.

4.3.3. Global optimization with reannealing

For the analysis of the influence of reannealing in the optimization process, we performed some experiments executing Simulated Annealing with reannealing intervals of 200, 450, 700 and 950 iterations. Again, 1000 executions were done in order to guarantee a statistical analysis for the three temperature schedule functions described before.

Fig. 9 shows the relation between the number of optimal solutions found by Boltzman schedule function versus the execution time for reannealing intervals from 200 to infinite (*i.e.*, no reannealing). Reannealing interval affects the number of optimal solutions in this case. As the interval decrease, the number of optimal solutions decrease too. The best configuration is with no reannealing, demonstrating that it is not interesting to use reannealing with T_{Boltz}. It happens because the temperature decreases slowly at the beginning of the annealing process. With the reannealing, the temperature increases for higher values before the search in the design space reaches a path trending to the optimal solution.

When the temperature schedule function is modified to Exponential, the behavior is opposite. As the reannealing interval decreases, more optimal solutions are found. Fig. 10 shows the relation between optimal solutions found and execution time for this temperature schedule configuration.

The same occurs for the Fast temperature schedule function, shown in Fig. 11. As the reannealing interval diminishes, the number of optimal solutions increases. This behavior is maintained for ever small intervals. A high improvement in the number of optimal solutions is obtained for reannealing intervals in the order of 100 iterations, as shown in Fig. 12. As the temperature decreases very fast, the reannealing allows to avoid local minima. Thus, it increases the chances of finding the correct path to the optimum solution. Also, we can observe the existence of an optimum value for the reannealing interval which returns the maximum number of optimal solutions.

4.3.4. Analysis of state generation function

The variation of the state generation function is also a factor that can change the convergence of the Simulated Annealing algorithm. Two of these functions are analyzed here: Boltzman and Fast. The combinations of temperature schedule function and state generation function produce distinct results for the synthesis of the differential amplifier. Fig. 13 shows

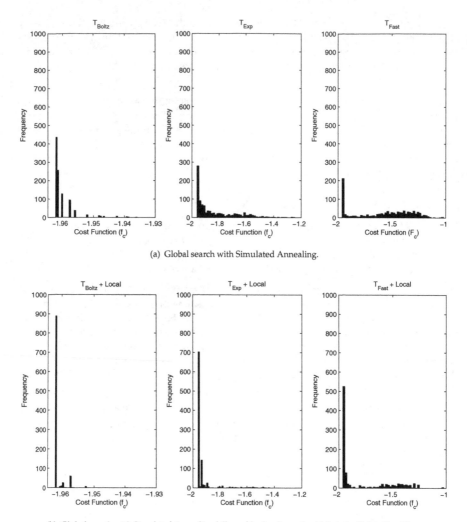

(a) Global search with Simulated Annealing.

(b) Global search with Simulated Annealing followed by local search with Interior Point Algorithm.

Figure 8. Frequency histograms of the final cost found by the optimization process for three different temperature schedule functions: Boltzman, Exponential and Fast. Obs.: x-scales are different in each chart for better visualization purpose.

the number of optimal solutions returned by the algorithm after 1000 executions for 6 combinations.

We can notice that there are a great improvement in the quality of the solutions using Boltzman temperature schedule together with Boltzman state generation function. This is the best combination, according to that was theoretical predicted in Section 2.

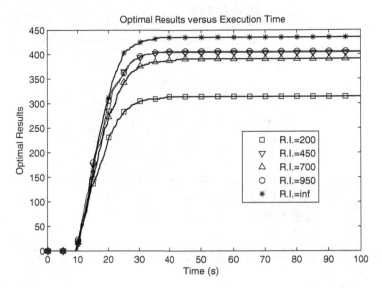

Figure 9. Optimal results versus execution time for the global optimization of a differential amplifier with Boltzman temperature schedule function and different reannealing intervals.

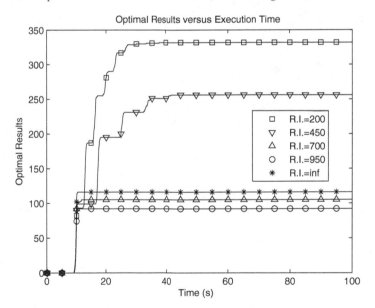

Figure 10. Optimal results versus execution time for the global optimization of a differential amplifier with Exponential temperature schedule function and different reannealing intervals.

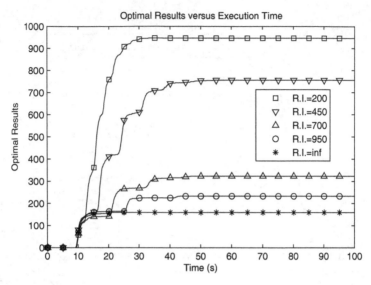

Figure 11. Optimal results versus execution time for the global optimization of a differential amplifier with Fast temperature schedule function and different reannealing intervals.

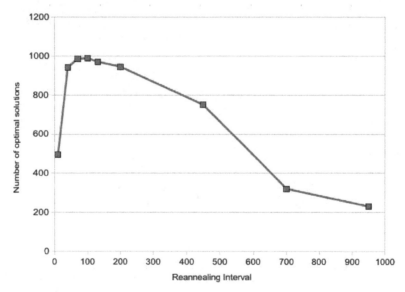

Figure 12. Maximum number of optimal results returned by the optimization process versus reannealing interval for Fast temperature schedule. The optimum value for the reannealing interval is near 100.

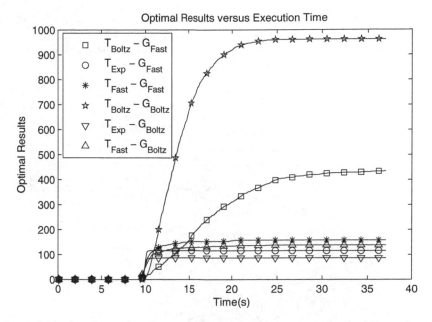

Figure 13. Number of optimal results returned by the optimization process for the differential amplifier for different annealing functions and temperature function schedules.

4.3.5. Analysis of best SA options for the differential amplifier

Results presented before allow us to suppose that the temperature schedule function affects directly the quality of the solutions generated by the global optimization algorithm. The Boltzman schedule, followed by a post-processing with a local search algorithm, demonstrate best convergence to the optimal point, at the expenses of a larger execution time. This additional time, however, is not a problem if we consider that the chances of finding the optimal (or near the optimal) solution are increased. For our 2-variables problem, this additional time is irrelevant (about 10s for 1000 executions). For more complex circuits with dozens of variables, the execution time can be a factor of concern. It is increased exponentially with the number of free variables, since the design space grows fast with the number of free variables. We can estimate the design space size $D_s(X)$ as:

$$D_s(X) = \prod_i \frac{x_{i(ub)} - x_{i(lb)}}{x_{i(step)}} \tag{28}$$

where $x_{i(ub)}$ and $x_{i(lb)}$ are upper an lower bounds of variable x_i, respectively, and $x_{i(step)}$ is the minimum step allowed for variable x_i. It is clear that the exploration of the entire design space is hard for a problem with several free variables. An alternative, in this case, is to use the Fast temperature schedule with reannealing, which is also efficient in the design space exploration. Both Boltzman followed by local search and Fast with reannealing achieved the optimal solution in about 90% of the cases. These configurations are candidates to be tested in a larger circuit.

5. Operational amplifier design

In order to apply simulated annealing in a more realistic and practical operational amplifier, we syntesized a folded cascode in CMOS IBM $0.18\mu m$, regular Vt, $1.8V$ technology node. The schematics of this amplifier is shown in Fig. 14.

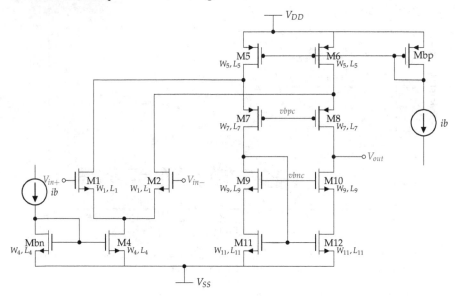

Figure 14. Schematics of a CMOS folded cascode amplifier.

The modeling of this circuit for the proposed optimization process is simple and similar to the previous described modeling of the differential amplifier. The SPICE netlist and the testbench are the information necessary to describe the circuit and bias. The specifications are simulated by an external electrical simulator (HSpice), which returns, for a given set of variables, the electrical characteristics of the circuit. In our design there are 15 free variables, summarized in Tab. 6. It leads to a very large 15-dimensional design space, which is difficult to explore and find the minimum cost value. It is possible to limit the design space inserting constraints in the cost function related to the operation region of each transistor, forcing the devices to operate at saturation ($V_{DS} > V_{GS} - V_T$) and strong inversion ($V_{GS} > V_T$) regions. The specifications and design goals for this circuit are shown in Tab. 7. In the output is connected a capacitive load of $3pF$. We expect to size the circuit optimizing gate area and power dissipation while maintaining the constraints of GBW, low-voltage gain, phase margin and slew rate inside a given range.

Using Boltzman for both temperature schedule function and state generation function, followed by local search with interior point algorithm, we find the final results shown in the third and fourth columns of Tab. 7 for global and global followed by local searches, respectively. It is possible to note that all design objectives were reached, while keeping all devices in the specified operation region. There is an improvement in the multi-objective design goal with the post-processing local search. The final gate area is $145.13\mu m^2$ and

Variable	Final values (our work)	Final values - GENOM ([3])
W_1	11.58 μm	14.91 μm
W_4	22.39 μm	6.99 μm
W_5	14.13 μm	36.78 μm
W_7	30.72 μm	63.04 μm
W_9	7.16 μm	31.45 μm
W_{11}	6.58 μm	7.32 μm
L_1	0.73 μm	1.38 μm
L_4	0.71 μm	1.94 μm
L_5	0.29 μm	0.37 μm
L_7	0.52 μm	0.91 μm
L_9	0.87 μm	0.89 μm
L_{11}	4.54 μm	2.19 μm
$vbnc$	0.0579 V	0.001 V
$vbpc$	-0.0408 V	-0,0449 V
ib	36.78 μA	48.51 μA

Table 6. Free variables and final results found for the folded-cascode amplifier optimization.

dissipated power is 133.2μW. The advantages of this approach is that the resulting circuit is already validated by electrical simulations and does not need to be verified in another design stage.

We can make a direct comparison of the results obtained by this work using SA with other approaches, such as the tools that use genetic algorithms as main optimization heuristic. Although it is difficult to perform a fair comparison with other works in the literature, mainly because the experimental setup in general can not be reproduced with the provided information and there is no standard benchmarks in analog design automation, it is still interesting to compare the general performance of our methodology with other results over similar circuits and design objectives.

In this sense, the results presented by [3] with the GENOM tool are passible to comparison, because the same experimental setup can be reproduced - although some implementation details are not available, such as the parameters of the electrical model. This tool is based on a variation of genetic algorithm as the main optimization heuristic. The folded cascode was implemented in UMC 0.18μm technology. The final results obtained by GENOM for the same circuit synthesized by our approach are summarized in the fiftieth column of Tab. 7.

We can see that both methodologies present similar results for the design constraints. By the other side, both power dissipation and gate area depicted by our approach using Simulated Annealing are about half the final values provided by GENOM. Power dissipation was decreased in 45.5% and gate area in 49%, a great improvement in circuit performance. These results prove that SA is a powerful heuristic for the design of micro-power operational

Specification	Objective	Global (SA Boltz)	Global+Local	GENOM ([3])
GBW	>12MHz	14.86 MHz	14.98 MHz	15.35 MHz
Av0	> 70dB	73.04 dB	70dB	70.61dB
PM	> 55°	76.87°	78.76°	79.6°
SR	> $10V/\mu s$	$10.98V/\mu s$	$11.37V/\mu s$	$15.36V/\mu s$
Area	minimize	$188.25\mu m^2$	$145.13\mu m^2$	$284.7\mu m^2$
Power	minimize	$129.9\mu W$	$133.2\mu W$	$244.6\mu W$

Table 7. Design performance and final results found by the optimization process for the folded-cascode amplifier.

amplifiers. Again, it is important to note that the comparison between the results can not be exact because some parameters in the device electrical model and other configurations are not equal. The final values for the free variables are shown in Tab. 6. We can see that the gate widths of the transistors trend to be larger than the gate lengths and that the magnitudes are similar in both approaches.

6. Conclusion

The design of analog integrated blocks and the search for an optimum design point in a highly non-linear design space evolve different approaches and choices. Simulated Annealing and its variations are a good option for the exploration of this kind of problem. This chapter presented some implications of the algorithm tuning over the final results. We could demonstrate that the correct configuration of SA options can lead to good solutions near the optimality in reasonable execution time. Although it is not clear that some configuration is suitable for sizing all types of analog blocks, it is possible to notice that the approach is correct and, with minimum adjusts for different circuits, SA can be used as a general optimization algorithm, providing good solutions. A direct comparison with a tool based on genetic algorithms for the synthesis of a folded cascode operational amplifier showed that better results can be obtained with the correct design space exploration with SA. As future work, the analysis of parameter variation in the optimization methodology for design centering must be implemented.

Acknowledgements

We would like to thank CNPq and Fapergs Brazilian agencies for supporting this work.

Author details

Lucas Compassi Severo, Alessandro Girardi,Alessandro Bof de Oliveira, Fabio N. Kepler and Marcia C. Cera
Federal University of Pampa – UNIPAMPA, Alegrete Campus
Av. Tiaraju, 810, CEP 97546-550, Alegrete-RS, Brazil

7. References

[1] Aguiar, H., Junior, O., Ingber, L., Petraglia, A., Petraglia, M. R. & Machado, M. A. S. [2012]. *Adaptive Simulated Annealing*, Vol. 35 of *Intelligent Systems Reference Library*, Springer, pp. 33–62.

[2] Allen, P. E. & Holberg, D. R. [2011]. *CMOS Analog Circuit Design*, The Oxford Series in Electrical and Computer Engineering, 3rd edn, Oxford.

[3] Barros, M., Guilherme, J. & Horta, N. [2010]. *Analog Circuits and Systems Optimization based on Evolutionary Computation Techniques*, Vol. 294 of *Studies in Computational Intelligence*, 1st edn, Springer.

[4] Degrauwe, M., Nys, ., Dukstra, E., Rijmenants, J., Bitz, S., Gofart, B. L. A. G., Vitoz, E. A., Cserveny, S., Meixenberger, C., Stappen, G. V. & Oguey, H. J. [1987]. Idac: An interactive design tool for analog cmos circuits, *IEEE Journal of Solid-State Circuits* SC-22(6): 1106–1116.

[5] der Plas, G. V., Gielen, G. & Sansen, W. M. C. [2002]. *A Computer-Aided Design and Synthesis Environment for Analog Integrated Circuits*, Vol. 672 of *The Springer International Series in Engineering and Computer Science*, Springer.

[6] El-Turky, F. M. & Perry, E. E. [1989]. BLADES: an artificial intelligence approach to analog circuit design, *IEEE Trans. on CAD of Integrated Circuits and Systems* 8(6): 680–692.
URL: *http://doi.ieeecomputersociety.org/10.1109/43.31523*

[7] Geman, S. & Geman, D. [1984]. Stochastic relaxation, gibbs distributions, and the bayesian restoration of images, *IEEE Transactions on Pattern Analysis and Machine Intelligence* PAMI-6(6): 721–741.

[8] Girardi, A. & Bampi, S. [2003]. LIT - an automatic layout generation tool for trapezoidal association of transistors for basic analog building blocks, *DATE*, IEEE Computer Society, pp. 11106–11107.
URL: *http://doi.ieeecomputersociety.org/10.1109/DATE.2003.10028*

[9] Girardi, A. & Bampi, S. [2007]. Power constrained design optimization of analog circuits based on physical gm/id characteristics, *Journal of Integrated Circuits and Systems* 2: 22=28.

[10] Glelen, G., Walscharts, H. & Sansen, W. [1989]. Isaac: A symbolic simulator for analog circuits, *IEEE Journal of Solid-State Circuits* 24(6): 1587–1597.

[11] Harjani, R., Rutenbar, R. A. & Carley, L. R. [1989]. OASYS: a framework for analog circuit synthesis, *IEEE Trans. on CAD of Integrated Circuits and Systems* 8(12): 1247–1266.
URL: *http://doi.ieeecomputersociety.org/10.1109/43.44506*

[12] Hershenson, M., Boyd, S. P. & Lee, T. H. [2001]. Optimal design of a CMOS op-amp via geometric programming, *IEEE Transactions on Computer-Aided Design* 20(1): 1–21.
URL: *http://www.stanford.edu/boyd/opamp.html*

[13] Ingber, L. [1996]. Adaptive simulated annealing (asa): Lessons learned, *Control and Cybernetics* 25(1): 33 – 54.

[14] Ingber, L. [1989]. Very fast simulated re-annealing, *Mathematical Computer Modelling* 12(8): 967 – 973.

[15] Liu, B., Fernandez, F. V., Gielen, G., Castro-Lopez, R. & Roca, E. [2009]. A memetic approach to the automatic design of high-performance analog integrated circuits, *ACM Transactions on Design Automation of Electronic Systems* 14.

[16] Mandal, P. & Visvanathan, V. [2001]. CMOS op-amp sizing using a geometric programming formulation, *IEEE Trans. on CAD of Integrated Circuits and Systems* 20(1): 22–38.
URL: *http://doi.ieeecomputersociety.org/10.1109/43.905672*

[17] Nye, W., Riley, D. C., Sangiovanni-Vincentelli, A. L. & Tits, A. L. [1988]. DELIGHT.SPICE: an optimization-based system for the design of integrated circuits, *IEEE Trans. on CAD of Integrated Circuits and Systems* 7(4): 501–519.
URL: *http://doi.ieeecomputersociety.org/10.1109/43.3185*

[18] Press, W., Teukolsky, S., Vetterling, W. & Flannery, B. [2007]. *Numerical Recipes: The Art of Scientific Computing*, 3rd edn, Cambridge University Press, New York, chapter Section 10.11. Linear Programming: Interior-Point Methods.

[19] Razavi, B. [2000]. *Design of Analog CMOS Integrated Circuits*, 1st edn, McGraw-Hil.

[20] Szu, H. & Hartley, R. [1987]. Fast simulated annealing, *Physical Letters A* 122: 157–162.

[21] Vytyaz, I., Lee, D. C., Hanumolu, P. K., Moon, U.-K. & Mayaram, K. [2009]. Automated design and optimization of low-noise oscillators, *Transactions on Computer-Aided Design of Integrated Circuits and Systems* 28(5): 609–622.

Permissions

The contributors of this book come from diverse backgrounds, making this book a truly international effort. This book will bring forth new frontiers with its revolutionizing research information and detailed analysis of the nascent developments around the world.

We would like to thank Marcos de Sales Guerra Tsuzuki, for lending his expertise to make the book truly unique. He has played a crucial role in the development of this book. Without his invaluable contribution this book wouldn't have been possible. He has made vital efforts to compile up to date information on the varied aspects of this subject to make this book a valuable addition to the collection of many professionals and students.

This book was conceptualized with the vision of imparting up-to-date information and advanced data in this field. To ensure the same, a matchless editorial board was set up. Every individual on the board went through rigorous rounds of assessment to prove their worth. After which they invested a large part of their time researching and compiling the most relevant data for our readers. Conferences and sessions were held from time to time between the editorial board and the contributing authors to present the data in the most comprehensible form. The editorial team has worked tirelessly to provide valuable and valid information to help people across the globe.

Every chapter published in this book has been scrutinized by our experts. Their significance has been extensively debated. The topics covered herein carry significant findings which will fuel the growth of the discipline. They may even be implemented as practical applications or may be referred to as a beginning point for another development. Chapters in this book were first published by InTech; hereby published with permission under the Creative Commons Attribution License or equivalent.

The editorial board has been involved in producing this book since its inception. They have spent rigorous hours researching and exploring the diverse topics which have resulted in the successful publishing of this book. They have passed on their knowledge of decades through this book. To expedite this challenging task, the publisher supported the team at every step. A small team of assistant editors was also appointed to further simplify the editing procedure and attain best results for the readers.

Our editorial team has been hand-picked from every corner of the world. Their multi-ethnicity adds dynamic inputs to the discussions which result in innovative outcomes. These outcomes are then further discussed with the researchers and contributors who give their valuable feedback and opinion regarding the same. The feedback is then collaborated with the researches and they are edited in a comprehensive manner to aid the understanding of the subject.

Apart from the editorial board, the designing team has also invested a significant amount of their time in understanding the subject and creating the most relevant covers. They scrutinized every image to scout for the most suitable representation of the subject and create an appropriate cover for the book.

The publishing team has been involved in this book since its early stages. They were actively engaged in every process, be it collecting the data, connecting with the contributors or procuring relevant information. The team has been an ardent support to the editorial, designing and production team. Their endless efforts to recruit the best for this project, has resulted in the accomplishment of this book. They are a veteran in the field of academics and their pool of knowledge is as vast as their experience in printing. Their expertise and guidance has proved useful at every step. Their uncompromising quality standards have made this book an exceptional effort. Their encouragement from time to time has been an inspiration for everyone.

The publisher and the editorial board hope that this book will prove to be a valuable piece of knowledge for researchers, students, practitioners and scholars across the globe.

List of Contributors

Gholam Reza Karimi and Ahmad Azizi Verki
Electrical Engineering Department, Engineering Faculty- Razi University, Kermanshah, Iran

Luis M. San-José-Revuelta
University of Valladolid, Spain

Laurence Miègeville
Department of Electrical Engineering, POLYTECH Nantes, University of Nantes, France
Research Institute on Electrical Energy of Nantes Atlantique, St Nazaire, France

Patrick Guérin
Department of Industrial Engineering and Maintenance, IUT Saint-Nazaire, University of Nantes, France
Research Institute on Electrical Energy of Nantes Atlantique, St Nazaire, France

Ivan Zelinka and Lenka Skanderova
Department of Computer Science, Faculty of computer science, 17, listopadu 15, 708 33 Ostrava-Poruba, VSB-TUO Ostrava, Czech Republic

Yan Zhang
Beijing Key Lab for Terahertz Spectroscopy and Imaging, Key Laboratory of Terahertz Optoelectronics, Ministry of Education, Department of Physics, Capital Normal University, Beijing, 100048 China

Igor Arambasic, Javier Casajus Quiros and Ivana Raos
ETSI Telecomunicacion, Universidad Politecnica de Madrid, Spain

Raymond Kwan and M. E. Aydin
University of Bedfordshire, United Kingdom

Cyril Leung
University of British Columbia, Canada

Manish Jha and Bithin Datta
James Cook University, Townsville and CRC CARE, Adelaide, Australia

Zhiru Shi, W.A.C. Fernando and A. Kondoz
I-Lab, CVSSP, University of Surrey, Guildford, United Kingdom

Yiqiang Sheng and Atsushi Takahashi
Department of Communications and Integrated Systems, Graduate School of Science and Engineering, Tokyo Institute of Technology, Tokyo, Japan

Fran Sérgio Lobato, Elaine Gomes Assis and Valder Steffen Jr
Universidade Federal de Uberlândia, Brazil

Antônio José da Silva Neto
Universidade do Estado do Rio de Janeiro, Brazil

Ali Sadollah and Ardeshir Bahreininejad
Faculty of Engineering, University of Malaya, Kuala Lumpur, Malaysia

Lucas Compassi Severo, Alessandro Girardi, Alessandro Bof de Oliveira, Fabio N. Kepler and Marcia C. Cera
Federal University of Pampa – UNIPAMPA, Alegrete Campus Av. Tiaraju, 810, CEP 97546-550, Alegrete-RS, Brazil

Printed in the USA
CPSIA information can be obtained
at www.ICGtesting.com
JSHW011459221024
72173JS00005B/1143

9 781632 404664